TREE AND SERPENT WORSHIP

OR

ILLUSTRATIONS OF MYTHOLOGY AND ART IN INDIA

IN THE

First and Fourth Centuries after Christ

FROM THE SCULPTURES OF THE BUDDHIST TOPES

AT

SANCHI AND AMRAVATI

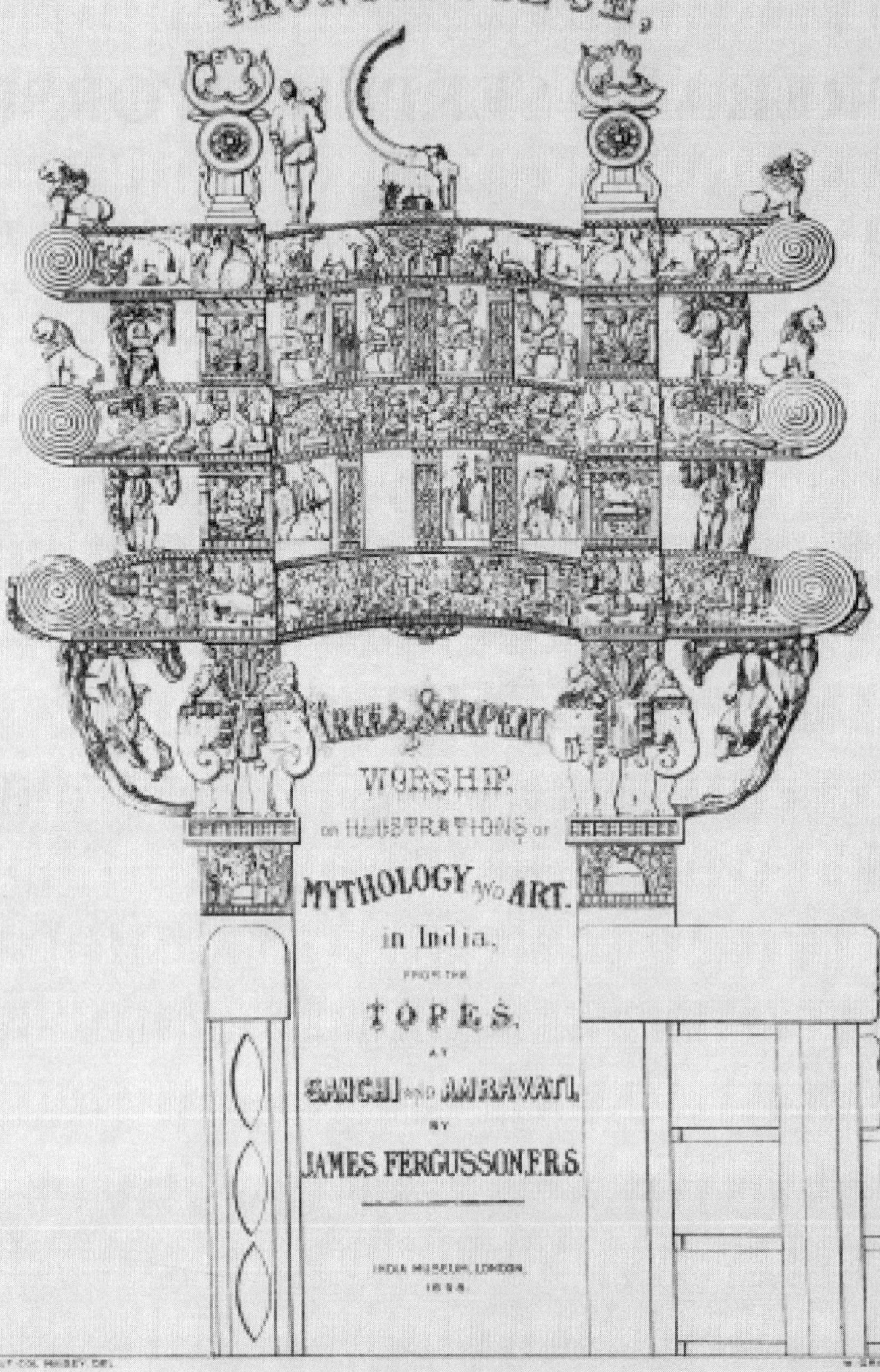

ELEVATION OF NORTHERN GATEWAY SANCHI

TREE AND SERPENT WORSHIP

OR

ILLUSTRATIONS OF MYTHOLOGY AND ART IN INDIA

IN THE

First and Fourth Centuries after Christ

FROM THE SCULPTURES OF THE BUDDHIST TOPES

AT

SANCHI AND AMRAVATI

JAMES FERGUSSON

THIRD EDITION

REVISED, CORRECTED AND IN GREAT PART RE-WRITTEN

Published by

Facsimile Publisher
12 Pragati Market
Ashok Vihar, Ph-2
Delhi-110052
facsimilepublisher.com

Distribution Network
gyanbooks.com
India, USA, Canada, UK, Australia, France

ISBN : 978-93-5324-591-7 (HB)
First Published, London, 1873 (Second Edition)

2nd Impression 2020

Printed at: Gyan Press, Delhi.

Tree and Serpent Worship

Author: James Fergusson

TREE AND SERPENT WORSHIP:

OR

ILLUSTRATIONS OF MYTHOLOGY AND ART IN INDIA

IN THE

First and Fourth Centuries after Christ.

FROM THE SCULPTURES OF THE BUDDHIST TOPES

AT

SANCHI AND AMRAVATI.

PREPARED UNDER THE AUTHORITY OF THE SECRETARY OF STATE FOR INDIA IN COUNCIL.

SECOND EDITION.

REVISED, CORRECTED, AND IN GREAT PART RE-WRITTEN.

BY

JAMES FERGUSSON, ESQ., D.C.L., F.R.S., M.R.A.S., ETC.

AUTHOR OF "PICTURESQUE ILLUSTRATIONS OF INDIAN ARCHITECTURE," "HISTORY OF ARCHITECTURE," ETC. ETC. ETC.

LONDON:
INDIA MUSEUM,
1873.

Wm. H. ALLEN AND CO., 13, WATERLOO PLACE, S.W.
Publishers to the India Office.

POSTSCRIPT.

Since this work was published, I have been informed by Mr. James Burgess of Bombay that the winged figures with human heads and birds' feet represented in the Buddhist sculptures are called Gandharvas by those in India learned in such matters, and not Garuḍas as I had assumed. As I also find that Dr. C. Leemans of Leyden, in his descriptions of the sculptures of Boro Buddor in Java, applies the same term to them, I have no doubt that this is the correct appellation, and they must be promoted from the sixth to the fourth place among the eight orders of heavenly beings depicted by the Buddhists.

The reader is therefore requested, on page 111 and after page 131, where Plate XXVI. is described, to substitute Gandharva for Garuḍa wherever these Harpy-like figures are mentioned. The only true Garuḍa who then appears in the Sanchi sculptures is that in Plate XX., Figure 3, where he follows immediately and appropriately after the seven-headed Nâga.

PREFACE TO SECOND EDITION

In the preface to the first edition I tried to explain, in as clear language as I could command, what were the disqualifications under which I laboured in undertaking a work of this sort. My ignorance of the learned languages of India and my not having made a special study of ancient and more especially of Buddhist myths were serious drawbacks. Against these, however, I could place my practical knowledge of Indian art and architecture, and long familiarity with Indian modes of expressing their feelings in material representations. It would no doubt be desirable, but it must be confessed extremely difficult, perhaps impossible, to find any one combining in his own person both these classes of qualifications; and, if this is so, it certainly seems expedient that the architect or artist should come first to arrange the materials and point out their affinities, and so prepare them for the study of any scholar or student of religious history who might come afterwards.

However this may be, I cannot in any way regret that I undertook the task, for this reason, at least, if for no other, that if I had not done so, no one else that I know of, in this country at all events, would have undertaken it. No professional author could have devoted the years requisite to its performance without remuneration,—and that the nature of the work does not admit of,—and no amateur that I am acquainted with, has, with the requisite leisure, that devoted love of the subject which would induce him to enter on so thankless an undertaking, and to submit to all the annoyances which its performance is only too certain to entail on him. I consider the attempt, however, well worthy the sacrifice of any amount of time and feeling which it may give rise to, for the more I study them the more convinced I am that the plates of this work—I speak of the plates and the plates only, wholly irrespective of the text—are the most valuable contributions that have been made to our knowledge of Buddhist history and art since James Prinsep's wonderful decipherment and translation of the Aśoka inscriptions.

These plates present us with an entirely new but most interesting picture of religion, life, and manners in India in the first centuries of the Christian era, and carry back our knowledge of Indian art to the time when it comes in contact with that of the Greeks in Bactria, to whom it is now quite clear that the permanent lithic art of the Indians owes its first original impulse. Points which were either wholly unknown or only hazily suspected before these Plates were made available for their investigation.

When the first edition of this work was published I fully expected that before a second was called for I should have had considerable assistance in unravelling the mysteries of the Plates from the criticism of the press. In this I have been, I am sorry to say, disappointed. Certain inadvertencies and inelegancies have been pointed out, and I hope all removed,[1] but I am not aware of any suggestion for the improvement of the work, or any addition to our knowledge which has accrued from that source.

From one review I expected a great deal, but unfortunately in vain. The late Professor Goldstücker was so struck with the importance of the subject, and the new light it threw on the origin and early history of Buddhism, that he volunteered to write a review of the work for the Quarterly Review. With that amiable weakness, however, which was the bane of his career, he undertook far more work to oblige friends and others than he could possibly perform, and this essay though, as I understand, far advanced, never was completed. The last time I saw him shortly before his lamented death, he told me that, as it was now too late for the Review, he would write it out and let me use it or any part of it as an appendix in any new edition of the work. He died very shortly after this, and I am sorry to say the essay has not been found among his papers. I regret this, not only because nothing that came from the pen of so distinguished an orientalist could be without interest and instruction, but because his earnest notice of the work, whether in praise or blame, might have induced others to read it with more attention than has hitherto been done.

Considerable light has, however, been lately thrown on the subject by the publication in India of Grant's Gazetteer of the central provinces, and by two papers on Serpent Worship which have appeared, one by Vishvanath Mandlik in the ninth volume of the Journal of the Bombay Asiatic Society, and the other by Pratapachandra Ghosha, in the thirty-ninth volume of the Bengal Society's Journal, which add very considerably to our knowledge of the subject; and as my collection of photographs increases I am daily acquiring fresh proofs of the prevalence of this and other cognate forms of worship in India.

From these and other sources[2] I might no doubt by myself have improved this edition considerably, but for the great advance that has been made I am indebted

[1] I am indebted to Professor Max Müller for three corrections, which I would acknowledge with gratitude, were it not that he has thought proper to convey them in a manner so studiously offensive as quite to cancel any such feeling on my part.

[2] Had it been in my power to do so, I would probably have made more use of Colonel Maisey's MS. notes in this edition than I have done, but before returning to India he borrowed his MS. from the library at the India Office, and took it with him and has it now in India.

to my friend the Rev. Samuel Beal. From his intimate knowledge of Buddhist literature and art acquired during his residence in China, he was enabled to identify the Wassantara Jâtaka, the conversion of Kaśyapa and other subjects portrayed in the bas-reliefs. These he communicated to me by letter privately without any stipulation, so that I might have appropriated his knowledge as my own. To prevent any misapprehension, however, on this subject, I induced him to embody his discoveries in a paper published in the Journal of the Royal Asiatic Society (Vol. V., N.S., p. 164 et seqq.). I do not agree with him in all his identifications, and where I differ have stated my reasons for my opinion. Where we agree I have always endeavoured to acknowledge my obligations, which, as will be perceived, have modified to a very considerable extent the views put forward in the first edition with regard to the ethnography of the people represented, and the interpretation of many of the sculptures.

The drawings made by Lieut. Cole, and the casts he brought home have also enabled me to render my description of the Sanchi Tope much more full and complete; and the photographs of the Cuttack Caves and those from other parts of India, which I have acquired since 1868, have added very considerably to my general knowledge of the subject, and enable me now to speak with confidence where before I could only express hesitating or doubtful opinions.[1]

From all these causes I trust it will be found that this second edition is a very great improvement on the first. I have not thought it necessary or expedient to alter the early part of the Introductory essay to any extent. It makes no pretence to an exhaustive treatment of the subject, and suffices as an introduction to the Indian part which has been greatly extended and I trust improved. The description of the two Topes themselves and of their sculptures have been to a great extent re-written, and a sufficient number of the subjects have been identified to make the history and purpose of the whole sufficiently intelligible. The small balance that remains can

---

[1] In the introduction to the second edition of his archæological reports, which has just reached this country, General Cunningham disputes the extent of the interval of time I have allowed between the Topes at Sanchi and Amravati, stating (page xxiii.) that he understands I have been led to adopt this difference of age chiefly on the difference of styles I have observed in the sculptures of the two monuments, especially in that of the naked female figures. For reasons given elsewhere (J. R. A. S., Vol. VI. p. 213 to 274) I would hardly care to notice his opinion on this subject, but as others may share his misconception, I may as well explain that I never did or never would base the age of buildings on so frail a foundation. The human form is not progressive, and it depends very much on the skill of the sculptor and local circumstances whether a nude figure of the first or fourth century differs from one in the eleventh or fourteenth. I have examples of both ages so similar that it would puzzle most people to say to which age they belonged, and no satisfactory conclusion can, I conceive, be drawn from such data. But architecture is progressive in all countries where true styles prevail, and when its sequences are once grasped the conclusions derived from them as to age are absolute and indisputable. I therefore base my conclusions as to the dates of the monuments in question:—first, on their architecture; secondly, on the progress of ritual or costume; thirdly, on history and tradition; fourthly, on sculptures, decorative as well as figures; and, lastly, on inscriptions, which in that early age are painfully uncertain and untrustworthy. If the General will carefully peruse what is said on these subjects in this edition I think he will see reason to withdraw his objections.

easily be explained by any one resident among Buddhists, who will no doubt be able to recognise the legends, but this will hardly add much to our present knowledge of the age or purpose of these buildings or of the art with which they are adorned.

Whatever its shortcomings, I trust I may at least claim for my book the merit of directing attention to an important class of myths which have hitherto been too much overlooked by those who have turned their attention to such subjects. If, too, I am not very much mistaken, it throws very considerable new light on the origin and early history of Buddhism, and on that of the superstitions out of which that religion took its origin and early forms. Be this as it may, I feel sure that it carries our knowledge of architecture and sculpture of India to a remote period where all before was dark, and beyond which it now seems vain to expect that our researches will be able to penetrate much further back into the night of time. A good deal, no doubt, yet remains to be done to fill up all the details, but the outlines are complete, and the Plates of this work present us with a picture of religion, manners, and arts of India at a remote and hitherto dark period of her history such as has not been found elsewhere, and, as such, as I cannot but think is well worthy of the attention of all those interested in the welfare or antiquities of that great and most poetic region of the globe.

J. F.

Langnam Place,
March 1873.

PREFACE TO THE FIRST EDITION.

THE story of this book is simple, but it seems necessary it should be told in order that much which it contains may be appreciated at its true value, and not taken for what it does not pretend to be.

When in the autumn of 1866 arrangements were being made in this country for the great Paris Exhibition, to be held in the following year, Mr. Cole suggested to me that it would afford an excellent opportunity for forwarding my designs for a dissemination of knowledge of Indian art and architecture. Having then just completed my "History of Architecture," and having consequently the requisite leisure, I fell readily into his views; and after due consideration it was arranged that I should exhibit a large collection of Photographs of Indian Architecture which I possessed, together with others to which I had access. It was felt, however, that a mere collection of Photographs, without some more prominent object to draw attention to them, would hardly answer the purpose. I therefore proposed, that, in addition, some casts of Indian sculpture or architectural fragments should be added, not only to give a character to the exhibition, but also to enable students to judge of the merit of the objects from specimens of the true dimensions.

I next examined, among other places, the collection in the India Museum, then at Fife House, for the purpose of obtaining the requisite models for casting; and after carefully going over the whole, fixed on four examples of sculpture from the Amravati Tope as those best suited for my purpose. I had long been familiar with these marbles, as they had been sent to this country by Colonel Mackenzie before 1820, and were the principal ornaments of the old Museum in Leadenhall Street. I had often admired them when there, and considered them so curious and so interesting that, had an opportunity occurred, I would have thought it well worth while to make a voyage to India specially for the purpose of exploring the Tope, and of examining the numerous antiquities I knew to exist in its neighbourhood. I was therefore not a little astonished at being informed that a large collection of marbles from the same monument were stored in the coach-houses of the establishment.

On investigation I found that Mr.—now Sir Walter—Elliot, when Commissioner in Guntûr in 1845, had excavated a considerable portion of the monument, and sent down to Madras the results of his explorations. They lay there, exposed to the wind and rain, for ten or twelve years, and then were sent home, and, after a short sojourn in the Docks, were deposited where I found them, in consequence of their being no space in the Museum itself for their exhibition.

This most unexpected discovery made a considerable alteration in the plan of campaign. It was now determined, instead of casting any, to send four or five specimens of the marbles themselves to Paris, and to bring out and photograph the whole to the same scale, so as to enable them to be pieced together, so that a restoration of the monument might thus be effected. In this project I was warmly seconded by Dr. Forbes Watson, the Director of the Museum, who lent me every assistance which the means at his disposal afforded, and notwithstanding numerous difficulties,—it was mid-winter, and the snow on the ground the graeter part of the time—the task was successfully accomplished in consequence of the intelligence and untiring zeal of Mr. Griggs, the photographer attached to the establishment.

As soon as a complete set of the photographs was obtained, I set to work to piece them together, and by processes explained in the text obtained two elevations of the outer Rail, shown on a reduced scale in Plates XLVIII. and XLIX., and one of the inner Rail, Plate LXXV., all which were exhibited in Paris with the marbles, and some 500 other Photographs of Indian architectural objects. During the three or four months, however, which I had spent poring over these Photographs, I had not only become familiar with their forms, but had acquired a considerable amount of unexpected knowledge of ancient Indian art and mythology. The greater part of this was quite new to me, but seemed of sufficient importance to justify me in making it public; and in pursuance of this object, I exhibited the photographs and read a paper on the subject to the Royal Asiatic Society in June 1867, which afterwards was printed in their Journal, vol. III. of new series, p. 132. et seqq. This paper, however, was very far from exhausting the subject, or from illustrating the monument to the extent which seemed desirable, and I in consequence appealed to the Secretary of State for India in Council for assistance to enable me to publish the whole of the Photographs, with such explanations as might seem desirable. Sir Stafford Northcote entered warmly into the project, and the Council most liberally granted the permission and funds necessary for its execution, in the section of the India Museum devoted to the reproduction of works of artistic value.

It was then intended that the work should consist of thirty or thirty-two Photographic Plates and eighteen or twenty Lithographs, with the accompanying explanations, but should be confined wholly to the Amravati Tope. It was then also agreed that the price should be limited to three guineas, on the principle adopted in the Department, that the public should obtain this and other similar works at prices calculated only to cover the cost of production. In the course, however, of the investigations required for carrying out this project, I lighted on a beautiful series of drawings of the Sanchi Tope, made in 1854 by Lieutenant-Colonel Maisey, of the Bengal army, and which were then in the Library of the India Office; and at the same time received from Lieutenant Waterhouse, R.A., a set of Photographs of the same monument. The sculptures of this Tope bore so directly on the subject in hand, that, having now ample means of illustrating the Sanchi Tope also, I determined to publish it as a sequel to that at Amravati. As the work progressed, however, it became apparent that this was in reality putting the cart before the horse. That at Sanchi was the oldest of the two Topes; and it would be reading the book backwards to publish first the more modern example. I in consequence again applied to the India Council, and my proposal being met in the same liberal spirit, the work has assumed its present form and price.

When this stage was reached it became a very serious question what form the text of the work ought to assume. The great danger to be avoided was apparently the assumption that the Tree and Serpent Worship portrayed in the illustrations of this work should be considered as a mere local Indian superstition. In order either to enlist the sympathy of European scholars, or to place it on its true basis, it seemed indispensable to explain how far that form of worship had prevailed in other countries, and to what extent it underlaid or influenced other forms of faith. To do this fully and completely was quite incompatible with the scope of the present work, even if I had been qualified to attempt it. At the same time, however, I could not but feel that to have made the text a mere description of the two Topes, and to announce it as such, was simply to seal the book against general readers, and to relegate it to the small and I fear diminishing body of enthusiasts who are supposed to delight in grubbing in the despised local antiquities of India. On the other hand, to treat it from a scientific and more cosmopolitan point of view required an author who not only knew Sanskrit and Pali sufficiently well to read the ordinary texts, but who could also decipher inscriptions and pronounce on paleographic puzzles. He ought also to have devoted some years study at least to the Western branch of the subject, from the early Grecian to its latest Finnish developments.

To none of these accomplishments can I make the smallest possible pretensions. My knowledge of Indian languages is confined to the vernacular dialects, and I had never devoted any special attention to Tree or Serpent Worship in the West before I undertook this work. I am therefore wholly dependent on translations, which are seldom complete and not always trustworthy, for my knowledge of the Eastern branch of the subject, and to a moderate course of reading for the Western. A more cautious or prudent man, aware of the numerous pitfalls which such a course must lead him across, would have declined the undertaking altogether; and all I can plead in excuse for my temerity is, that in all instances I have tried to write well within what I believe to be my real knowledge. So much indeed is this the case that my impression is, that the work is more exposed to criticism for what it omits than for what it contains, and I in consequence lay myself open to the reproach of seeming ignorant of what it may be assumed ought to be known to everyone treating of such a subject. It would have been far easier to write an introduction twice or three times as long, and to have left it to the reader to discriminate between the wheat and the chaff; but I have thought it better to put forward only what I felt I could substantiate, and to leave the fuller development of the subject to more competent scholars.

At the same time, though fully aware of my shortcomings in a literary point of view, I felt that I probably was as competent as any other person I could name to treat of the subject of the Topes and their sculptures from an architectural or archæological point of view. Long personal familiarity with Indian monuments, and loving study of them, extending through half a lifetime, had given me a readiness in discriminating their peculiarities, which I am sorry to think very few possess; and I felt, therefore, some confidence in undertaking this part of the work.

Whether I was justified in this or not, others must judge; but at all events, I felt and feel to be only too true, that if I did not undertake it there was no one else, so far as I knew, who possessed the leisure, combined with the love of the subject, necessary for the task. Unless I availed myself of the opportunity, I could not but fear that the illustrations of the work might lie dormant for another half century—as those of the Mackenzie Collection have done—or at least for another quarter of a century, as has been the fate of those presented to the nation at so much trouble and expense by Sir Walter Elliot.

There was still another course open, which was to delay the appearance of the work till this time next year. Another twelve months' study and preparation might have enabled me to make my text much more complete than it now pretends to be; but even then it would not have been perfect. Personally I should no doubt have gained considerable credit to my own reputation by such a course, but so convinced do I feel that the illustrations of this work are in themselves — wholly irrespective of the text—the most valuable contribution that has been offered to the students of Indian antiquities for many years past, that I at once abandoned any such idea. The text has gone on *pari passu* with the plates, and my last sheet was sent to press before the last lithograph was ready for proving. The work has not consequently been delayed one hour for anything I have done, and I am sure I have been right in acting thus. Still I might have been induced to delay the appearance of the work if I had been able to enlist the co-operation of persons in India who have local opportunities of acquiring knowledge regarding the subject. I have, however, found it so difficult to explain by correspondence, with strangers, what it is exactly that I wanted to know, and still more difficult to disabuse their minds from the idea that it was not a mere antiquarian crotchet on my part, that I am afraid that very little would be gained in that respect by delay. The real way to interest strangers is to show them what has been done, and to let them see what still remains undone. When this is once brought home to them, I feel convinced that there are hundreds of intelligent officers and others in India who both can and will at once supply the required information.

In the meanwhile, however, I must not be understood as complaining. General Cunningham, Colonel Meadows. Taylor, Professor Cowell, Dr. Balfour, and Dr. Best, have contributed most important appendices to this work. Dr. Reinhold Rost has afforded me most valuable assistance in passing the sheets through the press, while Prince Frederick of Schleswig Holstein, and many others, have given me most useful information and aid. Still the subject, in its present form at least, is new, and it will require the co-operation of a considerable number of qualified individuals before it can be placed on an intelligible and secure basis.

This last is the fact to which, in conclusion, I would wish especially to direct attention. If this work is really of the importance and interest which from its illustrations I believe it really is, the very limited number of copies to which this edition extends will soon be exhausted, and the work must appear again either in a similar or a more popular form. Whether in that event it will also be more complete or perfect depends more on others than on myself. If those who are more competent, or who have special opportunities of gaining knowledge, will aid either by criticisms or communications to the public press, or by imparting information to me privately, a great deal may easily be done. I urge this the more earnestly, because it seems to be only by such co-operation, either in such a book as this, or under some more competent leadership, that we shall be able to follow the worship of the Tree or the Serpent through all their ramifications, or to trace them back to their source. My conviction, too, is that the subject will well repay any trouble that may be bestowed upon it, for if I mistake not it is the oldest — it was at one time the most prevalent, and it is now the most curious of all those forms of worship through which man ever attempted to approach or to propitiate the Divinity.

J. F.

20, Langham Place, November, 1868.

NOTE.

THE difficulty as to the correct mode of spelling Indian names has presented itself with more than usual prominence in the following pages. The rule which it has been attempted to follow is, in the first instance, to leave all names which are already familiar to the English ear in the forms in which they have been adopted into our literature. Thus, such names as Cashmere, Cambodia, Ellora, Amravati, &c., have been left as they are usually written. Such familiar terms Râjâ, Nâga, Hindû, &c., which occur at every page in the latter part of the work, and regarding the pronunciation of which there can be no doubt, are generally written without any accents. All other Indian proper names are accented according to the method of transliteration most usually adopted by Indian scholars. This is done not only to indicate to the English reader the correct mode of pronouncing the word, but also to prevent any ambiguity as to the word or person intended.

It has been a little difficult to follow out these rules strictly on all occasions, but this is at least what has been attempted throughout.

CONTENTS.

INTRODUCTORY ESSAY.

PART I.—WESTERN WORLD.

PART II.—EASTERN ASIA.

THE TOPE AT SANCHI.

CHAPTER I.

CHAPTER II.

THE TOPE AT AMRAVATI.

CHAPTER I.

CHAPTER II.

CONCLUSION.

APPENDIX:

LIST OF ILLUSTRATIONS.

PHOTOGRAPHS AND LITHOGRAPHS.

SANCHI.

FRONTISPIECE—Elevation of Northern Gateway.

SANCHI—*continued.*

AMRAVATI.

AMRAVATI—*continued.*

WOOD ENGRAVINGS.

NOTES

ON

TREE AND SERPENT WORSHIP.

INTRODUCTION.

PART I.—WESTERN WORLD.

THERE are few things which at first sight appear to us at the present day so strange, or less easy to account for, than that worship which was once so generally offered to the Serpent God. If not the oldest, it ranks at least among the earliest forms through which the human intellect sought to propitiate the unknown powers. Traces of its existence are found not only in every country of the old world; but before the new was discovered by us, the same strange idolatry had long prevailed there, and even now the worship of the Serpent is found lurking in out-of-the-way corners of the globe, and startles us at times with the unhallowed rites which seem generally to have been associated with its prevalence.

Although the actual worship of Trees is nearly as far removed from our ordinary forms of faith as Serpent Worship, still it can hardly be considered as more than an exaggerated perversion of many of the ideas now current; and we can hardly wonder that in an early stage of human civilization, it may have assumed considerable importance. There is such wondrous beauty in the external form of trees, and so welcome a shelter beneath their over-arching boughs, that we should not feel surprise that in early ages groves were considered as the fittest temples for the gods. There are also, it must be remembered, few things in nature so pleasing to the eye as the form or the colour of the flowers which adorn at seasons the whole vegetable kingdom, and nothing so grateful to the palate of the rude man as the flavour of the fruits which trees afford. In addition to these were the multifarious uses to which their wood could always be applied. For buildings, for furniture, for implements of peace or war, or for ornament, it was indispensable. In ancient times it was from wood alone that man obtained that fire which enabled him to cook his food, to warm his dwelling, or to sacrifice to his gods. With all their poetry, and all their usefulness, we can hardly feel astonished that the primitive races of mankind should have considered trees as the choicest gift of the gods to men, and should have believed that their spirits still delighted to dwell among their branches, or spoke oracles through the rustling of their leaves.

Where we miss the point of contact with our own religious notion, is when we ask how anyone could hope that a prayer addressed to a Tree was likely to be responded to, or how an offering presented to such an object could be appreciated. Originally it may have been that a divinity was supposed to reside among the branches, and it was to this spirit that the prayer was first addressed; but anyone who has watched the progress of idolatry must have observed how rapidly minds, at a certain stage of enlightenment, weary of the unseen, and how willingly they transfer their worship to any tangible or visible object. An image, a temple, a stone or tree may thus become an object of adoration or of pilgrimage, and when sanctified by time the indolence of the human mind too gladly contents itself with any idol which previous generations have been content to venerate. It is so much easier than to strive actively to realise an invisible ideal which even the highest intellects too often fail to reach.

In the same manner, when it comes to be more closely examined, the worship of the Serpent does not seem so strange as it might at first sight appear. As was well remarked by an ancient author, "The serpent alone of all animals, without legs or "arms, or any of the usual appliances for locomotion, still moves with singular "celerity;"[1] and he might have added—grace, for no one who has watched a serpent slowly progressing over the ground, with his head erect, and his body following apparently without exertion, can fail to be struck with the peculiar beauty of the motion. There is no jerk, no reflex motion, as in all other animals, even fishes, but a continuous progression in the most graceful curves. Their general form, too, is full of elegance, and their colours varied and sometimes very beautiful, and their eyes bright and piercing. Then, too, a serpent can exist for an indefinite time without food or apparent hunger. He periodically casts his skin, and, as the ancients fabled, by that process renewed his youth. Add to this his longevity, which, though not so great as was often supposed, is still sufficient to make the superstitious forget how long an individual may have been reverenced in order that they may ascribe to him immortality.

Though these qualities, and others that will be noted in the sequel, may have sufficed to excite curiosity and obtain respect, it is probable that the serpent never would have become a god but for his exceptional power. The destructive powers of tigers or crocodiles are merely looked upon as ordinary exaggerations of a general law, but the poison fang of the serpent is something so exceptional, and so deadly in its action, as to excite dread, and when we find to how few of the serpent tribe it is given, its presence is only more mysterious. Even more terrible, however, than the poison of the Cobra is the flash-like spring of the Boa—the instantaneous embrace and the crushed-out life—all accomplished faster almost than the eye can follow. It is hardly to be wondered at that such power should impress people in an early stage of civilization with feelings of awe; and with savages it is probably true that their religions generally sprang from a desire to propitiate by worship those powers from whom they feared that injury might be done to themselves or their property. Although, therefore, fear might seem to

[1] Eusebius, Præ. Evan., I. 9 (p. 66, Gaisford).

suffice to account for the prevalence of this worship, on looking closely at it we are struck with phenomena of a totally different character. When we first meet Serpent Worship, either in the Wilderness of Sinaï, the Groves of Epidaurus, in Sarmatian huts, or Indian Temples, the Serpent is always the Agathodæmon, the bringer of health and good fortune. He is the teacher of wisdom, the oracle of future events. His worship may have originated in fear, but long before we become practically acquainted with it, it had passed to the opposite extreme among its votaries. Any evil that ever was spoken of the serpent, came from those who were outside the pale, and were trying to depreciate what they considered as an accursed superstition.

If fear were the only or even the principal characteristic of Serpent Worship, it might be sufficient, in order to account for its prevalence, to say, that like causes produce like effects all the world over; and that the serpent is so terrible and so unlike the rest of creation that these characteristics are sufficient to explain everything. When more narrowly examined, however, this seems hardly to be the case. Love and admiration, more than fear or dread, seem to be the main features of this faith, and there are so many unexpected features which are at the same time common to it all the world over, that it seems more reasonable to suspect a common origin. In the present state of our knowledge, however, we are not in a position to indicate the locality where it first may have appeared, or the time when it first became established among mankind.

In so far as such glimmerings as we possess enable us to guess the locality of its origin, I would feel inclined to say that it arose among a people of Turanian origin, the primæval inhabitants who first settled on the banks of the Lower Euphrates, and that it spread thence as from a centre to every country or land of the Old World in which a Turanian people settled. Apparently no Semitic, or no people of Aryan race, ever adopted it as a form of faith. It is true we find it in Judea, but almost certainly it was there an outcrop from the older underlying strata of the population. We find it also in Greece, and in Scandinavia, among people whom we know principally as Aryan, but there too it is like the tares of a previous crop springing up among the stems of a badly-cultivated field of wheat. The essence of Serpent Worship is as diametrically opposed to the spirit of the Veda or of the Bible as is possible to conceive two faiths to be; and with varying degrees of dilution the spirit of these two works pervades in a greater or less extent all the forms of the religions of the Aryan or Semitic races. On the other hand, any form of animal worship is perfectly consistent with the lower intellectual status of the Turanian races, and all history tells us that it is among them, and essentially among them only, that Serpent Worship is really found to prevail.

Human Sacrifices.

The almost universal association of human sacrifices with the practice of Serpent Worship would render it extremely desirable to ascertain, if it were possible, how far the connexion between the two is real, or to what extent the juxtaposition may be only accidental. The subject is, however, very seriously complicated by the circumstance of the very different form which the rite took in various ages, and the different points of view from which it must consequently be at times regarded.

In its earliest and simplest form, human sacrifice seems merely to have been regarded in the nature of a tithe. A cannibal savage shared with his cannibal god the spoils of victory as he did the products of the chase, or he sought to sanctify his revenge or his sensuality by making his deity a participator in his crimes. Another form arose from the idea that death was only a change, and that the future state was little more than a continuation of this world. It became consequently necessary for his enjoyment of it, that a man should be accompanied by his cattle, and his slaves, male and female, and in its most refined form the wife voluntarily sacrificed herself to rejoin her beloved husband. A third form sprung from a higher and more religious motive: it arose from a conviction of man's own unworthy and sinful nature as compared with the greatness and goodness of God, and the consequent desire to atone for the one by the sacrifice of whatever was most dear, and to propitiate the favour of the deity by offering up whatever was most precious and most beloved—even one's own, and it might be only, child. A fourth form, equally compatible with the highest civilisation, was the national sacrifice of one to atone for the sins of the many. Serpent Worship is associated in a greater or less degree with all these forms of the human rite, and so much so that it is nearly correct to say that wherever human sacrifices prevailed, there Serpent Worship is found also, though the converse does not appear so capable of proof. Serpent Worship did continue to exist when, at least, human sacrifices had ceased to be performed, though even then it is not quite clear whether it was not only from the disuse of one of two things which had once been associated.

In Egypt human sacrifices never assumed the position of a religious or domestic institution. The victorious king dedicated the prisoners taken in war to the gods, but beyond this it does not seem to have been carried; and Serpent Worship in Egypt seems likewise to have been sporadic and of little importance.

In Judea, so long as any traces of Serpent Worship prevailed, the idea of human sacrifices seems to have been familiar, but after Hezekiah's time we simultaneously lose all traces of either.

So long as Greece was Pelasgic, Serpent Worship and human sacrifices went hand in hand, but with the return of the Heraclidæ, the latter went out of fashion, though the former still lingered long, but in a modified form. In Rome, on the other hand, as we shall presently see, the worship of the Serpent was a later introduction, but as it strengthened, so did the prevalence of human sacrifices; and till Christianity put a stop to them they certainly were considered an important means of appeasing the wrath or propitiating the favour of the gods. It may, in Rome, have been to some extent derived from Etruria, or encouraged by the example of Carthage, where human sacrifices certainly prevailed till the destruction of the city, and wherever Moloch—"horrid king"—was worshipped; and in all these instances the practice seems to have risen and fallen with Serpent Worship.

In Mexico and Dahomey, where in modern times human sacrifices have been practised to an extent not known elsewhere, there too Serpent Worship was and is the typical and most important form of propitiation; while in India, there can be little doubt but that the two existed together from the earliest time. The sacrifice of men could not, however, stand before the intellectual acumen of the Aryan, and was utterly antagonistic to the mild doctrines of the Buddhist. It consequently was abolished wherever it was possible to do so; but the more innocent worship of the Serpent cropped up again and again wherever neglected, and remained in many places long after the sister form had practically lost its meaning. Both still exist in India at the present day, but not apparently practised together or by the same tribes. It is not, however, by any means clear whether the dissociation is real, or whether we merely assume it is so in consequence of our ignorance of the subject. Human sacrifices, especially among the Khonds, have attracted the attention both of governments and of individuals; while it is only now that attention is being turned to the modern forms of Serpent Worship.

Notwithstanding all these coincidences—and they might easily be extended—it must not be overlooked that nowhere can we trace any direct connexion between the two forms of faith. No human sacrifice was anywhere made to propitiate the serpent, nor was it ever pretended that any human victim was ever devoured by the snake god. In all instances, as just mentioned, the serpent is the Agathodæmon, the bringer of health or good fortune, the protector of men or of treasure, and nowhere was it sought to propitiate him by sacrifice of life beyond what was necessary for food, nor to appease him by blood offerings.

When the subject has been more thoroughly investigated than has hitherto been the case, it may be possible to trace a more direct connexion between the two forms of faith than we are now able to do. At all events we shall then be in a position to say whether it was a real partnership or only an accidental juxtaposition. In the meanwhile, all that is required in this place is to draw attention to the subject, and to point out a coincidence which is so remarkable that when investigated it may hereafter lead to the most important results.[1]

Egypt.

In an attempt to investigate any form of ancient mythology from an historical point of view, we naturally turn first to Egypt; for not only was Egypt the earliest civilized of all the countries of the ancient world, in so far at least as we at present know, but she was pre-eminently the parent of all idolatries. With the Egyptians all knowledge was considered as divine, and whatever they saw, they worshipped. Their gods had been kings; their kings were gods; and all the animal kingdom was considered worthy of worship in a greater or less degree. From bulls to beetles, or from crocodiles to cats, it made little difference; all came alike to a people so essentially religious as the Egyptians seem to have been.[2] It is little wonder, therefore, that Serpents, and it may be Trees, should be included in their multifarious Pantheon, and it is easy to detect numerous instances of the honours bestowed on both. Still it would be straining the argument beyond its legitimate issue to describe the Egyptians as in any sense an essentially Tree or Serpent worshipping people. The serpent was worshipped on the banks of the Nile among other animals, perhaps in some instances

---

[1] As human sacrifices hardly form part of the subject of the work, I have not thought it necessary to encumber the text of this section with notes or references. The subject has been exhaustively treated by Kalish, in his Commentary on Leviticus XXIII. p. 381 to 416. I am also much indebted to an unpublished essay by Sir John now Lord Acton, where the whole question is treated with his usual depth of learning.

[2] If any animal was pre-eminently worshipped in Egypt, it probably was the Bull Apis, and as the Bull is still worshipped in India simultaneously with the Serpent, we might, reasoning backwards, be led to believe that the Serpent in Egypt may have been, like the Bull, as important as the Nâga in India. These analogies are, however, I am afraid, not to be depended upon; and after all, was the Bull in Egypt more essentially an object of worship than a Cat or an Ibis? Or than any other animals we find embalmed in these tombs?

with a certain degree of pre-eminence;[1] but on the whole the accounts are hardly sufficient to enable us to say that the serpent was more honoured than his associated animal gods. At the same time it must be admitted that the serpent very frequently appears in the sculptures of the Temple walls, and frequently in a place of honour, as on the brow of the king, or as a prominent ornament of his dress, but hardly ever there with that pre-eminence he attained in other countries.

The relative position of Tree Worship among the Egyptians seems to be almost the same. It is true that the important part which the Tamarisk (Ἐρίκη) plays in the legend of Isis and Osiris, as told by Plutarch,[2] might tend to a somewhat different conclusion, and the prominence given to the other tree (Μηθίδη), which marked and shaded the tomb of Osiris in the same legend, might lead to the belief that a form of Tree Worship prevailed in Egypt before the multifarious Theban pantheon was elaborated. The authority, however, for these facts is not such as can be relied upon, and the sculptures again do not favour the belief that Trees were considered as divine on the banks of the Nile, though they may justify the belief that the Sycamore was sacred to the goddess Netpe, and the Persea to Athor.[3]

The great test of such a subject in Egypt are the sculptures which cover the walls of the Temples. These are the Bible of the Egyptians, in so far at least as we know it. Any one studying these with that object might easily pick out fifty or a hundred examples which would tend to show that the Egyptians were both Tree and Serpent worshippers; but, on a fair review of the whole subject, these would probably be found to be only a fractional part of the nature worship of the Egyptians, and neither the most prominent nor the most important.[4] In spite, therefore, of the passages in classical authors which may be quoted against this view, it would probably be incorrect to include the ancient Egyptians among the votaries either of the Serpent or of Trees.

JUDEA.

The earliest distinct allusion which we have to those mysterious properties which the ancients attributed to certain Trees, is to be found in the second and third chapters of Genesis. The planting of the Trees of Life and Knowledge in the Garden of Eden is there described in minute detail, and judging from subsequent forms of the story, their custody seems to have been intrusted to the serpent. Taken by itself, this narrative has always appeared one of the least intelligible parts of the Pentateuch, and numberless theories have been formed to account for what seemed so completely outside the range of ordinary human experience. With the knowledge we now possess, it does not seem so difficult to understand what was meant by the curse on the serpent, or the prohibition to eat the fruit of the trees. When the writers of the Pentateuch set

---

[1] Herodotus, II. 74. Ælian, de Animal. XVII. 5. Clemens Alex. III, 2. p. 93.

[2] Plutarch, de Iside et Osiri, 11. Wilkinson's Ancient Egyptians, vol. V. p. 261, et seq.

[3] Wilkinson, vol. IV. p. 391, plates 36 and 54, &c.

[4] On such a monument, for instance, as the Sarcophagus of Menephthah, in Sir John Soane's Museum, where the Serpent occurs more frequently than on any monument of the same extent I am acquainted with, and in a more important character, there is not one instance in which it can be said he is being worshipped. He is the representative of heaven—is a good or evil genius—a protector or destroyer—a mere hieroglyphic—anything, in short, but never a god.—See Bonomi's published account of the Sarcophagus: Longman, 1864.

themselves to introduce the purer and loftier worship of the Elohim, or of Jehovah, it was first necessary to get rid of that earlier form of faith which the primitive inhabitants of the earth had fashioned for themselves. The serpent, as the principal deity of that early religion, was cursed "above all cattle, and above every beast of the field;"[1] and in future there was to be for ever enmity between the serpent and "man of woman born." The confusion of ideas on this subject seems to have arisen from the assumption that the curse was directed at the reptile as such, and not rather at a form of worship which the writers of the Pentateuch must have regarded with horror, and which they thought it necessary to denounce in the strongest terms and in the form they believed would be most intelligible by those to whom it was addressed. The tree it was not necessary should be cursed; the fruit of the tree of knowledge had been eaten, and no further result could be obtained by access to it, while the tree of life was guarded by a cherub with a flaming sword, and all approach prevented. Its fruits could not then be obtained, nor have they to the present day.

The two chapters which refer to this, however,—as indeed the whole of the first eight of Genesis,—are now generally admitted by scholars to be made up of fragments of earlier books or earlier traditions belonging, properly speaking, to Mesopotamian rather than to Jewish history, the exact meaning of which the writers of the Pentateuch seem hardly to have appreciated when they transcribed them in the form in which they are now found. The history of the Jews and of the Jewish religion commences with the call of Abraham, and from that time forward the worship of Serpents and Trees took an infinitely less important position, though still occasionally cropping up, often when least expected, but apparently not as a religion of the Jews, but as a backsliding towards the feelings of the pre-existing races among whom they were located.

There is apparently no mention of serpents, either in the Bible or in any of the traditions in connexion with Abraham or his immediate descendants; but that Patriarch "planted a grove at the well of the covenant (Beersheba), and called there "on the name of the Lord"[2]—a circumstance the more worthy of note, as it is the earliest mention of a form of worship to which continual allusions are afterwards made in Jewish history. The oak, or rather the terebinth tree, under which Abraham is said to have entertained the angels at Mamre, became an object of extreme veneration to his descendants, and, if we may trust Eusebius, was worshipped down to the time of Constantine.[3] The pious zeal of that emperor led him to desecrate its altars, and apparently to cut down the sacred tree to make way for a Christian church which he erected on the spot, and which was then or afterwards dedicated to St. George.[4]

With the time of Moses the indications became more distinct and palpable. We gather from the context in the Bible,[5] and still more from the narrative of Josephus,[6] that the tree or bush on Horeb, from which the Lord appeared to Moses as a flame, had been considered sacred before that event. It was, indeed, apparently in consequence of its sanctity that it was chosen for the delivery of the oracle, while the conversion on

---

[1] Genesis, iii. 14. [2] Genesis, xxi. 33. [3] Eusebius, Vita Constantini, III. 53.

[4] The oak now pointed out at Hebron as Abraham's tree is in quite another locality.

[5] Exodus, iii. 5. [6] Josephus, Antiq. Ju. II. 12. 1.

that occasion of Moses' rod into a serpent brings these two names into the juxtaposition in which they are so frequently found. This miracle on Horeb would, however, be more impressive and more to the point were it not that it was repeated by Aaron before Pharaoh, and copied by the Egyptians;[1] but at the burning bush it stands alone, and without any apparent motive for its exhibition there, except the appropriateness of the combination.

With the Brazen Serpent in the Wilderness[2] we tread on surer ground; it is the first record we have of actual worship being performed to the Serpent, and it is also remarkable, as the cause of this adoration is said to have been its healing powers. From the readiness with which this explanation was adopted by the Jews, it would seem as if that characteristic had been ascribed to the Serpent before that time. We now, however, learn it for the first time, though we afterwards become so familiar with it in Greek mythology, where the Serpent himself represents Æsculapius, and is the indispensable concomitant of Hygeia.

From this time we lose the sight of the worship of the Serpent from the narrative of the Bible, till it somewhat unexpectedly reappears in the time of Hezekiah. We then learn that the brazen image that Moses had set up, had for more than five centuries been preserved in the Temple, and that "unto those days the children of Israel did burn incense to it."[3] It was only then, after six centuries of toleration, that it was resolved to put an end to this idolatry, together with the kindred worship of the Groves. In the intermediate period there is hardly any expression that countenances the belief that the worship of Serpents generally prevailed among the Jews, unless it be one in the Wisdom of Solomon, where it is said, "They worshipped serpents void of reason,"[4] in strange contrast with the New Testament expression, "Be ye wise as serpents."[5]

Neither in the Bible, however, nor in the Talmud,[6] is there anything that would justify the assertion that Serpent Worship, even in the most modified form, prevailed among the Jews after its abolition by Hezekiah. It cropped up again, as we shall presently see, in the Christian sect of Ophites, but probably in this instance the superstition was derived from Persia.

The case is different with the worship of Trees or Groves. The first form of this appears to have arisen from the veneration paid to natural groves, and the worship offered therein to Baal[7] and other foreign gods, but the Grove or Asherah is also frequently an image, no doubt like that emblem so often represented on the Assyrian sculptures.[8] This is an artificial tree, such as might have been placed alongside of the Brazen Serpent within the Temple at Jerusalem.[9]

It hardly admits of doubt but that this worship of the Asherah or of Groves was a true and essential form of Tree Worship, but it seems to have been local, and

---

[1] Exodus, vii. 8.

[2] Numbers, xxi. 9.

[3] 2 Kings, xviii. 4.

[4] Wisdom, xi. 15.

[5] Matthew, x. 16.

[6] I make the assertion on the authority of Mr. Deutsch, of the British Museum, who has kindly looked through the Talmud for me with reference to the question.

[7] 2 Kings, xvii. 16.

[8] Lord Aberdeen's black stone, History of Architecture, W.C. 75; see also British Museum Sculptures, and Layard's and Botta's plates, *passim*.

[9] 1 Kings, xvi. 33; 2 Kings, xxi. 3, xxiii. 4 & 6; Isaiah, xvii. 8, xxvii. 9, &c.

entirely opposed to the spirit of the Jewish religion. As a rule it is reprobated by their chroniclers and prophets, and eventually disappears. Had it ever been really adopted by the Jewish legislators, we might perhaps be able to ascertain more correctly its origin and affiliations. Possibly we may do so when the Assyrian antiquities are more completely investigated than they now are. For the present we must rest content with the knowledge that both Trees and Serpents were worshipped in Judea, and hope that some new light may some day be thrown on the subject.

Even, however, if in abeyance, we can hardly suppose that Serpent Worship was extinguished in Judea, inasmuch as immediately after the Christian era we found it bursting forth again with wonderful exuberance in the sects of the Nicolaitans, the Gnostics, and more especially that called the Ophites (Οφῖται). Of the latter, Tertullian tells us, "they even prefer the Serpent to Christ, because the former brought the "knowledge of good and evil into the world. They point also to his majesty and "power, inasmuch as when Moses raised the Brazen Serpent in the Wilderness, "whoever looked on it was healed; and they even quote the Gospels to prove that "Christ was an imitation of the serpent, because it is said, 'As Moses lifted up the "'serpent in the wilderness, so must the Son of Man be lifted up'" (John, iii. 14).[1] Epiphanius describes these ceremonies in the following terms: "They keep a living "serpent in a chest, and at the time of the mysteries entice him out "by placing bread before him. The door being opened he issues forth, "and having ascended the table folds himself above the bread.[2] This "they call a perfect sacrifice. They not only break and distribute "this amongst the votaries, but whosoever wishes it may kiss the "serpent. This the wretched people call the Eucharist. They con-"clude the ceremonies by singing a hymn through him to the Supreme "Father."[3]

No. 1.

CISTA, FROM A ROMAN COIN OF ADRAMYTTIUM.

There are other paragraphs to the same effect, and the representations of serpents and Serpent Worship in the so-called Gnostic form are too numerous and too familiar to require further notice here.

We have no means of knowing how long this worship of the Serpent continued to prevail in Syria—most probably down to the seventh century, when the Mahomedan invasion swept away a large mass of the parasitic superstitions which had fastened themselves on Christianity; but the literature of that age is so mixed up with fables and misrepresentations, that it is very difficult to write confidently about anything it describes.

Except the instance above alluded to, of the Terebinth at Mamre, I am not aware of any authentic instance of direct Tree Worship in Syria after the Christian era,[4] but there may be, though, as they have not hitherto been looked for, they may still remain unknown.[5]

---

[1] Tertullian, de Prescript. Hereticorum, c. xlvii.

[2] Pigraque labetur circa donaria serpens.—Ovid, Amor. Eleg. lib. ii.

[3] Epiphanius, lib. i. Hæres: XXXVII. p. 267, et seq.

[4] On the Roman imperial coin representing the Temple at Baalbec, a cypress as sacred to the sun is the *numen*, shown in the centre, through the opening in the great Propylon, where in almost every other instance the statue of the Deity is represented. (Donaldson, Architectum Numismatica. N. 34. Eckhel. III. 355, &c.)

[5] Though not bearing directly on the subject, the "Legend of the True Cross" is a curious example of a cognate superstition. Like most Mediæval legends, it is so childish that it would be hardly worth while to

Phœnicia.

In addition to the Tyrian coins and other monuments which in themselves would suffice to prove the prevalence of Serpent Worship on the seaboard of Syria, we have a direct testimony in a quotation from Sanchoniathon, an author who is supposed to have lived before the Trojan war.[1] This passage is in itself so curious as throwing light on the feelings of the ancients on this subject, that it may be worth while to quote it nearly entire. "Taautus attributed a certain divine nature to dragons and " serpents, an opinion which was afterwards adopted both by the Phœnicians and " Egyptians. He teaches that this genus of animals abounds in force and spirit more " than any other reptiles; that there is something fiery in their nature; and though " possessing neither feet nor any external members for motion common to other " animals, they are yet more rapid in their motion than any others. Not only has " it the power of renewing its youth, but in doing so receives an increase of size and " strength, so that after having run through a certain term of years it is again absorbed " within itself. For these reasons this class of animals were admitted into temples, and " used in sacred mysteries. By the Phœnicians they were called the good dæmon, " which was the term also applied by the Egyptians to Cneph, who added to him the " head of a hawk to symbolize the vivacity of that bird."

After this, Eusebius or Philo go on to quote several other authors to the same effect, among others the Magian Zoroaster, who describes the hawk-headed deity as "the chief,

---

allude to it, but it contains an earlier oriental element, which may be considered as throwing some light on the old form of worship.

The legend relates that when Adam was on his death-bed, he sent Seth to try and regain admission to Paradise. This, of course, was impossible, but he was allowed by the angel who guarded it to look in at the gate. He saw, among other things, the tree which had borne the fatal fruit, its roots then extending to hell, but its upper branches reaching to heaven. The angel gave him three seeds, recommending him to place them in Adam's mouth, when he died. He did so, and they produced three trees, a cedar, a cypress, and a pine. These afterwards united into one, and their branches performed many miracles. Solomon cut down the tree, and tried in vain to use its trunk to support the roof of his palace. It disdained such a use, and was consequently thrown across the Brook Cedron to be trodden upon. It was rescued from this ignominy by the Queen of Sheba, and buried below the Pool of Bethesda, which owed its healing properties to its virtues. It came to the surface when wanted for the Cross, and afterwards was buried in Calvary, where it was recognized by the Empress Helena in consequence of its miraculous healing powers. It was taken to Persia by Chosroes, and recovered by Heraclius, and afterwards, as is well known, throughout the middle ages a piece of the wood of the True Cross was prized by emperors and kings beyond all other earthly possessions. So great, indeed, was the demand that it was endowed with the property of self-multiplication, but even this did not suffice to bring it into contempt, and as late as 1248 Philip Augustus erected the Sainte Chapelle to enshrine a morsel of the wood of the tree of Paradise. The Sainte Chapelle may thus be considered as the last, as it probably is among the most beautiful, temples ever erected to Tree Worship.

All this is so silly that the only excuse for alluding to it is, that throughout the earlier past there runs a thread of oriental myth different from the clumsy inventions of ordinary mediæval miracle mongers, and this, if properly investigated, might perhaps throw some light on the feelings with which sacred trees were regarded in ancient times, and tell us something of the causes which led to their being so universally worshipped.*

[1] Eusebius, Præ. Evan. I. 9. (p. 66, Gaisford). See also Müller's Fragmenta, III. 572.

---

* The following authorities for the legend are quoted by S. Baring Gould, in his "Myths of the Middle Ages" from which the above is abridged; Vita Christi, Troyes, 1517; Legenda Aurea de Jacques de Voragine; Geschiedenis van het Heylighe Cruys; Speculum Historiale, by Gottfried von Viterbo, &c.

the best, and most learned of the gods;" but from the context it appears that there is here some confusion between the Serpent god and the eagle-headed deity of the Assyrians, who is generally supposed to represent Nisroch,[1] and whose image so frequently occurs in the Sculptures. It scarcely, however, admits of a doubt but that this eagle-headed deity of the Assyrians became the Garuda of the Hindu mythology, who, before the time when Eusebius wrote, had taken so important a position in the Serpent Worship of the Hindus, as we shall afterwards see, but still it is not clear how the confusion between the two objects crept into the passage as we now find it. Eusebius certainly understood the quotation as applying to the serpent, but the ascription to the serpent of these qualities cannot, I fear, be relied upon. It suffices to show, however, what importance the Christian writers of the fourth century were inclined to attribute to the Serpent Worship of the Gentiles.

The coins of Tyre represent in some instances a tree with a serpent coiled round its trunk, and on either hand two rude stone pillars (Petræ Ambrosiæ?) or an altar with two serpents rising from the angles of its base. Others represent the serpent coiled around a rude stone obelisk, with the Tyrian Hercules contending with a serpent.[2]

Taken in conjunction with the above quotation, these, with others that might be quoted, suffice to show that the serpent was honoured, perhaps worshipped, in Tyre from an early period down to the time of Alexander. More, probably, might be found if looked for, but they are not necessary for our present purpose.

Mesopotamia.

As hinted above, the Garden of Eden was supposed to have been situated somewhere on the Lower Euphrates, and the story of the earlier patriarchs down to Noah (Xisuthrus) being common to the narratives of Berosus and Moses, we naturally turn to Babylonia in the hope of being able to point out the mythical relations of that strange faith which is first mentioned as existing in that country. Unfortunately, long before the Greeks or any foreign travellers visited Babylonia, the great wave of the dominion of the Semitic Assyrian had passed over it, and nearly obliterated all traces of the earlier Chaldean forms, and as strangers ignorant of the language, it is hardly to be expected that they would have dug up the fossil remains of an extinct religion. The earliest native historian (Berosus) lived after the time of Alexander (B.C. 270?), so that he too was likely to pass over what had been so long forgotten. The one chance that now remains to us for recovering it is from the cuneiform inscriptions. Serpent Worship, so far as I know, has not yet been looked for among them, and till they are examined with special reference to the inquiry, it is impossible to say where it may or may not be found. In the meanwhile, Sir Henry Rawlinson informs us, that Hea, or Hoa, the third person in the Babylonian trinity of great gods, may be considered as the serpent deity, "since there are very strong "grounds for connecting him with the serpent of Scripture, and the paradisaical "traditions of the tree of knowledge and the tree of life."[3]

---

[1] Layard, Nineveh and its Remains, abridged edition, p. 46.

[2] Maurice, vol. VI. pl. 5. p. 273.

[3] Herodotus translated, &c., by Geo. Rawlinson, vol. I., p. 600.

The only direct testimony we have of Serpent Worship in Babylon is in that part of the Book of Daniel which is now printed separately in the Apocrypha,[1] and which gives an account of the destruction of Bel's great Dragon which they of Babylon worshipped. The story told there of the fraud of the priests and the indignation of the people at the destruction of their god all bear so strong an impress of probability that it is difficult to doubt their truth.

The story as it stands, except in its catastrophe, is not unlike one related by Ælian,[2] as occurring in Egypt, in the days of Ptolemy Euergetes. The description of the serpents of Metele is nearly identical with this of Babylon, but there the only result was that the prying priest went mad, and for all we know the serpent continued to receive his daily dole for long afterwards.

Heredotus, strange to say, deserts us in this difficulty, and the only indication in Diodorus is in his description of the three statues that adorned the great Temple of Belus; that of Rhea being accompanied by two very large silver images of serpents, each weighing 30 talents; and that of Juno, standing with her right hand resting on a serpent's head.[3]

No mention of Tree Worship has, so far as known, been brought to light in Babylonia, but in Assyria it is among the most common forms of idolatrous veneration. The representations of this on Lord Aberdeen's black stone has already been alluded to, and it occurs at least twenty times as a principal object in Layard's plates, and very frequently also in Botta.[4]

It can hardly be doubted but that this is the Asherah or Grove so frequently mentioned in the Bible, and is a true form of Tree Worship; but no thorough investigation has yet been made by any one competent to the task, in order to ascertain how and where it arose, or what the exact ideas were which it represented. Judging *à priori*, I would feel inclined to suggest that the Serpent Worship was a peculiarity of the Turanian Babylonians of the old Chaldean Empire—Tree Worship that of the Semitic Assyrians; but a great deal has yet to be done before this can be either positively affirmed or rejected, and the reasons for even suggesting it will be more easily understood when our present task is further advanced.[5]

Greece.

In attempting to explain the phenomena presented by the architectural history of Greece, it seems necessary, as a basis for any reasoning on the subject, to assume the existence in that country of two distinct and antagonistic races at one period of the

---

[1] Story of Bel and the Dragon, v. 23, et seq.

[2] Ælian, de Animal. XVI. 39.

[3] Diodorus, II. 9. 5.

[4] Monument de Ninive, 5 vols. folio. Paris, 1846–50.

[5] One instance may be as well quoted here, not as bearing directly on the Babylonian form of worship, but from its similarity to representations we find on coins* elsewhere in India.

The cylinder from which the representation is taken is in the collection of Mr. Steuart, and is engraved in Lajard's Culte de Mithra, Plate VI., Fig. 4, but without any indication by which its agé could be determined. My impression is, that many of these cylinders, and this among the number, are more modern than is generally supposed, and may come down to Achæmenian times.

* J. A. S. B., vol. VII., Plate XXXII.

No. 1A.

Cylinder, with Tree and Serpent, From Lajard.

story. The one race is represented by the tombs, or so-called treasuries, of Mycenæ and Orchomenos, and the megalithic polygonal masonry of the walls of the most ancient cities. To the other belongs the chaste intellectual refinement of the Doric order, while between the two intervenes the elegant and ornate Ionic as a compromise combining the peculiarities of each.

The first class of buildings have been ascribed to the Pelasgi; and though considerable difference of opinion exists as to the exact ethnological position of those people, and whence they came, there seems no valid objection to assuming that they were a people of a race entirely different to the Hellenes, who afterwards superseded them. If not of purely Turanian race, they must have been so closely allied to that family that, till the contrary is shown, they may be considered as belonging to it.

In like manner the Ionic order as certainly represents an Asiatic. To some extent it may be a Semitic clement in the population of Greece, while the Doric remains the exponent of the intellectual refinement to which the Aryan element attained during the short but dazzling outburst of their greatness.

The same distinction seems indispensable in treating of the mythology of ancient Greece. Assuming the Veda and the Zend Avesta to be exponents of the religious feelings of the Aryans, it is impossible to understand—if language is any test in such a matter—how a people speaking a tongue so purely Aryan as the Greek, could so completely have relapsed into a Turanian ancestral worship as we find that of Greece in its great age. Unless a great substratum of the inhabitants of Greece belonged to the Turanian family, their religion, like their language, ought to have presented a much closer affinity to the earlier scriptures of the Aryan race than we find to be the case. The curious anthropic mythology of the Grecian Pantheon seems only explicable on the assumption of a potential Turanian element in the population, though the study of the language fails to reveal to us its existence.

Such an hypothesis is still more indispensable when we refer to the Tree and Serpent Worship that certainly prevailed to a greater or less extent during the whole period of Grecian history, though of course more prominently during the earlier part. Here again it is necessary to make a further distinction. All the earlier myths refer to the destruction of serpents or of serpent races. This continues down to the return of the Heraclidæ; after that time, when Hellenic supremacy was assured, we meet with a kindlier feeling. The serpent then became the oracle—the guardian of the city, or the healing god,—the Agathodæmon in short. In Greece, as everywhere else, when a new faith once feels secure in its position, it no longer objects to the forms which it superseded, and these by degrees crop up again, and eventually become part at least of the outward faith of people whose real sentiments may, nevertheless, be most diametrically opposed to such superstition.

One of the oldest and most celebrated myths of Greece relates the destruction of the dragon[1] Python by Apollo, and his taking possession of the oracle which the

---

[1] There seems to be no real or scientific difference in Greek between the word Δράκων and Ὄφις. Generally, however, Draco is applied to the larger, and serpent to the smaller kind of snakes. Draco would hardly be applied to an asp or cobra; nor Ophis to one of the great guardian serpents so frequently alluded to. I can hardly admit, however, the popular definition :—Anguis aquarum, Serpens terrarum, Draco templorum.

serpent guarded.[1] Cadmus fought and killed the dragon that devoured his men, and sowing its teeth raised soldiers for his own purposes. In Indian language, he killed the Nâga Râja of Thebes, and made sepoys of his subjects. The tradition of the close of the career of Cadmus and his wife is even more suggestive of Serpent Worship than the events of their life. Their conversion into serpents as a cure for ills that had become unbearable, and the respect with which it is represented they were afterwards regarded, point to a form of faith that must have been at that time familiar to the inhabitants of Greece.[2]

The Argonautic Expedition was undertaken to recover a fleece that hung on a sacred tree, guarded by a dragon that Jason and his companions would have been unable to cope with, unless they had been aided by the enchantments of Medea. But the great destroyer of serpents in those days was Hercules. Most appropriately was he represented as strangling two serpents sent by Juno to destroy him while he was yet in his cradle. His adventures in the Garden of the Hesperides is the pagan form of the myth that most resembles the precious serpent-guarded fruit of the Garden of Eden, though the moral of the fable is so widely different. His fight with the many-headed Lernean Hydra, on the other hand, suggests the origin in the West of many-headed serpents with which we are becoming so familiar in the East. In the earlier representations, apparently, he had only seven heads, but afterwards, as was also the case in India, they were indefinitely multiplied.[3] A still earlier, perhaps the earliest, mention of this mythological animal is in Homer, who speaks of a three-headed snake as adorning the baldrick of the buckler of Agamemnon.[4] As a Grecian peculiarity, this many-headedness might be passed over, but it is interesting as bearing on the subject we have specially in hand.

Though generally represented as the destroyer of Serpents, Hercules, on the other hand, is said to have been the progenitor of the whole race of Serpent-worshipping Scythians, through his intercourse with the Serpent Echidna.[5] There is nothing, however, inconsistent in this. The age in which he is said to have lived was one of transition between two civilizations. An old Turanian Serpent-worshipping race were, in Greece, passing away with their religion, to make place for the Aryans and their more intellectual form of faith. Hercules was the popular embodiment of all the favourite myths of the age; and to him consequently was ascribed the destruction of whatever was old wherever it was destroyed, as well as the perpetuation of whatever remained wherever it was known to have been preserved.

---

[1] Python terræ filius draco ingens. Hic ante Apollinem ex oraculo in Monte Parnasso responsa dare solitus erat.—Hyginus, fab. 140. If we may trust Lucian, de Astrologia, p. 544, at Delphi a virgin delivers the oracle, (hence, the symbol of the constellation Virgo,) and a dragon speaks from under the tripod, because the constellation Draco appears among the stars.

[2] Ovid's Metamorph. III. 1. and IV. 9.

[3] In the eastern corridor of the Uffizi, at Florence, there is a marble sarcophagus of a good age (68), on the front of which are sculptured the labours of Hercules. The Hydra is here represented with the head and shoulders of a human being, the lower part only from the waist downwards being serpentine. From the shoulders rise seven serpents. The difference between them and the Indian examples is, that each of the serpents at Florence have a separate neck and head. In India they are generally combined. In other respects the images are identical.

[4] Iliad, XI. 38.

[5] Herodotus, IV. 9.

After the return of the Heraclidæ, serpents—as hinted above—seem to have been kept at Delphi and in the caves of Trophonius;[1] in both instances, apparently, for oracular purposes. But the great centre of Serpent Worship was Epidaurus, where stood the famous temple of Æsculapius and the grove attached to it, in which serpents were kept and fed down to the time of Pausanias. Some of these, according to him, were of great size, measuring, he says, 30 cubits in length.[2] It is not, however, clear whence the myth of Æsculapius came, and when it was introduced into Greece. There was a temple dedicated to this god in Alexandria, in which a huge serpent was kept;[3] but this worship is as likely to have been taken there by the Greeks, as brought thence, though the name and many features may be thought to betray an Egyptian origin.

Perhaps the most remarkable event connected with the Epidaurian serpent was the embassy sent from Rome in the year 462 A.U.C. under Quintus Ogulinus. The description of the advent of the divine serpent is one of the most animated passages in Ovid's Metamorphoses,[4] and which, so far as the main facts go, is confirmed by Livy,[5] Valerius Maximus,[6] and Aurelius Victor.[7] That such an embassy was sent, and brought back a serpent, seems undoubted, as also that it was received with divine honours by the populace of Rome, and it may also be admitted that the plague was stayed after its arrival, but whether in consequence of it or not is another question. The Romans thought it was, and Serpent Worship was established in Rome from that time forward. On the other hand, we learn from Pausanias'[8] mention of it, that the Æsculapian serpent continued to be venerated in Greece till after the Christian era.

Another, and almost as interesting an example for our present purposes, occurred in Athens. When Minerva contended with Neptune for the city, she created the olive, which became sacred to her, and planted it on the Akropolis and handed over the care of it to the Serpent God Erechthonios. He is sometimes represented like the giants, as only half a serpent, the body of a man, the lower extremities as serpentine. Such, however, was not the usual or popular belief, inasmuch as we learn from Herodotus,[9] that when the Persians were approaching Athens the inhabitants, though warned by the oracle, refused to leave their homes till they learned that the great serpent, the guardian of the citadel, had refused its food, and left the place. When their Serpent God had deserted them, there was no longer any hope, and they fled.

There can be no doubt but that the ancient Tree and Serpent Temple stood where the Erechtheum now stands, and, being destroyed by the Persians, was rebuilt afterwards in its present form. The tree, I believe, occupied the Caryatid Portico, the serpent the lower cell adjoining, where also the well of Neptune seems to have been situated. The fane of the goddess occupied the higher level, and was approached by a different entrance.[10] Be all this as it may, the real point is that here we have in

---

[1] Pausanias, II. p. 137.
[2] Loc. cit. 175.
[3] Ælian, de Animal. XVI. 39.
[4] Metamorph. XV. 5.
[5] Liv. X. 47.
[6] Val. Max. 1, 8. 2.
[7] Au. Victor. XXII. 1.
[8] Loc. supra cit.
[9] Herod. VIII. 41.
[10] I am aware that in this distribution of the parts I differ from Beulé, who excavated this temple, and published the result of his researches. It would be out of place to attempt to give my reasons here, but my objections to his plan are not given without due consideration.

Athens a temple dedicated to Tree and Serpent Worship, and perhaps the only one specially so devoted which is now standing in Greece.[1]

Besides, however, the prominent instances in which the snake figures in Greek mythology as the representative of the gods, or as delivering its oracles, or guarding sacred places or things, its influence occasionally crops up in places where we should least suspect it, Nothing, for example, can well be more curious than the story of Alexander's birth, as told by Plutarch.[2] That Olympias his mother should have kept tame snakes in the house is scarcely to be wondered at, as Illyria is a country where they abound, and where also their worship was prevalent. It is curious, however, that it should be thought worthy of record that one was found in her bed, and that Philip should have believed in the possibility of the serpent being the real father of Alexander the Great. The same view is taken by Lucian,[3] who seems to adopt without hesitation the idea that Alexander was born of a serpent. Even Cicero[4] does not discountenance the story when he tells us that on the occasion of the illness of Ptolemy, one of Alexander's generals, from a poisoned wound, the serpent of Olympias appeared to him in a dream, having a root in his mouth. This Serpent, who, from the context we are led to infer, was the father of Alexander, then pointed out the place where the herb grew, and the wound cured by its application.

It is possible that the story may have arisen from some connexion with the Bacchic mysteries, into which Olympias was initiated, and in which serpents always played a prominent and important part, and we know that Alexander wished to connect his eastern conquest with that of the Indian Bacchus,[5] but explain it as we will, the myth is curious as arising in so advanced a stage of Grecian enlightenment.

The traces of Tree Worship in Greece are even fuller and more defined than those of the Serpent *Cultus* just alluded to. In this instance we have fortunately an elaborate treatise on the subject by a thoroughly competent scholar,[6] to which the reader is referred, and the slightest possible notice will consequently suffice for our present purpose.

As each succeeding Buddha in the Indian mythology had a separate and different Bo Tree assigned to him, so each god of the classical Pantheon seems to have had some tree appropriated as his emblem or representative. Among the most familiar are the oak or beech of Jupiter,[7] the laurel of Apollo, the vine of Bacchus. The olive is the well-known tree of Minerva. The myrtle was sacred to Aphrodite. The apple or orange of the Hesperides belonged to Juno. The populus was the tree of Hercules,[8] and the plane tree was the "numen" of the Atridæ.

Of all these the oldest and most celebrated was the oak, or rather grove at Dodona, originally founded by the Pelasgi,[9] it may be some sixteen centuries before the Christian era: it remained an oracle till the time of Constantine.[10] It thus

[1] If the sculpture of the Western Pediment of the Parthenon had not been so completely destroyed, I believe we should have found the Olive Tree of Minerva, and the Serpent at its base occupying the central position between the contending deities. I have seen it so restored, but I fear there is no real authority for it.

[2] Plutarch, Vita Alex. II.

[3] Lucian, dial. Mort. XIII. 1. Pseudo Kallisthenes, I. 10.

[4] Cicero de Divinat., II. 66.

[5] Arrian, V. 2 and 3. Quintus Curtius, VIII. 10. 12.

[6] Bötticher, Baumcultus der Hellenen. 8vo. 1856, p. 554, pl. 63.

[7] Pausanias, I. p. 40, VII. 643.

[8] Pliny, 12. 2.

[9] Strabo, VII. p. 327.

[10] Aristides, I. p. 84, II. p. 12. Max. Tyr. 14. 1.

certainly survived, even if its foundation did not precede, that of its great rival, the serpent oracle of the neighbouring Temple of Delphi. It was from the branches of this time-honoured tree that the sacred pigeons, combining the rustling of their wings with that of the leaves, made up those sounds which were interpreted as oracles throughout the whole period of Grecian history. It was not, however, only as a shelter for the sacred pigeons, or that the wind might rustle through their leaves and agitate the bells that hung among their branches, that the trees of the Dodonian grove were held to be sacred. Tradition ascribed to them the power of speaking for themselves, and even when cut down, as in the case of the ship Argo, a piece of the sacred oak inserted either in prow or keel, had the power of communicating to these adventurous navigators the will of Jove.[1]

It is not quite clear whether or not any structural temple, properly so called, ever was erected in the grove at Dodona. None certainly is described by Pausanias or anyone else, and on the whole, the context seems to bear out the conclusion that the grove was the *ἱερόν*, and that except altars and minor adjuncts it was not profaned by any works of human hands.

The laurel at Delphi was as celebrated as Dodona's oak. It was under its shade that Python the son of Earth sought refuge when wounded by the arrows of Apollo, and where his oracle existed before the Sun god conquered it.[2] The earliest temple here was constructed of laurel wood, afterwards of bronze, and only in later days of stone, when apparently the oracle and with it the site of the tree were included in the sanctuary.

The story of Daphne need hardly be alluded to.[3] It is so well known, and so is the continual use of the laurel throughout classical antiquity as a sacred emblem of Apollo, as a sign of victory, the indispensable accompaniment of every triumph, and also as a healing power almost as important as the serpent of Æsculapius.[4]

In the opening cantos of the Iliad there is a scene which may serve as well as any other to illustrate the feelings of the Greeks on this subject.[5] When the host was detained in Aulis, and Agamemnon was sacrificing under the shade of a sacred plane tree, a serpent creeps from under the altar, and, climbing the tree, devours deliberately, one after the other, the eight nestlings of a sparrow. The ninth one was the mother bird herself, thus prophesying the nine years they were to tarry before they conquered the wide-streeted Troy. To authenticate the wonder, the serpent was then metamorphosed by Jupiter into stone, and we learn afterwards, that the tree was considered as sacred, inasmuch as Pausanias saw the wood of it preserved in the Temple of Diana in the second century.[6] That nothing may be wanting to complete this as an illustration of their worship, it was while the Greeks were detained at Aulis that Agamemnon was—like Abraham—constrained to sacrifice his child, but as a goat was accepted for the one, so the Grecian hero was saved from a similar sorrow by the substitution of a deer by the goddess Diana. This looks like a period of transition, when at least the most objectionable features of the old faith were becoming obsolete, and might practically be set aside.

---

1 See Bötticher, Baumcultus, pp. 113, 164.
2 Euripides, Iph. in Taur. 1245.
3 At conjux quoniam mea non potes esse.
Arbor eris certe, dixit, mea.—Ovid, Meta. I. 558.
4 See Bötticher, pp. 338–393.
5 Pausanias, IX. 748.
6 Homer, Iliad II. 304, et seq.

It would be easy to multiply these instances of Tree and Serpent Worship among the Greeks to almost any extent; but enough has probably been adduced to show how important a part it played in the mythology of Greece during the whole period of her independent history. When to this we add the knowledge of the purely anthropic and ancestral character of her popular Pantheon, we cannot but feel how little title Greece has to that purely Aryan rank which her language would seem to assign to her. There must always have been a very large admixture of Turanian blood in the veins of the inhabitants of that country, varying, of course, in extent in the different states, but except, perhaps, in Sparta, nowhere entirely evanescent.

Italy.

It does not appear, from anything that has yet been brought to light, that the Etruscans were either worshippers of Serpents or of Trees. It is true the evidence is not conclusive, and is at best merely negative. We have none of the scriptures of the people. We cannot read their inscriptions, and such temples and religious edifices as remain are all of late date, contemporary with the advanced Roman civilization, and when consequently they may have been weaned from their earlier superstitions. It may also be observed that Serpent and Tree Worship are exactly those forms which are least likely to leave permanent traces of their existence except through the traditions of the people in some form of writing. When the Tree or Grove is cut down all traces of it are soon obliterated, and natural decay alone is quite sufficient to cause its complete disappearance, and when the Serpent dies there is no longer a god or an image of one in the sanctuary.

These considerations must make us pause before giving any very decided opinion on the subject; for, reasoning *à priori*, the Etruscans were just such a people as one would suspect of being likely to indulge in such a form of faith.

Their *quasi* Turanian origin, their ancestral worship, the importance they attached to sepulchral rites, the very absence of temples of a permanent character, and many other circumstances, would lead us to expect to find this worship among them, but till it is found it is needless to insist on what at best are mere analogies.

One, however, of the first religious acts of the Romans brings us back to an old line of memories. When Romulus, so says the tradition, had slain Acron king of Cenina in single combat, he hung the "Spolia Opima" on an ancient oak on the Capitoline Hill, which the shepherds before that time had considered as sacred, and there marked out the boundaries of the Temple of Jupiter, which was the first and became afterwards the most sacred of Roman temples.[1]

On the other hand, almost the only tradition that seems to give a local and indigenous form to Serpent Worship is that connected with Lanuvium, a place sixteen miles south of Rome. Here we learn from Ælian there existed a large and dark grove, and near it a temple of the Argive Juno. In this place was a vast and deep cave, the abode of a great serpent. To this grove the virgins of Latium were taken annually to ascertain their chastity, which was indicated by the dragon.[2] If the serpent accepted the offering, not only was their purity considered as established, but a good and fertile season was sure to result from the success of the ordeal.[3] A similar

---

[1] Livy, I. 10. [2] Ælian, Var. Hist. IX. 16. [3] Propertius, Eleg. VIII. 4.

oracle seems to have existed in Epirus, where a circular grove once stood surrounded by a wall in which the sacred serpents were kept, descended it is said from the great Python of Delphi, and here dedicated to Apollo. On the great festival of the year a virgin priestess entered the grove naked, holding in her hand the sacred food. If they took it readily, a fruitful harvest and a plentiful year were sure to follow, if they refused, it was considered as the gloomiest of auguriès.[1] The one difference between the two oracles being that in the Eastern oracle the serpents were not called upon to decide as to the chastity of the priestess, but merely to prophesy as to the prospects of the year.

Except in the instance of Lanuvium the traces of this primitive religion became infinitely more scarce in Italy than they were found to be in Greece, but whether this arises from their non-existence, or merely because they were not recorded, is by no means clear. As mentioned on a previous page,[2] the actual worship of the serpent was introduced from Epidaurus to Rome 462 A.U.C., but the fact of such an embassy being sent on this occasion indicates a degree of faith on the part of the people, which could only have arisen from previous familiarity.

In the Augustan age, enlightenment was too far advanced for such a primitive form of faith to have any real hold on the public mind. Indeed, when such a treatise as that of Cicero "De Natura Deorum" became popular many much more advanced beliefs than that in serpents were trembling in the balance, but the poets still delighted in referring to those forms which time and mystery had long rendered venerable. Ovid's Metamorphoses are full of passages referring to the important part which the Serpent performed in all the traditions of Classic Mythology.

Every one is familiar with the circumstances of the two snakes sent by Minerva to destroy Laocoon,[3] for his attempt to undeceive the fated Trojans. Their task accomplished, they sought refuge behind the shield of Pallas in her temple in the town. Still more characteristic was the appearance of a serpent from the tomb, when Æneas was sacrificing to the manes of his father Anchises,[4] and his hesitation as to whether the unexpected apparition should be considered as the *genius loci*, or an attendant on his deceased parent.

In the other poets there are numerous allusions to Serpents and Serpent Worship, which in themselves, taken separately, would not be of much importance, and which consequently it would be tedious to quote, though taken altogether, with the other information we possess, they do indicate a prevalence of reverence for the serpent in Rome greater than might be expected from so enlightened and so freethinking a community. There is one passage, however, in Perseus[5] which it is impossible to pass over. It is that in which the satirist orders "two serpents to be painted "on the wall to indicate that the place is sacred." The form of this painting we learn from several examples at Pompeii and Herculaneum,[6] where two of somewhat conventional form, and in very conventional attitudes, approach an altar or some object which their presence seems intended to sanctify. There is every reason to suppose that such representations were much more common than the few remains

[1] Ælian, de Animal. XI. 2.

[2] *Vide ante*, p. 15.

[3] Virgil, Æneid. II. 200 and 227.

[4] Ibid, V. 84, et seq.

[5] Pinge duos angues:
Pueri, saçer est locus.—Sat. I. 112.

[6] Antichità d'Ercolano, IV., p. 65, pl. xii.; Mazois, II. pl. 24, &c.

we possess might at first sight lead us to suppose, and that the serpents were also frequently represented as the *genii loci*,[1] and as mixed up with Mithraic or Tree Worship.[2] The instances in which this occurs are so numerous that if collected together they would appear at first sight to make out a strong case, but notwithstanding all this the inhabitants of Imperial Rome cannot fairly be said to have been either a Tree or Serpent worshipping race. It is curious to observe, however, how some of the great men among the Romans still cherished the remnants of this superstition. Scipio Africanus[3] is reported to have believed that he had been nursed by a serpent, and Augustus allowed it to be understood that his mother Atia had received him from a serpent, remembering probably the story of Olympias, the mother of Alexander the Great.[4] The people of Rome, it is said, on one occasion showed more sympathy with the young Domitius (afterwards Nero) than with his half-brother Britannicus, because "serpents had once watched over his childhood."[5]

The Emperor Tiberius[6] kept a tame serpent for his amusement, but when he found it one morning eaten by ants he drew the augury that he must henceforward guard himself against an attack from the many-headed multitude. Hadrian, it is said, procured a large serpent from India, which he placed in the Temple of Jupiter Olympius at Athens,[7] which he had just rebuilt.

It is a difficult question to determine how far the representation of serpents on coins may be taken as indicating the existence of Serpent Worship in the cities to which they belong, or to what extent they should be considered as merely heraldic, like other animals or plants which were emblematic of other cities.[8] If they might be enlisted, the coins of Tyre[9] would go far to confirm what we gather from other sources (*ante*, p. 10) of the prevalence of Serpent Worship there. The most remarkable series, however, of coins of this class are those known as Cistophoroi, belonging to certain cities of Asia Minor. On the obverse of these there is generally in the centre a bow case supported by two serpents standing erect, the one apparently male, the other female, and accompanied by emblems, the meaning of which is not easily determined. On the reverse they generally have a cista mistica, half open, and from it a serpent is issuing (Woodcut No. 1). Around this there is a wreath of vine leaves and grapes, indicating clearly a connexion with the Bacchic mysteries, where such a cist was employed, and in which serpents always performed an important part.

No. 2.

ROMAN PROCONSULAR COIN OF TRALLES.

All these serpent coins belong to the Roman period, the earliest apparently being struck during the pro-consulship of Q. Tullius Cicero (brother of the orator) B.C. 91, and after being the coinage of Asia Minor for more than a century they fade into

[1] Antichità d'Ercolano, vol. I. pl. xxxix.

[2] The Serpent always plays an important part in all representations connected with the worship of Mithra. In the recently discovered Mithraic Temple under the church of St. Clemente, at Rome, the whole of the face of the altar, behind that occupied by the principal divinity, is devoted to the apparently co-ëqual Serpent God.

[3] Gellius, Noct. Att. VI. 1.

[4] Suetonius in Aug. c. 94.

[5] Tacitus, XI. 11.

[6] Suetonius, Vit. Tib. 72.

[7] Xiphilin, Rom. Hist. Script. III. 358.

[8] The British Museum has recently acquired an imperial copper coin representing an image of Diana Artemis on the summit of a tree, and two serpents guarding its base, apparently against the attacks of two men, who seem to be attempting to get possession of the image of the goddess, by cutting down the tree on which it is placed.

[9] Maurice, Indian Ant. VI. p. 273.

the imperial coinage of the empire.[1] Those which have been found up to the present time belong to the following ten cities (Pinder says eleven, but Parium is doubtful), Pergamos, Thyatira, Smyrna, Ephesus, Sardes, Laodicea, Adramyttium, Tralles,[2] Apamea, and Nysa. As will be observed, this list comprises all the Seven churches of Asia, with the exception of Philadelphia, and it is by no means clear that it, too, may not be eventually included. Is this coincidence accidental? If not absolutely, it certainly is nearly correct to assert, that no people adopted Buddhism except those among whom Serpent Worship can certainly be traced as pre-existing, and it appears probable that the worshippers of the serpent should in like manner be more open to the influence of Christianity than the refined and sceptical Greek or Roman.

This is not the place to attempt the investigation of such a subject, even if the materials existed for the purpose, but I may state, that my impression is, that these coins and other evidence[3] do prove the existence of a form of Serpent Worship in the cities of Asia Minor till after the Christian era. And, if I am not mistaken, the presence of such a form of faith may have influenced the early spread of Christianity in these cities to an extent not hitherto suspected.

Germany.

We look in vain through the classical authors for any trace of Serpent Worship among the Germans, nor indeed ought we to expect to find any among a people so essentially Aryan as they are, and always were; while, on the other hand, we have not in Germany, as we find in Greece, any traces of that underlying race of less intellectual Turanians who seem everywhere to have been the Serpent worshippers all the world over.

By whatever name they may have been known, these Ophite races seem, in Europe at least, never to have penetrated far inland from the shore of the sea. The deeply-indented coasts of Greece thus presented a singularly favourable locality for their settlement. They swarmed up the rivers of France, and the shores of such an inland sea as the Baltic was also well suited to their habits. They were adepts at draining lakes or embanking the estuaries of the rivers on which they settled. Fish seems to have been their principal food, and fishing consequently their chief occupation. What domestic animals they possessed they pastured on the alluvial plains which were kept clear of forests and fertilized by the floods. Such a people were, however, utterly incompetent to deal with the forests that covered the soil of Germany, and incapable of that steady organization of labour without which success in agriculture is impossible; especially under so rigorous a climate, and conditions so unfavourable as those which the surface of Germany must have presented to the earliest settlers there.

If, however, we find no traces of Serpent Worship among the purely Teutonic races, the evidences of Tree Worship are numerous and complete. Tacitus, in his Germania

---

[1] The best account, so far as I know, of these coins is in a paper by M. Pinder, in the Transactions of the Akad. der Wissenschaften. Berlin, 1855. As what is said in the text is mainly based on this, it will not be necessary to refer to it again.

[2] Those of Tralles have also the Indian humped bull on the obverse (pl. 1, figs. 18 and 20), though what this may mean it is impossible to say.

[3] Herodotus, I. 78.

alludes to it frequently. In one place he distinctly states that the Germans have no images, and decline to enclose their gods within walls, but consecrate groves and woods, within which they call on the name of God.[1] They called together the people of their own race in woods sanctified by the auguries of their forefathers or pristine awe,[2] and sacred groves and trees are mentioned by name both by him and Cæsar.[3] The most frequent mention, however, of the sacred groves and trees of the Germans is to be found in the earlier Christian writers, who, when narrating the events that accompanied the conversion of the nation to Christianity, relate how these were cut down and destroyed, in order that the old superstitions might be eradicated. These have been collected and arranged by Grimm[4] with his usual industry and intelligence, so that it is hardly necessary here to go over the same ground again. The conclusion he arrives at (p. 60) is that "individual gods might have dwelt on hill-tops, or in " caves, or rivers, but the festal universal religion of the people had its abode in " *woods*, and nowhere has another temple yet been found."

The first care of the Christian missionaries, wherever they went, was to cut down the groves of the Pagans, and to desecrate their ancient places of worship, or to speak more correctly, to consecrate them to their own religion by the erection of a chapel or church within their sacred precincts. They soon discovered that by the first course they only excited the wrath and enmity of the natives, by the latter they conciliated them, and drew them insensibly towards the purer faith; but they fail to tell us how long these quasi converts persisted in venerating in their hearts the god-like grove rather than the miserable stone and mortar house in which the priests told them their new god alone consented to dwell.

It would be well worth while, if anyone would take the trouble, to trace how long trees and groves continued to be objects of veneration after the Germans were converted to Christianity. One of the last and best known examples is that of the "Stock am Eisen" in Vienna, the sacred tree into which every apprentice, down to very recent times, before setting out on his "Wanderjahre," drove a nail for luck. It now stands in the centre of that great capital, the last remaining vestige of the sacred grove round which the city has grown up, and in sight of the proud cathedral of the Christian, which has superseded and replaced its more venerable shade.[5]

Sarmatia.

If a line were drawn from the shores of the Caspian Sea north of the Caucasus to the mouth of the Vistula or Dwina in the Baltic, it would be coincident with one

---

[1] Tacitus, Germ. 9.

[2] Prisca formidine, Loc. cit. 39.

[3] Loc. cit. 40. 43. Cæsar, Ann. 2. 12; 4. 73.

"The Khonds use neither temples nor images in their worship. They cannot comprehend, and regard as absurd the idea of building a house in honour of the deity, or the expectation that he will be peculiarly present in any place resembling a human habitation. Groves kept sacred from the axe, hoar rocks and hill tops, fountains and the banks of streams, are in their eyes the fittest places for worship."—Major Charteris MacPherson, Journal Royal Asiatic Society, vol. XIII. p. 235.

[4] Deutsche Mythologie, c. IV. pp. 57 to 77.

[5] The festival of the Christmas tree at the present day, so common throughout the whole of Germany, is almost undoubtedly a remnant of the Tree Worship of their ancestors.

of the oldest routes of communication between the east and the west. If we are correct in assuming that Tree and Serpent Worship had their origin in the East, it was most probably by this road that any traces of them that are found in the north of Europe must have found their way thither. It was on this route that Hercules met the serpent-maiden Echidna, and where she gave birth to the Eponymous hero of the Scythian nation.[1] Here, too, resided the Amazons, the female warriors, whose institutions seem so mysteriously connected with Serpent Worship. At the far end of this route Procopius tells us that "in his day the barbarians worshipped forests "and groves, and in their barbarous simplicity placed trees among their gods."[2]

In Sarmatia, according to Erasmus Stella, "for some time they had no sacred rites; "at length they arrived at such a pitch of wickedness that they worshipped serpents "and trees." The Samogitæ, we are told, worshipped the serpent as a god, and if any adversity befel them, concluded that their domestic serpents had been negligently served. In Lithuania the people "believed vipers and serpents to be gods, and "worshipped them with great veneration." Jerome of Prague, in the fifteenth century, according to Silvius, saw these wretched idolaters offer sacrifices to serpents. Every householder had a snake in the corner of his house, to which he gave food and offered sacrifice. Cromer[3] charges the Prussians with the same idolatry, and Masius[4] mentions a royal town near Wilna where in his day (*adhuc*) serpents were worshipped by many of the inhabitants, and in Livonia it is characteristically added that the inhabitants were accustomed to sacrifice their most beautiful captives to their serpent gods.[5]

None of these indications are worth much in themselves, and the authorities on which they rest are not such as will bear the test of critical examination, but the general impression they leave is, that Serpent Worship must have prevailed in Eastern Europe to a great extent during the middle ages. It seems incredible that the authors named, and especially such a work as that of Olaus Magnus, should be so full of anecdotes of serpents and Serpent Worship in a country where nothing larger than a viper or adder naturally is found, if there were not some foundation for their belief.

Olaus Magnus,[6] quoting from Crantzius and Mechavita, states that the Poles worshipped their gods, Fire, Serpents, and Trees,[7] in woods. This state of things, he says, lasted in Poland down to the year 1386, when the prince and his brethren were converted to Christianity; but he adds, that though nearly extinguished, these superstitions still linger (1555) in remote parts of Norway and Wermelandia. In addition to this, however, we have evidence which it seems impossible to doubt, that

---

1 Herodotus, IV. 9.

2 De Bello Gotico, II. 471, Bonn, 1833.

3 De Rebus Polon. III. 43.

4 De Diis German. c. 29.

5 This paragraph is abridged from Deane's Serpent Worship, p. 245, et seq. I have not been able to verify the references.

6 Lib. III. ch. 1.

7 Rubenus, a Benedictine monk, being ordered to visit Dorpat in 1588, "on his way passed through the "sacred woods of the Esthonians. He saw there a pine tree of extraordinary bigness, the branches of which "were full of pieces of old cloth, and the roots covered with many bundles of hay and straw.

"He asked what was the meaning of it, and was answered that the inhabitants adored that tree, and that "women after a safe delivery brought these bundles. They had also a custom at certain times to offer a tun "of beer, &c." Bayle's Dictionary, English translation, 1737, vol. IV. p. 928.

both Trees and Serpents were worshipped by the peasantry in Esthonia and Finland within the limits of the present century (see Appendix A), and even then with all the characteristics possessed by the old faith when we first become acquainted with it.[1]

SCANDINAVIA.

Among the problems that perplex the investigator of northern antiquities there are few that present so many difficulties as those which concern the advent of Woden, and the origin of the religion of which he was the chief. Hitherto a solution has frequently been sought in a connexion supposed to exist between the northern religion and that known in India under the title of Buddhism. By assuming Woden to have migrated from the east, and brought that religion with him, the difficulties which perplex the subject have to a certain extent been assumed as explained. The more closely, however, the question is examined the less hope does there appear to be that a solution can be reached in this direction.

There are not, perhaps, in the whole world two religions so diametrically and so essentially opposed to one another as Buddhism and Wodenism, nor two persons so different as the gentle Sákya Muni, who left a kingdom, family, and friends to devote fifty-three years of his blameless life to the attempt to alleviate the sufferings of mankind, and Odin, "the terrible and severe God, the Father of slaughter: he who "giveth victory and reviveth courage in the conflict: who nameth those that are "to be slain."[2]

The leading doctrinal characteristic of Buddhism in its early form is its atheism; the Scandinavian, on the other hand, had Woden, Thor, Freya, and a host of minor gods, rulers of men during their lifetime, and continuing the active personal interference with the affairs of men after their elevation. Among the practical characteristics of Buddhism there was, first, the remarkable extension of the Jewish Commandment, "Thou shalt do no murder" into "Thou shalt not kill," including in the prohibition everything that had life; while the greatest glory of the northern hero was the number of his enemies he had slain, and nothing escaped from his joyous bloodthirstiness. Another peculiarity of Buddhism was the negation of all worldly pleasures and enjoyments. It is hardly possible to conceive anything more incongruous than would have been the presence among the roistering mead-drinking warriors of the north, of a yellow-robed ascetic, sworn to celibacy, living on alms, and devoting his life to pious contemplation; his one hope and highest aspiration being, that after infinite transmigrations he might be so purified by suffering that he might eventually obtain absolute rest by annihilation and absorption into the original essence of all things. How different this from the northern Walhalla. "The heroes," says the Edda,[3] "who are received into the palace of "Odin have every day the pleasure of arming themselves, of passing in review, "of ranging themselves in order of battle, and of cutting one another to pieces; "but so soon as the time of repast approaches they return on horseback all safe

---

[1] Der Ehsten abergläubische gebraüche, &c., von J. W. Boecler, beleuchtet von F. R. Kreutzwald. St. Petersburg, 1854.

[2] Mallet, Northern Antiq. (Bohn's edition), p. 21.

[3] Mallet, Northern Antiq., p. 104.

"and sound to the hall of Odin, and fall to eating and drinking. Though the "number of them cannot be counted, the flesh of the boar, Sæhrimnir,[1] is sufficient "for them all; every day it is served up at table, and every day renewed entire. "Their beverage is ale and mead. One single goat, whose milk is mead, furnishes "enough of that liquor to intoxicate all the heroes. Odin alone drinks wine; "wine is for him both meat and drink. A crowd of virgins wait on the heroes "at table, and fill their cups as fast as they empty them."

This, certainly, is not Buddhism, at least as that religion is known to us by anything that has hitherto been published on the subject. How far the revelations of the sculptures of the Sanchi Tope and Cuttack Caves may induce us to change our opinions of the earlier forms of that faith remains to be seen. There is, certainly, a much greater similarity between the Buddhism of the Topes and the Scandinavian mythology than between it and the Buddhism of the books, or as preached by Sákya Muni; but still the gulf between the two is immense, and if any traces of the doctrines of the gentle ascetic ever existed in the bosoms of Odin or his followers, all that can be said is, that they suffered fearful shipwreck among the rocks of the savage superstitions of the north, and sank, never again to appear on the surface of Scandinavian mythology. If the two religions came anywhere in contact it is at their base, and before the Indian form was reformed in the sixth century, B.C., for underlying both there seems to have existed a strange substratum of Tree and Serpent Worship; on this the two structures seem to have been raised, though they afterwards diverged into forms so strangely dissimilar.

As will be seen in a subsequent part of this work, recent discoveries have narrowed, to a certain extent, the gulf which separated them at the time of their greatest development, and it is by no means impossible that if we are able to go further back they may be found to approximate still more closely. We do not however, at present, see much prospect of reaching a point where the two may come in contact, except at the point where they both start from their fundamental Serpent Worship; but the inquiry is too new, and the facts yet gathered are far from being sufficient to enable us to speak with anything like certainty, except regarding the later forms of either of these faiths.

The myth of the Yggdrasil ash is told in considerable detail in the Prose Edda, though its meaning will hardly be understood till we are more familiar with the corresponding features in Indian mythology.

"It was under the ash, the chiefest and holiest seat of the gods, that they "assembled every day in council. The branches spread over the whole world, and "even reach to heaven above. It has three roots, one stood over Mimir's well, in "which wisdom and wit lie hidden; and one over Niflheim, a place where those "wicked people are sent who die from natural causes, and this root it is, that is "continually gnawed by the serpent Nidhögg, with whom in Hwergelmir there are "so many snakes that no tongue can recount them.[2] The third root of the ash is

---

1 Mallet, Prose Edda, 429.

2 Pliny refers to the connexion of the serpent with the ash, but in a different sense (XVI. 13). He says snakes will not rest in its shadow, but shun it at a distance, and adds, from "personal experience," that, "if a "serpent is so surrounded by a fence of ash leaves that he cannot escape except by passing through fire, he will "prefer the fire rather than pass through the leaves."

" in heaven, under it is the holy Urdar fount; it is here the gods sit in judgment. " Near this sit the three Norns or fates, who fix the lifetime of all men. In its " branches sits an eagle who knows many things, and a squirrel, Ratatösk, runs " up and down, and seeks to cause strife between the Eagle and Nidhögg. Four " harts run across the branches of the tree and bite the buds." In addition to this is the great Midgard serpent Jörmungand, "who being of parentage of bad " augury, was thrown by All-Father (Odin) into the ocean, but the monster grew " to such an enormous size, that holding his tail in his mouth, he encircles the " whole earth."[1]

Without continuing these quotations further at present, enough has perhaps been brought forward to show that Yggdrasil is in the first place a reminiscence of the trees of fate and knowledge of the Garden of Eden, though wisdom lay in a well of water at the root of the northern tree, of which Odin drank and gained knowledge,[2] instead of eating its fruit, which, with an ash, was not a probable form of the myth. It is also probably enough to enable us to recognize in the eagle, the Garuda, and in the Nidhögg, the Nâgas of eastern fable, though the squirrel does not there appear to have been necessary to keep alive the enmity that always existed between them. And in Thor fishing for the Midgard serpent, and the part he is to play at the end of all things, we may without difficulty recognize a reflex of the churning of the ocean and the renewal of all things by Vishnu through the instrumentality of the great serpent. As might be expected from the nature of the country and style of its historians, we have fewer accounts of the actual form of the worship than of its doctrinal importance. Still we are told[3] that in front of the great Temple at Upsala "there grew a huge tree of unknown kind, that spread with " large boughs, and was green both summer and winter," and near the same temple a sacred grove, every tree and every leaf of which was considered the most sacred thing in the world.[4] It was called Odin's Grove, and in it the most solemn sacrifices were performed, especially every ninth year, when nine human victims were sacrificed from among the captives if in time of war, or nine slaves if in time of peace.

The serpent is not mentioned as an actual object of worship in any written history; though no doubt the superstition prevailed with the others down to the time when the whole was abolished in the ninth century on the introduction of Christianity. Yet we are told that in the sixteenth century, "There are house " serpents which are accounted in the northern parts of Sweden as household gods; " they are fed with sheep and cows' milk and to hurt them is a deadly sin." The same author tells us that "serpents rest deep under the roots of birch trees, the " multitude of them cause heat with their breath, and so keep the leaves green in " winter."[5] All this is foolish enough, but the thousand and one stories about serpents which crowd the pages of the good Archbishop of Upsala suffice to show that even in his day the superstition had not died out among the common people, and though serpents were no longer worshipped, the time when they were so was

[1] Translation of Prose Edda, 410, et seq.
[2] Page 411.
[3] Olaus Magnus, III. 5.
[4] Mallet, p. 113.
[5] Olaus Magnus, XXI. 47 and 48.

not yet forgotten.[1] At the same time it seems tolerably clear that such a serpent mythology as existed in Sweden could never have sprung up naturally in so northern a climate, where all the snake tribe are so insignificant. It must have been imported from the East, though we have yet to learn by whom this was done, and at what exact time it was effected.

France.

We seem to know less of the primitive worship of the early inhabitants of Gaul than of that of almost any other country of Europe. This may arise partly because the Gauls were so far civilized before the classical authors became acquainted with them, that their old beliefs had lost much of their individuality and freshness, while they were not so far advanced or civilized at the time when Christianity blotted out the old religions, as to feel sufficient interest in them to care to record their forms. A good deal also is no doubt due to the fact that the subject has not been carefully investigated by any competent authority since the new school of criticism was introduced. The French antiquarians do not yet seem to have discovered the safe channel between the whirlpools of credulity and the dry sand banks of frigid scepticism.

Nearly all that we know of the religion of the ancient Gauls is gathered from the celebrated passage in Cæsar's Commentaries,[2] when he pauses from the narrative of his exploits to describe the civil and religious institutions of the people he had conquered. In this account there is absolutely no mention of either Tree or Serpent Worship; on the contrary, he tells us that their principal deity was Mercury, not probably the god known by that name in the Roman Pantheon, but it may be Woden or some such synonym. After him came Apollo, Mars, Jupiter, and Minerva. Rather a strange selection, and stranger classification if we are to accept them as the Roman gods whose names they bear; but most probably they were local deities who, to his apprehension, more closely resembled these gods than any other his readers might be acquainted with.

Cæsar's assertion that the Druids were the priests, and by inference the only priests of the Gauls, is considerably modified by the subsequent testimony of both Strabo[3] and Diodorus[4] who divide the priests into three classes, the Bards, the Druids, and the Soothsayers. All these authors agree in describing the principal rite to consist in sacrifices, performed apparently in the open air, and by inference in groves. They also agree in stating that human victims were frequently immolated in what appears to have been considered the most solemn and acceptable of their sacred rites.

---

1 Castren, in his Travels in Lapland, gives some very curious details about the feelings of the Lapps with regard to Serpent and Tree Worship at the present day. According to their traditions, Snakes, like men, live in societies, each with a captain and subordinate officers; once a year each community meets in general assembly, and not only has each serpent the right to bring his own grievances forward, but the jurisdiction of the chief extends to men who have slain or offended any of his subjects. *Reise Erinnerungen aus den Jahren* 1838–44, pp. 66–77. A good deal of information on this subject will be found in a Swedish work by Hylten-Cavallius, entitled Wärend och Wirdarne, p. 142, for the worship of Trees as at present existing, and pp. 329 to 332 for that of Serpents.

2 De Bello Gall. VI. 13, 20.

3 Geographica, IV. 275.

4 Hist. V. 31.

Notwithstanding the silence of the principal authorities, we are not without evidence as to Tree Worship having prevailed. Maximus Tyrius,[1] for instance, distinctly asserts that the "Celts worship Jupiter, but under the form of a tall oak tree;" and Pliny[2] describes in detail the veneration of the Druids for the oak, especially the mistletoe, which grew on the oak, the ceremony accompanying its removal being apparently in Pliny's eyes the most important of those connected with the worship. It is, however, more from Christian writers that we acquire a conviction that Tree Worship prevailed extensively among the Celts.[3]

There is, for instance, the famous pear tree, that grew at Auxerre in the fourth century, which was hung with trophies of the chase, and venerated as god by the people to such an extent that its destruction by the Holy Amator was considered a triumph, not only worthy to be related at length in the life of Genarius,[4] but sung in indifferent Latin verse some centuries afterwards by Herricus.[5] From the Life of St. Amandus[6] we learn that groves and trees (*arbores et ligna pro diis colerent*) were worshipped in the north of France, near Beauvais (Belvacence), and the destruction of the tree, which was dedicated to the devil (*arborem quæ erat dæmoni dedicata*), is recorded as a most meritorious act.

The second Council of Arles[7] denounced those who venerated trees, or fountains, or stones, and declared those guilty of sacrilege who neglected to destroy them. That of Tours[8] issued a similar decree, almost in the same words. These instances might no doubt be multiplied to almost any extent if anyone would take the trouble to look for them, but, as before mentioned, the French archæologists have hardly turned their attention to the subject.[9]

The traces of Serpent Worship in Gaul are so few and so evanescent that, in ordinary circumstances, an author would be justified in asserting that it did not exist among the Celts any more than it did among the Germans, and in passing by the subject altogether. Such a superstructure, however, has been raised on a passage in Pliny[10] that it is impossible to treat it thus. Among the many marvels and puerilities of his Natural History, there is none more absurd than that of the egg (*anguinum*) produced by the breath of a number of serpents, who meet together for the purpose of producing it, apparently on midsummer eve. It is projected by them into the air, and must be caught in a blanket before it falls, and the fortunate possessor must be on horseback, and gallop off with it; for if the snakes catch him before he crosses running water, a worse fate than Tam o' Shanter's will befall him! This fable is reported on the authority of the Druids, and it is added that this *anguinum* is considered a charm by them. It is, I believe, the only passage in any classical

---

1 Diss. 8. ed. Reiske, I. 142.: Κέλτοι σεβοῦσι μὲν Δία, ἄγαλμα δὲ Διὸς Κελτικὸν ὑψηλὴ δρῦς.

2 Hist. Nat. XVI. 95.

3 My conviction is, that the circular church at Lanleff in Brittany was originally dedicated to Tree Worship. There is nothing Christian about its form or sculptures. The centre never was roofed, or intended to be so, though the aisles were, and there seems no good reason for doubting that the Yew Tree which adorned its centre, till within the last few years, was really the "Numen" for which this temple was built, probably in the tenth century of our era.

4 Act. Sanctor. Bolland, 31 Julii, p. 203.

5 Quoted by Grimm, Deutsche Myth. (2d ed.), p. 69.

6 Acta Benedict. sec. 2, p. 714.

7 Arles Concil. II. can. 23.

8 Concil. Tur. II. can. 16.

9 On Tree Worship in Gaul, see D. Monnier, Traditions Populaires comparées. Paris, 1854. p. 716. ff. See also Rude Stone Monuments by the Author, pp. 24—26.

10 Hist. Nat. XXIX. 3.

author that connects the Druids with serpents, or by implication would lead us to suspect that some superstition regarding serpents may have existed in Gaul.

If the records of the early provincial Christian councils in France were examined, it is possible that some denunciation of Serpent Worship may be found. If General Penhouët[1] is to be trusted, there are frequent traditions of the destruction of serpents by the early Christian missionaries, and these may fairly be construed as meaning Serpent Worshippers, if such passages exist; but till they are abstracted and published, no argument can be based on them.[2]

There is still one argument which has occasionally been hinted at in the previous pages, which may be considered as tending to show that Serpent Worship may have prevailed among the Celts. They certainly indulged in human sacrifices, and where this custom prevails, we generally find Serpent Worship accompanying it. The converse also is generally true. The worshippers of the serpent were those who, so far as we know, were most addicted to the sacrifice of men. If this proposition could be established absolutely, it would be a sufficient proof of the prevalence of Serpent Worship in Gaul, but the premises are as yet much too far from being established to enable us to draw any such definite conclusion from them. They may eventually be brought to do so. At present it must suffice to indicate the form of the argument without attempting to base any theory on so slender a foundation.

On the whole, therefore, we are probably justified in assuming that Tree Worship did exist among the Celts as among the Germans till their conversion to Christianity; but, on the other hand, there seems to be no sufficient evidence to show that they were worshippers of the serpent, and if the Druids were priests of the Celts, which there seems no reason for denying, there is nothing to connect them with that faith, though no doubt they may not only have tolerated but indulged in local superstitions, as many Christians do at the present day.

At the same time recent researches have brought to light circumstances which would lead us to believe that there existed in France an earlier pre-Celtic race

---

[1] The Rev. Bathurst Deane, Worship of the Serpent, p. 283, et seq.

[2] The following curious particulars were furnished me by my friend Sir Vincent Eyre, of ceremonies witnessed by him in company with several English gentlemen at Luchon, in May 1869, and published by him in the Athenæum in July of that year. They certainly are not an evidence of Serpent Worship, but look very like a reminiscence of a triumph over Serpent Worshippers.

"Some singular rites and ceremonies, which appear to have been handed down from remote heathen times, are still to be found in full force at Luchon, in the Pyrenees, where it is customary, on the eve of St. John, to sacrifice living serpents, by means of a fiery and somewhat cruel ordeal, in the following manner:—A hollow column, composed of strong wicker-work, is raised to the height of about sixty feet in the centre of the principal suburb, and interlaced with green foliage up to the very top, while the most beautiful flowers and shrubs procurable are artistically arranged in groups below, so as to form a sort of background to the scene. The column is then filled with combustible materials, ready for ignition. At an appointed hour,—about 8 p.m.,—a grand procession, composed of the clergy, followed by young men and maidens in holiday attire, pour forth from the town chanting hymns, and take up their position around the column. Meanwhile, bonfires are lit, with beautiful effect in the surrounding hills. As many living serpents as could be collected are now thrown into the column, which is set on fire at the base, by means of torches, armed with which about fifty boys and men dance around with frantic gestures. The serpents, to avoid the flames, wriggle their way to the top, whence they are seen lashing out laterally until finally obliged to drop, their struggles for life giving rise to enthusiastic delight among the surrounding spectators.

"This is a favourite annual ceremony for the inhabitants of Luchon and its neighbourhood, and local tradition assigns to it a heathen origin."

allied to the Esthonians and Finns. They may have been Serpent Worshippers, but they seem to have been obliterated by the Celts in very early pre-Christian times, and their fossil remains have not yet been examined to a sufficient extent to enable any positive opinion to be formed on the subject.

Great Britain.

If we have reason to complain that the French archæologists have not turned sufficient attention to their pre-historic antiquities, the same reproach cannot certainly be applied to those of this country. From the days of Aubrey and Stukeley to the present day volume after volume has issued from the press, and the transactions of learned societies are full of papers on the subject. Every barrow has been explored, every antiquity measured and described, and it must be added every etymology has been enlisted, and every scrap of evidence gathered together and amplified, till a fabric has been raised of such marvellous magnitude that it is startling to find on what slight foundation it rests, and how soon it would topple over if the breath of reason could only be brought to bear upon it. In the meanwhile, however, every upright stone has become a Druidical remain, and every circle or line of stones an Ophite temple. There was a time, according to our antiquaries, when the Druids ruled absolutely in this land, and when, under their auspices, Serpent Worship was as essentially the religion of the people as Christianity is now. The belief that this was so has become from reiteration so engrained, that modern science will probably have a harder task to extirpate it, than the Romans had to abolish the real Druids, or the early Christian missionaries had to induce the people to forsake the worship of the serpent in countries where it prevailed in reality.

Fortunately the controversy lies in a very narrow compass. There are, I believe, only two very short paragraphs in any classical authors which mention Druids in connexion with Britain, and not one that mentions Serpent Worship, and no English author prior, at all events, to the 13th century alludes to either the one or the other.[1]

Of the two classical passages, that in Tacitus applies strictly to the Isle of Mona (Anglesea), and will be referred to hereafter. The other is that in Cæsar's Commentaries,[2] and is so important that it must be quoted at length, and in its own language. After describing the Institution of the Druids in Gaul, he goes on to say: "Disciplina "(Druidum) in Britannia reperta, et inde in Galliam translata esse existimatur, et "nunc qui diligentius eam rem cognoscere volunt, plerumque illo discendi causa "proficiscuntur." Had this slight allusion not slipped from Cæsar's pen, there would have been absolutely no evidence of the existence of Druids in England; and after all it hangs on the value to be assigned to the word "existimatur," it is thought or believed! Neither Cæsar or any other Roman ever said he saw a Druid in this country; they never mention their temples or sacred places, and no one ever assisted at their rites. Still, with this paragraph before us, and with the knowledge that the majority of the

---

[1] I make this absolute statement with considerable confidence, not only because no paragraph of the sort has been quoted by any of the advocates of this faith, but because there is a very full and careful index to the "Monumenta Historica Britannica," and the word Druid does not occur in it.

[2] De Bello Gall. VI. 13.

inhabitants were Celts, it cannot be denied but that Druids may have existed in England, but even then their connexion with Serpent Worship rests wholly on that very apocryphal passage in Pliny (vide *ante*), in which he asserts that the Druids used the *anguinum* as a charm.

The other paragraph is more to the point.[1] In the year 61 A.D., Paulinus Suetonius was called away to suppress a revolt in the Island of Mona. He there met the army of the natives on the shore, and saw that the women and Druidesses were rushing about with dishevelled locks, and torches in their hands, urging the men to the contest.[2] When the rebellion was suppressed, the sacred groves in which their human sacrifices had been performed were cut down, and we are led to infer Druidism suppressed. Tacitus then goes on to narrate with infinitely more detail the far more important revolt of Boadicea, but, strange to say, in that great national uprising there is absolutely no mention of Druids, either in his narrative or in that of Dion Cassius.[3] No groves were cut down, no rites abolished, when it was suppressed; and if any legitimate inference can be drawn from such silence, no Druids existed in the more civilized parts of England.

From whatever point of view the subject is looked at, it seems almost impossible to avoid the conclusion that there were two races in England,—an older and less civilized people, who,[4] in the time of the Romans, had already been driven by the Celts into the fastnesses of the Welsh hills, and who may have been Serpent Worshippers and sacrificers of human victims, and that the uncritical Romans confounded the two. They seem rather to have dwelt on the picturesqueness of the naked blue-painted savage as a contrast with those races they were familiar with, as a Catlin revels in the manners and virtues of the Red Indian in contrast to the vices and effeminacy of his more civilized oppressor.

Be this as it may, it is principally from Welsh Triads, so-called, and the Welsh bards, that we depend for our knowledge of the Druids and their doings, and Serpent Worship in this country. If we knew when the works of the Welsh bards were reduced to the form in which we now find them, and if we could depend on the translations we have, some light might no doubt be thrown on our subject.[5] It is, however, an unfortunate peculiarity of the Celtic mind that when they attempt to elucidate the history of their country from their annals, they adopt a species of logic totally distinct from that followed by the Saxon, so that it becomes impossible to use the information they offer. Still it does not seem reasonable to doubt but that remnants of the Druidical religion, and perhaps also of Serpent Worship, may have lingered in the Welsh hills long after they had disappeared from the plains. Where we do find tradition attaching them to any of the monuments of the plain, it is through

---

[1] Tacitus, Ann. XIV. 29.

[2] If I wanted an illustration of this scene, I do not know where I could find a better than on the walls of the Caves at Ajanta. The original copy of the picture was unfortunately burnt in the fire at the Crystal Palace in 1866; but it is engraved in Mrs. Spier's Life in India, p. 302.

[3] Dion Cassius in Xiphilinus' Abridgment, LXII. 1 & 4.

[4] Norris's Cornish Drama, II. 401.

[5] Skene's translation of the four most ancient Welsh poems, which has just been published, has gone far to set this question at rest. It cannot be said that the word Druid does not occur in them, but if we were not looking for it, it is hardly in such a manner as would attract attention, and the part they play is most insignificant, besides it is by no means clear to what age or authority such references really belong.

Welsh agency and almost within sight of the hills, as at Stanton Drew in Somersetshire,[1] where the sainted Keyna, the daughter of a Welsh king changed the Serpents and Serpent Worshippers who opposed her residence among them into the stones of the well known circles there. The still more celebrated example at Whitby where

> " A thousand snakes each one
> Were changed into a coil of stone
> When Holy Hilda prayed,"

I am afraid owes its origin more to the presence of innumerable ammonites in the cliffs than to the pre-ëxistence of any Snake Worshippers on the spot.

Beyond this, though we do occasionally find traditions of the serpent, they are few and far between, and of uncertain origin; one, for instance, is related by Mathew Paris, of St. Albans.[2] Writing in 1260 (?) he relates that the Saxon Abbot Aldred filled up a great hole which once was the abode of an immense dragon, in a place which was still called the Wurmenhert. This appears to have been surrounded by a circular vallum, which we infer still existed in the 13th century, though no trace of it now remains. The circular enclosure and the crypt may be considered as certain, they so exactly resemble the Irish Raths; but the dragon is, I fear, too far off to be depended upon, though it is one of the most authentic traditions we possess.

If this is so, it may be asked, what is the evidence on which the Druidical origin of such monuments as Stonehenge and Avebury have been assumed? The answer fortunately is simple—absolutely none. It never was pretended that any direct testimony existed, and the negative evidence is perfectly complete. No ancient author, no one, in fact, anterior to the invention of printing, ever refers to any stones or stone temples, circular or in any other form, as connected with the worship of the Druids or the Celts. On the other hand, every tradition that exists, whatever their value may be, points to the Arthurian age as that to which they owe their origin.

If it is further asked, what evidence there is to connect these temples with Serpent Worship, exactly the same answer must be given—not one tittle has yet been adduced. The one direction in which it seems probable some such connexion may be established, is from their similarity to the Indian examples, which it is the object of this volume to describe; but whether these will be sufficient for this purpose can only be decided when the argument is fully elaborated. Meanwhile are we correct in calling them temples at all? The one peculiarity of Celtic worship that seems best established, is the love of trees—their fondness of groves for their sacred rites. Is it probable that they would select the downs of Wiltshire, especially such a spot as that where Stonehenge stands, for the site of their greatest temple—a spot where no tree ever grew or could grow? That they might erect a tomb or cenotaph among the graves of their forefathers seems probable enough; and if Avebury was a battle field, that would account for the locality where it is found, but it seems difficult to suggest a reason for their being where they are on any other hypothesis.

This, however, is not the place to examine the evidence on which the age or purposes of these monuments is to be determined. It is, however, impossible to pass over the subject entirely in silence, as reference will occasionally have to be made to

---

[1] Archæologia, XXV. p. 198.

[2] Vitæ Abbatum, p. 40.

them in the following pages; while unfortunately nine people out of ten in this country at the present day believe that Stonehenge and Avebury were built by the Druids; that they were Dracontia or Serpent Temples; and every one can point out the altar stones on which the human victims were sacrificed, and in fact knows all about their religion and rites, and it may be added believes in their primæval antiquity. Till these erroneous impressions are dispelled, the subject we have in hand can hardly be rendered intelligible.[1]

A far more promising field for the investigation of Serpent Worship in Britain occurs in Scotland, on the east coast, north of the Forth. In that country, once known as Pictland, there exists even at the present day a great number of Megalithic monuments, many of which are covered with sculptures of a class totally distinct from those found anywhere else, and which have hitherto baffled the ingenuity of antiquaries. Among them the serpent appears frequently and so prominently that it is impossible to doubt that he was considered as an object of veneration by those who erected those monuments, while on the other hand Serpent Worship could hardly have originated in the north of Scotland, where the snakes are so few and contemptible. Mr. Stuart[2] enumerates twenty-three representations of the serpent on these stones, thirteen times accompanied by emblems, ten times without them. In some instances, such as the Newton stone, the serpent is evidently the object for which the stone was set up, and he is accompanied by the broken sceptre, which may either be a hieroglyphic for God or King, or may only mean "holy" or "great," or some such adjective, but it certainly implies distinction, if not consecration.

The age of these sculptured stones is known with tolerable certainty, inasmuch as the greater number of them have either the Cross itself or Christian emblems engraved upon them, and these must therefore be subsequent to the age of St. Columba, who arrived in Scotland apparently in 563, and died in 597. Many of those also which have only Pagan emblems are so nearly identical with the Christian stones that they must be about the same age. Some, however, are ruder and simpler, and the series fades back into the plain unsculptured Menhir, of which many exist in the same district. There seems, indeed, to be no essential break either, so far as design or purpose is concerned, between the rude unchiselled blocks of Carnac and Avebury and such elaborate Christian obelisks or Swenos stone at Forres, or the group that once surmounted the mound at St. Vigeans.[3]

We shall probably not err far if we regard these traces of Serpent Worship in the north-east of Scotland as indicating the extreme western limit to which an oriental superstition seems to have extended, and which may probably, as hinted above, be traced through Scandinavia and the eastern provinces of Europe to the shores of the Black Sea, where it was in almost immediate contact with those places where we know it afterwards flourished. The Edda seems sufficient to prove that a form of Serpent Worship did certainly prevail in Scandinavia in the early centuries of the Christian era; and nothing seems more probable or more in accordance with Pictish

---

[1] The argument with regard to the age and use of these monuments has, since this was written, been more fully developed by the author in his work on Rude Stone Monuments. Murray, 1871.

[2] Sculptured Stones of Scotland, vol. II. p. lxxiv.

[3] All these will be found described in Stuart's "Sculptured Stones," above referred to, and also in Colonel Forbes Leslie's "Early Races of Scotland." Edin. 1866.

traditions,[1] than that it should have passed thence into Scotland, and should have left its traces everywhere between the Orkneys and the Firths.[2] There is no evidence, however, of Serpent Worship, in this form at least, having passed south of the Forth. The traces of it that may exist in England or Ireland—if any—most probably belong to an earlier pre-historic people, and may have been introduced by another and more southern route.

Africa.

We tread on surer ground, when leaving Serpent Worship in its most attenuated form, and in the uncongenial climate of its furthest extension to the north and west, and turn to Africa, where it always was at home, and where it now flourishes in all its pristine vigour. Serpents are, and always must have been, so numerous and important in Africa, that it is there, if not in Mesopotamia, that we should, *à priori*, expect their worship to have been first introduced, and it is by no means impossible that it was so. We know so little, however, of what happened in Africa in ancient times—except in Egypt—that it is difficult to speak with any confidence on the subject, and the institutions of Egypt were so abnormal and so exclusively their own, that we cannot reason from them to any general conclusions. Perhaps, when the subject is carefully looked into, more may be ascertained than is now known, but our present purpose is with the worship as it exists at the present day, or did in recent times.

One of the best known examples of modern Serpent Worship exists in Upper Egypt, at a place called Sheikh Haredi, from a tomb of a Mahomedan saint of that name, which exists on the spot. The account given of the place by Norden,[3] who visited it in 1738, with a mere change of names, is an exact counterpart of what might have been found in Pausanias or any ancient author describing the grove of Esculapius, at Epidaurus. When anyone was so unwell as to require his services, an ambassadress was sent in the person of a spotless virgin—as at Lanuvium—and if his godship pleased he came out of his cave, hung himself around her neck, and allowed himself to be carried in procession to the sick man's bedside. Here he stayed, as Norden irreverently suggests, a length of time proportionate to the gifts offered to his priests, and then returned alone to his dwelling. Dr. Pococke's episcopal dignity seems to have been so offended by the monstrosity of the superstition, that he abuses the serpent and his attendants, but he confirms in every particular Norden's account. He was told that it had been there since the time of Mahomet; that they sacrificed to it sheep and lambs. They added that when a number of women visit him, which they do once a year, he comes out and twines himself about the neck of the most beautiful.[4]

From Wilkinson[5] we learn that the worship still continues, but has fallen somewhat into disrepute of late.

---

[1] Skene's Chronicles of the Picts and Scots, p. xcv. et seq.

[2] There are some traditions in Northumberland, such as that of the Laidley Wurm of Spindleston Heugh, and there was a Wurm hill at Lambton, and at other places in the neighbourhood (Walter White, Northumberland and the Border, p. 249, et seq.). All this would perfectly accord with the theory that it was the result of a Scandinavian course of immigration which reached these two points on the coast.

[3] Travels in the East, ii. 40.

[4] Pococke in Pinkerton's Voyages, xv. p. 269, et seq.

[5] Handbook of Egypt, 301.

It does not seem to be a matter of much doubt but that the Serpent was extensively worshipped in Abyssinia before the introduction of Christianity in the fourth century. All the lists of their kings which have been brought home by Bruce, Rüppell, and others, commence with "the Serpent" and his progeny, though we are not told when he reigned nor where. We are further told that when Ábreha and Átzbeha founded Axum 340 A.D., "that one portion of the people of Ethiopia "then worshipped the Serpent, the rest followed the Law of Moses. Abuna Abba "Salâmâ then introduced Christianity, and the inhabitants were baptized," &c.[1]

It is by no means clear whether the great dragon who is said to have lived at Axum[2] was the image of a god or merely a serpent, more probably the former, as he was burst asunder by the prayers of nine Christian saints. Be all this as it may, we have the direct testimony of Bruce[3] that the Shangalla, in that neighbourhood, "worship various trees, serpents, the moon, planets, and stars in certain "positions;" and more instances might no doubt be found if looked for. It is, however, on the west coast that the worship flourishes in all its pristine vigour.

Although no one has resided long enough on the Guinea coast with learning and leisure sufficient to write anything like an exhaustive treatise on the religions of that country, we have what is nearly of equal value for our purposes in a series of narratives of Portuguese, Dutch, French, and English travellers, extending over more than two hundred years. Those anterior to 1746 have been digested by Astley[4] into a continuous narrative and description; and in 1760 President de Brosses,[5] of the French Academy, wrote a lucid account of what was then known on the subject, and from that time various travellers have added to our knowledge. The best and fullest of the modern narratives are those of M. Répin,[6] a surgeon in the French navy; and that of Capt. Burton and Commodore Wilmot,[7] who went on an official mission to Dahomey in 1863. The one point on which we desire more information is as to the extent of this form of faith, and as to the ethnological relations of the people who practise it. We are told, for instance, that when the Dahomans invaded Whidah in 1726, they killed the sacred snakes, and otherwise outraged the religious feelings of the Whidans.[8] Both countries are now united under one rule, and apparently with one religion. Was it otherwise 140 years ago? and can the distinction now be traced? These and such like questions are well worthy of more attention than they have hitherto received, for if we are ever to understand the ancient peculiarities of this faith, it must be by a thorough study of the best living examples.

Hitherto we have been only gathering together, as it were, the fossil remains of an extinct religion, whereas in Africa not only does Serpent Worship flourish at the present day, but it exists in conjunction with all those peculiarities of which only traces can be found elsewhere. Ancestral worship, accompanied by human sacrifices on the most lavish scale, is the leading characteristic of the Dahoman religion, and

---

1 Dillmann in Zeitschrift der Morgenländischen Gesellschaft, vol. VII. p. 338, et seq.

2 Ludolf. Comment. iii. 284?

3 Travels, ii. 554.

4 Astley's Collection of Voyages, 4 vols. quarto, London, 1846.

5 De Brosses, du Culte des Dieux Fetisches, &c. 12mo. Paris, 1760.

6 Le Tour du Monde, 1863, p. 9, et seq.

7 Mission to the King of Dahomey, 2 vols. 8vo. Murray, 1864.

8 Capt. Snellgrove's Narrative in Astley, iii. 489.

with it we have the institution of a female warrior class, which we have hitherto only known through the beautiful Amazonian fictions of the Greeks or the legends of the Hindoos, as to the Strî-râjya, but in Dahomey the institution exists to this day in all its hideous savagery.

The three gods worshipped in Whidah, or to speak more correctly, the three classes of gods, are Serpents, Trees, and the Ocean;[1] the same trinity represented by Minerva, Neptune, and Erechthonios as was established in the Erechtheum, in the Akropolis of Athens, more than three thousand years ago. Of these, the serpent called Danh gbwe, or the earthly serpent, is the first. "It is esteemed the supreme bliss and "general good. It has 1,000 Danh-si, or snake wives, married and single votaries, and "its influence cannot be meddled with by the two others, which are subject to it."[2]

The ancestor of the present race of serpent gods is said to have deserted from the Ardrah people ages ago, in consequence of their wickedness, on the eve of a battle, and to have been received by the Whidah people with the highest honours.[3] He is reported to be still alive, as all these gods are immortal, though it need hardly be added, no European has seen him, but his descendants seem to be among the most beautiful, and certainly are among the most harmless of their kind.

Des Marchais gives a full description of the worship addressed to this god, and a picture of a procession, in which the king, the king's wives, and all the nobles took part,[4] bearing presents and offerings to the serpent god. Prayers are addressed to him on every occasion, and answers are returned by the snakes in conversation with the high priest. The one thing we seem to miss is the Esculapian character. It may be that this is included in his characteristic of an omniscient and all-powerful god, but it does not seem to be especially mentioned.

Women, when touched by the serpent, are said to become "possessed." They are seized with hysteria, and often bereft of reason. When so affected they are secluded in hospitals prepared for their reception, and generally afterwards are considered as priestesses,—Fetish women,—though returned to civil life. The bulk of the priestesses are girls devoted either before their birth or at a very early age to the service of the god. They are brought up in the temple, taught singing, dancing, and various accomplishments exactly as the nautch girls are in the temples of Southern India, and when of age are married to the god. On this occasion they are marked with the image of the god by pricking the skin with needles and rubbing in indigo, or some blue dye, which is indelible.[5] This seal is said to be set upon them by the god himself,[5] but, as in Greece, no one dare to divulge his mysteries.

Besides this earthly serpent, there is another, the heavenly one, commonly called Danh. It is the rainbow, and makes the Popo beads, and confers wealth on man. Its emblem is a coiled and horned snake of clay, in a pot or calabash.[6]

---

[1] Bosman in Astley.

[2] Burton, vol. II. p. 139.

[3] Des Marchais' (1725) Voyages, ii. p. 135, et seq.

[4] A copy of this plate is given in Astley, vol. III. plate 7.

[5] From Suetonius we learn that when Atia, the mother of Augustus, was touched by the serpent in the temple of Apollo, she was marked with a stain (macula) like a painted serpent, so that she did not afterwards dare to appear in the public baths.—Sueton. in Aug. c. 94.

[6] Burton, ii. 148.

The second god in the Dahoman Pantheon is represented by lofty and beautiful trees. They are prayed to and presented with offerings in times of sickness, and especially of fever. The most revered of these is the cotton tree (Bombax), whose wives equal those of the snake, and the Loco, the well-known poison tree of the West African coast. The latter numbers few Loco-si or wives, but, on the other hand, has its own fetish pottery, which may be bought in every market.[1]

The youngest brother of the triad is Hu, the ocean. The Huno, or ocean priest, is now considered the highest of all, a fetish king at Whidah, where he has 500 wives. The offerings to this god are rice, corn, oil, beans, and also cloth, cowries, and other valuables; but at times the king sends as an ocean sacrifice, from the capital, a man carried in a hammock, with the dress, the stool, and umbrella of a noble. A canoe takes him out to the sea, and he is thrown to the sharks.

The human sacrifices or "customs," as they are usually called, of Dahomey, are one of the most remarkable religious observances of the world. They have been frequently described, but by no one so fully or intelligently as by Captain Burton, in his volumes we have just been quoting from.[2] They are divided into greater and lesser customs. At the former not less than 500 or 600 victims are sacrificed; at the latter, at which Captain Burton and his companions assisted, 30 or 40 seem to suffice. The idea seems to be that when the king leaves this world it is necessary his wife, his servants, and his domestic animals should accompany him, and they are all slaughtered accordingly. The lesser customs are an annual act of ancestral worship in honour of the departed king, and also to keep up his stock, though in the land of the immortal this seems unnecessary. Besides that, whenever a battle is fought or any great event happens, a messenger is despatched to propitiate the late king by keeping him "*au fait*" in the news of his late kingdom. It is said the present king would not be unwilling to do away with, or at least to modify, some of the most revolting features of this great slaughter, but that his subjects would regard such an act as a neglect of his most sacred duties, and he might lose his throne as a punishment for such impiety.[3]

None of the works above referred to make it clear what the negro's ideas of immortality are, probably because none such exist. That they have an idea of a future state, and that they consider this world as merely one of transition, is evident. All pass on to the next and better world, but with the same wants, feelings, and desires that they possessed while sojourning here, and apparently with the same distinction of rank. The last king, however, is the one especially honoured, and the reigning monarch, when he dies, expects the chief worship to be paid to him, and no doubt he is the one who takes the greatest interest in sublunar affairs. They never rise apparently to the rank of gods, but if they do not die they are at least very soon forgotten.[4]

When contemplating this, to us, strange religious development, the question inevitably arises, How far are we to consider this Dahoman worship as a living

---

[1] Burton, ii. p. 140, l. 141.

[2] Burton. As almost the whole work is devoted to this subject, it is needless to specify pages.

[3] Burton, ii, 176.

[4] Among the Zulus the snake is held in great respect, and is not willingly killed; as their dead ancestors are supposed to reappear in the form of snakes.—Colenso, on the Pentateuch, p. VI. p. 142.

fragment of the oldest religion of the world, or how far it may have grown up in more modern times?

The traditions of the country are, as might be expected, far too vague to be of any avail in such an enquiry, and we are left to draw our conclusions from such information as we can gather elsewhere. We know from the Egyptian monuments that neither the physical features nor the social status of the negro have altered in the slightest degree during the last 4,000 years. If the type was then fixed which has since remained unaltered, why not his religion also? There seems no *à priori* difficulty. No other people in the whole world seem so unchanged and unchangeable. Movements and mixtures of races have taken place everywhere else. Christianity has swept Serpent Worship out of what were the limits of the Roman world, and Mahomedanism has done the same over the greater part of Northern Africa. Neither influence has yet penetrated to the Gold Coast, and there apparently the negro holds "his old faith and old feelings fast" in spite of the progress of the rest of the world. It may be very horrible, but so far as we now know it is the oldest of human faiths, and is practised with more completeness in Dahomey than anywhere else, at least at the present day.

America.

There are few things in connexion with the ancient mythology of America more certain than that there existed in that country before its discovery by Columbus extreme veneration for the serpent. Whether or not this should be designated "worship" is not so clear. The total absence of any native literature renders it extremely difficult to realise the exact interpretation to be put on any observed phenomena, and we gather very little trustworthy information from the early Christian missionaries or historians. They were either too ignorant or too prejudiced to take a dispassionate view of what they saw, and were too much inclined to see the serpent of Eve, or the deluge of Noah, in the vague traditions of the natives; though, to account for these, they were obliged to make St. Thomas missionary to Mexico—before that kingdom or city was founded—as well as first Bishop of Madras. The consequence is, that we are dependent either on a very imperfect examination of the Sculptures, or on very vague oral traditions, for our knowledge of the subject; and it need hardly be added, that with only such data it is extremely difficult to arrive at any satisfactory conclusion. At the same time, however, it must be admitted that if a systematic examination of such data as exist were undertaken, with special reference to Tree and Serpent Worship, a great deal might yet be effected; but as no one has yet attempted the investigation, the subject must for the present be left in its original obscurity.

The principal deity of the Aztec Pantheon seems Tezcatlipoca, or Tonacatlecoatl, literally the Sun Serpent. According to Sahagun, in his character of God of Hosts, he was addressed by the Mexican high priest: "We entreat that those who die in "war may be received by thee, our father the sun, and our brother the earth, for "thou alone reignest."[1]

---

[1] Squier's Serpent Symbol in America, p. 162.

The name of the primitive goddess, the wife of Tezcatlipoca, was Cihuacohuatl, or Tonacacihua, the female serpent or the female sun. She, according to the Mexicans, gave to the light at a single birth two children, one male the other female, to whom they refer the origin of mankind.[1]

A still more remarkable myth is that of Quetzal-coatl, literally the feathered serpent. He is by some represented as born of a pure virgin in the province of Tollan; by others as a stranger coming from a "far countrie," some time between the sixth and ninth century of our era. Be this as it may, he was the great law-giver and civilizer of the inhabitants of Anahuac. He taught them religion, gave them laws, instructed them in agriculture and the use of metals, and the various arts of life. He is generally represented as an old man, with a white flowing beard and venerable aspect. He was, in fact, the Lycurgus and the Bacchus of Central America, and having finished his mission he withdrew, like the former, it is said, by sea, promising to return. So implicitly was this believed by his subjects, that when the Spaniards appeared on the coast they were joyfully hailed as the returning god and his companions. Alas! they came only to destroy them and their institutions.

If all the evidences bearing on this legend were thoroughly sifted by some one competent to the task, I feel confident they would result in an historical residuum; and if so, it would throw great light on one of the most perplexing problems connected with the civilization of the New World.

As we shall see presently, Serpent Worship was the faith of a great and prosperous kingdom in Cambodia at the time just indicated as the age of the Mexican prophet; and it is more than probable that the worship prevailed in China and the islands to the eastward at that time. Is it possible that it may have crossed the Pacific, and landed on the western coast of America, and, finally, bloomed in Anahuac? If such a solution were possible, it would explain many similarities between the religion and arts of the Old World and the New, which are now extremely puzzling, for want of some such evidence of intercommunication.

On the other hand, if we may trust the antiquaries of the United States, there are great serpent mounds formed of earth, 1,000 feet long and more,[2] which would seem to prove that before the present race of Red Indians inhabited the states Ohio and Iowa, a race of Serpent Worshippers occupied their places, and they may have been the ancestors of the Toltecs. When, however, we remember with what curious credulity Stukeley manufactured a Dracontium out of Avebury, and Bathurst Deane saw a serpent seven miles long in the groups of Menhirs at Carnac, we must pause before we feel sure that these American mounds do really represent serpents at all. This point cannot be settled without much more accurate surveys and more cautious observers than have yet turned their attention to the subject.

If it should turn out that these are really representations of the great serpent, and that this worship is indigenous in the New World, we are thrown back on the doctrine that human nature is alike everywhere, and that man in like circumstances and with a like degree of civilization does always the same things, and elaborates

---

1 Gama, Descripcion Historica y Cronologica de las pedras de Mexico, 1832, p. 39.

2 Smithsonian Contributions to Knowledge, vol. 1. See also Squier's Serpent Symbol, p. 137 to 141.

the same beliefs. It may be so, but I confess it appears to me that at present the evidence preponderates the other way. It should be mentioned, however, that in America the snake that is worshipped is always the indigenous rattlesnake. Whether as separate images or as adorning the walls of the temples of Yucatan, this characteristic seems invariable, and in so far would favour the local origin of the faith. The greatest difficulty of the investigation arises from almost absolute destruction of all the monuments of the capital by its barbarous conquerors, and the consequent paucity of real reliable data on which to found our conclusions.

It seems, however, impossible to read the numerous evidences which Müller[1] has collected together with so much industry not to feel convinced that Serpent Worship did prevail all over the continent. In Peru apparently with qualities similar to those of the Serpents in the Old World.[2] But in Mexico, and among the North American Indians, occasionally with attributes of terror which were never ascribed to him on this side of the Atlantic. Quetzalcoatl is always an exception to this inference; and on the whole it seems more reasonable to suppose that these characteristics are to be ascribed more to the horror of the Christian narrators than to the feelings of the worshippers. We have no native accounts, and depend consequently wholly on those who looked on the worship from an outside and antagonistic point of view.

If, however, we may trust Bernal Diaz, he tells us that living rattlesnakes were kept in the great temple at Mexico as sacred and petted objects. They were kept in a cabin of diversified form, in which a quantity of feathers had been strewed, and there they laid their eggs and nursed their snakelings. They were fed with the bodies of the sacrificed, and with dogs meat.[3] The same author tells us that on Cortes' march to Mexico they arrived at a place called Terraguca, which the Spaniards called the Town of Serpents, on account of the enormous figures of these reptiles which they found in the temples, and which the natives worshipped as gods.[4] But though it is impossible to read any of the narratives of the conquerors without being struck with the frequency with which sacred Serpents and Serpent Worship are spoken of, it is always as a thing accursed, and to be avoided; never as an object worthy of attention, or to be inquired into, and their narratives consequently throw very little light on the subject. The sculptures would do more; but it will require a long and patient investigation by some one competent person on the spot before their evidence can be considered as available; at present we know very little of what they may contain.

It need hardly be remarked that human sacrifices were found accompanying Serpent Worship in America almost to as great an extent as in Dahomey. Even here, however, it is probable we must make a distinction which may be of some importance. In Africa the sacrificial rites seem to be purely ancestral. In America they were made to propitiate gods, not apparently the ancestors of the reigning family, nor nearer to them in time than Quetzalcoatl. The principal object seems always to have been augury to obtain from the gods an indication of their will, which does not seem to have been the case in Dahomey. It was also no doubt considered that the sacrifice itself was agreeable to the deity, and it was expected that the oracle,

---

[1] Amerikanische Urreligionen. Basel, 1855.

[2] Müller, p. 366.

[3] Bernal Diaz, translated by Lockhart, i. 233.

[4] p. 125. See also pp. 3, 7.

which was the declaration of his will, would be favourable in proportion to the number of the victims.

It is by no means improbable that when looked for, Tree Worship will also be found to have prevailed extensively in the New World. Mr. Tylor mentions two instances that came under his notice.[1] The first was a venerable deciduous cypress, with a stem sixty feet in circumference near its root, and with a fountain gushing up within the hollow of the trunk itself. It was hung all over with votive offerings, besides hundreds of locks of hair, teeth, and bits of ribbon. The other was treated in the same manner, and had the valuable property for whoever touched it, that all feeling of weariness left him. Müller also finds traces of Tree Worship all over the continent of America, and generally in juxtaposition, if not in actual connexion, with that of the Serpent.[2] But here again we must pause for further information before attempting to generalize.

---

[1] Anahuac, 215, 265.

[2] Amerikanische Urreligionen, 494. See also 107, 124, 264, *et seq.*

PART II.—EASTERN ASIA.

Persia.

The Eastern branch of our subject has been even less investigated by European scholars than those divisions noticed in the previous pages. This has arisen partly from a less degree of familiarity with Eastern tradition, but more probably because until the very recent discoveries in Cambodia and at Amravati no very tangible data existed on which any satisfactory conclusions could be based. The subject is now, however, assuming a very different aspect, and before long it may be hoped that great light will be thrown on the Tree and Serpent Worship of the western world, from a study of those forms of that faith which we now know existed at one time in India.

With Persia the case is slightly different. We know of no material remains of Snake Worship in that country, and learn very little from native history. The Zend-Avesta is the work from which at first sight we might expect most, not only from its antiquity, but because of its doctrinal character. It is, however, of very little use for our present purposes, inasmuch as it, like the Vedas, embodies the religious belief only of the Aryan, or as they are called here, the Iranian branch of the Persian people, and it need hardly be repeated here that they are not, and never were, Serpent Worshippers anywhere. If, indeed, there is one point which comes out more clearly than another in the course of this investigation, it is that Serpent Worship is essentially that of a Turanian, or at least of a non-Aryan people. In the present state of the enquiry it would be too bold a generalization to assert that all Turanian races were Serpent Worshippers; and still less can it be affirmed that all who looked on the Serpent as a God belonged to that family of mankind. It is safe, however, to assume that the whole tendency of the facts hitherto brought to light, lies in that direction; and it seems probable that eventually the worship of the Serpent may become a valuable ethnographic test of the presence of Turanian blood in the veins of any people among whom it is found to prevail.

At the time when the Greeks became acquainted with Persia, the whole country, under the influence of the Achæmenian kings, had been brought to acknowledge Zoroasterism with its elemental Fire Worship as their principal form of faith. This religion in its purity,—if we know it in that state,—was the faith which the Iranians brought with them from their original seats when they separated from the Indian Aryans, and was practically their common faith both in India and in Persia. In the latter country, however, in the time of the Achæmenidæ, it was strangely mixed up with Magism, a religion of much more Semitic, or even, it may be suspected, Turanian form, and the two were at that time so blended in the Grecian accounts at least that it is now impossible to separate the one from the other.

When the Greeks first turned their attention to the religion of Persia we gather from what they tell us that Tree and Serpent Worship had ceased to be regarded as the religion of any important body in the state, though the probability is that it may have been followed to a considerable extent by large classes of people in that vast empire. As, however, the Persians despised, and the Greeks did not observe the Ophites, we are left almost entirely at the mercy of the Mahomedan historians and poets of the eleventh and following centuries for such faint glimmerings of truth as can be picked up, and anyone who has ever opened one of their books will know what blind guides they are in such an investigation. It is doubtful whether even the critical skill of European scholars will ever sift a substratum of tangible history out of the fables of Firdausi or Mirkhond. At present the task has hardly been attempted, and when it has, with only a small modicum of success.

By far the most important and most interesting person in ancient Persian history, for our present purposes at least, is Zohák. According to all accounts he came from Arabia, and took his title, Bívar-asp, from his body guard of 10,000 horsemen by whom he was always accompanied.[1] His genealogy from Tází or Táj, the eponymous of the Arabs, is given both in the Bundehesch and the Mojmil.[2] His father is represented as a simple possessor of flocks and herds, but he is said to have conquered Central Asia, and to have fixed his residence at Babel.[3] His reign, or rather that of his dynasty, is said to have lasted 1,000 years, when he was overthrown by Feridún, with the assistance of Gavah the blacksmith, by whom the original line of Jemshid was then restored.

Feridún has been identified almost without doubt with Thraêtaona of the Zend-Avesta, celebrated as the slayer of the three-headed Serpent Dahâka, who was the creation of the evil power Angra Mainyus,[4] or more popularly Ahriman.

Zohák is represented by all the Mahomedan historians as having two snakes growing at his back, one from each shoulder, and they add that it was necessary to appease these monsters by sacrificing daily two young men in order that their cravings might be satisfied with their brains.[5] All this has hitherto been mysterious enough, but as we shall presently see, all women of the Nâga race had one serpent between their shoulders, and all men—in India—one with three, five, or seven heads; the two of Zohák seem an earlier form, being the exact duplication of those of the females, and it is also probable that the *three* heads of the Zend-Avesta[6] include the human head between the two snakes. We shall be in a better position to judge of this presently, but whatever explanation we adopt, it seems only to be an earlier form of a myth with which we are now becoming familiar in India. The human sacrifices are only what we find so universally accompanying Serpent Worship all the world over.

The most startling novelty with regard to Zohák is the assertion that he came from Arabia, where we have no reason to suppose that Serpent Worship then pre-

---

[1] Justi Bundehesch, 1868, Glossary, s. v. Béwarásp. Handbuch der Zendsprache, 1866, Glossary, s. v. Dahâka.

[2] Windischmann, Zoroastrische Studien, pp. 30, 37, c. 39.

[3] Is it possible that this is the Arab dynasty which, according to Berosus, ruled in Babylon in the 13th century B.C.? Rawlinson's Ancient Monarchies, vol. I. p. 193.

[4] Windischmann, quoting from the Yaçna, IX. 8, p. 29. *See also* Westergaard in Weber's Indische Studien, vol. III. p. 416.

[5] Mojmil (156); Windischmann, 37; Sháh Námeh, Atkinson's translation, p. 14.

[6] Tribus oribus præditum, tribus capitibus. Masaudi, III. p. 252, and the Mahomedans, on the contrary, always speak of "Two Serpents borne on the shoulders of Dahák."

vailed. Perhaps it only means right bank of the lower Euphrates, which to a man writing in Afghanistan, or the north-east of Persia, might be so described; the original seat of the empire being Babylon would bear that interpretation. Moses of Chorene[1] would try to persuade us that Zohák was identical with Astyages the Mede, but as his assertion seems to rest more on a verbal coincidence than on historical evidence, too much reliance must not be placed upon it. The Serpent dynasty most probably reigned in Media rather than in Persia proper, but they must have been extinct before the time of Cyrus, though whether all this is so or not can only be determined after more careful examination than it has yet met with.

One remnant of the race of Zohák seems to have survived in Cabul, and it would be especially interesting to us, if we knew more about it, as it seems the connecting link between the Persian and Indian Serpent Worship. According to the Mojmil, "When Táj, the primogenitor of the Arabs, was settled in Babel, one of his sons "married a daughter of Feridún and settled in Cabul, and his son was Rustem's "maternal grandfather."[2] We find further particulars of the family in the Sháh Námeh. When Zál the son of Sám went to Cabul he found Mihráb, a descendant of Zohák, on the throne, and having fallen in love with his daughter, Rudabeh, he was forbidden by the Mubids to marry her, because the chief of Cabul was of the family of Zohák, the Serpent King. The father too from this circumstance dreaded the resentment of Manuchehr if he allowed the union, and not without reason, for the king ordered Sám to destroy Kábul by fire and sword, and especially the house of Mihráb, then ruler of the serpent race, and all his adherents were to be put to death.[3] Fortunately for the lovers the difficulty was got over, and the result was the birth of Rustem, the most wonderful hero of Eastern romance. The point of interest to us, however, is, that it is probably to the preservation of this race of Serpent Worshippers that we owe that remarkable development of Buddhism, which distinguished the valley of the Cabul river between the decline of the Greco-Bactrian kingdom and the rise of the Mahomedan power in that quarter.

One of the last material traces of Serpent Worship that is found in Persia occurs in a bas-relief at Nakshi-Rustem, near Persepolis. It represents Ormuzd bestowing the circlet of royalty on Ardishir Babegán the first king of the Sassanian line (A.D. 226). Beneath the feet of the horse on which the god (?) is seated, lies Ardevan, the last of the Parthians, and round his head are twisted two writhing snakes,[4] not such as probably adorned the shoulders of Zohák, but still sufficiently important to mark that the sculptor intended to represent the Parthian as of the hated race of Zohák, the follower of the accursed Ahriman, whom Ormuzd tramples under foot while bestowing the emblem of royalty on the Zoroastrian, Fire-Worshipping Sassanian.

The more closely it is looked at the more probable does it appear that not only in this instance, but throughout the whole ancient history of Persia, the so-called dualism is much more an ethnographical expression than the result of any theological

---

[1] History of Armenia, Postscript to Book I. "Les déscendans d'Astyages établis en Arménie portoient encore le nom de Vischabazouni, ce qui signifie Race de dragon. Cette dénomination leur venait du nom du roi des Mèdes."—St. Martin, I. 285.

[2] Windischmann, 37.

[3] Atkinson's translation of Sháh Námeh, p. 77 et seq.

[4] Ker Porter, vol. I. plate xxiii.; Flandin et Coste, Voyage en Perse, plate clxxxii.

elaboration. It was the opposition of Turan to Iran, of Zohák to Zoroaster, of Ormuzd to Ahriman—an Aryan race, with their pure elemental worship, intruding into a country occupied by a Serpent-worshipping people of Turanian origin, but instead of totally abolishing and ignoring the religion of the conquered, forcing it into an unnatural combination with their own. All this, however, was carried out in such a manner as to represent their own as the source of all that is good and elevated, and that of the subject race as the origin of all that is evil and accursed.

The answer to the question whether Tree Worship did or did not prevail in Ancient Persia will mainly depend on the signification scholars may eventually agree to assign to the Homa or Soma worship, which forms so important a ceremonial observance both in the Vedas and the Zend-Avesta. If the Soma plant always was the Asclepias acida or Sarcostema viminalis, which is now used by the Brahmans for that purpose, it cannot be called Tree Worship in the sense in which the term is used throughout this essay. The Asclepias is a creeping shrub, almost without leaves, and only remarkable for a milky juice, to which the most important virtues are ascribed. It is now used as freshly expressed,[1] but in former times was fermented so as to produce intoxication.

On the other hand, Windischmann, who had probably rendered himself more familiar with the spirit of the Zend-Avesta than any other scholar, thus expresses himself on the subject. "Homa is the first of the trees planted by Ahura-Mazda "in the fountain of life. He who drinks of its juice never dies. According to the "Bundehesh, the Gogard or Gaokerena tree bears the Homa, which gives health and "generative power, and imparts life at the resurrection. The Homa plant does not "decay, bears no fruit, resembles the vine, is knotty, and has leaves like jessamin, "yellow and white."[2]

In another place he says, "From this it appears that the White Homa or the "Tree Gokard is the Tree of Life which grew in Paradise."

In Persian mythology the Homa was also personified as a god, and converses with Ahura-Mazda with regard to the origin of all things, as if he were co-equal in knowledge with the great god of the Persians himself. Whatever form, however, it may have taken, our author adds, the Soma was unquestionably the greatest and holiest offering of ancient Indian or Iranian worship.[3]

It would require a much more intimate knowledge of the subject than can be obtained from such translations as have been made, or such books as have been published, to speak at all definitely regarding the Homa. From such data as are available it would appear that the Homa had its origin in the same myth as the Trees of Life and Knowledge which grew in Paradise, and that it passed through a stage of Bacchic mystery, though whether the vine or some other plant was then the Homa is by no means clear; and at last it sank into the present innocent Soma form, which, however, can hardly be regarded as anything but a reminiscence of its former greatness and importance.

---

[1] Haug, Essays, p. 247 ff. Wilson, Introduction to the Rig-Veda-Sanhitâ, vol. I. p. xxxvi. et seq.

[2] Ueber den Somacultus der Arier. p. 131.

[3] Windischmann, Zoroastrische Studien, pp. 89, 167, 251.

We shall have frequent occasion to speak of the Bodhidruma or Tree of Knowledge of the Buddhists, in the sequel. It is the principal object of worship at Sanchi, and among the most important at Amravati. It will only be possible to ascertain what connexion may have existed between it and the Gaokerena of the Persians, or the Homa, when some competent Scholar, familiar with both Zend and Sanskrit, looks through the original authorities with special reference to this inquiry.

Though sufficiently absurd, the following legend from the Sháh Námeh is curious. Sikander, after the conquest of India, went to Mekka, and thence to a country where there were two trees, one male, one female. The first spoke during the day, the latter at night. Whoever had a wish went there to have his desires accomplished. Sikandar longed for length of days. When he came under the tree a horrible sound arose and rung in his ears; and on his asking what it meant, the attendant priest replied that fourteen years of his life still remained. Again he asked, "Shall I see "Rúm and my mother and children before I die?" The answer was, "Thou wilt "die at Karshán."[1]

The oldest known authority for this legend is the Pseudo-Kallisthenes, who wrote apparently about the year 200 A.D.[2] As he relates it, there were two trees, one of the Sun, which spoke in the Indian language, and one of the Moon which spoke Greek.[3] In the Mediæval fables, the "leafless tree" was introduced between these two. This tree is mentioned by Marco Polo,[4] and under the name of the "Arbre Sec" was one of the favourite myths of the Byzantine and of early Christian travellers, though it is even now by no means clear where it grew; my impression is that it was in Seistan, though others place it in Khorassan, nor do we know what exact meaning the Mediævalists attached to the fable.

One thing only seems clear, from their constant and reiterated reference to it, that a tradition of an earlier Tree Worship existed in Persia even at that late date, indistinct of course, but when we reflect that the worship must have been abolished, though certainly it was not obliterated, as early as the rise of the Achæmenian dynasty, 2,000 years before Marco Polo's time, the wonder is, not that it should be indistinct, but that the faintest reminiscences of it should then remain.

Unfortunately the classical authors afford us little or no assistance in regard to Tree Worship in the countries westward of India, except the identical remark of Quintus Curtius, in speaking of the inhabitants on the banks of the Indus, "Arbores maxime colunt,"[5] there is no passage bearing, so far as I know, directly on the subject.

The Chinese travellers are hardly more communicative; but Hiouen-Thsang does mention a great Pipal tree of Peshawar,[6] under whose shade the four preceding

---

[1] Atkinson, Translation, p. 507.

[2] Zacher, Pseudo-Kallisthenes. Halle, 1867, p. 102.

[3] Loc. p. 161.

[4] Marsden, p. 109. For an exhaustive note on the position of this tree and on the legends connected with it, I must refer my readers to the edition of Marco Polo's travels, edited by Col. Yule, C.B., published by Murray, 1871. At page 120 et seq. vol. 1, he will find all that is known or can well be said on the subject.

[5] Hist. Alex. VIII. 9.

[6] Histoire de la Vie de Hiouen-Thsang, I. p. 83.

Buddhas had reposed, and under it the last had predicted the appearance of the great Kanishka, who in consequence had erected alongside of it, about the Christian era, the largest and tallest of all the Stupas of which we have any record. This tree seems to have existed and been reverenced down to the time of Baber (in 1504), who mentions it as the great tree of Bekram.[1] The Gûrh Katri he describes as close to it was probably the remains of the Monastery of Kanishka. Even its site cannot now be ascertained.

CASHMERE.

Although from its position on the map, Cashmere might fairly be considered as an integral part of India, still its circlet of mountains has been sufficient to keep it distinct and separate, and we consequently find there vestiges of the old faith better preserved than in most places on the plains. Another circumstance which has tended also in the same direction is that the Aryans on entering India do not seem to have turned aside to conquer or at least permanently to occupy the valley. If they entered India by crossing the Indus at or near Attock,—and there seems no good reason for doubting that this was so,—this seems so strange that we feel almost inclined to believe that Cashmere was really then in the state described in the earliest legends, a great lake, or at least a valley so filled with water and so swampy as to be unfit for human habitation. Though this may not be quite true we are no doubt justified in assuming that 4,000 or 5,000 years ago a much larger portion of the valley was under water than is the case now, and the real snakes may then have been relatively more important than their Nâga successors afterwards became.

Be this as it may, Cashmere has always been considered, in historical times, as one of the principal centres of Serpent Worship in India, and hitherto it has been principally from her legends that what little was known of the Nâgas has been gathered.

Cashmere is also fortunate in possessing in the Râja Tarangiṇî something more like a connected history than almost any other country of India, and from its pages, with the incidental notices by classical, Chinese, and Mahomedan authors, we are enabled to form a tolerably distinct view of the subject.

Although from the context there is a strong presumption that Snake Worship prevailed in the valley from a very early period, still we have no direct testimony to the fact till the century before the Christian era, when the King Dâmodara having, it is said, offended some Brahman was converted into a snake,[2] and still, it is said, haunts the spot. He was succeeded by three Tartar princes, Hushka, Jushka, and Kanishka, known from history and from their coins to have been Buddhist, and to have reigned about the Christian era. In the reign of their successor Abhimanyu we are told that "in consequence of the disuse of the prescribed institutes, and the "abolition of every form of sacrifice, and a departure from the lessons of the Nîla "Purâṇa, the Nâgas were particularly incensed, and visited the offences of the people "with severe and unseasonable storms of rain and snow, and those especially perished

[1] Leyden's translation of Memoirs of Baber, 157, 264.

[2] Wilson's Abstract of the Râja Tarangiṇî in Vol. XV. Asiatic Researches, p. 22. All the future references to this work are derived from the same source, which seems better and more trustworthy than the translation by Troyer. The volume and the page will, therefore, only be quoted.

"who had adopted the Bauddha heresy."[1] Gonerda III., who succeeded this king, prosecuted the reform which that prince had commenced.

The ancient ritual, according to the Nîla precepts,[2] was restored, and the worship of the Nâgas and the offering of sacrifices re-established.[3] During the following centuries we have several legends of Nâgas, but the faith of the kings is seldom mentioned, and seems to have oscillated between Snake Worship, Buddhism, and Hinduism, but as our historian belonged to the latter faith his testimony is not always quite to be depended upon. When Hiouen-Thsang entered the valley in 632, in the reign of Báláditya the last king of the Gonerdiya race,[4] he found the Buddhist religion still very prevalent in the valley, though he admits that the king only interested himself in the heretics and in the temples of their gods, and despised the faith of Buddha.[5] He repeats the usual story of the valley having been a lake, but adds, "50 years after the Nirvâṇa (B.C. 493?) a disciple of Ânanda converted the Nâga "Râja, he quitted his tank, built 500 monasteries, and invited sages and saints to "come and dwell in them."[6]

It is not, however, only in the valley that our Chinese traveller repeats the Hindu legends about serpents and their power, but at every stage of his journey from Cabul to Cashmere, he everywhere finds some spot where a dragon king or Nâga Râja resided, and played an important part in the legendary history of the land. These legends, as might be expected, were found in the seventh century very much altered from their more primitive forms, but they are interesting, in the first place, as showing how essentially the north-west corner of India was at one time the seat of Serpent Worship, and also, in what manner it was eventually—except perhaps in Cashmere—amalgamated with Buddhism.

Among these legends one of the most pertinent to our present purpose is that of a member of the family of Śâkya—that of Buddha—who when travelling in Udayana—the Kamboja of the Hindus, lying northward from Peshawar—fell in love with a serpent king's daughter. He was eventually married to her, and by the advice and with the assistance of his father-in-law, killed the king of the country and obtained the sovereignty. Though his wife had obtained and was confirmed in the possession of a human body, a nine-headed snake occasionally appeared at the back of her neck, which on a certain occasion her husband cut off at a single blow while she was asleep. The result was blindness, of which she was afterwards cured by Śâkya-muni himself, and her son Uttarasena was present at the distribution of his relics at Kuśinagara, where the great ascetic obtained Nirvâṇa.[7]

---

[1] A. S. XV. p. 24.

[2] A. S. XV. p. 25.

[3] The Nîla Purâṇa has not hitherto been seen by any European, but an abstract of its contents will be found in an Appendix to this work. At my request Mr. J. Muir, the well-known Sanscrit scholar, wrote out to Sir D. Macleod, the Chief Commissioner in the Punjab, and he procured two copies from Cashmere, which were placed in the hands of Professor Cowell, who kindly undertook to make the required analysis. It is not exactly what it was expected to be, and probably is only a modern form of an older ritual which has perished, or at least has not yet been found.

[4] Journal Royal Asiatic Society, IV., N.S., p. 98.

[5] Vie et Voyages de Hiouen-Thsang, traduites par Stanislas Julien, 3 vols., Paris, 1853 and 1858, II. 180.

[6] Hiouen-Thsang, I. 168.

[7] Hiouen-Thsang, II. 141.

An almost equally curious legend is told of a Buddhist priest (Bhikshu) who became a serpent, because he had killed the tree Elâpatra, and resided in a beautiful lake or spring near Takshaśilâ (Taxila). In our traveller's day when the people of the country wanted fine weather or rain, they went to the spring accompanied by a priest (Śramaṇa) "and snapping their fingers, invoke the dragon, and immediately "obtain their wishes."[1] In these legends the chief characteristic of the Serpents throughout the East in all ages seems to have been their power over the wind and rain, which they exert for either good or evil as their disposition prompts.[2]

A curious confirmation of the prevalence of Nâgas in the North-west of India is obtained from the Buddhist account of the proceedings consequent on the Third Convocation held B.C. 253. Missionaries were then sent to all the neighbouring countries. Among others Majjhantiko was dispatched to Kashmîra and Gandhâra.[3] A Nâga king of that country, named Aravâlo, endowed with supernatural powers, by causing a furious deluge to descend was submerging all the ripened crops in these countries. The Nâgas and their King tried every means to terrify the missionary, but were subdued by his calmness and address; "whereupon the Théro "propounded his doctrines, and the Nâga king attained the salvation and state of "piety in that faith." In like manner "in the Himawanta (Himalaya) regions, 84,000 "Nâgas were converted, and the Nâga king placing the Théro on a gem-set throne "respectfully stood by fanning him. On that day the inhabitants of Kashmîra and "Gandhâra, who had come with offerings to appease the wrath of the Nâga king, "bowing down to the Théro (instead of the Nâga king) stood reverentially by his "side," &c. These extracts from the Mahawanso,[4] depict faithfully the Buddhist belief on the subject two centuries before Hiouen-Thsang's time, though not from personal observation. The account is further interesting, because these in the north-west were the only Nâgas to whom missionaries were sent by Aśoka. Either it was that the others had been converted before, or that Cashmere and the mountain countries east and west of it, were the most prominent seats of the faith.

These accounts by native authorities are fully confirmed by such scanty notices as we glean from classical authorities; Onesicritus tells us that two ambassadors sent to the king of Cashmere by Alexander, brought back news that the king of the country cherished two large serpents of fabulous dimensions.[5] Maximinius of Tyre tells us, that when Alexander entered India, Taxilus (King of Taxila) showed him a serpent of enormous size which he nourished with great care and revered as the

---

1 Hiouen-Thsang, II. 152. General Cunningham visited this spring at Hassan Abdul in 1863, and found it still revereneed. Other legends are told at pp. 49, 99, 133, &e.

2 This power over the weather, which is one of the leading characteristics of Nâgas, has led to their being confounded with the Vedic Ahi. In their origin and purpose I believe the two to have been perfectly distinct, but in the process of time the one legend borrowed from the other till the two have become so mixed up together that it will now be extremely difficult to separate them again. My own impression is that the Vedic myth is an adaptation of a local superstition; borrowed in fact from the Serpent-worshipping aborigines among whom the Aryans were settled.

3 In this wide sense Gandhâra seems to include all the countries westward of the Indus as far as Candahar. Relics of this missionary, as we shall presently see, were deposited in No. 3 Tope at Sanchi.

4 Turnour, Translation, pp. 72 and 73.

5 Strabo, XV. 698.

image of the god whom the Greek writers, from the similitude of his attributes, called Dionysus or Bacchus.[1]

The latest authority we have, is that of Abulfazl, who tells us that in the reign of Akbar (1556—1605) there were in Cashmere 45 places dedicated to the worship of Śiva, 64 to Vishṇu, 3 to Brahmâ, and 22 to Durgâ, but there were 700 places in the valley where there were carved images of snakes which the inhabitants worshipped.[2]

All this is fully confirmed by the architecture of the valley; with very few exceptions, all the ancient temples of Cashmere seem to have been devoted to Serpent Worship. They stand in square courts which were capable of being flooded and were crossed by light bridges of stone, some of which still remain. Even at the present day some of these temples are unapproachable without wading, in consequence of the water which surrounds them, and all might be rendered so by a slight repair to their waterworks. There being, of course, no images in the sanctuaries long prevented antiquaries from perceiving the form of faith to which they were dedicated.[3] But where the deity is a living god and mortal, when he and his worshippers pay the debt of nature, they leave no material trace to recall the memory of their past existence.

CAMBODIA.

There is another country on the other side of the Bay of Bengal the study of whose antiquities is nearly as important to the elucidation of Serpent Worship in India, as those of Cashmere, though in a totally different sense. In the last-named country we look for the "incunabula" of the faith, in Cambodia for its fullest known development. The ruined cities of Cambodia have, however, been only so recently discovered, and are yet so little known, that it is extremely difficult to feel sure on many points connected with their history or purposes.[4] Whatever doubt may,

---

[1] Maxim. Tyr. Diss. XIII. ed. Lip. 140.

[2] Ayeen Akbaree, Gladwin's Translation, p. 137.

[3] The great Temple at Martand is generally supposed to have been dedicated to the Sun. I believe in consequence of some fancied nominal similarity, but, like the others, it seems really to belong to the Nâgas. There is no image in the sanctuary, and no inscription, and the stone of which it is built is unfortunately so friable that there is a difficulty from photographs to make out the sculptures. To me they all seem provided with snake-hoods, but whether this is so or not, can only be determined by some one on the spot.

[4] The temples were first discovered by M. Mouhot, a French naturalist, in 1858–60, but he did not pretend to any knowledge of their history. They were afterwards visited by Dr. Bastian, who has written voluminously regarding them, but either it is that he knows nothing about them, or for some reason he is afraid to commit himself to any statements on the subject. The greatest amount of information has been obtained from the photographs of Mr. J. Thomson, and his personal communications. From these sources a tolerably connected account is condensed in my History of Architecture (II. p. 713, et seq.), to which the reader is referred. Since that time, Messrs. Edmiston and Douglas, of Edinburgh, have published a selection of Mr. Thomson's photographs, with explanatory text taken principally, with my consent and collaboration, from my work above referred to. At the present moment a work is in the press, in Paris, by M. Garnier, Lt. de Vaisseau, who on the death of his chief, succeeded the Captaine La Grée in the "Exploration Scientifique de la Riviére Mekon." The work will contain plans and views of the principal ruins of Cambodia, and is accompanied by a carefully compiled and elaborate text, which throws considerable light on the subject. M. Garnier has kindly communicated to me the proof sheets of his work, but I am sorry to say I cannot quite agree with him, either as to their age nor the purposes to which the temples were dedicated. I am afraid it is, that we have both a great deal to learn regarding them, but meanwhile it seems expedient that both views should be submitted to the public for their decision.

however, exist on other points, it seems certain that the great suburban Temple of Nakhon Vat was, at least originally, wholly dedicated to Serpent Worship. Every angle of every roof is adorned with a grim seven-headed serpent, with a magnificent crest of what is apparently intended for feathers, and every cornice of every entablature is adorned with a continuous row of these seven-headed deities, but without crests. The former may be counted by hundreds, the latter by thousands. But it is not only these; every balustrade, every ridge, almost every feature of the building bears the same impress. The arrangements too of the temple are such as are suitable for Serpent Worship, and that only. There is no image in the sanctuary, and no worship represented in the bas-reliefs. No cross-legged figures of Buddha are seen anywhere, though they crowd the faces of the nearly contemporary temples of Boro Buddor in Java, and no Buddhist legends can be traced in any of the sculptures that cover the walls of this most magnificent of temples. Everything seems taken from the Râmâyana and Mahâbhârata and other heroic poems of the Hindus, nothing from the Jatakas of the Buddhists. All the courts are tanks to contain water, and everything recalls the temples of Cashmere, but with ten-fold magnificence. Neither in India, nor so far as is known anywhere else, is there another temple displaying the same amount of patient labour devoted to the elaboration of appropriate ornament over so extended a surface as in this newly-discovered temple. It is 600 feet square at base, and rises to a height of 180 feet in the centre, while every part is covered with carvings in stone, generally beautiful in design, and always admirably adapted to their situation, and to tell the story they were meant to convey.

It does not seem clear that the other temples in the city of Nakhon Thom are dedicated to Serpent Worship in the same manner as the one just alluded to. They are, however, so completely overgrown with jungle that photography hardly helps us in this instance. They were more extensive, and seem to have been as elaborately ornamented as the one temple of which we have some knowledge, but so far as can at present be made out, they seem rather to have been dedicated to some bastard form of Buddhism than to the worship of the Serpent in the form in which it is found at Nakhon Vat.

The question that principally interests us at this stage, is to ascertain how this marvellous development of Serpent Worship arose in Cambodia, and at what time.

The first impulse would be to assume that it was indigenous, but this certainly does not seem to be the case. The architecture of the temple is, if anything, classical —Roman Doric. The ornaments—bassi-relievi—are all subjects borrowed from the Râmâyana or Mahâbhârata, and fade gradually into the myths of the Hindu religion. The people are Indian. The natives, wherever they appear, are represented as an abject race, and are very cruelly treated by the superior race who were the builders of the temple, and the carvers of the bas-reliefs.

Another theory, which at first sight seemed plausible, was that the worship had reached Cambodia from the north. We know from Hiouen-Thsang that Serpent Worship was to be found in Koutche in the north of Thibet,[1] we know that the Strî Râjya, or Amazon kingdom, was in Thibet,[2] and we have so many traces of Serpent

[1] Mémoires, I. 4.

[2] Asiatic Researches, XV. 48.

Worship all along the north of the Himalaya, Hindu Kush, and Caucasus, that it looks like a Scythian or northern form of faith, and may have leaked through the mountain ranges into both Cashmere and Cambodia, radiating from a common northern centre.

When more closely looked into, this theory seems as untenable as the last. The communication between Thibet and Cambodia is barred by ranges of mountains, which have hitherto proved practically impassable either as trade routes or for military operations. The southern country could only be reached through China, and Serpent Worship, could hardly have passed through that country without leaving more traces of its passage, or bringing with it more evidences of Chinese civilization than appears to be the case. We know so little, however of the local superstitions of China that we must again pause before expressing any decided opinion on this subject.

The only remaining hypothesis that suggests itself is that they came from India direct by sea. When we turn to their own traditions for any confirmation of this, the answer is distinct, "Our ancestors came from Myang Rom, or Romavisci, not far from Takçasila" (Taxila).[1] Startling as this may at first sight appear, there are many circumstances which not only take away from its strangeness, but seem to render it probable. In the first place Taxila, as just pointed out, was one of the great centres of Serpent Worship. The country they claim to have migrated from is, by the ancient Sanskrit authorities, called Kamboja.[2] Their capital they call Inthapattapuri (Indraprastha), and that of Siam was Ayuthia (Ayodhyâ), the two capitals of the Mahâbhârata and Râmâyaṇa, and almost all the other principal towns throughout the country bear Sanskrit names. If Halifax, Boston, and New York, are evidence of an English people having settled in America, the names of the Cambodian cities are equally conclusive in this respect.

Another argument which seems as important as any other, is the similarity of the style of architecture in the two countries. This is not only traceable in the arrangement of their temples, but in the details. The Cashmere pillars are curiously like those of the Grecian Doric order,[3] those of Cambodia are even more classical, but resemble Roman Doric. Nothing similar to either as yet been discovered between the two points, but there is an amount of classical influence apparent in the sculpture at Amravati which seems to supply a connecting link.

The improbability of such a migration is considerably lessened by the knowledge that an Indian colony did reach Java, by sea of course; did introduce there their own faith, and built those wonderful temples of Brambanan and Boro Buddor, which in many respects resemble, though they do not rival, those of Cambodia. All this has been rendered more probable within the last few years by the discovery of Serpent Worship existing to the extent it does at Amravati, near the mouth of the Kistnah, the very country whence navigators set sail who were about to cross the bay of Bengal going to the Gold Coast,[4] and there seems now to be no doubt but that this

---

[1] Bastian, Völker des Östlichen Asien, I. p. 393.

[2] Wilford, A.R., VI. 516., VIII. 336; Muir, Original Sanscrit Texts, II. 368. ff. &c.

[3] Essay on the Arian order of Architecture as exhibited in the Temples of Kashmir, by Captain A. Cunningham, J.A.S.B., September 1848.

[4] Ptolemy, VII. 1.

was Thatûn or Suverna Bhumi near the mouth of the Sitang river to which Aśoka sent the missionaries Sono and Uttaro after the third Convocation 253 B.C.[1] At that time and down to the fifth or sixth century A.D. Thatûn was the point by which the trade of India reached the far east, and that consequently by which the Indians almost inevitably reached and kept up their communication with Cambodia.[2]

Every day since attention was turned to the sculptures at Amravati, fresh evidence of the prevalence of Serpent Worship in Central India has come to light, and it seems now tolerably clear, either that serpent races passed down the valley of the Indus, across Central India by the valley of the Godavery, and thence by sea to Cambodia; or that they passed from Takshaśilâ direct by land to Amravati, and thence to the Golden Chersonese. If a straight line is drawn on the map between these two first-named places it passes over Sanchi and other spots where Snake Worship once prevailed, and on the whole this route seems to be the one the emigrants would most probably have taken; but we are only yet on the threshold of the inquiry, and must wait for further information before deciding.

The time when this migration took place is even more difficult to fix, but it appears to have first commenced in the fourth century, (after 318,) to have been continued in the fifth and sixth, and probably reached its height in the era of the religious disturbances and persecutions in India in the eighth and tenth centuries. Cambodia was conquered by the Siamese between the years 1351–74, the capital destroyed, and depopulation set in. From that time Serpent Worship seems to have declined and to have been entirely superseded by Buddhism, which probably coexisted with it during a greater part of the time in varying degrees of ascendency, but which is now the faith of all the civilized Indo-Chinese provinces.[3]

The Cambodian legends which refer to the colonization of the country and the building of the city of Inthapattapuri, are all extremely similar to those related by Hiouen-Thsang, when speaking of the Kamboja whence they are said to have come, as noticed above. In all the dragon king's daughter is the principal personage, and from her the royal race claim to be descended. In the Cambodian legend it is related that the banished prince, Phra Thong, was driven, after a long sea voyage, on an island where grew a wonderful Talok tree, "Grewia inæqualis." He ascends its branches to look about him, but the tree grows faster than the celebrated beanstalk of Jack, and he fears he shall never see his mother earth again. In descending, however, he finds himself in a wonderful grotto in the hollow of the tree, where he meets with the dragon king's daughter, and marries her. The father consents to their union, and

---

[1] Mahawanso, ch. XII., p. 71.

[2] "The cradle of Buddhism in Burmah," by R. F. St. A., St. John, in Phœnix, vol. II., p. 180, et seqq.

[3] The kingdom and city seem to have been at the height of their prosperity when they were visited by the Chinese traveller in 1295/97, whose account of the country was translated by Abel Rémusat, and published in the first volume of the "Nouveaux Mélanges Asiatiques."

He mentions the great serpent with nine heads that formed the parapet of the bridge, and which still exists in ruins, and the 54 statues of divinities, each holding a serpent in his hand (p. 107). He also mentions the golden tower of the palace where the king slept, and where formerly dwelt a fairy in the form of a nine-headed serpent, who was considered as the protectress of the kingdom. He does not, it is true, enumerate Serpent Worship by name as one of the religions of the country, and Buddhism as only the second of the three, but it may be hid under the names of the other two (p. 110), or it may be that he overlooked the suburban temple of Nakhon Vat, to which that form of worship may have been confined in his day.

builds the city of Nakhon Thom for their residence, where he comes frequently to visit his beloved daughter; but the people complain of his presence, and his ungrateful children frighten him away by placing an image of the four-faced Brahma over the gate of the city.[1]

Another form of the legend is, that king Pathumma Surivong, while reposing under the wonderful tree, saw the dragon king's daughter bathing with her companions in a neighbouring lake, fell in love and married her, and went to the underground abode of his father-in-law, where he spent a fortnight. According to this legend he behaved much better to the old Serpent than Prince Phra Thong.

According to a third form, Indra had come down from heaven, but had neglected to bring any female attendants with him; feeling the loneliness of his situation, took up with the dragon king's daughter, who bore to him Ketumalea, the father of Pathumma Surivong, who seems really to have been the founder of the city.[2]

We have a date twice repeated, 957–8 A.D., for the accession of the last-named king, and if the names above quoted were really or closely connected with one another, as the legends would lead us to suppose, the migration and all the subsequent events down to the founding of the city really took place in the tenth century. If we were to draw our conclusions from the legends alone, this view must probably be adopted; but the context, and the indications from Indian experience, incline me to extend the time between the first migration and the building of the city to four or five centuries; but it is at present little more than guess work, in so far as the earlier dates are concerned. The circumstance that interests us most is the important part played in these legends by Nang Nakh, the Serpent king's daughter, and the description of her father and his kingdom. Foolish and legendary as all this may appear at first sight, it assumes considerable importance when we find it resulting in some of the most wonderful temples which the world ever saw, and in the most remarkable devolopment of pure Serpent Worship anywhere to be found.

China.

It is extremely difficult to ascertain anything that is at all satisfactory regarding the worship of the serpent in China. No scholar, so far as I know, has investigated the subject, nor has any traveller devoted special attention to such indications of it as may exist in the country. We are consequently left to such stray passages as are scattered here and there in the various authors who treat of Chinese subjects, and without knowing exactly what reliance to place on the information so afforded. It is

---

[1] The Serpent King was, it appears, a Sabbatarian, at least he devoted every seventh day to prayer. Bastian, I. 397. See also Trans. R.A.S., vol. II. p. 94, where Col. Low reports, "Every seventh day the mighty "Râja Nâga issues forth from his palace, and having ascended a high mountain, pours forth his soul in ardent "devotion."

[2] All these legends are taken from Bastian's Völker des Östlichen Asien, pages 393 to 439. They are so mixed up together and with extraneous matter that it is impossible to quote separate pages, even if it were worth while.

nevertheless impossible to observe the very important part the Dragon plays in the imagery and decoration of Chinese temples, on the dress and ornaments of the kings, or on the standards of the army, without feeling that some important symbolism is concealed beneath its almost universal employment. It is true that in modern times the dragon has been invested with wings, and teeth, and claws, and transformed into a monster more horrible than any nightmare that ever disturbed the sleep of a mediæval herald; still it is difficult to avoid the conviction that if we could trace him far enough back, we should find that he was developed out of something much more nearly resembling "a beast of the field."

To take one instance among many, Kæmpfer[1] relates that two heaven-sent Serpents watched over the first washing of Confucius, for which a spring burst forth from the floor of the cave in which he was born. It would be interesting, for many reasons, to know when this tradition arose, and whether it is really Chinese or imported from India. Confucius was nearly contemporary with Buddha, and at a slightly subsequent time[2] was teaching doctrines so similar to those of the Indian philosopher, that now that they have got mixed up together in China, it is extremely difficult to discriminate what belongs to each. The connexion between Buddhism and Serpent Worship will be sufficiently apparent in the following pages. It would be curious if Chinese philosophy could be traced to the same or any similar source.

The following is another example. "Father Martin, one of the Jesuits who "obtained a settlement in China, says that the Chinese delight in mountains and "high places, because there lives the dragon, upon whom their good fortune depends. "They call him the father of happiness. To this dragon they erect temples, shaded "with groves."[3] This is exactly what we would expect, but when we meet with such a passage as this we are forced to ask, If this be so, why has not everybody seen it, and why have not others told us the same story?

The most satisfactory evidence I have obtained regarding Serpent Worship in China is from a Chinese work, entitled "The Great Cloud Wheel Rain asking "Sutra." It is an Imperial work, printed in its present form under the auspices of Keen Lung, A.D. 1783, and forms part of a great collection of Buddhist standard works. It is supposed to be spoken by Buddha in the "beautifully adorned Great "Cloud Circle Hall of the Nâga-Râja Nanda Upananda, and consists of a succession "of Dhâraṇis imparted by Buddha to the dragons for the sake of those who in "their worship desired rain."[4]

The most curious part of the book is the plates. These represent, first, a Nâga temple, which very much resembles—though the likeness is, of course, accidental—the tabernacle of the Jews. The shrine is a tent, standing in a rectangular enclosure surrounded by canvas screens. The furniture consists of an altar and four lighted

---

1 Japan, 426. See also Life of Confucius, Chinese Classics, vol. I. p. 59,

2 Confucius was 8 years old when Buddha died.

3 The Rev. Bathurst Deane, quoting Cambray, Mémoires Celtiques, p. 163.

4 The work in question was lent me by the Rev. S. Beal, a thoroughly competent Chinese scholar, who furnished the above particulars. His opinion is, that the work even in its present form is older than the 13th century, though the woodcuts may be more modern. See also J. R. A. S. XX. 170.

candles. Seven tables, or stands, are laden with cakes (shewbread), and as many with fruit; and seven lamps take the place of the seven-branched candlestick. There are four woodcuts representing the deities worshipped in the temple. One of these is reproduced in fac-simile in the annexed woodcut. It is a form of the Serpent God which was invented in India in the twelfth or thirteenth century, and with which we shall presently become familiar.[1] A human head and body, ending in a serpentine form from the waist downwards, but with the much more characteristic accompaniment of a degenerate serpent hood. In the first figure in this Chinese work, the Nâga has three serpents rising behind its head; in the second, five; in the third—that in the woodcut—seven; and the last, nine serpents. The lower extremities of the first and second are spotted like serpents. This one and the fourth have scales more like those of a fish. In India between the third century B.C. and the twelfth A.D., we find serpent hoods ranging from three to seven heads, but never the human body terminating in a serpent downward, till after the last quoted date.

No. 3.

NÂGA, FROM CHINESE SUTRA.

Although all this may have been derived from India, and in its present form probably was so, still it is interesting to find it practised in China so long after it has been forgotten there. At the same time, however, as hinted in speaking of Cambodia (p. 52), it is by no means clear that both India and China may not have borrowed their Serpent Worship from some common centre in Thibet. We are not yet, however, in a position to say whether it penetrated to China by the southern route it afterwards certainly took, or whether it may not have reached it by the north, or from a common centre in Tartary.

OCEANIA.

It has long been known that Serpent Worship prevailed to a considerable extent in some at least of the islands in the Pacific, but the notices of it that I have met with are singularly vague and unsatisfactory. No one with the requisite local knowledge has yet thought it worth while to collect and arrange the facts, so as to render them available as historical data; and till this is done, it is impossible to employ usefully even such information as we possess.

My own impression is that, wherever we find human sacrifices prevailing, or what—if we dare put such words together—we ought rather to designate as religious cannibalism, there Serpent Worship will be found also. In the Fiji islands it certainly exists. Degei, one of their principal gods, is supposed to be enshrined or

[1] Vide infra, page 73.

to exist in the form of a serpent, lying coiled up in a cave of Navata, a mountain on the coast of Viti Levu. Some traditions represent him with the head and part of the body of a serpent, the rest of him being of stone, emblematic of his everlasting and unchangeable nature.[1]

The savages of Australia, it is said, believe in the existence of a gigantic serpent, who created the world by a blow of his tail, and who is the cause of earthquakes. Nothing will induce them, however, to reveal to the white man the rites with which they worship the serpent, but which are reported to include human sacrifices and cannibalism.[2]

Traces of Serpent Worship are found at Suku and Kedal, and other places in Java, but there apparently not connected with Buddhism,[3] but as a local superstition of the natives; and other instances might be quoted, if it were worth while, or they could be depended upon. So little, however, is this the case, that the subject would hardly have been worth mentioning at all, were it not that one of the most interesting problems connected with the subject is the supposed connexion between the Serpent Worship of the Old World and that of Central America. Is it possible it could have migrated viâ the Fiji Islands and the Marquesas? There does not seem to be any other route which presents greater probabilities, if we are prepared to concede the previous question that America did borrow her Serpent Worship from the East; but as yet this is far from being settled.

Ceylon.

We must wait for further information before we can speak with anything like certainty, either regarding the extent to which Serpent Worship prevails in Ceylon, or with reference to any material evidences which may attest its existence in former days. Except Mr. Upham's,[4] no work that I am aware of treats of the subject, and no drawings except his have been published which afford any information regarding it. Though far from being exhaustive, Mr. Upham's work is sufficient to show how imperfect the conversion of the natives to Buddhism has been, and to what an extent the worship of the Nâga still prevails. In Ceylon, however, it seems now to be mixed up with Demon Worship and the worst superstitions of the Hindu Pantheon to such an extent as to be barely recognizable, and it will require considerable labour to resolve all these superstitions into their component parts.

In addition to this, I have seen native drawings of mythological subjects, which show a greater admixture of Serpent Worship than would be found in similar representations on the continent of India; and I have also had access to original drawings by Europeans in which the three or seven-headed Nâga is found adorning almost every sacred spot in the country.[5] The difficulty is to judge from such

---

[1] Seemann, Mission to Viti, p. 290.

[2] Manuscript information.

[3] Sir S. Raffles, Java, vol. ii. p. 47. Crawfurd's Dictionary of the Eastern Archipelago, sub vocibus.

[4] History and Doctrine of Buddhism in Ceylon, by Ed. Upham. London, 1829.

[5] Mr. Nicholl, the artist who made the drawings from which all the architectural subjects in Sir J. Emerson Tennent's work were engraved, recently showed me his original sketches. Everywhere at Anurâdhapura, Pollonarua, Dambool, &c. the Nâga appears prominent. The engraver, not knowing what it was, has converted it into a head-dress, which it requires a very practised eye to recognize as a seven-headed snake.

materials as exist what is really old and what may have been added; this, however, any competent antiquary on the spot could very easily determine.

In the meanwhile, however, numerous photographs of the antiquities of Ceylon have reached this country,[1] and they show in the first place that the entrance of all the larger temples are guarded by Wardens, who invariably have hoods of Serpents with seven heads. Buddha is also sometimes apparently so adorned. Once certainly on the Great Cave at Dambool with a three-headed Serpent hood; but the most striking image yet known to exist in Ceylon is at Mehentele. Here, carved in high relief on the face of a rock, is a great five-headed snake rising seven or eight feet out of the deep waters of a tank, in which the lower part of his body is hid. His hood measures six feet across, and taken in conjunction with its accompaniments it is one of the most imposing and awe striking images of a Nâga known to exist in that country.

In so far as they have been translated the testimony of the Buddhist scriptures seems to be as distinct as such evidence can be expected to be, that Ceylon was inhabited by a Nâga race of serpent worshippers when converted to Buddhism, the legends say in the sixth, but more probably in the third, century, B.C. Whether Gorresio, the translator of the Râmâyana, is correct in asserting that the Râkshasas whom Râma encountered in that island were Nâgas or not, is a question that must be left to Sanskrit scholars to decide. It does not appear that the passages are so understood by the modern Hindus. Snakes never appear as Râma's opponents in any of the thousand and one representations of that famous war; but Gorresio may be correct nevertheless, and it would be interesting to know.[2]

The three Ceylonese historical works which have been translated—the Mahâwanso, Ratnâcari, and Râjâvali—all commence with an account, more or less detailed, of the conversion of the Nâgas of Ceylon by Buddha himself.

The account in the Mahâwanso is to the following effect[3]: "In the fifth year "of his Buddhahood, the vanquisher of the five deadly sins perceiving that a conflict "was in hand between the Nâgas Mahodaro and Chûlodaro for possession of a gem-"set throne, out of compassion to the Nâgas visited Nâgadwîpo."[4]

At that time this Mahodaro was a Nâga king of a Nâga kingdom, 500 yojanas in extent, bounded by the ocean. His sister had been given in marriage to a Nâga king of the Kanawaddhamâno. mountain, and her son claimed the throne by inheritance, &c. "To them the vanquisher preached a sermon of reconciliation. "Both parties rejoicing thereat, made an offering of the gem-set throne to the divine "sage. The divine teacher alighting on the earth, seated himself on the throne, and "was served by the Nâga kings with celestial food and beverage. The lord of the

---

[1] These photographs have been principally taken at the expense of Government, and though they only at present represent the two old capital cities, it is intended to extend the series to other localities, and when this is done and they are accompanied by the requisite letterpress, Ceylon will possess a more complete illustration of its antiquities than any other possession of the British Crown.

[2] When so good a Sanskrit scholar as Muir doubts, it would be presumptuous in me to advance an opinion See Sanskrit Texts, II. 436.

[3] Mahawanso translated by the Hon. G. Turnour, p. 4.

[4] The translation limits the term Nâgadwipo to the northern portion of Ceylon, but on what grounds does not appear. The context seems to imply the whole island.

"universe procured for 80 koṭis of Nâgas, dwelling on land and in the water, the "salvation of the faith, and the state of piety" (p. 6).

The maternal uncle of Mahodaro, the Nâga king of Kalyâṇî, who was preparing to join in the war is also converted, and at parting Buddha promises to return, meanwhile bestowing on the Nâga king the gem-set throne, and having planted the Râjâyatana tree, at parting addressed them thus, "Oh, Nâga kings! worship this my "sanctified tree; unto you, my beloved, it will be a comfort and a consolation."

The same story is told, with slight and unimportant variations, in the other two histories, and from that time forward the Mahâwanso teems with Nâga legends; they seem, however, all to refer to the continent of India rather than Ceylon, and will be alluded to when necessary hereafter. The conversion of the island seems to have been complete in the time of Aśoka, B.C. 250,[1] and as the earliest of the scriptures we have were not reduced to writing in their present form before the fifth century after Christ, we must not expect from Buddhist authorities any admission of a faith adverse to Buddhism existing in the island at that date.

This, however, is just one of those cases in which the monuments are so useful to supplement the "litera scripta." If they were examined we should see how far the conversion was radical, and to what extent the people still adhered to their old faith. My impression is, that after more than 2,000 years, their conversion is still far from being complete. Whenever any competent person will look below the surface, I am very much mistaken if the old Serpent Worship is not found still practised by the aboriginal races in all remote parts of the island; but it is useless speculating when real information can be so easily obtained.

Whatever may be the result of the investigation into the Serpent Worship of Ceylon, there is no doubt whatever about the prevalence and importance of Tree Worship in that island. The legend of the planting of the Râjâyatana Tree by Buddha has already been alluded to, but the history of the transference of a branch of the Bo Tree from Buddh-gayâ to Anurâdhapura is as authentic and as important as any event recorded in the Ceylonese annals. Sent by Aśoka (250 B.C.) it was received with the utmost reverence by Devanampiyatisso, and planted in a most conspicuous spot in the centre of his capital.[2] There it has been reverenced as the chief and most important "numen" of Ceylon for more than 2,000 years, and it, or its lineal descendant sprung at least from the old root, is there worshipped at this hour. The city is in ruins; its great dagobas have fallen to decay; its monasteries have disappeared; but the great Bo tree still flourishes according to the legend, "Ever green, never "growing or decreasing, but living on for ever for the delight and worship of "mankind." Annually thousands repair to the sacred precincts within which it stands, to do it honour, and to offer up those prayers for health and prosperity which they believe are more likely to be answered if uttered in its presence. There is probably no older idol in the world, certainly none more venerated.[3]

---

[1] Throughout this work the year 250, as a date easily remembered, is assumed as that of Aśoka. It is probable that the true date of his accession is 270, and as he reigned 35 years, his death took place in 235 B.C.; 250 B.C. is therefore a fair mean, and has the merit of involving no hypothesis as to the chronology of the period.

[2] Mahawanso, chap. xviii.

[3] Sir Emerson Tennent, Col. Forbes Leslie, Chapman, and indeed everyone who has written about Ceylon, mention the fact. The drawings of it also are numerous.

India.

In every essential respect the religious history of India is extremely similar to that of Persia, but with one curious accidental difference, which influenced to a considerable extent their outward aspect and ultimate fate. From the accession of the Achæmenidæ till the old religions were practically swept away by the Mahomedan invasion, all the countries of Central Asia were united under one sceptre, and subject to one code of laws. The consequence is, that the Turanian, the Semitic, and the Aryan races, which successively occupied those countries known as Persia in its widest sense, all became more or less amalgamated into a homogeneous people, and their religions were also to the same extent fused into one great whole. The Ayran religion of Ormuzd was united in bonds of most unholy matrimony with the Turanian form of Ahriman, and the Magian religion acted as a flux to unite the two, at least to such an extent as probably to defy all the efforts of modern analysis to separate them again into their original elements.

The case of India was widely different. No native tradition represents India as ever united under one rule. When the Greeks visited it they found it divided into 122 different nations,[1] and the number probably was never less, it may have been more, till towards the end of the seventeenth century, when the Moguls under Aurangzebe nearly succeeded in rendering their sway paramount in India; but just as the house of cards was about to be completed, it fell to pieces from the inherent want of cohesion in the parts.

This circumstance renders the history of the religions of India very much more perplexed and more difficult to follow; but once the subject is mastered the Indian form becomes not only more instructive, but also very much more interesting to the student of comparative mythology.

No important Semitic element apparently ever existed among the populations of India, but from the earliest historical times we find two well defined and perfectly distinct races. One, the Aryan, or Sanskrit-speaking race, who entered India, it is generally supposed, across the Upper Indus, and eventually spread themselves throughout the whole of the valley of the Ganges, and the countries between the Vindhya and the Himalaya mountains. The other, known as the Dravidians, of Turanian affinities and speaking Tamul, or languages closely allied to it, entered India probably earlier than the Aryans, but across the Lower Indus, and now occupy the whole of the southern part of the peninsula nearly up to the Vindhya mountains.[2]

There seems to be no difference of opinion among Indian ethnologists with regard to these two great divisions of the people, but it is not quite so clear whether there was not a third occupying the countries north of the Vindhyas and between them and the Himalayas, in which they have been superseded by the Aryans. The language of the superior race has so completely taken possession of every department of literature at the earliest period to which our knowledge extends, that we

---

[1] Arrian, Indica, VII.

[2] Comparative Grammar of the Drávidian or South Indian family of Languages, by the Rev. R. Caldwell, B.A. London, 1856.

have no written record of the existence of this aboriginal people; and the blood of all has in modern times been so mixed by migration and colonization, that it seems impossible to dig back to the roots through the jumble of languages and races that now exists in the valley.[1]

The mode in which the question presents itself as bearing on the present inquiry is this:—It may safely be asserted that no Aryan race, while existing in anything like purity, was ever converted to Buddhism, or could permanently adopt its doctrines. If we take, for instance, the three leading features of that faith, atheism, metempsychosis, and absence of caste, they are essentially Turanian, and found everywhere among people of that race, but are distinctly opposed to the feelings of the Aryans wherever they are found. It is quite true that the Aryans may, during their 2,000 years residence in India before Buddha's time have become so mixed with the native tribes, and so impure, that some of their families may have temporarily adopted the new faith. So far as we now know this seems especially to have been the case in the early ages of Buddhism, but when that religion assumed the essentially Turanian form which it obtained from the changes introduced by Nâgârjuna about the Christian era, the two forms of faith became absolutely antagonistic, which they had not been before.

On the other hand, it does not appear that the Dravidian races ever were essentially, or to any great extent, serpent worshippers, or ever were converted to Buddhism. It may be too bold a generalization, in the present state of our knowledge, to assert that no race ever permanently adopted Buddhism who had not previously been Serpent Worshippers—but, if not quite true, it is nearly so; and though Serpent Worship is found south of the Kistnah, it is below the Ghâts and among races who cannot be classed as pure Dravidians. In like manner, though there were Buddhists in Drâviḍa-deśa, there are hardly any traces of Buddhist buildings or establishments now to be found south of Amravati.

If this should eventually prove to be the correct view of the case, it becomes necessary to assume the existence in the valley of the Ganges of a people differing from Dravidians and more closely allied to the Thibetans, the Burmese, and other Indo-Chinese races. Some kind of Buddhism probably existed beyond the Himalayas before Śâkya-muni's time. It still flourishes there, and seems indelible in all these lands. In India it did attain great prevalence and power during a thousand years, and no doubt something like it existed also there before the time of Śâkya-muni; but so little hold does it seem to have had on that people that it is now so completely washed out, that there hardly exists a single true Buddhist, certainly not a Buddhist establishment, between the Himalayas and Cape Cormorin.[2]

Assuming this view of the matter to be correct, it is evident that any traces of Serpent Worship that may be found in the Vedas or earlier writings of the Aryans must either be interpolations of a later date and concessions to the superstitions of the subject races. If we may trust a paper recently published in Bombay, such references do exist, and the Sárpa rájní "the queen of the serpents or the queen of

---

[1] If I understand him correctly, this is the opinion of Brian H. Hodgson, late of the Bengal Civil Service, as expressed in a series of papers he is now publishing in the "Phœnix Monthly Magazine."

[2] In a recent statistical report on the population of Bombay, I see "Boodists" enumerated among the sects. Who are they?

" all that moves " is alluded to in the Rig Veda and certainly mentioned in the Aitareya Bráhmana and other writings of that class. "The Black Yajur Veda," our author adds, "contains more prayers to Serpents and Serpent Worship than the Rig Veda. " In the Sanhitá of this Veda are prayers to the Sarpás who are addressed as inhabiting " the heavens, the skies, the rays of the sun, the water, the vegetables, &c."[1] In all these instances it will, however, be observed that it is the Sarpás or Serpents properly so called that are thus addressed, in subsequent times the Nâgas take their places, and though in some instances it is difficult to discriminate between the two, the latter have always more affinity to humanity and human form than the pure Sarpás.[2]

The traditions from which the Râmâyaṇa was compiled also represent a state of Aryan society so comparatively pure, that, except in cases above alluded to (p. 58), there is probably no mention of Nâgas there. But the heroes of the Mahâbhârata were much less pure a race Their origin, their polyandry, and other peculiarities, all point to the Himalayas; and from this work, consequently, we may expect some light on Serpent Worship. The poem, however, was compiled—in its present form at least—by Brahmans long after the events it describes; and although many ancient fragments are encrusted in its more modern form, little even of its narrative can be accepted as true history.

One of the most remarkable coincidences connected with the subject of Serpent Worship arises from the fact that the Mahâbhârata, which may practically be considered as one of the books of the Hindu Bible, opens, like the Pentateuch, with a curse on the Serpent. What is even more curious is that in both instances the same "equivoque" as to the name exists: read carelessly or in a translation, the curse in the Hindu epic is on the reptile, not on its worshippers, just as happens in the Bible, where, however, the conciseness of the narrative does not enable us to rectify the meaning from the context. In the Indian poem, however, the story of the great sacrifice for the destruction of the Serpents is so mixed up with historical and human action that it is evident at once that the ambiguity[3] about the name, is only seized upon by the Hindu poets as an excuse for introducing the supernatural into an ordinary human transaction, and to enable them to give rein to that exuberance of fancy which is the curse of their poetic effusions.

Passing over the first canto, which is a general introduction to the whole poem, the next three (ślokas 657 to 2197), are wholly occupied by the affairs of the Nâga

---

[1] Serpent Worship in Western India by Rao Sahib Vishnath Narayan Mandlik. J. B. B. R. A. S. IX. pp. 188–9.

[2] M. Vivien de St. Martin, in his "Géographie du Veda," pp. 103–4, states that the Aryans ascribed to the Dasyus the power of controlling the elements, and of granting or withholding rain at their pleasure. If this were so, it was not to the people themselves, but to their Serpent God, that this power should have been ascribed by the writers of the hymns of the Vedas. I confess, however, that my reading of the work in Wilson's translation does not bear out this attribution.

[3] In the Âdi Parva the word used for serpent is almost invariably "Nâga." In the Vana Parva, where Bhîma gets into trouble with Nahusha in the form of a real serpent or boa, it is as usually "Sârpa;" but as is mentioned in a very learned paper in the J. B. B. R. A. S., vol. IX. p. 183, it is difficult to distinguish at this day between the Nágas and the Sárpas. The two words, in their religious acceptation, are now practically treated as equivalent. Sárpa is the more comprehensive term, and means anything that moves. Nâgas are treated as a species of superior Sárpas, and Nâga now specially means the most venomous serpent—the Cobra di Capello.

race, commencing with the marriage of the two sisters Kadrû and Vinatâ with the Rishi Kaśyapa, and the strange desires of the two with regard to their progeny. These led to Kadrû, the eldest, being the mother of 1,000 Nâgas, who were the progenitors of the whole serpent raee. The names of her principal deseendants are then given,[1] some of which have already been quoted, others will frequently be referred to in the sequel; such, for instanee, as Śesha, Vâṣuki, Airâvata, Takshaka, Karkotaka, Kâliya, Aila or Elâpatra, Nîla and Anîla, Nahusha, and others. Her sister, on the other hand, became the mother of Garuḍa, who, in consequence of the trick played by Kadrû on her sister, became the all-powerful enemy of the Nâga raee, and hence also the mother's curse, from whieh sueh fatal eonsequences flowed.

When divested, however, of its poetic garb, and all its mythological rubbish, the story of the Mahâbhârata, in so far at least as Serpent Worship is concerned, does not seem difficult to understand, and may be succinctly narrated.

The Lunar race, to which the heros of the great war belonged, were a second great horde of the Aryan race, who seem to have entered India across the Upper Indus at least 1,000 years after the purer so-called Solar race. The first seat to which we can trace them back seems to be Takht-i-Bahai, north of Peshawar.[2] Thence, passing through the Punjâb, we find them settled at Hâstinapura, between the Jumna and Ganges, about the thirteenth century B.C., when the real aetion of the poem commences.

The first transaction in which the Nâgas appear, is the burning of the forest of Khâṇḍava.[3] Simply, it seems, that when the family at Hâstinapura became too numerous, it was determined to found a second capital, and for this purpose the spot where Delhi now stands was cleared by burning the forest which then oecupied its site, and dislodging the Nâgas who occupied the spot. The Nâgas were proteeted by the Buddhist deity Indra. But, attacked by the Vedic god Agni, the Brahman poet represents them as all perishing except their king Takshaka.

Subsequent to this the relations between the Pâṇḍus and the Nâgas seem to have been of the most friendly description. Arjuna, in his first banishment, marries first Ulûpî,[4] the daughter of a Nâga king at the foot of the Himalayas, near Hurdwar; and shortly afterwards he formed a still more important connexion, by marrying Chitrângadâ, daughter of Chitravâhaṇa, the Nâga king of Manipur, by whom he had a son, Bhabra-vâhana, who played so strange a part in a subsequent episode, when his father, in the performance of the Aśwamedha, or horse sacrifiee, again visited Manipur.[5] From these and other minor particulars it would seem that the author of the Mahâbhârata wished to represent the Aryans of that day as cultivating friendly relations with the aborigines. The real quarrel took place some time after the great war was ended, and in this manner:—Parîkshit, the grandson of Arjuna, had sueceeded to the throne; and one day, while hunting in the forest, incensed at the

---

[1] Âdi Parva 1551, et seq.

[2] Bellew, Report on the Yusufzais, p. 136. Some very curious sculptures have recently been discovered at this place, but they are all long subsequent to the age of Bhârata, and betray a Bactrian, or at least a Western, influence, which gives them a character very different from anything found in India. They are all Buddhistic; but with a strong infusion of Græco-Bactrian feeling.

[3] Âdi Parva, Fauche's translation, 8050, et seq.

[4] Loc. 7788.

[5] Wheeler's History of India, vol. I., p. 404.

contumacious silence of a hermit,[1] insulted him by hanging the dead body of a snake round his neck. His son and disciple cursed the king for this insult to his father, and invoked the aid of Takshaka, the king of serpents, to avenge it. The consequence was, that on the eighth day from that time Parîkshit was bitten[2] by Takshaka, who is always represented as king of Takshaśilâ.[3] It was to avenge this assassination of his father, that Janamejaya undertook the great sacrifice for the destruction of the Nâgas.[4] Thousands—myriads—had already perished, when the slaughter was stayed at the intervention of Astîka, a Brahman, though at the same time the nephew of Vâsuki, the serpent king of the eastern Nâgas.[5] It is probable the remnant either, like Astîka, become converts, or at least promised submission to the dominion of the Aryans. We consequently hear no more of them for three or four centuries, till at last, about the year 691 B.C., we find a Nâga dynasty on the throne of Magadhá;[6] and it was under Ajâtaśatru, the sixth king of this race, in the year 623, that Buddha was born, and the great regeneration of the subject races was inaugurated.

The sequel of the story of the Mahâbhârata is told with great vividness in the Nâgânanda,[7] a Buddhist drama, ascribed to Śrî Harsha Deva, of Canouge (A.D. 610 to 648).[8] It is there narrated that Vâsuki, in order to save the remnant of the Nâga race which was threatened with extermination by their terror for Garuḍa, agreed to supply their insatiate enemy with a Nâga victim daily. This went on till the bones of the Nâgas whitened the plain, when Jîmûta Vâhaṇa, the hero of the drama, moved by the agony of the mother of one of the victims, offered himself in the true spirit of Buddhism as a willing substitute for the doomed Nâga. This devotion and self-sacrifice so astonishes Garuḍa, that feeling ashamed of previous voracity, he abandons his claim to his daily meal, restores life to those he had devoured, and all ends happily.

If we knew more of the local ethnology of India, all this narrative might probably be authenticated to an extent which it is now impossible to attempt. It is curious to observe that in Manipur, the scene of Arjuna's marriage with Chitrângadâ, and his slaughter by her son, that at the present day the peculiar god of the Royal family is a species of snake, called Pa-kung-ba, from which the family claims descent. When it appears, it is coaxed on to a cushion by the priestess in attendance, who then performs certain ceremonies to please it. This snake appears sometimes, they say, of great size; when he does so, it is indicative of his being displeased with something. So long as he remains of a diminutive form, it is a sign he is in good humour.[9]

In the immediate neighbourhood of Manipur there are numerous tribes of aboriginal people, still called Nâgas. From their name and locality it might be supposed they must be Serpent Worshippers; but no one has yet observed that form of faith among them. The subject must, therefore, be remitted for further inquiries.

---

1 Âdi Parva, 1696, et seq.

2 Idem, 1801.

3 Idem, 678, 830, et seq.

4 Idem, 2073, et seq.

5 Idem, 1025, et seq.

6 Wilson's Vishnu Purâna, p. 467. Lassen's Ind. Alt. I. (2d ed.) App. p. xxxviii. et seq.

7 "Or the Joy of the Snake World," translated by P. Boyd, B.A., with an introduction by Professor Cowell. London. 1872.

8 Journal R.A.S. New Series, IV., 87.

9 Account of the Valley of Munipur, by Major Macculloch: Records of Government of India, No. XXVII. 1859.

The locality of Janamejaya's sacrifice is said in the Mahâbhârata to have been the Kurukshetra, the famous battle-field of the Pâṇḍus and Kurus, north-west of Delhi, but another and more probable site is still pointed out at Agrahaut, in Orissa.[1] There, within the precincts of a very old and remote, but now ruined, temple, may be seen numerous small models of temples, said to have been placed there by Janamejaya, to represent those princes who could not be present on the occasion. They are probably not so old; but it is strange to find the traditions of the Mahâbhârata still clinging to these spots, and Serpent Worship still prevailing there. At least, not far from this—at Sumbulpore—in 1766, Mr. Motte and another[2] went to visit a great snake that had been worshipped there since the world began! They saw him emerge from his cave, which he does every seventh day,[3] and accept the offering of a goat which his worshippers had provided. After devouring it he took a bath in a canal that surrounded his dwelling-place; and from the mark he left in the mud at the edge, Mr. Motte estimated his diameter to have been about two feet. He does not even guess his length, but it must have been considerable. When Major Kittoe visited Sumbulpore in 1836 he was still alive,[4] and probably is so still; and I have no doubt but that numerous other deities of the same sort could easily be found if only looked for; but attention has never hitherto been direeted to the subject.

If anywhere it certainly is about Sumbulpore, or to the westward of it that the ancient history of India would lead us to look for traces of Nâga Worship. The names of the two Nâgpûr provinces are certainly derived from the mythic snake, "and the significance of their joint relation to the mysterious serpent gods or serpent "races of Indian mythology is enhanced when we find the Rajas of Chota Nágpúr "claim to be Nágabansís, or serpent descended, and have, or till lately had, the "lunettes of their serpent ancestor engraved on their signets as proof of their "lineage."[5] M. Grant then goes on to enumerate the Rajas of Garhá Mandla—of Kárond—and the chief of Khairághur, and others, as equally claiming Nâga descent. The Raja of Bastar, he adds, a Rajput, succeeded to a Nâga line, which, in an inscription, dated 1073, A.D., claimed to be descended from Kasyapa, the mythical progenitor of the sun, but who, through Kadrû, one of his wives, is said to be the progenitor of the Serpent race. "But perhaps," he adds, "the most curious "relic of serpent connexion left in the provinces is at the Temple of Buran Deva, "in Chattisgarh, which is evidently of very early origin. It contains no image but "that of a Cobra, and lying near are two inscriptions, one containing a list of "22 kings, who trace their descent to the union of a snake god with the daughter "of a holy man who lived south of the Narbadá." "The inseription taken in "connexion with the snake image[6] may, perhaps, imply that the Haihaya King at

---

[1] Asiatic Researches, XV. 257.

[2] Asiatic Register, vol. I. p. 82.

[3] Vide ante, note, p. 51. Is it possible that the period of creation in Genesis being limited to seven days is a part of the primæval Ophite faith?

[4] J. A. S. B. vol. VIII. p. 478.

[5] Grant, Introduction to Gazetteer of Central Provinces, p. lxiv.

[6] Another serpent temple of even greater celebrity is found at Bhadravati (Bhándak), 16 miles N.W. of Chanda. It is supposed, by the Chanda Brahmins, says Major Lucie Smith, to have been crected by Yuvanaswa in honour of the serpent who aided him in his contest with Bhím, and is the only temple in the district dedicated to Snake Worship. Report on the Land Revenues of the Chanda District, p. 28.

" the time was a Snake Worshipper, or, if a Buddhist, as there is reason to think, " that his Buddhism was tainted with Serpent Worship." (p. lxv.)

After enumerating various other reasons for believing in the importance of the Serpent Worshippers in Nâgpur, Mr. Grant adds, "Whether the Nágas of the Hindu " legends were Scythian Buddhists, as is supposed by Sir H. Elliot, or not, it seems " probable that they were a race apart, in the early centuries of the Christian era, " and there certainly seems reason for inferring the existence in, and round Central " India, of a small but powerful foreign element, distinguished by its reverence, " whether religious or ancestral, for Serpent Gods and progenitors." (p. lxix.)

These extracts might be continued to any extent, but it is better to refer the reader to the paper itself, which is full of learning and research. Enough has been abstracted to show that Serpent Worship certainly did prevail in these central provinces at one time, and to make it probable that when looked for more traces will be found than were noticed even by the talented author of the Gazetteer and his assistants.

Before leaving this part of the subject it may be well to point out that the abode of these Nâgas, whether described in Hindu poems or Buddhist legends, is always underground, they never appear on earth except when they have daughters to marry, or other important business to transact, and having accomplished this they return instantly "to their dark abodes, deep in the bowels of the earth," where mediæval rhapsodists placed our Hell.

One of the Nâga Rajas, Nalo or Nala, is said to have resided in an underground palace or city called Majerika[1] or Manjerika,[2] apparently under the centre of Jambudwipa. Vâṣouki's abode, as mentioned above, was under, but near Manipur, Ulûpî's near the Himalayas, and the Râja Nâga of Cashmere resided far below the bottom of his lakes. Both Hindu poets and Buddhist fabulists exhaust all the language of hyperbole in describing the magnificence and splendour of their subterranean palaces. They are such as Milton described, and Martin painted. There the Nâga Kings enthroned in state ruled over myraids of subject Nâgas of various degrees, and either through their subjects, or more rarely personally, took a part in the affairs of mankind, as related above, or as is found at every turn in almost every Hindu or Buddhist legend.

Rise of Buddhism.

As has been frequently suggested in other works,[3] the great characteristic of the ancient as well as of the modern history of India is the constant recurrence of one typical phenomenon which controlled the destiny of the nation in all ages to which our knowledge extends. From the earliest dawn of tradition to the present day the great underlying stratum of the population of India seems to have been of Turanian race, very unwarlike, and incapable of any great rise in civilization, except through admixture of blood. These consequently easily fell a prey to the hardier and more warlike races bred in the countries now known as Bokhara and Affghanistan,

[1] Turnour, Mahawanso, p. 185.
[2] Spence Hardy's Eastern Monachism, p. 247.
[3] History of Architecture, by the Author, vol. II., p. 446, et seqq. &c.

and the result has been that at periods of from five to ten centuries, horde after horde has crossed the Indus, and settled in the fertile plains of India. For awhile these retained their freshness and vigour, but by degrees, partly from the enervating effects of the climate, but more from intermixture with the aboriginal races, they sunk to the lower level of the indigenous inhabitants, and in their turn became a prey to the next horde that followed the steps of their forefathers across the Indus.

For our present purpose it is not necessary to inquire when the first great immigration of the Aryans or Dravidians took place, or when they first settled in the north and south of India respectively. It is sufficient that we are able to state that the less pure horde of the Aryans, known as the Lunar race probably reached the Ganges about the thirteenth or fourteenth century B.C. From that time till the third or fourth century, or for more than one thousand years, no horde of any race, so far as we know, crossed the Indus. This may, in a great measure, be owing to the existence of the powerful empires of Assyria and Persia on the other side of the river, which may have kept the barbarians in check, or to local causes we cannot now detect. Be that as it may, the fact that interests us here is, that during this long period the blood of the Aryans had become so mixed and so impure that the Veda was no longer possible as a rule of faith, and when Śâkya-muni availed himself of the opportunity so afforded, to revive the religion of the aboriginal Turanians, his call was responded to in a manner which led to the most important consequences, in a religious point of view, not only in India, but to all the Turanian families of mankind.

So far as we can now see, Buddhism was little more than a revival of the coarser superstitions of the aboriginal races, purified and refined by the application of Aryan morality, and elevated by doctrines borrowed from the superior intellectual resources of the Aryans. Buddha himself was undoubtedly of purely Aryan race, being the descendant of a junior branch of the Solar kings of Ayodhyâ. Burmese traditions represent his son Rahula as assuming the garb of a priest;[1] but the Hindus, with more probability, record his succeeding to the throne of his grandfather, and we gather from them, that the dynasty retained its Brahminical faith till its extinction shortly afterwards.[2] The dissemination of the Buddhist religion seems wholly due to the accident of its having been adopted by the low caste kings of Magadhá, and to its having been elevated by one of them to the rank of the religion of the State.

As a part of the reform which Buddha introduced, ancestral worship was abolished, and the sepulchral tumulus became instead the depository of relics of saints; Serpent Worship was repressed, but the sister faith of Tree Worship was elevated to the first rank.[3] Absolute negation of sensual enjoyment, which to the Turanian in all ages is as the

---

[1] Bigandet, Life and Legend of Gaudama, p. 229.

[2] Wilson's Vishnu Purana, p. 463.

[3] When in 1866 I wrote the second volume of my History of Architecture, I, after hazarding the assertion "that before the Aryans reached India, the inhabitants of the valley of the Ganges seem to have been Tree and "Serpent Worshippers," then added, in speaking of the Buddhist reform (p. 448): "Serpent Worship was utterly "rejected, but Tree Worship was adopted as an important part of the new faith." When in the following spring I discovered the Amravati sculptures in the coach house at Fife House, I hastened to add as an erratum on the last page a recantation or at least modification of this assertion. Further investigations now incline me to go back to my old faith. The serpent, I believe, was rejected by Buddha and his earlier followers, but cropped up again among other mediæval corruptions, and, as we shall presently see, became an important element in Buddhist mythology.

breath of life, was elevated into a crucial test of faith, and asceticism became ultimately the one path to salvation. There is every reason to believe that human sacrifices were common in ancient India. War was the normal state of its kingdoms, and persecution is too essentially a characteristic of the Aryan races not to have flourished there. On the other hand, the Buddhist expanded the Jewish commandment "Thou shalt do no murder" into "Thou shalt not kill," and extended it to the meanest of created beings. No history we know of ever recorded a war waged by Buddhists as such,[1] and toleration of the faith of others was one of the most marked characteristics of the new religion. No faith was ever so essentially propagated by persuasion as that of Buddha, and though the Buddhists were too frequently persecuted even to destruction, there is no instance on record of any attempt by them to spread their faith by force in any quarter of the globe.

The Turanian of course had no caste, so that institution was put aside only to be revived when a second upheaval of local superstitions under Aryan influence, on the decay of Buddhism, brought Śivaism and Vishnuism to the surface, together with all the monstrosities of the modern Hindu pantheon.

Although doubts have been expressed as to the exact date of Buddha's birth to the extent of about 60 years, the usual chronology,[2] which is that adopted throughout this work, represents him as born at Kapilavastu, a small principality on the north of the Ganges, in the year 623 B.C., and he died at Kuśinagara, not far from the place of his birth, 543 B.C., in the eighth or eighteenth year[3] of the reign of Ajâtaśatru, the sixth king of the Nâga dynasty of Magadha, who was then the lord paramount of Northern India.

The name of Śiśunâga is applied by the Brahmans to the first king of this dynasty; the Buddhists give it to the tenth, and add the following legend:—On a certain occasion one of the chief of the courtezans bore a child to one of the Lichchhawi Rajas, but the child proving an abortion was put into a basket, and at night thrown on a dungheap. A certain Nâgarâjâ, the tutelar of the city, observing it, encircled it with its folds, and sheltered it with its hood. The people who congregated there made a noise, "Śu, Śu," to frighten the snake, and on examining the basket found the abortion matured into a male child with every mark of greatness on it. In consequence of this incident he received the name Śiśunâga, and in time ascended the throne of Magadha.[4] The second convocation was held 100 years after the death of Buddha, during the reign of his son Kálásoka, and we gather, though somewhat indistinctly, that his successors, including the nine Nandas, till the accession of the celebrated Chandragupta (B.C. 325), were Nâgas or Serpent

---

[1] Whether or not the events depicted in Plate XXXVIII. should form an exception to this rule will be discussed hereafter.

[2] I have myself no doubts as to the correctness of the usually received date, and have published my reasons for this belief in the Journal of the Royal Asiatic Society, vol. IV., New Series, p. 133. For the convenience of readers, however, the conclusions I have arrived at in these chronological researches will be found in the table at the end of this volume. The reasoning on which they are based will be found in the journal of that society, but the results have meanwhile been adopted as data throughout this work.

[3] Turnour, Mahawanso, xlvii., lii.

[4] Turnour's Introduction to the Mahawanso, p. xxxvii. See also Bigandet, Life of Gaudama, p. 362, et seq.

Worshippers pure and simple.[1] They certainly were considered as of very low caste; hated by the Brahmans, and were not loved by the Buddhists.

With the Mauryan kings Buddhism seems to have entered on a new phase; at least in Aśoka's inscriptions we have no trace of the worship of either Buddha himself, nor of Trees nor Serpents. Pure abstract morality seems to have been the form it then took or was intended to take.[2] But in the Mahâwansó, one of the great events of Aśoka's reign, is the despatch of a branch of the Bo Tree of Buddh Gayâ to Ceylon,[3] showing that form of faith to be then prevalent; and in the Caves of Orissa, which may be anterior to the Christian era, we find both Tree and Serpent Worship prevailing.[4] There are, however, few periods of Indian history during which such scanty materials exist for settling any point, either historical or mythological, as during the two centuries and a half before the Christian era. We know very little indeed of what happened during that period, and we hardly see where light is to come from to illumine those dark ages.

Immediately preceding the Christian era a great revolution took place in Buddhism under the influence of Nâgârjuna,[5] one of the most important names connected with the history of the religion. Although we cannot fix the date of this patriarch with absolute certainty, we can within very narrow limits. The quotation from the Thibetan Târanâtha in Vassilief's work[6] places him between 14 years B.C. and 28 A.D., both dates reconcileable with a not very long life. But we have another means of ascertaining it even more satisfactorily. Nâgârjuna was the ruling spirit in the great council or convocation held under Kanishka, the Tartar king of Cashmere and Northern India. In a tope erected by this king at Manikyâla a number of Roman consular coins were found around the principal deposit. These date from 73 to 33 B.C.,[7] and as we cannot suppose they were deposited there till some time after the year in which they were coined, the building of this tope by Kanishka must be placed within the thirty years that preceded the Christian era.

At that time the Buddhists were divided into eighteen sects, grouped into four great divisions,[8] a circumstance from which we may infer that Buddhism was torn by internal dissensions, and might have perished without the impulse given by this fresh importation of Tartar blood from the north. At the same time also we learn that Milinda, king of the Eastern Panjâb, had silenced the Buddhist priests in argument, and driven them from the country across the Himalaya to Rakshita Tal and Manasarovara.[9] At this critical juncture the youthful Nâgârjuna appeared. He was then a monk in the celebrated monastery of Nâlanda in Behar[10]—the Monte Cassino of India,—and proclaimed himself the restorer of the old faith. According

---

1 Mahá Padma and Nanda, the only two of their names we know with certainty, are both names of serpents. Their coins I believe to be those depicted, J. A. S. B., vol. VII., pl. LX., No. 1 to 9. On all these the serpent is the principal symbol.

2 J. A. S. B., VII. p. 219; J. R. A. S., XII. 153.

3 Vide ante, p. 59.

4 Vide Appendix H.

5 His name is singularly suggestive, being compounded of "Nâga," a serpent, and a tree, "Arjuna," under which he was born. Vassilief, &c. Bouddhisme, 213.

6 Le Bouddhisme, 201.

7 Cunningham, Bhilsa Topes, 130.

8 Asiatic Researches, XX. 92, 297.

9 Cunningham, Bhilsa Topes, 130.

10 This Monastery took its name and probably owed its original sanctity to a dragon or Nâga called Nâlanda, who resided in a pool close by. General Cunningham saw in 1861–62 the tank in which he resided. Report to Government for those years, p. 12.

to this prophet the words uttered by Śâkya Muni during his life-time had been heard and noted down by the Nâgas, who had kept them to themselves in their own abode, till such time as mankind should become worthy to receive them. Nâgârjuna gave out that he had received these documents from the Nâgas and was commissioned to proclaim them to the world.[1] This gave rise to an entirely new school of Buddhism known as Mahâyâna, or as M. Julien translates it,[2] the "Grand Véhicule," as opposed to Hînayâna or the "Petit Véhicule;" the distinction between the two being in almost every respect identical with that which exists between Evangelical and Mediæval Christianity.

This is another of those curious historical coincidences that exist between Christianity and Buddhism, and there are few so startling. In the first three centuries after the death of its founder, Buddhism was a struggling sect, sometimes petted, sometimes persecuted, but in spite of all we are told in subsequent legends, never spread to any great extent among the people. Three hundred years after Buddha, Aśoka did for Buddhism exactly what Constantine did for Christianity. He adopted it, made it the religion of the state, and with all the zeal of a convert, used every exertion to assist in its propagation. Six hundred years after Buddha, Nâgârjuna and Kanishka did for the eastern faith what St. Benedict and Gregory the Great did for the western, they created a church with a Hierarchy and a Doctrine. We must go on further still for four centuries more, to Buddhaghosa (A.D. 410) and to Hildebrand, before we find our Mediæval churches quite complete, with the priesthood quite segregated from the laity, and the system perfected in all its parts. In the sixteenth century after Christ came the reformation, and with it the restoration of Evangelical Christianity. Before the sixteenth century after Buddha came a reformation, but it was one of extermination of the faith, is so far as India was concerned. Śankara Âchârya was the Indian Luther, but his aim was widely different. Whatever may have been the abuses and corruptions they had crept into Buddhism in the eighth and tenth centuries of our era, they were replaced by a faith much less pure, and far fuller of idolatrous absurdities than that which it superseded. What the western reformers aimed at, was to restore the Christian Hînayâna. In the east the reform came from without from the professors of another religion, not from within, and hence the different fate of the two faiths. In Europe Christianity was invigorated by the struggle, in India Buddhism perished altogether.

The consequence of all this is, that we are now very much in the position of a foreign investigator who might have entered some great conventual establishment in Europe in the fourteenth or fifteenth century to study Christianity. Worse than even this; it is as if the monasteries of the middle ages had lasted for four or five centuries longer without any reform or light from without, and that then an attempt should have been made to ascertain within their walls what primitive Christianity originally might have been. The explorer would have found lives and legends of saints in abundance; miracles and divine communications without end; ponderous tomes of scholastic divinity, and a marvellously falsified history. Instead of the Bible, he would have been referred to that mass of beautiful but purely legendary fictions which, in the course of centuries, had attached themselves to the name of the Virgin

---

[1] Vassilief, Bouddhisme, 119.

[2] Voyages de Hiouen-Thsang, *passim*.

Mary, and to all the members of the Holy family. All this, too, he would have found mixed up with the stories from the Old Testament, and from the lives of Mediæval saints in most marvellous confusion. If among all these works he chanced to light on the Bible, it certainly would not be pointed out to him as the one true Life of Christ, or as the basis of the Christian faith. We would, no doubt, appreciate the Gospels of Buddhism if we found them; but all that has yet been disinterred from the monasteries of Thibet, or the libraries of China or Ceylon, is in its present form subsequent to Buddhaghosa; more than one thousand years after the death of the founder of the religion, and long after the Nâga revelation had superseded the original faith. We are thus precisely in the position of the student of Christianity who had only the library of some Mediæval monastery at his command. In so far as books are concerned, we depend almost wholly for our knowledge of the Life of Buddha on the Lalita Vistara,[1] and other works of the same age and class. The Lalita Vistara, however, was reduced to its present form in the fourteenth century of Buddha, and is the exact counterpart in purpose and authenticity to the Legenda Aurea, and similar works of the Christian middle ages. It is true all these Buddhist books profess to be founded on earlier works, and no doubt this to a considerable extent is true; but till the sculptures of the Topes at Sanchi and Amravati were brought to light we had no test by which the authenticity of these earlier works could be recognized when found, we were left very much to our own powers of critical discrimination to say what is original and what may have been added to suit the tastes and feelings of an age long subsequent to the events.[2]

Looking at what has been done within the last twenty years, it is not impossible that we may recover even the original Sûtras, the Vinaya and the Abhidhârma, as they are said to have been compiled by Upâli, Ânanda, and Kâśyapa immediately on the death of Śâkya Muni,[3] or at all events we may hope that the keen criticism of modern scholars may be able, at least to some extent, to separate the wheat from the chaff, and restore to us a tolerably correct picture of primitive Buddhism as it existed before the Christian era. Notwithstanding all the difficulties of the task, considerable progress has already been achieved in this direction. Burnouf's contributions are invaluable,[4] while the works of Barthélemy St. Hilaire,[5] of Bigandet,[6] and Vassilief,[7] are most useful résumés of what is known. The Germans also and our own scholars have collected a mass of materials, and discussed and dissected a number of problems which will clear the way for a correct understanding of many questions whenever a serious attempt is made to combine the whole into a consecutive history.

In the meanwhile it is of the utmost importance that everything should be gathered together and published that can throw any light on Buddhism anterior to the time when the books we now possess were reduced to their present form. The

1 Translated from the Thibetan by Foucaux. Paris, 4to., 1847.

2 If anyone would wish perfectly to realize the position of Buddhist scholars at the present day, let him read carefully any one of the many versions of "Lhystoire du Noble et Vaillant roy Alexandre le Grand," as compiled in the middle ages, and compare it with the narrative of the life of the same monarch as related by classical authors. Having done this, he will appreciate the difficulty in which Oriental scholars are now placed as regards the early history of Buddhism in the life of the founder of that religion.

3 J. A. S. B., vol. I. p. 6; Asiatic Researches, XX. 42, &c.

4 Introduction à l'Histoire du Buddhism Indien; Lotus de la Bonne Loi, &c.

5 Le Bouddha et sa Religion. Paris, 1860.

6 The Life or Legend of Gaudama. Rangoon, 1866.

7 Le Bouddhisme, ses Dogmes, son Histoire, et sa Littérature, traduit du Russe par La Comme. Paris, 1865.

only written documents which certainly belong to the earlier epoch are the edicts of Aśoka, engraved on the lâṭs at Delhi, Allahabad, and elsewhere; and on rocks at five or six places in India, extending from the shores of the Bay of Bengal to Guzerat, and to the Himalayas and Peshawar on the north. Except that at Bhabra,[1] these are neither doctrinal nor historical. They are dry moral precepts, and so unlike to Buddhism as now known, that, but for collateral secondary evidence, it might very well be doubted whether they belonged to that religion at all, or it might be disputed, as was done by the late Professor Wilson, whether they were written by Aśoka. The Bhabra inscription and further investigations have set these questions at rest. But the picture these inscriptions afford us of Buddhism 250 B.C. is a wonderful contrast to what we find in the Lalita Vistara of Thibet,[2] as compiled in the eighth or ninth century of our era, or any other written records of the religion which we possess.

Next in importance to these inscriptions are the sculptures of the two Topes, illustrated in this work. It may now be considered as certainly ascertained that the gateways at Sanchi were erected within the limits of the first century of our era, and the earlier ones were, therefore, contemporary with Nâgârjuna. They are not pure, but they are purer than anything of their kind now known to exist elsewhere. Buddha never appears in them as an object of worship. The Dagoba, the Chakra or wheel, the Tree, and other such emblems are reverenced. The Serpent does appear but rarely, and we have very little of the absurd supernatural fables which afterwards form the stock of the legends. But what is more interesting is, that there are certain Jatakas or parables relating to the life of Buddha in pre-existing states as a Bôdhisatwa, which are repeated in these sculptures almost literally as they are found in modern works now-current in Ceylon and other Buddhist countries,[3] a circumstance only too painfully characteristic of the whole literature of India. The poem or the fiction remains fixed and unalterable; the history is distorted and changed, till the events can hardly be recognized.

The sculptures of the Tope at Amravati are three centuries more modern than those at Sanchi, and represent a state of affairs much more in accordance with modern notions. Buddha is worshipped, but the Nâga is his co-equal. The Dagoba, the Tree, the Chakra, are all reverenced; and almost all the legends of modern times may probably be traced in its sculptures, though in a purer form than in the books. Sanchi may be taken as the nearest approach we possess to an illustrated Bible of the Hînayâna period, four hundred years before the oldest Buddhist book we possess; and Amravati as a pictorial illustration of the Mahâyâna three centuries after its promulgation, and just before Fa-Hian[4] visited the country and gave us the earliest description we have of the faith by any outsider, since at least the very meagre and unsatisfactory accounts of the Greeks.

In the frescoes that cover the walls of the Caves at Ajanta is found a third picture three centuries later than the sculptures at Amravati, this time representing

---

[1] J. R. A. S., XVI. p. 367.

[2] These inscriptions will be found reprinted, in so far as it is necessary for present purposes, in Appendix B.

[3] The most prominent of these at Sanchi is the Wassantara Jataka, which occupies the whole of the lowest beam of the northern gateway, and will be found described in its proper place further on.

[4] Foĕ-Kouĕ-Ki, translated by Rémusat, &c., 4to., Paris, 1836.

the state of Buddhist belief just before its decline. Owing to the unfortunate fire at the Crystal Palace these are not now available for purposes of illustration, but they may become so hereafter. Even, however, if we possessed drawings or photographs of them, they could never be so important for the history of the faith as the sculptures of the two Topes of Sanchi and Amravati, which represent it before the existence, in their present form, of any of the books we now possess. Our regret, however, at the loss of these copies, is very much lessened, in so far as our present purposes are concerned, by the knowledge that there were no traces of Serpent Worship in the paintings. The only representations of the Nâga found at Ajanta are among the sculptured decorations of the doorways or in detached bas-reliefs outside the caves,[1] where they may be considered as accessory or subordinate to the principal form of worship. For a history of Buddhism, the paintings are of great interest; as illustrating either Tree or Serpent Worship, they are comparatively unimportant.

The same remark applies to the frescoes in the Caves at Baugh, and generally to the western Caves. The tendency of the migration from Takshsaśilâ seems to have been southward, and towards the East, and never to have descended into the Cave region of the northern Ghauts. On the other hand, the most recent example I am acquainted with of any great Nâga sculptures belonging to the classical age of Indian art, is the well-known bas-relief at Mahavellipore,[2] on the eastern shore, about forty miles south of Madras, and executed apparently in the twelfth or thirteenth century. This is carved on two great masses of granite rock, and extends about 90 feet north and south, by 30 or 35 feet in height. On the northern or right-hand portion, a group of elephants, beautifully executed, is advancing towards the centre, and above them some thirty figures, interspersed with lions and other animals, are all turning in the same direction. On the left-hand rock the lower part was evidently intended to contain the representations of the rest of the animal kingdom, but is only commenced. The upper portion has a number of human figures, equal to that of the other half of the bas-reliefs, and all equally turning towards the centre. Among them there is certainly one God of the Hindu pantheon, probably Śiva, but his emblems are so destroyed that it is impossible to feel quite sure. Below him is an ascetic, and close by a small temple with an image in the cell; but here again it is impossible from the photograph to say which god it is intended to represent. The artist has utilized the edge of the northern rock, so as to give his

No. 4.

BUST OF THE NÂGA RAJA AT MAHAVELLIPORE.
[*From a Photograph by Dr. Hunter.*]

[1] I possess some hundreds of *sculptured* representations of the Nâga. I never saw or heard of a *painted* Nâga anywhere.

[2] This bas-relief was described by Bishop Heber and Mrs. Graham. A notice of it by Mr. Goldingham appeared in the Asiatic Researches, vol. V. A view of it was published by Daniell; but the best is that by Messrs. Babington and Hulston, in the Transactions of the Royal Asiatic Society, vol. II., plates I. and II. I have several photographs of it by Dr. Hunter, of Madras, lying before me. The upper part of the principal figure was lying on the ground half buried in the sand when these gentlemen visited the place. Dr. Hunter had it raised and photographed, so that nothing essential is now wanting to complete the picture.

principal figures a higher relief than could be obtained in the flat portions, and also to heighten their effect by having a shadow behind them. But unfortunately from this cause they were so exposed that the upper portion has been broken away. When Mr. Babington drew them, in 1827, only the lower part of the great Nâga was remaining, but the bust has now been recovered from the sand in front, where it was found lying, and is represented in the woodcut (No. 4), on the previous page. His wife below him was quite perfect, with a three-headed snake hood, and presents us with a form not found either at Sanchi, Amravati, or Ajanta. The Nâgas here, both male and female, are represented as Serpents from the waist downwards, but with human busts. They all have, however the Snake hood of from three to seven heads canopying their own: in the same manner as in the Chinese woodcut, No. 3, introduced on page 56, where this more modern form of the Nâga has been adopted; and, below all the half-human beings at Mahavellipore, the simple Serpent himself rears his head.

No. 5.

Síva with Nâgas from Hullabeed about 1300 A.D.
[*From a Photograph.*]

No. 6.

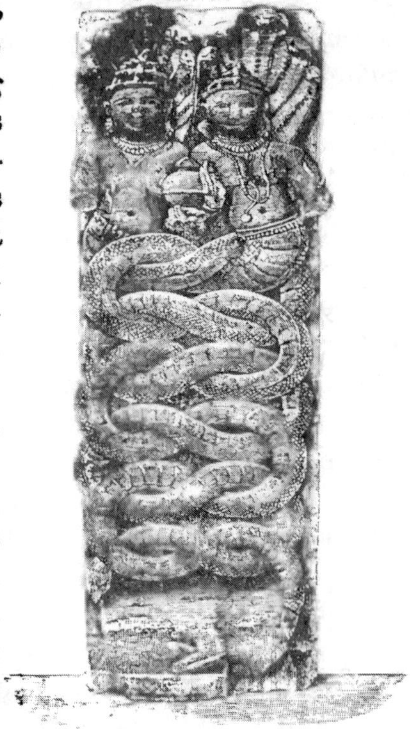

Nâga and Nâgnî.
[*From a Photograph.*]

Though this great rock sculpture is probably the grandest exhibition of Serpent Worship in India, the same form is found at Hullabeed and in the Caves at Iwulli, both probably in the thirteenth century, while in Cuttack there is scarcely a temple on the walls of which repeated examples of the half-human Nâgas may not be found. Generally they are represented there as females with five or seven-headed hoods, and not as the principal gods or objects of worship, but as subordinate Devatas, sanctifying and guarding the place.[1]

In other parts of the country they are ranged in groups in front of the Temples where they are worshipped. Sometimes simple serpents with very exaggerated hoods. At others with three, five, or seven heads. Often as single Nâgas or Nâgnîs, and very frequently as the two together with their tails intertwined in a true-love knot, as in the annexed woodcut (No. 6).

Over the doorway of a Cave at Cuttack is a representation of a three-headed Nâga, which I am inclined to believe may be the oldest sculptured representation of this

[1] I have photographs of all these Temples, which range from the 12th to the 15th centuries, but they have not yet been published.

form of divinity now known in India.[1] It may be three centuries before Christ. From that time, at Sanchi and Amravati, in other caves at Cuttack on the rocks at Mahavellipore, and the caves of Western India and the temples throughout the land we have an inexhaustible supply of illustrations[2] of the worship of this God and of the changes his form underwent during nearly 2,000 years. If these were put together they would form as curious a picture as anywhere exists of the more modern form of one of the primæval religions of the world.

Hindu Religion.

It might have sufficed for our present purposes to have stopped when we had brought the history of Serpent Worship in India to the point when the Buddhist scriptures were rescued from the keeping of the Nâgas and revealed to mankind. As this happens to be also the time when the Gateways were added to the tope at Sanchi, we might have left the sculptures to tell their own tale, and continue the history of Nâga worship from that point. It will add, however, very much to the clearness of what follows if we anticipate still further, and describe briefly what took place afterwards.

Speaking broadly, the modern religions of India may be divided into two great groups or classes, that of Śiva and that of Vishṇu. It is extremely difficult to offer even a plausible conjecture as to the origin of the former, or to guess when it first came into vogue. It has been attempted to identify Śiva with the Rudra of the Vedas, and it may be so, but it is certainly a local, not an Aryan form of faith, and seems originally to belong rather to the south than to the north of India. It may have existed there as a native local superstition for any length of time, but it only rose to eminence on the decline of Buddhism. Its principal teacher, if not its founder, in its present form, seems to have been Śankara Âchârya, who may have lived in the eighth or ninth century.[3]

There does not seem to be a trace of Tree Worship mixed up with Śivaism, nor any real connexion with Serpent Worship. It is true Śiva is occasionally represented holding a cobra or other venomous snake in his hand; serpents are also sometimes twisted round his neck or entwined with his hair; but in all these instances the serpent is a weapon, an implement of terror, not an object of worship. As the destroyer, everything that can add to the terrible was represented with him. In his hands the serpent is as a sword or trident, and, like his chaplet of skulls, merely meant to overawe and impress the beholder. It never is many-headed and never seems the guardian god. It is only the earthly serpent taught to do the will of its master.

Occasionally the serpent does appear in a more religious aspect in connexion with this form of faith. He is sometimes represented as entwined round the Lingam, and in some southern temples two serpents are sometimes seen erect with

---

[1] J. A. S. B., VII. pl. XL.

[2] From my own collection of photographs I think I could furnish at least one hundred illustrations.

[3] Asiatic Researches, XVII. 180. (A.D. 750?)

their heads above the Lingam, on either side as if worshipping it. In all these instances, however, the serpent is subordinate. It seems nothing more than we would expect to find in a country where Serpent Worship was at one time so prevalent, that the apostles of the new faith should represent the older as doing homage to the new god. In so far as the materials available enable an opinion to be formed, the amount and nature of the Serpent Worship we find mixed up with Śivaism is just what we might expect when a new form of faith superseded an old one. Much of the more ancient worship passes into the new, partly because the priests desire to conciliate the votaries of the old, partly in order to exhibit the triumph of the new god, but more perhaps because nothing is so difficult to kill as an old superstition, and the more unreasonable it is, the harder it dies.

When we turn to the Vaishṇava group of religions, we find a very different state of things. This religion is descended from a group of faiths in which the Serpent always played an important part. The eldest branch of the family was the Nâga worship, pure and simple; out of that arose Buddhism, as frequently hinted above, and on its decline two faiths—at first very similar [1] to one another—rose from its ashes, the Jaina and the Vaishṇava. The first named was the purest and most direct descendant of Buddhism, retaining more of its doctrinal purity, and less of the local element, and consequently less Serpent Worship than the other. Still the Nâga is almost always to be found in Jaina temples, and placed where it evidently was intended to be an object of worship, but subordinate to the saint to whom the temple was dedicated.

The Vaishṇava faith, on the other hand, arose contemporaneously with the Sivite, on the ruins of Buddhism, but with much less of the appearance of being a local indigenous superstition; on the contrary it bears many marks of being a foreign introduction, as if imported at some remote period by some of the immigrant races, and after rotting and fermenting for ages in the fertile soil of India, at last found the means of coming to the surface between the eighth and the tenth centuries. Garuḍa, Vishṇu's Vâhana, the enemy of the Nâgas, is almost certainly the hawk-headed deity of Assyria; and in all the avatars of Vishṇu we find more traces of western superstition than in anything Śivite; but what interests us most here is, that the Nâga appears everywhere in Vaishṇava tradition. There is no more common representation of Vishṇu than reposing on the Śesha, as the seven-headed snake is called by the Brahmans, contemplating the creation of the world. It was by his assistance that the ocean was churned and Amrita produced. He everywhere spreads his protecting hood over the god, or his avatars, and in all instances it is the seven-headed heavenly Nâga, not the earthly cobra of Śiva.[2]

---

[1] Asiatic Researches, IX. 270, and XVII. 285.

[2] Nothing is more common than to connect the worship of the Lingam with the impurities with which the Hindu religion is only too justly reproached. This, however, is a mistake. The worship of Śiva is too severe, too stern, for the softer emotions of love, and all his temples are quite free from any allusion to it. The contrary is the case with the Vaishṇavas, who abhor the Lingam. Love pervades all their myths, and their temples are full of sexual utterances generally expressed in the grossest terms. The existence of any such representation in a temple at once proves it to have been originally dedicated to the worship of Vishṇu, or some of his avatars.

The worship of the Tulsi plant, which is one of the commonest forms of Vaishṇava adoration, is another of those indications which point to a common origin for the two religions. It would, of course, be absurd to designate as Tree Worship the adoration of such a plant as Sweet Basil, but the descent from the "Ficus Religiosa" to "Ocymum Sanctum" is just such a change as might be expected to take place when a dogma is transferred from an older and higher faith to one of a less elevated character. Both symbolize the worship of the vegetable kingdom, and are a part of that curious association of men with animals and plants which is so marked a characteristic of both the Buddhist and Vaishṇava forms of faith.

The strongest evidence, however, of the connexion between the worship of Vishṇu and that of Buddha is found in the fact that the Hindus, even to the present day, recognize Buddha as the ninth avatar of Vishṇu. From a historical point of view they are no doubt correct in this: all the eight preceding avatars refer to events that certainly preceded the time of Śakya-muni, and when we understand them they may point to a long chain of tradition out of which Buddhism arose, and into which it fell again, which, when philosophically examined, may throw a flood of light on the origin of Buddhism and of Indian religions generally.[1]

At present it must suffice to point out, that the group to which Buddhism belongs comprises Tree and Serpent Worship as the base, combined with the association of men with animals, especially monkeys, either in consequence of the doctrine of metempsychosis, or as the origin of that belief. These grew into Buddhism, and then bifurcated into the Jainism and Vishṇuism of modern times.[2]

It is extremely difficult in the present state of our knowledge, to say to what particular section of the Indian population this group of religions belongs. We know that they were anti-Aryan, yet they do not appear to belong to the Dravidian group. The peculiar deity of the latter I fancy must have been Śiva, and his worship is antagonistic in every essential to those religions composing this family. We must pause till we know more of the ethnology of India before we can decide this question in anything like a satisfactory manner.

Meanwhile, however, the similarity of this family of religions points to an identity of race which can hardly be mistaken, and my own impression is that they belong to the aboriginal races once inhabiting India to the northward and eastward of the Vindhya range of hills. For the present, Scythian is a term that might possibly be applied with advantage. It is sufficiently vague, but perhaps near enough to the truth to be useful.

The subject is only mentioned here because it will recur again and again in the following pages and unless these generalizations are borne in mind, the sequel will

---

[1] The 10th or coming Avatar of Vishṇu is Kalki, or the Horse, of which we shall have several opportunities of speaking when we come to describe the sculptures of the Amravati Tope, where the horse frequently appears as an important character, but with a rôle not easily understood. The Chakra or Wheel, which occupies the principal place among Buddhist emblems both at Sanchi and Amravati, afterwards becomes one of the principal emblems of Vishṇu. But perhaps the most striking coincidence is to be found at Puri. The Temple there probably occupies the site where the tooth relic of Buddha was long enshrined, and the worship of Vishṇu under the name of Jaganath, as there practised, is little else than very corrupt Buddhism.

[2] It would take a volume to discuss, and an unlimited number of references to establish these conclusions At present I will only refer to two inscriptions; that at Buddh Gayâ, Asiatic Researches, vol. I. p. 284, and that of Belgola, vol. IX. p. 270.

hardly be intelligible. The sculptures at Sanchi and Amravati may not suffice to settle these questions, but if I am not mistaken they throw as much or more light upon them than any other documents that have yet been brought to light.

Modern Worship of Trees and Serpents in India.

Few probably have read the preceding pages without a desire to inquire whether Serpent Worship exists in India at the present day, and if so, to what extent it prevails? If the inquiry were addressed to even our best-informed Indian authorities, the reply would probably be negative. We have actually possessed India now for more than a century. The Asiatic Society was established in 1784. Since then, with the branch societies in Madras and Bombay, and the Asiatic Societies of England, France, and Germany, some hundreds of volumes have been published, containing some thousands of papers. As not one of these, before the publication of this work, was devoted to Serpent Worship, or even described it as existing, it might well be argued that it cannot possibly now be found there.

The truth of the matter, however, seems to be that attention has not hitherto been specially directed to the subject, and till this is the case, the most obvious evidences might be passed by without being noticed;[1] but since this work was first published a flood of light has been thrown upon the subject, and before long it may be expected that Serpent Worship will be acknowledged to be one of the most extensive of the minor faiths of India, and probably also as one of the most ancient, if not the oldest, of any of those now known to us.

In Forbes' Oriental Memoirs,[2] in Bishop Heber's Travels, and in fifty other places, allusions are made to the feelings of respect and reverence paid by the natives of India to snakes, and no one can reside long in the country without perceiving it; yet, except in Miss Frere's charming little volume, entitled "Old "Deccan Days," I hardly know a book in which snakes, and especially seven-headed snakes,[3] play an important part, or which reflects the feelings of the natives

---

[1] As an instance of this, I may perhaps be allowed to quote against myself what occurred at Ajanta. I spent a considerable time in exploring these caves, but my mind was full of architecture. I measured everything, drew every detail, and familiarized myself with every architectural affinity. But neither then nor subsequently* did I note the presence of any Nâgas. Now that my attention is turned to it, I find in drawings and photographs twelve or fifteen sculptured representations of the seven-headed Nâga, and there may be many more. I now also recollect seeing Nâgas in all the Jaina temples at Abu, at Sadree, and elsewhere, but then I passed them over. Now I cannot take up a photograph of any temple belonging to the group of religions which include the Buddhist, Jaina, or Vaishṇava faiths, without seeing snakes everywhere, but in places where neither I nor anyone else detected them before.

[2] Vol. II. pp. 329, 384, &c.

[3] In the narrator's narrative (p. xxvii.), the following singularly naïve and interesting passage occurs:—"All "the cobras in my grandmother's stories were seven-headed. This puzzled us children, and we would say to "her, 'Granny, are there any seven-headed cobras now, for all the cobras we see that the conjurors bring "'round have only one head each.' To which she used to answer, 'No, of course there are no seven-headed "'cobras now. That world is gone, but you see each cobra has a hood of skin, that is the remains of another "'head.' Although we have often looked for seven-headed cobras we never could find any of them." Had they not been converted to Christianity they might at least have believed in them, even if they had not seen them.

---

* I have twice published on the subject of these caves; first, on the Rock-cut Temples of India, folio, 1845, and subsequently, a volume on the same subject in 1864, illustrated by photographs by Major Gill.

regarding them. The stories of serpents there related are only an accidental selection out of thousands of similar legends, all which might easily be localized or traced to their source, and many of which will no doubt be investigated so soon as attention is really directed to the subject.[1]

Two instances of Serpent Worship, at Manipore, and Sumbulpore, have already been mentioned (pp. 64 and 65). Two others are still more remarkable. In the great temple at Madura the three principal images in the Tosak Khâna are a golden (?) image of Hanumân, another of Garuḍa, the Vâhana of Vishnu, but the terrible enemy of the snakes. Between these two stands an image of the seven-headed Nâga, richly jewelled, and under a splendid canopy. In the great temple at Seringham, likewise, the principal images are two golden statues of the seven-headed Nâga, larger apparently than that at Madura, and even more richly jewelled;[2] and I have no doubt that many other such might be found, but they have not yet been looked for.

In the meanwhile the following two paragraphs, introduced incidentally in two works recently published in London, may serve to indicate the class of illustrations which will no doubt be found everywhere when looked for. "At the Nág Kûán "or Serpent Well, in the city of Benares," says Mr. Sherring, "the Nág or Serpent "is worshipped. In a niche in the wall of one of the stairs is a figure representing "three Serpents (query, a three-headed Serpent), and on the floor is an emblem "of Mahâdeva in stone, and a snake crawling up it. The well is visited for "religious purposes only once a year, namely, on the 24th and 25th days of the "month of Sáwan, when immense numbers of persons come to it from all parts "of the city. The women come on the first day, the men on the second; they "offer sacrifices both to the well and to Nágeśwar, or the Serpent God."[3]

The other relates to Tree Worship. "In Beerbhoom once a year the whole "capital repairs to a shrine in the jungle, and makes simple offerings to a ghost "who dwells in a Bela Tree." "The shrine consists of three trees—a Bela Tree "on the left, in which the ghost resides, and which is marked at the foot with "blood; in the middle is a Kachmula Tree; and on the right a Saura Tree." "In

---

[1] No one at all familiar with the subject, who reads these tales, can fail to be struck with the similarity that exists between them and many of those collected by the brothers Grimm and others from German and Scandinavian sources, and also with some of the more ancient Grecian myths. The usual mode of accounting for this identity, which can hardly be accidental, is to assume that the tales were originally invented by Aryan nurses beside the cradles of the race in Balkh and Bokhara, and that they were carried east and west by their Alumni when they set out on their travels some 4,000 or 5,000 years ago. The results of my reading have led me to conclusions widely different from this fashionable hypothesis. My belief is that all the serpents and dragons, all the dwarfs and magicians of these tales, all the fairy mythology, in fact, of the east and west, belongs to the Turanian races. These, as I have frequently had occasion to mention, underlie the Ayran races everywhere in Europe as in Asia, and occasionally crop up here and there through the upper crust, often when least expected. So far as I understand the idiosyncrasy of the two races, nothing can be more antagonistic to the tastes and feelings of the Aryans than these wild imaginings; while few things, on the contrary, could be more congenial to the comparatively infantile intellect of the Turanian races.

[2] Both these groups were photographed by Captain Tripe, and published by him for Government with other views of the temples in which they are found. I had hoped to have obtained more information regarding them before again publishing, but have been unsuccessful.

[3] The Sacred City of the Hindus, by the Rev. M. A. Sherring. London, 1868, p. 89.

"spite of the trees being at the most 70 years old, the common people claim the "greatest antiquity for the shrine, and tradition says that the three trees that now "mark the spot neither grow thicker nor increase in height, but remain the same "for ever."[1]

There is no doubt whatever with regard to the worship of Trees in modern times, and numerous instances might be adduced if necessary.[2] The Bo Tree at Buddh Gayâ is worshipped now as it was in the days of Aśoka,[3] and the Tree at Anurâdhapura is, as mentioned above (page 59), the principal object of worship in Ceylon at the present day.[4] And all over India there are numerous examples which we may hope some day to see registered.[5]

When this work was commenced I made every effort to obtain from India information regarding the present existence of Serpent Worship, but though not so successful as I could have wished, I was able to obtain several documents on the subject of considerable interest. One of these is by Dr. C. E. Balfour, of Secunderabad, whose long study of native manners and customs especially qualify him to speak on the subject. The other is from Colonel Meadows Taylor, so well known for his various literary works connected with India, and who likewise is especially competent, by long residence and intimate knowledge of the natives, to speak

---

[1] Annals of Rural Bengal, by W. W. Hunter, B.C.S. London, 1868, p. 131.

[2] The following is extracted from a paper by a Bengal civilian, intimately acquainted with the country and people, in the "Cornhill Magazine," No. 155, for November 1872, p. 598 :—"The contrast between the "acknowledged hatred of trees as a rule by the Bygas," an important tribe in Central India, dwelling near the source of the Nerbudda, "and their deep veneration for certain others in particular, is very curious."

"I have seen the hill sides swept clear of forests for miles, with but here and there a solitary tree left standing. "These remain now the objects of the deepest veneration, so far from being injured they are carefully preserved, "and receive offerings of food, clothes, and flowers from the passing Bygas, who firmly believe that Tree to be the "home of a spirit."

[3] Buchanan Hamilton, in Martin's Eastern India, I. p. 76.

[4] According to a very interesting paper compiled by the Editor in a recent number of the "Indian Antiquary," the followers of one of the most influential, but at the same time most modern of Hindu sects in Western India, have adopted Tree Worship apparently for nearly the same motives as influenced the Buddhist of old. "After "the death," it is there said, "of Swâmî Nârâyan" (in 1829), "his disciples erected chaurâs or resting places, "and monuments to his memory, in all the villages, and beneath all the trees where he had at any time made "any stay. There they worship him, and they worship the Trees." Indian Ant., No. XI., p. 335.

[5] The following instance of Tree Worship which I myself witnessed is amusing, even if not instructive. While residing in Jessore I observed at one time considerable crowds passing near the factory I then had charge of. As it might be merely an ordinary fair they were going to attend, I took no notice ; but as the crowd grew daily larger, and assumed a more religious character, I inquired, and was told that a God had appeared in a Tree at a place about six miles off.

Next morning I rode over, and found a large space cleared in a village I knew well, in the centre of which stood an old decayed Date tree, hung with garlands and offerings. Around it houses were erected for the attendant Brahmins, and a great deal of business was going on in offerings and Pûjâ. On my inquiring how the God manifested his presence, I was informed that soon after the sun rose in the morning the Tree raised its head to welcome him, and bowed it down again when he departed. As this was a miracle easily tested, I returned at noon and found it was so!

After a little study and investigation, the mystery did not seem difficult of explanation. The Tree had originally grown across the principal pathway through the village, but at last hung so low, that in order to enable people to pass under it, it had been turned aside and fastened parallel to the road. In the operation the bundle of fibres which composed the root had become twisted like the strands of a rope. When the morning sun struck on the upper surface of these, they contracted in drying, and hence a tendency to untwist, which raised the head of the Tree. With the evening dews they relaxed, and the head of the Tree declined, thus proving to the man of science, as to the credulous Hindu, that it was due to the direct action of the Sun God.

regarding their forms of worship. Both these documents will be found printed in the Appendix. But by far the most satisfactory evidence on the subject will be found in two papers, one published in the journal of the Bombay branch of the Royal Asiatic Society,[1] the other in the journal of the Asiatic Society of Bengal.[2] The author of the first had not, unfortunately, seen this work when his paper was read, or it might have afforded some more direct information than it does. As it is, however, it contains better and more complete statistical information regarding this form of worship than anything that has appeared in print. Both from his learning and his local knowledge the Rao Saheb is entitled to be considered as an authority on the subject. The following extracts from his paper may be considered as fairly representing our knowledge on the subject at the present day.

After describing the Nágapanchamí festival as celebrated at present, and the vessels and ceremonies used on the occasion, he goes on to say:—

"The account which I have given above, is that of the festival as it is observed in the Konkana district, particularly to the south of the island of Bombay. The festival is, however, not confined to a particular portion of Western India. It is general. It is celebrated by all classes and sects of the Hindus; by the orthodox as well as by the heterodox; by the followers of the Vedas, as well as by those who reject the religious authority of those works. The ceremonial differs slightly in different places. In some districts the people observe a fast on the fourth day, i.e., the day preceding the Nágapanchamí. It is clear, however, that the festival obtains greater sanctity above the Ghauts than below, except perhaps in Gujarátha and in the province of Kánadá (or Canara). In the Sattara and Kolhapura districts, the private schools are generally closed on this day; the pupils are bathed, dressed in their holiday attire, and taken in a grand procession to some river, or other watering place outside the town or village. In native States and Principalities, the State and its officers supply richly caparisoned elephants and horses, detachments of infantry and cavalry, and kettledrums and other instruments of music, on the occasion of these processions. Battísa-sirálen, a town in the Sattara Collectorate (lat. 16° 57′, long. 74° 15′), is famous as a place of Serpent Worship at the present day. Snakes of a certain species (called Nágakulí) said to be not very poisonous are here actually caught on the day of the Nágapanchamí, and kept either in earthen pots or covered bámbú baskets. They are fed with milk and edibles, and worshipped in other respects, like the images and drawings above mentioned. The day after the Nágapanchamí, they are taken back to the jungles and set free. I will not at this stage offer any conjecture as to whether this Serpent Worship has any relation to other systems of religion; but I would here note a curious tradition in connexion with a tree of the species Gorakhachincha (Adansonia Digitata), or the tamarind of Gorakha, which exists at the above town. Tradition ascribes this tree to be the result of a miracle performed by a saint called Gorakhanátha or Gorakshanátha. It is related that Gorakhanátha, when he came to this town, struck his walking stick into the ground

---

[1] Serpent Worship in Western India, by Ráo Sáheb Vishvanath Náráyán Mandlik. J. B. B., R. A. Ṡ., IX., p. 169, et seq.

[2] The Vastu Yága, and its bearings on Tree and Serpent Worship in India, by Pratápachandra Ghosha. J. A. S. B., vol. XXXIX., p. 199 et seqq.

on the spot where the tree stands; and that it grew into a stately tree which is now an object of popular worship. The annual festival of this tree is held on the eleventh of the dark half of the month of Chaitra. Worshippers begin to come on the previous day, and leave the place on the third or the twelfth of Chaitra. About 50,000 pilgrims are said to assemble every year on this occasion. A large bazaar is held for five or six days, and considerable mercantile business is transacted. The priests officiating at the shrine of this tree, have large holes bored in their ears, from which depend heavy ear-ornaments. They are hence called Kána phátés, literally persons with torn ears. All classes of people offer worship to this tree, including the followers of the Vedas, as well as others.

"To resume the main subject of this paper. Besides the actual worship of living snakes at Battísa-sirálen, there are temples dedicated to the Serpent God in various parts of the Dekkan. Of these, the one at Bhomaparánden in the territories of His Highness the Nizam is one of the most celebrated.

"In the South of India, Canara is a district which may be said to be sacred to Serpent Worship. In the Canarese districts generally, the Nágapanchamí festival is celebrated, as in the Dekkan, on the fifth of the bright half of Sravaṇa. But in the Telanga and Tâmila districts, the ceremony is performed on the fourth of the bright half of either the month of Kártika, or the month of Vaisakha, or the month of Mágha, and this day is therefore called by the people of those parts 'Nágalu chavatí,' i.e., the Nága chatúrthí or the chatúrthí of the Nágas. There is not much difference in the mode of performing the worship. In the Canarese districts, stone images of the Nága are kept generally under the shade of the Peepul tree (Ficus Religiosa). Metal images are also made, and after being worshipped they are presented to the Bráhmanas. This ceremony is performed by the females of higher classes. An incarnation of Sesha, one of the nine great Nágas, is worshipped at various places in these districts under the name of Subrahmanya.[1] There is a town in South Canara, called Subrahmaṇya, 55 miles S.E. of Mangalore (lat. 12° 40, long. 75° 40′). This is sacred to the Nága or serpent god.[2] On the sixth day of the bright half of the month of Márgasírsha (November and December) occurs its annual festival; and that day is hence called Subrahmaṇya Sashṭhí or Subráya Sashṭhí. Thousands of Bráhmanas are feasted on this occasion.[3] Bráhmaṇas, bearing the order of Brahmachárí, are in particular request. Lepers and persons supposed to be under

---

[1] See also Dubois, Manners and Customs, &c., p. 450.

[2] In the jungle in the neighbourhood of the shrine of Subrahmaṇya above mentioned, grows a species of cane, called after the presiding deity, *Nâgaveta* or Nâga-cane. A walking stick of this cane is reckoned a sufficient protection against the poison of serpents.

[3] "A circumstance showing the practical influence of Serpent Worship in worldly affairs here deserves a prominent mention. A class of Bráhmaṇas called Haigé in Canara, have, amongst their ranks, persons who arrogate to themselves the title of Nâgapátrí, or the proper habitat of the Nâga deity. They are supposed to become possessed of the spirit of the Nâgadeva, and, in that state, are thought to be capable of foretelling future events. People invite them to their homes, and have a feast in their honour, called the Nâgamaṇḍala or an assembly of the Nâgas. The least expense for such a feast amounts to from three to five thousand rupees. Formerly, the Nâgapátrís were in great repute. Disputes were referred to them for settlement, and their word was generally the law. An invitation from one of the Nâgapátrís to a litigant was almost instantly obeyed. One of the first things a party had to do under the circumstances, was to give a feast to the Nâgamaṇḍala and spend thousands of rupees. These things began in time to be perceived by the people, and the power and influence of these priests has, I understand, considerably declined." J. B. B., R. A. S. IX., p. 179.

the influence of evil spirits, are brought to this place for cure, which popular belief ascribes to the miraculous power of the deity.

"The serpent, either as a Sarpa or a Nága, thus enters intimately into the economy of a Hindu's daily life. He is treated as a Dvija, or a twice-born, and sometimes gets the honours of a funeral, just like a human being. It is well known how anxious a Hindu is to have a male heir to perform his funeral obsequies and inherit his name and fortune. To beget a son is reckoned a religious duty, and a Bráhmaṇa is enjoined to discharge it, and thus free himself from the debt he owes to his progenitors. When the natural means fail, or threaten to fail, the supernatural powers are invoked. A solemn sacrifice, named Náráyaṇa-Nágabaḷi [or the sacrifice to the Náráyaṇa-Nága] is performed in order to secure progeny. People generally repair to some Tírtha or sacred place, and the serpent sacrifice is there made to propitiate the deities. It would occupy a paper by itself to describe the whole of this rite. The fact, however, that it is performed is sufficient for my present purpose, as showing the ramifications of Serpent Worship in this country. This rite is performed in honour of the Sarpádevatás, not the snakes we see, but to some spiritual beings of a higher order in whose existence the Hindus are taught to believe. It seems that this sacrifice is sanctioned by Vedic ritual, and this leads me to a short examination of Serpent Worship, and the Sarpás and Nágas, as mentioned in the Vedas. As far as my researches have yet extended, the earth is addressed as the Sarpa-rájní (i.e., the queen of the serpents, or the queen of all that moves)."

These extracts might be continued to almost any extent, but the above are probably sufficient for present purposes.

The paper in the Bengal journal, though as learned, is not so full of the class of information we are now seeking, as that from which the above extracts are taken. From it, however, we learn one or two facts which are worth recording. At p. 202 he says, "The Serpent Goddess is worshipped in the Euphorbia Antiquorum. The Goddess "Mother of the Serpents and Goddess presiding over them is Manasá, the object of love "and devotion, and, as the name implies, an allegorical creation." Again, at p. 214, he says, "Nágapanchamí is an auspicious day for the worship of the Nágas. On the "occasion Manasá is worshipped in the Euphorbia plant. This is an instance of "Tree Worship connected with serpents." The paper itself is, however, devoted to disquisitions of a class too deep for our present purposes.

Concluding Note.

If the preceding pages were intended to be anything like a complete or independent essay on Tree and Serpent Worship, it would have been necessary to expand them to at least twice their present extent, and to explore sources of information which are only available to those having special qualifications for the task, and who are prepared to devote to it much more time than I have at my command. This was far, however, from the intention with which it was undertaken. That object was two-fold: first, to render the sculptures of the Sanchi and Amravati Topes intelligible, by affording a means of comparison with the forms of the same worship existing in other parts of the world; and, secondly, to render them interesting to European scholars by showing that the forms of worship there portrayed are not merely the Totems of local Indian tribes, but really living parts of a great religious development that at one time overshadowed the earth with its strange fetishisms.

A fuller and more complete investigation of the subject would add one of the most curious as well as one of the most important chapters to our history of ancient mythology; but even if I were capable of undertaking it, it would be out of place here. What seemed wanted and was aimed at was only an introduction to that form of Buddhism which the sculptures at Sanchi and Amravati for the first time reveal to us, but which are, if I mistake not, destined to place the history of that religion on an entirely new basis. If what has been said above suffices to establish the fact that there was a connexion between one of the primæval religions of the western world and this form of Buddhism in the east, a step has been made in the history of mythology, the importance of which it is not easy to over-estimate, and which I trust may hereafter be developed by others to its full legitimate extent.

From all this, as well as from other sources, we gather that Serpent Worship has been obliterated or nearly so in the Valley of the Ganges by the successive waves of Aryan or Mongolian migrations that have swept over it; nor is it found except sporadically in any of the purely Tamulian countries on the Coromandel coast. On the other hand it seems to prevail in all the hilly countries south of the Vindhya Hills, from Canara to Cuttack, and in Cashmere and Nepaul;[1]—in all those regions, in fact, where foreigners have not settled to such an extent as to obliterate the old faith and feelings of the aboriginal tribes. In these countries Serpent Worship seems now to prevail and to be followed to an extent not hitherto suspected.

---

[1] In Katmandu a statue was recently erected to the memory of a late Raja. He is represented as seated cross-legged on the top of a pillar, under the canopy of the expanded hood of a gigantic Cobra

THE TOPE AT SANCHI.

CHAPTER I.

INTRODUCTORY.

BEFORE proceeding to describe the two buildings which form the subject of the present work, it may be convenient to point out, as briefly as possible, the general characteristics of Buddhist architecture, and to indicate the relations of these two monuments to the other members of the group to which they belong.

In the first place, it cannot be too strongly insisted upon, or too often repeated, that stone architecture in India commences with the age of Aśoka (B.C. 250). Not only have we as yet discovered no remains whatever of stone buildings anterior to his reign, but all the earliest Caves, either in Behar or in the western Ghâts show architecture in the first stage of transition from wood to stone. One half, indeed, of the most essential architectural features of the Caves at Bhâjâ and Kârlâ, and of the earliest at Ajanta, is wooden, and the wood still remains in some of them to the present day. Though some of these Caves are certainly earlier than the Christian era, none are older than the time of Aśoka.[1]

Whether looked at from an archæological, an architectural, or an ethnographical point of view, this wooden origin of Indian Buddhist architecture is one of the most interesting facts connected with the subject. To the archæologist it affords an assurance that in this instance, at least, we have got to the beginning of things, and that all beyond the first imitation of wood can only be rude masses of stone that in themselves tell no tales, and can only be dated from evidence external to themselves.

The architect, in studying this art, feels that for once he is assisting at the birth of a new style, and that during the five or six centuries to which this work refers (between B.C. 250 and A.D. 400), he is gradually watching the growth of an original form of art, which was uninfluenced by any external or foreign element, but left to its own innate powers of development.[2]

The steps by which the rail at Sanchi was elaborated into that at Amravati will be pointed out in the sequel, in so far as they are at present ascertained; and it forms as interesting an example of the natural development of style as anything in

---

[1] For particulars I must refer the reader to my History of Architecture, II., p. 456, et seq.

[2] The nearest approach to anything like this in the west, is to be found in Lycia. Its early tombs are as wooden as the Caves of India, but they fell almost immediately under the influence of Greek art, and became Ionic before they had time to develop themselves into a native Lycian style.

the history of architecture. There may, it is true, be some difference of opinion as to the beauty of the Amravati example, but there can be none as to its originality; and even those who may be inclined to dispute the taste displayed in its design, must admit that it is singularly appropriate to the purposes to which it is applied, and in richness of ornament one of the most elaborate pieces of architecture to be found in any part of the world.

It is perhaps, however, in an ethnographical point of view that this wooden origin of Buddhist architecture is most interesting. As I have frequently had occasion to point out in another work,[1] the Aryan races were not builders. They always had too firm a conviction of the immortality of the soul, and consequently of the existence of a future state, ever to care much for a brick or stone immortality in this world; and no material art satisfied the cravings of their higher intellectual powers. The Turanians, on the contrary, never rose to a distinct idea of an external God, nor of a future state, but supplied the place of the latter by metempsychosis and final annihilation, while their intellectual status never enabled them to create such a literature as would satisfy that hankering after immortality which is inherent in the human breast. It consequently happens that practically all the literature of India belongs to the Aryan or Sanscrit-speaking races, and all the buildings to the Turanians or those speaking Dravidian or cognate tongues. The result of this distinction, in so far as the present subject is concerned, is this: so long as the Aryans retained their purity of blood and supremacy of power, no permanent buildings were erected in India. On the other hand, if there is one fact with reference to Buddhism more clear than another, it is that it is the religion of a Turanian race. It was not so much a reform on the Vedic religion of the Aryans, as that when these had lost their purity from mixture with the subject races, Sâkya Muni, called on the aboriginal races to rise, and moulded their feelings and their superstitions into that form of faith we now know as Buddhism. It was when these Turanians first came into power that permanent architecture was thought of in India; and as they grew in strength, and their influence extended, so did their architecture acquire consistency, and spread over the length and breadth of the land. They had no literature, or next to none; at least we have not yet found one Buddhist book that was reduced to its present shape till nearly 1,000 years after the death of the founder of the religion;[2] but we have buildings everywhere, and it is this circumstance that renders their architecture so valuable in an historical point of view, and so interesting as an expression of a great ethnographic fact.

Without attempting too minute a classification, the Buddhist buildings erected in India since Aśoka's time may be arranged in four principal groups:—

1st. Topes or Stûpas, with their surrounding rails and lâṭs; two of the oldest known examples of these, which happen also to be among the richest and most elaborately ornamented, form the subject of the present work.

2nd. Chaityas. Both in form and purpose these are almost absolutely identical with the early Churches of the Christians, though several of those cut in the rock were almost certainly excavated before the Christian era.

---

[1] History of Architecture, Introduction, et passim.

[2] Max Müller, Chips from a German Workshop, I. p. 196.

3rd. Rails. Though these are so frequently found surrounding Topes, that they are generally considered parts of them, they often are represented enclosing trees and other sacred objects, and at others, as at Amravati, are so essentially the principal part of the monument that the Tope and other buildings which were enclosed ought to be considered as strictly subordinate to the rail which thus practically becomes the monument itself.

4th. Vihâras, or Monasteries, formed, in the earliest times, the residences of the monks or priests who were attached to the service of the Topes or Chaityas, but they afterwards became the independent abode of monastic communities, who had chapels or places set apart for devotional purposes within the walls of their monasteries.

Taking the last first, we are almost wholly dependent on rock examples for our knowledge of the arrangement and mode of adornment of Indian monasteries. Of these, probably not less than 800 to 1,000 examples are still known to remain in India, of all ages, and extending from a century or two before the Christian era to the time when Buddhism ceased to be a dominant religion in India which probably was in the middle of the eighth century of our era. They also are of all sizes, from the simple cell of a single anchorite to a great hall 80 feet square and more, and sometimes surrounded by sixteen or twenty cells for the accommodation of the monks. The difficulties of lighting naturally limited the extent of each individual example in the rock, but they are generally found in groups of twenty or thirty Vihâras, affording, when taken together, accommodation for a large religious community.

The ruins of a very large Vihâra, have been recently excavated at Sârnath, near Benares.[1] It had, however, been destroyed by fire, and nothing but the foundation of the walls now remains. A still larger one was cut through by the railway works near Sultangunge in Bhagulpur, and destroyed of course; but here also nothing but the foundations remained, sufficient to show the plan, but nothing more. In 1861–2 General Cunningham found the remains of the great Nâlanda Vihâra to extend 1,600 feet in one direction by 400 in another, and no doubt excavations might bring some interesting particulars to light regarding this most celebrated of Indian monasteries, but too much must not be hoped for.[2] It was built of wood and brick, and for more than 1,000 years it has been used as the quarry of the fertile district in which it stood.

At Sanchi there are the remains of several Vihâras. One of the best preserved is represented in Plate No. XXIII. of this work. Its date is comparatively modern, probably the seventh or eighth century, and its dimensions are so small—about 100 feet across—that it would hardly be worth notice were it not that it happens to be the best preserved specimen of a Buddhist structural Vihâra known to exist in India. It will be described further on.

As might be expected, the Chaitya Caves are much fewer in number than the Vihâras; not more than twenty have been described; and it is hardly probable that

---

1 J. A. S. B., Volume for 1844, p. 473.

2 General Cunningham's Report to Government for 1861–62, p. 11. *See* also "Ruins of the Nalanda "Monastery, by A. M. Broadley, B.C.S., Calcutta, 1872."

more than thirty exist. As before hinted, they are almost exact counterparts of the choirs of Christian churches, consisting of a central nave, at the inner end of which stands the Dagoba or Stone Altar, either containing, or simulated to contain, a relic. Round this and along either side runs an aisle, which is entered by one of three doors, which open outwardly under a gallery corresponding to the rood-loft of Christian churches. The central aisle was covered with a roof, supported by wooden ribs, like the hull of a ship turned upside down—semicircular internally, but of an ogee shape outside. In all the earlier Caves the ribs were put up in wood, and at Kârlâ and Bâjâ remain to this day as they were put up 1,800 or 1,900 years ago, but in later Caves their form was repeated in stone, and afterwards merged into a purely lithic ornament.

No. 7.

ORIGINAL REPRESENTATION OF THE FAÇADE OF A CHAITYA FROM RAIL AT BUDDH GAYÂ.
(From a drawing by Captain Kittoe.)

The only example of a structural Chaitya yet brought to light is a small one at Sanchi, which will be described when speaking of Plate XXII. Like the Vihâra it is small and so much ruined that it is not easy to feel sure how it was originally finished, but as a unique example it is well worthy of attention.

We should not, perhaps, be justified in asserting that the Stûpas[1] or Topes were at all times the most important monuments of the Buddhist. They have become so now, but that may be owing to their form and the solidity of their construction, which has prevented their decay, while the more complex structures of the Vihâras and Chaityas, and the frailer materials of which they were composed, have caused their disappearance. Judging from the glowing descriptions given by the Chinese travellers of the Saughârâmas (Halls of Assembly) which they visited, and the monasteries in which they were entertained, it would appear that they considered them at least as important.

The Tope is, however, a solid circular pyramid[2] of brick or stone, and from its form, and under similar circumstances, might have lasted as long as those of Egypt. Those, however,—especially in the valley of the Ganges,—have long been used as quarries by the inhabitants of these thickly-peopled plains, and have consequently disappeared, with very few exceptions. It is only in remote or in thinly-peopled districts that any examples are now to be found.

It scarcely admits of a doubt but that the Tope is the lineal and direct descendant of the funereal Tumulus which, from the very earliest age to which our knowledge extends, the Turanian races—and probably some others—raised over the graves of their dead. Such Tumuli exist all over the north of Asia; they are found in Asia Minor and in Greece. They crowd the cemeteries of Etruria. They are far from being uncommon in Germany, and are found in all parts of France. We all know what numbers of them dot the downs of Wiltshire and Devon, wherever an

---

[1] From the Sanscrit, *Stûpa*, a mound or heap.

[2] Clemens of Alexandria, Stromat. I. 15. *See* woodcut 9 at the end of this chapter.

open country enabled a pastoral people to depasture their flocks without the necessity of clearing away the forest; and they are frequent in Scandinavia, and over the whole of the north of Europe; but it is doubtful whether any sepulchral Tumuli now exist in India. If these were of earth, the probability is they would be washed away by the overflowing rivers or by the tropical rains, but they do exist in Afghanistan, grouped around the Topes.[1]

There are two peculiarities which distinguish the Tope of India from the Tumuli of other countries. The first is, that being of brick or stone the material enabled them to assume a rounded or domical form, while the earthen Tumulus was as generally straight-lined. The circular form seems to have been adopted to assimilate them with the roofs of their other sacred and domestic buildings, which we learn from the sculptures were always curvilinear in outline. The second peculiarity is, that, instead of being the last resting place of a body, they had become depositories of relics only. Precisely the same change took place in the Middle Ages, when the stone coffin became an altar, and the place of the deposit of relics and other treasures instead of containing a body. In India, where the practice of burning the dead seems generally to have prevailed, this probably took place from the first. It may, however, be considered as an argument in favour of the foreign (Scythian?) nature of Buddhism in India, that the Tope should have been domical from the first instead of straight-lined, and should always have been a relic-shrine, never apparently a tomb.

In addition to its primary and general use as a relic-shrine, the Tope in India was also very commonly used as a memorial tower to mark a sacred spot.[2] Of the 84,000 Stûpas which Aśoka is traditionally said to have erected, we gather from the Chinese travellers that one half at least were erected to mark spots were Buddha or some Bôdhisatwa had performed some miracle, or done something worthy of being recalled to the attention of the faithful.[3] When Messrs. Masson and Honigberger opened the Topes in Afghanistan, they found about one half contained relics; the remainder were "Blind Topes," and contained nothing.[4] The same probably will be found to be the case, though to a less degree, in other countries. Where the Tumulus was a grave in reality, the chances are that not one in a hundred would be a memorial tower, though these last would probably be the largest and most important.

No. 8.

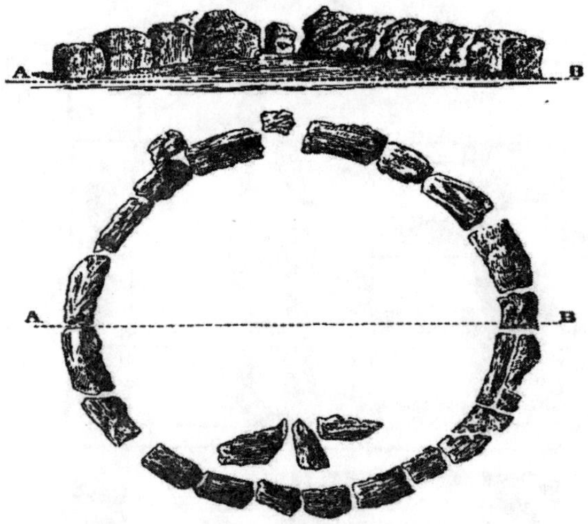

SEPULCHRAL CIRCLE AT AMRAVATI.
From a Drawing in the Mackenzie Collection.

The Rails which surround the Indian Topes are sometimes as important as the Tumuli themselves. In the case of Sanchi, and especially at Amravati, they are

[1] Masson, in Wilson's Ariana Antiqua, 61, et seqq.

[2] Properly speaking, the Tumulus containing a relic ought always to be designated "Dagoba," a word derived from "Dhâtu," a relic, and "Garbha," literally the womb, but here used as the receptacle or enclosing shrine. The memorial tower ought, on the contrary, always to be called "Stûpa," from the Sanskrit word Stûpa, a cairn or heap. The difficulty in applying these terms is, that there are no external signs by which the two can be distinguished, and till the contents of all are ascertained, any attempt at precision might only lead to errors.

[3] If anyone had the patience to classify them, this probably would be the result, at least so it appears in reading the travels of Fahian and Hiouen-thsang.

[4] Wilson's Ariana Antiqua, p. 68, et seqq.

certainly more so. Like the Topes, their origin is sepulchral. The circles of rude stones found all over Europe certainly are so, in most cases. They may sometimes enclose holy spots, and may possibly have in some instances been places of assembly, though this is improbable. Their application to the purposes of ancestral worship is, however, not only probable, but appropriate. Sometimes a circle of stones encloses a sepulchral mound, as at New Grange in Ireland,[1] and very frequently in Scandinavia[2] and Algeria.[3] In India rude stone circles are of frequent occurrence.[4] In the neighbourhood of Amravati alone there are some hundreds of them (Woodcut, No. 8), and all are sepulchral; but, like the Topes when adopted by the Buddhists, they were sublimated into a symbol instead of a reality.

Another circumstance of interest connected with the rail at Sanchi is, that it is only the first step from the wooden form. Its construction and general appearance will be easily understood from the annexed diagram (Woodcut, No. 9) and the photographs. From these it will be perceived that there is nothing lithic in its character. The three intermediate rails must, during construction, have been held in their places by some means not now apparent. The next pillar was pushed laterally to receive their ends in the mortices prepared for them, and the top rail was then fitted on to a tenon on the top of the post (as at Stonehenge), so as to hold the post upright and in its place. All this is good carpentry, but it is very clumsy masonry.

No. 9.

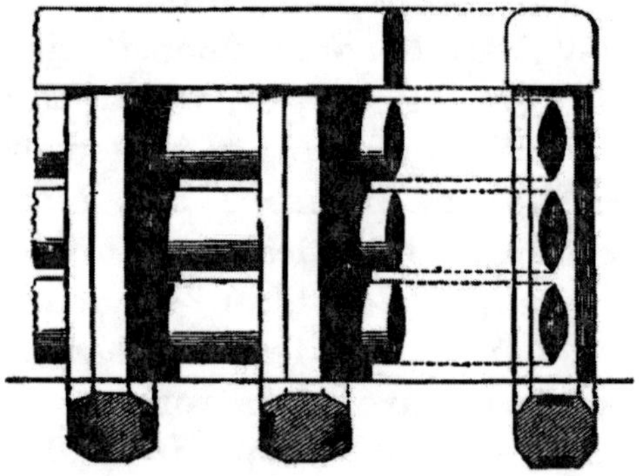

Great Rail at Sanchi.
From a Drawing by Colonel Maisey.

The next step in the elaboration of these rails is found on that surrounding the second Tope at Sanchi (B 2 on Map). This Tope is relatively much taller in form than the great Tope, which is an almost certain sign of a more modern age, though still anterior to the Christian era, and its rail earlier than the gates attached to the old rail of the great Tope. The innovation in this instance consisted in placing a centre disc on the pillar, ranging with the central rail, and two half discs at top and bottom[5] (Woodcut, No. 10). In the instance here given, too, the Serpent appears with the five heads, but whether this is a solitary instance or frequently repeated, we are not informed.

No. 10.

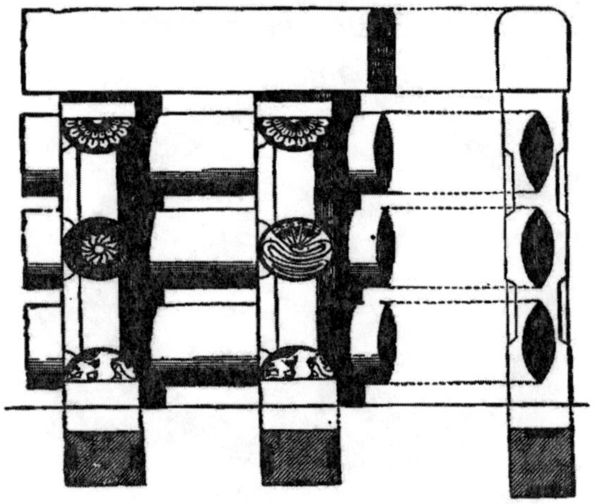

Rail of Second Tope at Sanchi.
From a Drawing by Colonel Maisey.

The Rail that enclosed the great Bo Tree at Buddh Gayâ was rectangular in plan, measuring 131 feet by 90, but in detail it very much resembled

---

[1] Archæologia, 1770, and frequently since described.

[2] Olaus Magnus, I. 29, and subsequently in every work on Sweden.

[3] Journal de la Société Archéologique de Constantine.

[4] For further particulars on this subject, *see* Rude Stone Monuments, by the Author, published by Murray, 1870.

[5] The probability seems to be that when the rail was in wood, nails with large heads or metal plates were used to keep the structure in form, as is still sometimes done in framed doors or gateways, and that these afterwards became ornaments, and were used architecturally, as we find it here and elsewhere.

that last described as surrounding No. 2 Tope, but rather more elaborately sculptured.[1] There is one inscription upon it, repeated five or six times over, but, as usual in such cases, it merely records that the rail was the gift of the Venerable Lady Kudangi.[2] The form of the characters used is so antique that the rail on which it is found might be as ancient as the time of Aśoka, and certainly was erected before the Christian era. Taking the whole evidence, however, as it now stands, I am inclined to ascribe to it the same date as the last-named rail, say about 150 B.C., a date which further investigation may shift 50 years either way.

The objects represented on the discs or semi-discs of the Buddh Gayâ rail are either portraits of men and women or of domestic animals and such like objects. But there are also winged horses and bulls and centaurs, reminiscences apparently of western forms, and monsters such as the Hindu imagination always delighted in. Nothing that can strictly be called Buddhism exists among the figure sculptures, but the Dagoba is worshipped four times, the Tree as often, the Wheel three times, and the Trisul emblem once. A feast is represented once, a boating scene once, and other scenes the meaning of which cannot now quite be made out.

Six pillars of another rail have been discovered by General Cunningham at Muttra, which differ considerably from any other now known. They are square, and about 4 ft. 6 in. high. In front of each is a female figure about half life size standing on a crouching dwarf, and above her head two kit-cat figures, generally male and female, in intimate relations with one another. The principal figures are nude, except the bead belt, which does not join in front, but are more exquisitely carved than any found either at Gayâ or Sanchi. So far as can be judged from the rails discovered there is absolutely no trace of Buddhism, as we now know it, about them, nor do we yet know how they were arranged, nor has anything been made public which would enable us to fix their date. From their style, however, I would guess them to be half way between Sanchi and Amravati, but more must be known before we can speak with anything like certainty regarding them[3] or their date.

The Buddhist rail, in the form in which it is found surrounding the great Tope at Sanchi, is especially interesting to Indian antiquaries, inasmuch as it was copied everywhere at that time, and became the favourite architectural ornament of the age. At Bhâjâ and Kârlâ, in the early Caves at Ajanta and at Kenheri, all the string courses and friezes are mere copies of this rail. Like the wooden triglyph of the Doric order, it was repeated through centuries in stone. It occurs on the central Dagoba at Amravati, but not on the rails or any of the surrounding buildings. It is not found, however, in any of the Caves of Ellora or Elephanta; indeed its use seems to have died out about the fourth or fifth century; but meanwhile its greater or less prevalence is no bad test of the real or comparative age of the building in which it is found.

---

[1] No details of this most interesting rail have yet been published, and no photographs are available. In the library of the India Office, however, there is a set of 46 drawings of its sculptures by Captain Kittoe, and they may generally be relied upon, as their author was singularly accurate both in his drawings and statements. Four woodcuts from these drawings are used as illustrations in this work.

[2] Cunningham, Report, 1861–2, p. 4. *Vide supra* woodcut No. 7.

[3] For all I know of the rail I am indebted to General Cunningham, who kindly sent me a photograph of five of the pillars, but with no further particulars than their general dimensions.

At Amravati all the three rails have circular discs covered with a lotus or water leaf ornament externally, and with figures sculptured on their internal faces. The top rail also is adorned with a frieze of figures internally, and on the outer face with a procession of men bearing a roll such as is used in Buddhist processions in Burmah at the present day. The whole rail, in fact, which is 14 feet in height, is covered with sculptured ornaments, and as it was at least 600 feet in length, it may perhaps be considered as the richest and most elaborate piece of screen work in the world.

The only connecting link which has been discovered between these two forms is in the Western Caves. In front of the great Cave at Kenheri, for instance, there is a low parapet wall, so weather-worn that it is difficult to make out its details. The annexed careful drawing (Woodcut No. 11)—which, however, is fully confirmed by photographs—shows it to possess most of the essential features of the Amravati rail. Each of the three intermediate rails has a disc, and the octagon pillars have a central circle and two half-circles. There is a waving line at top, and an animal frieze below.

No. 11.

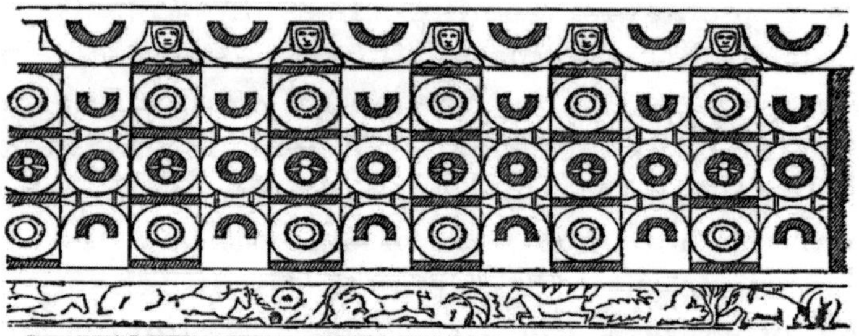

Dwarf Rail in front of Kenheri Cave.
From a Drawing by E. W. West, Esq.

Another rail similarly situated in front of the great Cave at Nassick, containing the Gotamiputra inscriptions (Woodcut, No. 12), shows still greater elaboration, and possesses all the features of the external face of the Amravati rail, excepting, course, the sculptures, which the scale, and probably the material would not admit of. Its animal frieze can be traced in the Photographs, but it is so completely weather-worn that it can only be indicated in the drawings. So far as I can make out, this Nassick rail is about the same age as that at Amravati; that at Kenheri is probably a little more modern. It is so weather-worn that it is difficult to determine its age with anything like certainty. My present impression is, that the Nassick rail belongs to the fourth,[1] the other to the beginning of the fifth century of our era. They are both examples of the completed design, and certainly long subsequent to anything found at Sanchi or at Gayâ or Muttra.

No. 12.

Rail in front of Nassick Cave.
From a Drawing by E. W. West, Esq.

So far as is at present known, the Amravati rail, besides being the richest of detached examples, was the last of its race. After the fourth or fifth century the rail became attached to the Tope in the form of a range of pilasters, and the procession

[1] Other reasons for this conclusion will be given further on when describing the architectural peculiarities of the Amravati Tope.

path, instead of being behind the rail, as at Sanchi, was on a terrace above the range of pilasters as at Manikyala.[1] In the Topes in Afghanistan it frequently degenerated into a mere ornamental band at some height from the ground, and gradually lost all trace of its original significance.

In Ceylon the top and intermediate rails were omitted. One or three rows of upright stone posts were arranged round the Dagobas,[2] as in the Thûparâmaya (Woodcut, No. 13), but not joined together. In theory these look much more like the rows of detached rude stone pillars of northern climes. In practice, however, they too look as if they have just passed through the wooden stage. Their form is so slender, and their ornaments so essentially wooden, that they can hardly have assumed their present shape directly from a rude stone obelisk. My own impression is that they were used as the supports of tapestry, which on festal occasions was hung between them. When Fa-hian visited Ceylon (A.D. 405), he was present when the Tooth relic was carried to Mehentele, which, like the procession of Jagannâth, was the great annual festivity of the place. On these occasions both sides of the roads were hung with paintings of the 500 different manifestations of Buddha, "painted in different colours, and executed with such care "as to appear living."[3] This is so exactly doing on canvas what we, about the same time, find done on stone at Amravati, that it seems hardly doubtful but that the one is the counterpart of the other, and for the Ceylonese form these tall thin pillars seem peculiarly appropriate.

No. 13.

View of the Thûparâmaya Dagoba, Anurâdhapura.

When thoroughly investigated there are few architectural arrangements that will afford a more curious illustration of architectural development than these Buddhist rails. Already we can trace them from the rude circular sepulchral enclosure, either in wood or stone, to such plain unadorned erections as those at Sanchi or Stonehenge, and thence to those of Buddh Gayâ; from that we can go on to that at Amravati, and till they lose themselves in the north of India. Many of the links are yet missing, though they will no doubt be easily supplied so soon as attention is really directed to the investigation.

Another interesting feature connected with these rails is the gateways attached to them. These are frequently represented in the sculptures at Amravati and the paintings at Ajanta, but the only examples known to exist in an erect position are those at Sanchi. They are more modern than the rails to which they are attached, being slightly subsequent to the Christian era; but still betray, like everything else in

[1] History of Architecture, Woodcuts, 978, 979.

[2] Transactions Royal Asiatic Society, III. pl. 17, 18, 20, &c.; History of Architecture, II. Woodcut, 1007.

[3] Foĕ-Kouĕ-Ki, p. 335. Beal's Translation, 157. These were afterwards known as the 500 or 550 Jâtakas to which frequent reference will be made in the sequel.

this style of architecture, their wooden origin. Such a form could never have been invented in stone; and the reason they are not more frequently found, is probably that they were generally executed in wood, even when attached to stone rails. The Chinese Pailoo is undoubtedly the lineal descendant of these gates; but even that is very generally at the present day constructed either wholly or partially in wood. It must, indeed, have required considerable courage to attempt such a construction in stone,[1] and the wonder is rather that several should have survived the wreck of eighteen centuries, than that so few should be found. The form of those at Sanchi and their sculptures form the first division of this work, and need not, therefore, be further enlarged on here; and as they are the only examples of their kind, no classification is possible.

The lâṭs or Stambhas form another group of early Buddhist monuments that must not be passed over. Four or five out of a larger number of those erected by Aśoka still exist, either standing, or in recognized fragments. They form, however, such excellent rollers for the British road maker, and such capital sugar or rice mills for the native zemindar, that the wonder is that so many are left. All those of Aśoka are similar to one another,—circular stone shafts of a single block, 30 or 40 feet in length, and surmounted by a capital with the falling leaf or bell-shaped form found at Persepolis. This form of the capital, together with the Grecian or rather Assyrian honeysuckle ornament with which it is generally associated, are two of the most valuable ethnographical indications which the architecture of this age affords. As we have every reason to suppose that the real architecture of Aśoka's time remained essentially wooden in all its forms, it is curious to observe him copying the details of the architecture of the countries of his allies, Antiochus or Antigonus, in his first attempts at a more permanent style in stone. So far as we now know, the use of these foreign forms was confined to lâṭs and detached objects, and they were not employed in bûildings, properly so called, till some time after their first introduction, and then very much modified from their original forms. The object for which Aśoka's pillars were erected was, that certain edicts might be engraved upon them, which he desired to enforce on his people. Those at Pathari and Erun were erected by the Guptas in the fifth century, and mark the change that had taken place in Buddhist feeling. His own personal greatness and glorification was the object of the king who erected the more modern examples, and no longer a disinterested desire for the religious welfare of his people, which seems to have been Aśoka's only motive. Intermediate between these two periods we have numerous examples. Some are cut in the rock, as at Kârlâ and Kenheri; but generally they are found attached to Topes. Two certainly at one time adorned each of the four entrances of the rail at both Sanchi and Amravati, and several of these still remain; most of them, however, are prostrate, though some are standing.

The capitals of the lâṭs of Aśoka were generally surmounted by a single lion or elephant[2] or other animal. At Sanchi and Kârlâ we have four lions seated back

---

[1] Henry of Huntingdon's description of the Trilithon at Stonehenge is curiously applicable here :—"Ubi lapides miræ magnitudinis in modum portarum elevati sunt, ita ut portæ portis superpositæ videantur."—Monument. Hist., p. 694.

[2] History of Architecture, Woodcuts, 969 and 970.

to back on their capitals, and at the former place sometimes a single figure of a man standing. My impression is, that wherever four animals are found surmounting a column, they were not intended as the final ornament, but as the support of a wheel—probably in metal—or some other Buddhist emblem. In other instances we have four men, and these overshadowed by the seven-headed serpent. At Amravati the lâṭs seem more generally to have been crowned by miniature Dagobas, but sometimes also by men, and by other emblems. As all these will be more particularly described in the sequel, where they occur in the Plates, it is not necessary to dwell more on their peculiarities in this place.

No. 14.

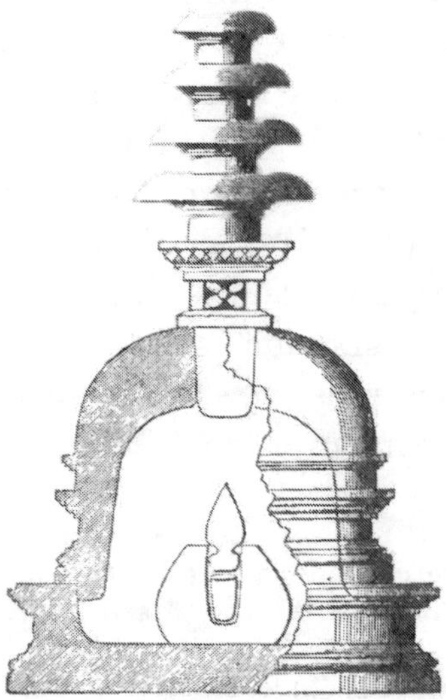

Relic Casket, from Manikyala,
In the possession of General Cunningham.

CHAPTER II.

Topes at Sanchi.—(Plates I. and II.)

The Topes at Sanchi, which it is proposed to illustrate in the following pages, form part of a great group of these monuments situated between the towns of Bhilsa and Bhopal, in Central India. They extend over a district seventeen miles east and west, and about ten miles north and south, in five or six different groups, and number altogether between forty and fifty tumuli of various dimensions. The smallest of them are no doubt mere burying places of local chiefs, erected over their ashes, and contain no objects of interest. Others are Dagobas, or relic shrines, in the correct sense of the word; while the great Tope itself (A. Plate I.) is a Chaitya or Stûpa,[1] erected apparently to commemorate some event in Buddhist history, or to mark some sacred spot.[2]

The great Tope at Sanchi (Plate II.) consists, first, of a circular basement 121 feet in diameter and 14 feet in height. On the top of this is a terrace or procession path, 5 feet 6 inches wide, within which the dome or tumulus itself rises in the form of a truncated hemisphere to a height of 39 feet. This was originally coated with chunan to a thickness of about four inches, but whether ornamented with painting or moulded plaster ornaments cannot be ascertained, owing to the very fragmentary state in which the coating now exists. On the top of the dome was a level platform, measuring 34 feet across. This was surrounded by a circular railing of stones, some of the pillars of which are still found among the ruins. Within this was a square Tee or simulated relic box, consisting of sixteen square pillars with rails, and measuring 11 feet 6 inches each way. Within this again was a circular support for the umbrella which invariably crowned these monuments.[3] When Captain Fell visited this monu-

---

1 Vide ante, page 88.

2 The whole of these Topes were carefully opened and examined by General A. Cunningham and Lieut.-Colonel Maisey in 1851, and the results published by the first-named officer, in his work on the Bhilsa Topes, by Smith, Elder, & Co. in 1854.

3 On one of the pillars of the rail at Buddh Gayâ there is a curious representation of these relic caskets, which is so unlike anything we find anywhere else that it is well worth quoting. Like the other three woodcuts taken from the sculptures of that race, and inserted further on, this one is from a drawing by the late Captain Kittoe, one of the set of 46 drawings of this rail, mentioned above, page 90 et seq.

No. 15.

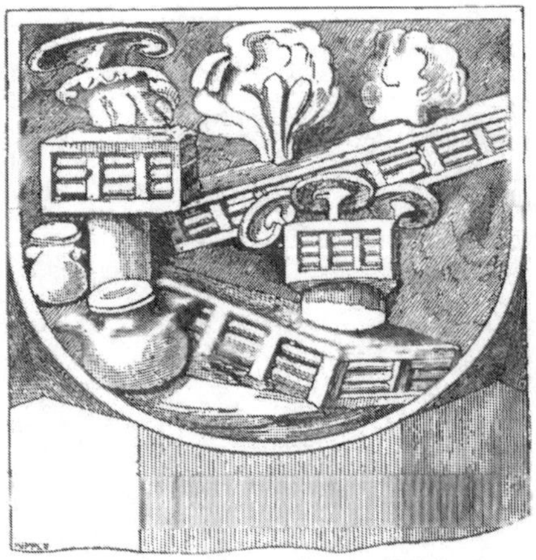

From a Pillar at Buddh Gayâ

In the foreground is a relic casket surmounted by three umbrellas, and standing within an oblong enclosure. To the left is another similar casket at the meeting of two rails; but this time guarded by a seven-headed Serpent, above whose head the sacred umbrella is expanded. In the second enclosure are two Trees, but of genera not easily determined, and on the ground two vessels, either containing offerings, or such as were used in sacrifice.

Notwithstanding the reliance that may be placed in Captain Kittoe's drawings, it is a pity this subject was never either cast or photographed, as it is one of the most curious and interesting representations of Relic Worship mixed with that of the Tree and Serpent which we possess, as well as one of the oldest. Its date probably being 100 to 200 years B.C.

ment in 1819,[1] all this was *in situ* and nearly perfect; but shortly afterwards some bungling amateurs dug into the monument, and so completely ruined it, that the form of its superstructure can now only with difficulty be made out.

The most remarkable feature, however, connected with this monument is the rail which surrounds it at a distance of 9 feet 6 inches from the base, except on the south, where the double flight of steps leading to the berm or procession path reduces the width to 6 feet 4 inches. As before mentioned, it is 11 feet in height, and consisted apparently of 100 pillars, exclusive of the gateways. Each of these was apparently the gift of an individual, and even the rails between them seem to have been presented by different persons. General Cunningham collected 176 short inscriptions from this rail,[2] all by different individuals, and each recording that the member on which it was engraved was the gift of some pious person, male or female, but all unfortunately unknown to fame. Not one, at least, has yet been satisfactorily identified.

There is absolutely no sculpture on the rail, but fortunately four gateways were added to it shortly after the Christian era, and these are covered with sculptured decorations of the most elaborate kind. Two of these are still standing, and the fragments of the other two are to be seen lying on the ground. The most perfect is the northern entrance, the rear elevation of which forms the frontispiece to this volume. The total height to the top of the central ornament is 33 feet 6 inches. The height to the under side of the lowest rail is 18 feet 6 inches in the centre, and the width of the opening between the two pillars is 7 feet clear. The greatest width is across the lowest rail, and measures within a fraction of 20 feet. The whole, as will be seen from the frontispiece and the photographs, is of a singularly wooden form, and is jointed and morticed together more like a piece of carpentry than a structure of stone.[3]

Number 2 Tope (B, in Plate I.) is very much smaller than that just described, being only 39 feet in diameter. It springs from a basement 6 feet in height, supporting a terrace or berm 5 feet 4 inches wide. Its section is that of a hemisphere stilted to the extent of 3½ feet. Its proportional of height, therefore, is 29 feet to 39, or as 3 to 4 nearly; that of the great Tope was only as 1 to 2, showing an advance, which is an almost certain indication of a more modern age.[4] The rail is 7 feet 6 inches in height, and elliptical in plan, in order to allow a clear space of 8 feet as well in front of the ramp as round the other parts of the building. The enclosure thus measures 69 feet by 74½ feet. As before explained, the rail is to some extent ornamented (Woodcut No. 10), but has no gateways of the same imposing character as those of the great Tope. The angle pillars are, however, ornamented as well as the intermediate rails, and afford some indications of great value. (See Plates XLII. and XLIII., which will be noticed hereafter.)

---

[1] J. A. S. B., vol. III. p. 490, et seqq. General Taylor, of the Bengal Cavalry, who was probably the first British officer that visited the monument, confirms the account given by Captain Fell. He discovered the Tope when encamped near it, during the campaign of 1818. Three of its gates were then standing, and a great part of the Tee still *in situ*.

[2] Cunningham, Bhilsa Topes, p. 235, et seq.

[3] All the above dimensions are taken from Colonel Maisey's MS. notes.

[4] Cunningham, Bhilsa Topes, p. 177.

As before mentioned, the great Tope seems to have been a "monumental tower." Nothing was found in it. This one, on the contrary, contained four steatite boxes, in which were placed relics "of Kâśyapa Gotra, missionary to the whole of the Himawanta," and of Madhyama, both these names being mentioned in the Mahawanso as missionaries sent by Aśoka to the Himalaya country,[1] thus confirming to the fullest possible extent the inscriptions on the box. Another contained relics of Mogaliputra, who was the head of the Buddhist church at the third convocation (B.C. 241), and altogether the Tope possessed memorials of ten of the principal personages of the Buddhist community during the reign of Aśoka. The three named above were well known before the Tope was opened, the other seven were less famous, but their connection can now be traced.[2]

There is another Tope at Sanchi, which is illustrated to some extent in this work. It stands near to the great Tope, and on the same platform (D 3, in plan, Plate I.). At first sight it appears only as a formless cairn of stones, but on examination it was found to consist of a dome 40 feet in diameter, standing on a base measuring 52 feet across and 6 feet high. The dome was originally crowned by a pedestal or Tee 4½ feet square, supporting a Chatta about 3½ feet diameter. Some fragments of the Rail are scattered about, but the principal ornament is the fragment of one of the Gateways, which is still standing (Plate XXI.), and though only about half the dimensions of those of the great Tope, is quite equal to them in elegance of design or richness of ornament.

The great interest of this Tope, or rather Dagoba, is that it was found to contain relics of Śâriputra and Mahâ Mogalâna, two of the principal disciples and followers of Buddha himself.[3] These were probably the most precious possessions of the fraternity at Sanchi.

As the other Topes at or about Sanchi are not illustrated in this work, it would be tedious and unnecessary to dwell on them here. They are all described and delineated in General Cunningham's work, to which the reader is referred for details. Some of them are of great value for the elucidation of the history of Buddhist art, but none equal, either in elaboration or in interest, to the three just enumerated.

History.

Although there are no data which enable us to ascertain positively the dates of the Sanchi Topes, there are certain indications which fix them within certain limits with a reasonable amount of certainty. One of the most distinct of these is in an inscription on a representation of a Tope on the Southern Gateway (Plate XVII.) now fallen and lying on the ground. It is to the effect that the beam on which it was found was "the gift of Ânanda, the son of Vaśishṭha, in the reign of Śrî Śâtakarṇi."[4] Unfortunately for our argument, there are several kings of the Ândhra

---

[1] Mahawanso, p. 74.

[2] These particulars are taken from General Cunningham's work, p. 285, et seqq. He and Colonel Maisey seem to have divided the "find" between them. Colonel Maisey's share is now on exhibition at South Kensington Museum; General Cunningham's is in his own possession.

[3] All these particulars are taken from Cunningham, Bhilsa Topes, p. 295, et seqq.

[4] Cunningham, Bhilsa Topes, p. 264.

dynasty who bore this name. The first reigned A.D. 10 to 28, according to my calculation; the second 64 to 120 A.D.,[1] and his long and prosperous reign would seem to afford a presumption that it was during his lifetime that these Gateways were erected. General Cunningham and Colonel Maisey both arrived at the conclusion that it was during the reign of the first Śâtakarṇi that they were added to the Rail;[2] and on the whole I am inclined to agree with them, but a second question arises on this point. The Gateways are not all of the same age. There is a considerable difference in style, and I quite agree in thinking with Colonel Maisey that the Gateway bearing this inscription is the oldest. But whether this is so or not, I feel little doubt but that the four Gateways of the great Tope, and the Gateway of No. 3, were all erected within the limits of the first century after Christ. The probability is that the South Gateway belonged to the first thirty years of it; in other words, was being carved while Christ was preaching at Jerusalem. The presumption is confirmed to the fullest possible extent by the style of architecture and of the sculpture, though it is difficult to make this argument available with those who are not intimately acquainted with the Caves of Kârlâ, Ajanta, and other contemporaneous examples.

The inscriptions on the Rails, though so numerous, do not contain a single historical name that can be recognized with certainty; but the style of the characters in which they are written is very similar to that used in the inscriptions of Aśoka, and never employed,—so far as is at present known,—after the Christian era.

For the Tope itself we have neither inscription nor architectural mouldings, and our Chinese travellers fail us here, as neither of them visited Sanchi, nor did any other mediæval writer; and no tradition exists among the Brahminical or Mahomedan inhabitants of the country as to the origin or date of this memorial of a long-forgotten faith.

In this difficulty the Mahawanso helps us a little.[3] It relates that when Aśoka was sent by his father to be governor of Ujjéni he tarried some time at Chaityagiri, or, as it is called elsewhere, Wessanagara,[4] the modern Besnagar, close to Sanchi. He there married Devî, the daughter of the chief, and by her had twin sons, Ujjenio and Mahindo, and afterwards a daughter, Sanghamitâ. The two last named afterwards entered the priesthood, and played a most important part in the conversion of Ceylon to Buddhism. Before setting out for Ceylon, "when Mahindo visited his royal mother at Chaitiyagiri," she established the thero in the superb Chaitya Vihâra, which had been erected by herself.[5] In all this it is true there is no mention of the Chaitya itself, and it may possibly have existed before Aśoka's time, but there is absolutely no proof of this, and till some one stone monument is discovered in India with an ascertained date anterior to 250 B.C., we must be content to commence our history there. On the other hand, the capital of the pillar (Plate XXXIX. Fig. 1) and the lions which surmount it are so similar to the works we know to be Aśoka's elsewhere, that we may safely assume they belong to his age. There is also a mutilated inscription, on which General Cunningham reads doubtfully his monumental title of Devânampriya.[6] If this is

---

[1] Journal Royal Asiatic Society, N.S., p. 122.
[2] Bhilsa Topes, p. 265.
[3] Mahawanso, p. 76.
[4] Turnour, Pali Annals, J. A. S. B., VII. p. 930.
[5] Mahawanso, p. 76.
[6] Bhilsa Topes, p. 259.

really his, it settles the question that the Tope was erected by him, though for what purpose he has not attempted to explain.

Without going further into the evidence, which is not necessary in this place, it may fairly be assumed that the great Tope is one of the 84,000 which Aśoka is traditionally said to have erected. If so, it is the only one of them all still remaining in India, and the oldest stone building in the country.[1]

The Rail may have been commenced immediately afterwards by the faithful of the congregation, and completed in 50 or 100 years. The Gateways were probably added to the then existing Rail at the time when the languishing religion of Buddha was restored to its pristine position by the eloquence of Nâgârjuna, backed by the political influence of the Turushka Kanishka.[2] Everything about them seems to indicate such a revival. If I might be allowed to state what I cannot prove, I would suggest that they must have been completed about or shortly after the death of Śâlivâhana, 78 A.D.

The superb Vihâra erected by the lovely Devî was, I am afraid, entirely of wood, and no trace of it consequently now remains.

The age of the second Tope seems intermediate between these dates. Its taller form shows it to be more modern than the great one, and the more ornate character of its Rail is a strong indication in the same direction. On the other hand, the character of its sculptures and the form of the letters in its inscriptions show that it is older than the Gateways of the large Tope, if we might guess, say by 100 to 150 years. It cannot well be more, for the ten persons whose relics it contains were all alive in the reign of Aśoka; and men do not become saints, and little bits of bone or beads that belonged to them do not become valuable, till their corporeal form is forgotten. Had they been buried here, it would have been otherwise; but we must allow a hundred years to have passed since their deaths before their relics were enclosed in steatite boxes and a Dagoba built over them. As a mean date I would be inclined to place No. 2 Tope at from 100 to 150 years B.C.

The third Tope is so ruined—as mentioned above—that there is nothing in its architecture that would enable us to fix its date. The Gateway may be of the same age as those of the great Tope, or slightly more modern; but even if this were ascertained it would not enable us to determine the age of the Tope itself. The gateway may have been added afterwards, as those of the great Tope certainly were. The fact of its containing relics of the companions of Buddha is equally useless for the purpose of fixing its date. They may have been brought here at any time. If, however, I am correct in a suggestion I will make in describing Plate XXXVIII., it may go some way towards settling this question. My impression is, that the scenes there depicted have reference to the acquirement or recovery of these very relics; and if this is so, the erection of this Tope is probably about contemporary with that of the greater one. According to this hypothesis, Aśoka conquered or recovered these relics from their original possessors, and erected this smaller Tope, as a chapel, for their

---

[1] General Cunningham's dates are, for the Gates, 19 to 37 A.D.; for the Rail, 250 B.C.; and for the Tope itself, 500 B.C. (page 270 et seq.) With regard to the two first I agree with him generally, but I think he exaggerates the age of the Tope, without assigning any valid reason for so doing. Assuming the Tope to have been erected by Aśoka, which I see no reason for doubting, this would hardly interfere with his date for the rail.

[2] Ante, p. 64. See also J. R. A. S., N. S., IV., p. 96.

reception. The Gateway, in that case, is at least two, it may be three, centuries more modern than the building to which it is attached.

There are six or seven other small Topes on the same platform as the great Tope (Plate I.). They are all, however, now merely formless heaps of loose stones, and none of them yielded any results to their explorers.

If we are thus enabled to fix the general age of the Sanchi Gateways with fairly approximative certainty, the next question that arises is to try and ascertain if there was a succession among them, and if so, which is the elder. No one who studies them attentively can, I think, fail to perceive the existence of a sequence, nor with the knowledge we now possess does it seem doubtful that the Southern Gateway was that first erected.

In the first place, Col. Maisey, whose artistic eye was so keen as to justify us almost in accepting his determination as decisive, was of this opinion. "The pillars," he says, "of the Southern Gateway are different in style from the others, and the buildings "and costumes struck me as having served as models for those of the other gates, which "though evidently the work of superior artists have not so original an appearance."

A more cogent reason than even this is their arrangement. Turning to the plan, Plate I., it will be seen from the position of the Tope on the platform, and the situation of the Chaitya, and other buildings, that the southern must always have been the principal façade, and the one consequently, where the first gateway would be erected. It is also the gateway in front of which were the steps leading to the berm, and consequently always must have been the principal of the four gateways. If this were so, it is almost equally certain that the northern gateway would be the next erected. Two gateways only a quadrant apart from one another would have been an intolerable architectural solecism. From similarity of style and its elephant capitals, the Eastern Gateway probably followed next; and lastly came the Western with its anomalous dwarf capitals, to be followed by the gateway of the small Tope, which has the same form of capitals, and resembles it very nearly in the style of sculpture.

This theory of succession rises almost to certainty when we look at it from another point of view. Admitting, which can hardly be disputed, that these gateways are derived from wooden originals, it is tolerably clear that the one most wooden in its form must be consequently the oldest, and this undoubtedly is the characteristic of the Southern Gateway. The relative height of the pillars to the under side of the capitals being as follows,[1]—

South	Gateway	- -	$6\frac{3}{4}$ diameter.
North	do.	- -	$5\frac{1}{2}$ do.
East	do.	- -	5 do.
West	do.	- -	$4\frac{3}{4}$ do.

a sequence which in itself is, I conceive, quite sufficient to establish the point, and taken with the other facts stated above, and those which are mentioned further on in the descriptions of the Plates, make it so certain, that in the following pages they will be described in this succession and treated as each belonging to one of the four quarters of the first century of the Christian era.

[1] It is impossible to state these proportions with minute accuracy. No two pillars and no two sides of the same pillar being exactly alike.

ETHNOGRAPHY.

It would add very much to the clearness of what follows, if, before proceeding to describe the individual bas-reliefs, it were possible to determine even approximately the races or classes of the people represented in the sculptures at Sanchi, as well as to what epoch of history the events depicted should be ascribed.

By the identification of the sculptures in the lowest beam of the Northern Gateway with the events of the Wassantara Jataka, one of the great difficulties which presented itself when the first edition of this work was published has been removed. The people dressed in kilts and with their hair twisted round their heads are now known to be Brahmanical or Buddhist ascetics, living in the woods and forests, and for the time at least practising asceticism. In appearance they differ entirely from the laity who in the sculptures are easily recognized by their costume. This consists of the dhotî, wrapped round the loins in precisely the same manner as it is at the present day; sometimes they have also a chudder or scarf over their shoulders; and all wear the turban. This last seems to be mingled with the hair, and twisted into the most fantastic shapes, more resembling the form now seen in Burmah than those usual in Bengal; but still it is fundamentally always a long strip of cloth wound round the head in what was no doubt then considered an elegant and fashionable form.

The costume of the women is more difficult to describe, though this is principally in consequence of its scantiness. Both at Sanchi and Amravati the women almost always wear enormous bangles about the ankles and wrists, and generally strings of beads round the neck, but their body clothing generally is limited to a bead belt round the body below the waist. From this belt slips of cloth are sometimes suspended, more generally at the sides or behind than in front, and sometimes also a cloth, worn something like the dhotî of the male sex, is also added, but when that is the case it is represented in the sculptures generally as absolutely transparent.

The most remarkable part of the female costume is the head dress, which is as voluminous as the body dress is scant. It is represented, Figs. 1., 2., and 3., Plate III., and seems to consist of two long plaits of hair mixed with beads, and a thick roll of cloth, so as to form a sort of tippet, almost covering the whole of the back of the wearer.

It is, however, not only in the Topes that this absence of dress is so conspicuous. In all the sculptures at Kârlâ, or Ellora, or Mahavellipore, or in the paintings in Ajanta, the same peculiarity is observable. Everywhere, indeed, before the Mahomedan conquest, nudity in India conveyed no sense of indecency. The wife and mother of Buddha are at times represented in this manner. The queen on her throne, the female disciples of Buddha, listening to his exhortations, and on every public occasion on which women take part in what is going on, the costume is the same.[1] It is equally remarkable that in those days these unveiled females seem

[1] When we first visited Japan in 1860, the females were seen "tubbing" in the public streets in the open light of day. Whatever it may be now, nudity conveyed no idea of indecency to the Japanese ten years ago.

to have taken part in every public transaction and show, and to have mixed with the men as freely as women do in Europe at the present day.[1]

All this is the more remarkable, as in Buddhist books modesty of dress in women is frequently insisted upon. In the Dulva, for instance, a story is told of the King of Kalinga presenting to the King of Kośala (probably Oude) a piece of muslin which afterwards fell into the hands of a lewd priestess. She, it is said, wore it in public, while it was so thin that she, notwithstanding this, appeared naked, to the great scandal of all who witnessed the exhibition.[2] The probability is, that the story and the book that contains it are of very much more modern date than our sculptures. It certainly is in direct conflict with their evidence.

The Ascetics are very easily distinguished from those just described. The costume of the men consists of a kilt, literally a kilt, not a cloth wrapped round the loins, but so far as can be judged from the sculptures, needle made, and fastened by a buckle or string. They also wear a cloak or tippet, which seems to be equally shaped and sewn, a thing apparently utterly unknown in India till the fashion of shaped garments was introduced by the Mahomedans.[3] Their head dress is also very peculiar; either it is that their hair was twisted into a long rope or plait like a Chinaman's, and then bound round the head in a conical form, or a piece of cloth or rope was similarly twisted. Their most marked peculiarity, however, is that they all wear beards, whereas no layman either at Sanchi or Amravati has a trace of a beard or of even a moustache. This is the more remarkable, as Nearchus tells us that the Indians daub their beards with various colours, so that some are white, others black, some red, some purple, and others green![4] Curtius tells us they never shave.[5] Diodorus assures us that they nourish their beards during their whole lives,[6] and received this custom from Bacchus, whom they call the bearded deity; and Strabo tells us they suffer their beards to grow without cutting, and dye them various colours by way of ornament;[7] and Solinus gives the same testimony.

It is probable that all these authorities spoke only of the people with whom they were most familiar, and who inhabited the banks of the Indus or the country now known as the Punjab. The bearded race would thus represent the Aryans who early settled in that country and probably occupied it almost exclusively at the time when the Greeks knew it best. The beardless people, on the other hand, would represent the less pure races who occupied the whole of the valley of the Ganges, and who were practically the people who were converted by the preaching of Buddha to the new form of faith.[8]

---

1 In India there are some tribes where the females still go nearly naked. The Putooas, for instance, described by Mr. Samuells, J. A. S. B., XXV. p. 295, have no other dress than a string tied round their waists, from which every morning they suspend a fresh bunch of leaves in front and another behind; literally the costume of our first parents in Paradise. In the south of India some of the females, of the races on the west coast especially, wear nothing above the waist, in curious contrast to the countries where the Mahomedans have held sway, where the women are now generally secluded, or, if appearing in public, are completely veiled.

2 Asiatic Researches, XX. p. 85.

3 Buchanan Hamilton, in Martin's Eastern India, II. 699.

4 Arrian, Indica, XVI.

5 Q. Curtius, VIII. 9. 22.

6 Diodorus, IV. 5.

7 Strabo, XV. 1024.

8 Only two instances of bearded men occur at Amravati. Both of them appear to be hermits or ascetics of the same class as those so frequently represented at Sanchi.

The costume of the female Ascetics differs from those of the laity even more than that of the men. They wear a petticoat striped like that of the other sex, and apparently gathered in at the knees, so as to form a neat and modest dress, and a cloak or tippet similar to that of the men is thrown generally over one shoulder so as to leave one breast bare, but sometimes both are covered. On their heads they wear a neat and elegant turban (Plate III., Figs. 4. and 5.). They wear no bangles nor ornaments of any kind.

Sculptures.

Although anyone may, by a careful study of the drawings and photographs, learn to discriminate between the different races of men represented in the sculptures, the task becomes very much more difficult when we attempt to ascertain what particular event each bas-relief represents, or to give a name to each individual scene. About one-half of the bas-reliefs at Sanchi, however, represent religious acts, such as the worship of the Dagoba, or of Trees, the Wheel, or other emblems. In all these cases there is no doubt or difficulty. There are also half-a-dozen scenes that can be identified with more or less certainty as representing events in the life of Śâkya Muni, and a considerable number of representations of scenes in domestic life, regarding which it will probably be impossible ever to feel sure that we know who the actors in them are. Nor is it of much importance here. Eating, drinking, and making love are occupations so common among mankind, that it matters little who the parties are who are so engaged in the Sanchi sculptures. But besides all these, there are several important bas-reliefs representing historical events, which it would be very interesting to identify if it were practicable. Generally the lowest architrave in each of the gateways is so occupied, sometimes both in front and back, as in the Northern Gate, and the two lowest in front of the Eastern, and two historical scenes are represented in Plate XXXVIII., one from the Western, the other from the Southern Gateway, both of which have fallen.

The two latter represent the siege of a city in order to recover and to obtain possession of some relics, and the triumphal return of the army with the precious deposit; and, as will be afterwards explained, it is probable that the caskets contain the identical relics that were enshrined in No. 3 Tope, and are now in this country. Be that as it may, the question is, who is the hero of the fight? and who brought home the relics to Sanchi? Assuming the sculpture to have been executed about the Christian era, does it represent a transaction in the reign of Aśoka more than two hundred years earlier, or did the king who erected the gates order these bas-reliefs to be executed to commemorate some great exploit of his own? If the king had engraved his own name on the gate, the latter would have been the probable solution, but the inscription only states that the sculpture is the "gift of Ânanda, the son of Vaśishṭha, in the reign of Śrî Śâtakarṇi." On the whole, therefore, considering that it is a religious monument, and the general self-denying character of Buddhism, it is more probable that the events represented had passed into the domain of religious history before they were sculptured on the gateways, and that they were actions sanctified by time.

Unfortunately the other inscriptions, though so numerous, afford us no assistance in this inquiry. It is probably correct to assert that there is not one single inscription, either at Sanchi or Amravati, which has any reference to the subject about or upon which it is engraved. They all record gifts, and gifts only, and it would be as reasonable to look for an explanation of the Resurrection or the Last Supper from the inscription of a memorial window in modern times, as to try and find out from those on the Topes what the sculptures represent.

Since the first edition of this work was published the investigation of these bas-reliefs has been placed on quite a new footing by the identification of the scenes represented in the lower beam of the Northern Gateway with the Wessantara Jâtaka and those of the right-hand pillars of the Eastern Gateway, Plate XXIV., with the conversion of the Kaśyapas and subsequent events.[1] These two seem quite certain, and many others have also been identified with more or less certainty, and will all certainly be explained when scholars familiar with the ordinary representations of such subjects in the East at the present day turn seriously to their investigation.

Meanwhile it is curious to observe how different the picture of Buddhism, which the pictures present to us, is from that we have been hitherto accustomed to. We have in Plate XXXIII. scenes from the life of Sâkya Muni up to the time when he attained Buddhahood, but no representation of him at Sanchi or at Gayâ after that event, unless I am correct in identifying the figure in the foreground of the bas-relief representing the conversion of the Kaśyapas as the gentle Ascetic. Be this as it may, we have not at Sanchi any of those cross-legged or curly-headed representations of the founder of the religion, or any statues of him preaching and teaching, which became common three centuries afterwards at Amravati, and are universal from that time to the present day. In lieu of this we have the worship of Trees, Dagobas, Wheels, and other figures. Omitting minor representations, where they are mere emblems or ornaments, or where they form parts of scenes which may be historical and where consequently they are subordinate, these occur in the following proportions on the five Sanchi Gateways:—

——	Trees.	Dagobas.	Wheels.	Śrî.[2]
South Gateway - - -	16	5	1	2
North do. - - -	19	8	2	3
East do. - - -	17	9	1	2
West do. - - -	15	10	2	1
Small Tope - - - -	9	6	4	2
	76	38	10	10

In other words, Trees are objects of decided worship, either by men or animals twice as often as the Dagoba itself, and the Wheel and Śrî a little more than one-fourth and one-eighth of these respectively. The Trisul ornament does not appear

[1] As mentioned in the Preface, I am indebted to the Rev. Mr. S. Beal for these and other identifications mentioned further on.

[2] See Woodcut, page 108, and description, page 112.

as the object of direct worship there; while no human being is represented as receiving the homage of his fellow men.

Besides war and worship, however, we have at Sanchi scenes of eating and drinking (Plate XXXVII.) which we hardly would expect to find on the gateway of a religious monument dedicated to Buddhism. The same thing, however, occurs on the Rail at Buddh Gayâ.

One other curious peculiarity is that, in these sculptures, elephants, monkeys, and other animals share with men in acts of adoration of the Dagobas and Trees, and seem in those early ages to have been considered as the equals of humanity.

All this will become clearer as we proceed and describe the bassi-relievi in detail, but all these put together prepare us for a picture of Buddhism in the first century A.D. very different from any we were led to expect from any books or pictures hitherto published on the subject.

It may seem premature, before describing the sculptures, to attempt anything like a criticism of their merits. It may, however, add to the intelligibility of what follows to point out how extremely different these are to the usual sculptures brought home from India, or represented in Hindu drawings. Neither at Sanchi nor at Amravati are there any of those many-armed or many-headed divinities who form the staple of the modern Hindu Pantheon. There are none of those monstrous combinations of men with heads of elephants or lions or boars. All the men and women represented are human beings, acting as men and women have acted in all times, and the success or failure of the representation may consequently be judged of by the same rules as are applicable to sculptures in any other place or country. Notwithstanding this, the mode of treatment is so original and so local, that it is difficult to assign it any exact position in comparison with the arts of the Western World. It certainly, as a sculptural art, is superior to that of Egypt, but as far inferior to the art as practised in Greece. The sculptures at Amravati are perhaps as near in scale of excellence to the contemporary art of the Roman empire under Constantine as to any other that could be named; or, rather, they should be compared with the sculptures of the early Italian Renaissance, as it culminated in the hands of Ghiberti, and before the true limits between the provinces of sculpture and painting were properly understood.

The case is somewhat different as regards the sculptures at Sanchi. These are ruder, but more vigorous. If they want the elegance of design at Amravati, they make up for it by a distinctness and raciness of expression which is wanting in these more refined compositions. The truth seems to be that the Sanchi sculptures, like everything else there, betray the influence of the freedom derived from wood carving, which, there can be little doubt, immediately preceded these examples, and formed the school in which they were produced.

It can now hardly be considered doutful but that this school of Indian art owes its origin to the influence of the Greek kingdom of Bactria. Of late years considerable collections have been made of Buddhist sculptures from ruined Topes in the neighbourhood of Peshawer.[1] These are in many respects extremely similar

---

[1] I speak confidently of these sculptures, as I have photographs of a considerable number, and specimens of others exist in this country. Unfortunately, no means exist as yet of conveying a knowledge of them to the public.

to those at Sanchi, but more closely allied to the classical type. In many of the Punjab examples the costumes and mode of treatment is almost purely western, but we are always able to trace the steps by which the Grecian design becomes Indianized, and changed into the type we find at Sanchi and Amravati.

Perhaps, however, the crowning point of interest in these sculptures is, that they complete our knowledge of the history of stone art in India. Hitherto we have been groping our way backwards with uncertain steps, never knowing at what conclusions we might ultimately arrive. As far back as the tenth or eleventh centuries we had abundant examples of structural buildings, and we found that each was perfect in the direct ratio of the age. The history of art in India, so far as we could trace it, was written in decay, and finding each example more perfect than the one that followed it, there was reasonable hope that some day we should find something that would stand comparison with the arts of the Western World.

Beyond the tenth century we were left for guidance almost wholly to the rock-cut examples. These, however, owing to the coarseness of the material out of which they were excavated, and the difficulties inherent in Cave art, could not be depended upon as trustworthy indications of the state of refinement of the arts in their age. In so far, however, as architecture is concerned, we learned from them that stone was first thought of as a building material about the age of Aśoka, certainly after the time of Alexander, and the commencement of the first intimate intercourse between the Western and the Eastern World.[1]

The knowledge that we have now gained of the early history of the art of sculpture in India, from the study of the examples at Sanchi and Amravati, enables us to point with equal certainty to Bactria as the fountain head from which it was introduced. We can thence follow it through the time when, from being a rude and imitative art, it rose to its highest degree of refinement in the fourth or fifth century of our era, at which time it had also become essentially localized. From that point our history is easy, though somewhat discouraging, from its downward tendency towards the present state of art in India. We are now also able to trace the Yavanas step by step, as they penetrated over the Upper Indus, and spread their influence and their arts across the continent of India to the very shores of the Bay of Bengal, at Cuttack, and Amravati. With almost equal certainty we can follow them as they crossed the bay, and settled themselves in Cambodia and Java. But the people who did all this were not Greeks themselves, and did not carry with them the Pantheon of Greece or Rome, or the tenets of Christianity. They were a people of Turanian race, and the form of worship they took with them and introduced everywhere was that of Trees and Serpents, fading afterwards into a modified form of Buddhism.

---

[1] See History of Architecture, by the Author, II. 455, et seqq.

No. 16.

Śrí, Consort of Vishnu.

From an image brought from Indore, engraved in Moor's Pantheon, Plate 30.

PLATE I.

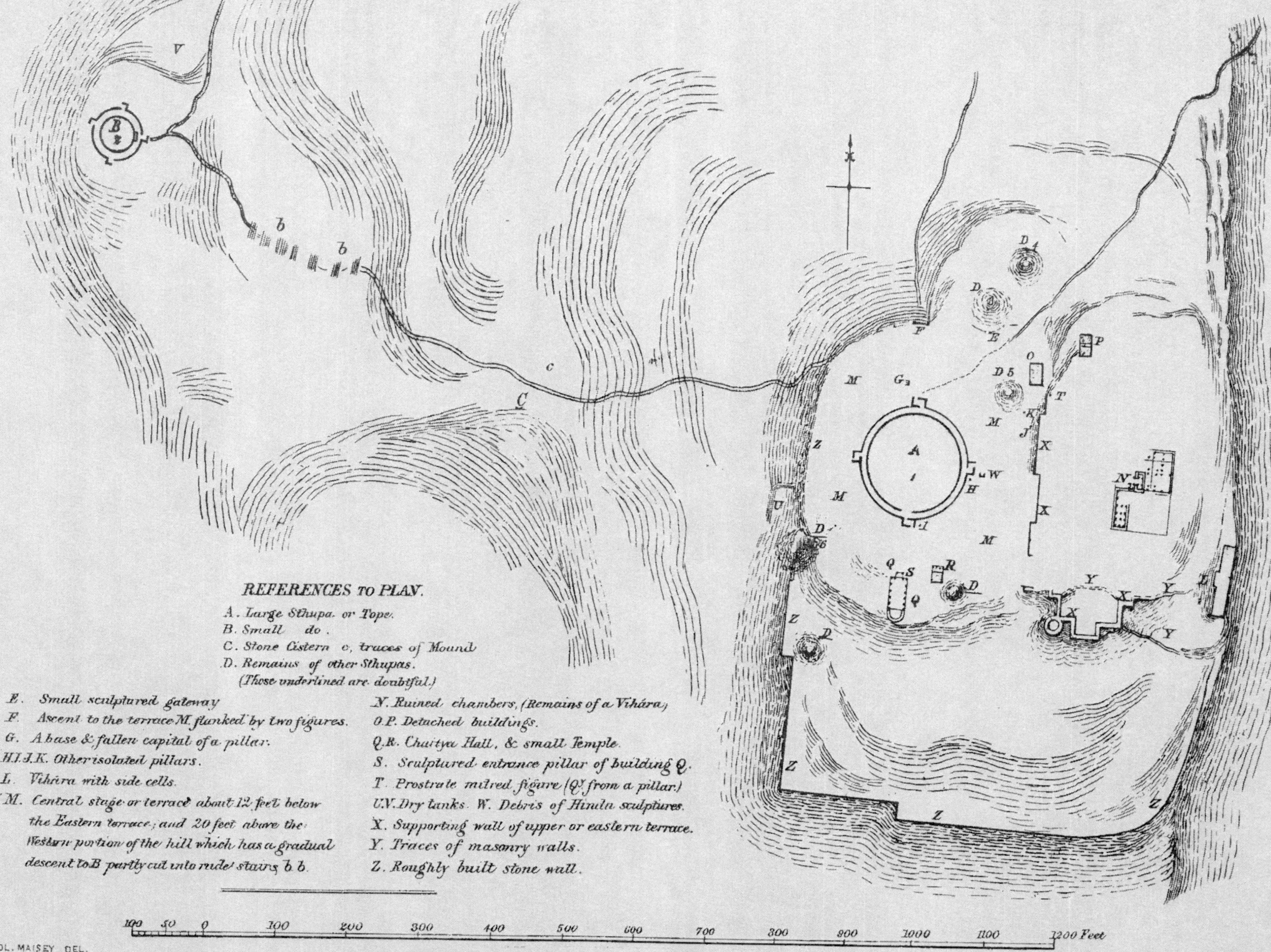

LT. COL. MAISEY DEL.

W. GRIGGS, LITH.

GROUND PLAN OF THE RUINS AT SANCHI.

SANCHI. PLATE II.

FIG. I.

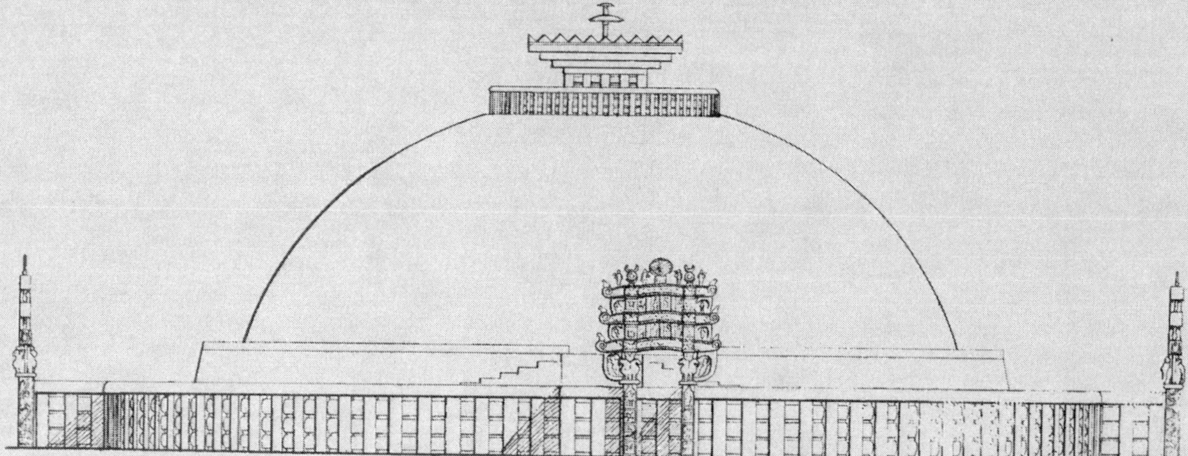

FIG. 2.

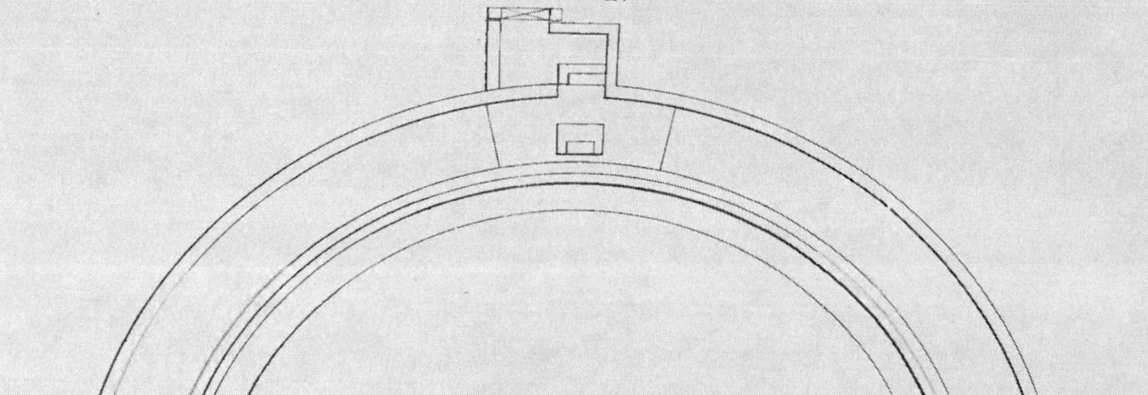

PLAN AND ELEVATION OF TOPE.

DESCRIPTION OF THE PLATES.

SANCHI TOPE.

FRONTISPIECE AND PLATES I. TO V.

THE frontispiece to the work is an elevation drawn to scale of the Northern Gateway of the great Tope, as seen from the inside. A photograph of the same subject will be found on Plate VII., and a comparison between the two is not only useful but interesting at starting, as it proves, in addition to their artistic merits, how exquisitely truthful Colonel Maisey's rendering is of these complicated subjects. Although reduced in scale to bring it within the size of the page, the drawing adds considerably to our knowledge of the bas-reliefs as reflected in the photograph. The elevation is also useful as showing the relative dimensions of the Gateway as compared with those of the Rail to which it was added.

Plates I., II., and III., have already been partially described. The first shows the relative position of all the monuments in the immediate neighbourhood of the great Tope at Sanchi, and includes all those which are referred to in the following pages. The other groups of Topes at Sonári, Satdhára, Bhojpur, and Andher, are described in detail by General Cunningham, in his work on the Bhilsa Topes; but as I possess no photographs or information regarding them beyond what is found in his work, they will not again be referred to in these pages. They are principally interesting in consequence of the relics which were found in the chambers in their interior, which throw considerable light on the history of Topes in general, and the purposes for which they were erected. They are, however, all smaller than those at Sanchi, and very inferior in richness of decoration, so that they add very little to our knowledge of the architecture of the Topes, or the mode in which they were ornamented. They are, besides this, in so ruinous a condition that photography would hardly be available for their illustration, and they possess no sculptured bas-reliefs of any description.

Plate II. contains a plan and elevation of the great Tope restored by Lieutenant-Colonel Maisey, from the fragments found by him on the spot. The details of their restoration and the measurements have already been given at page 96 et seq., and need not therefore be repeated here.

Plate III. contains various details in costume, &c., some of which have been referred to already, others will be noticed in the sequel.

Plates IV. and V. are complementary to Plate II., and represent the great Tope as photographed by Lieutenant Waterhouse from two slightly varied points of view. The first shows the North Gateway, nearly in front on the right hand, and a side view of the East Gateway on the left. In the foreground, but too much out of focus to enable its details to be distinguished, stand the ruins of the Gateway of the small Tope (No. 3), shown more in detail in Plate XXI., with which it will be described further on.

Plate V. represents the Tope with the Eastern Gateway, nearly in front, and the North Gate is seen sideways on the right hand. Between the two is seen the Rail, which is nearly perfect throughout this quadrant, and enables us to judge of its relative importance as compared with the Tope itself. The berm or platform from which the dome springs, is also distinctly visible in both these photographs.

In neither view is it possible to distinguish any remains of the stucco which once covered the whole of the dome. Fragments of it are still found lying about, sufficient to show that its thickness was about four inches; but there is nothing to enable us to determine whether it was painted, or whether it was covered with ornaments in relief, as there is every reason to believe was the case at Amravati. From such representations of Topes as are found among the sculptures at Sanchi, the inference would rather seem to be that the surface was plain, but that on great festival occasions it was adorned with wreaths and garlands hung on pegs, and it may also have been adorned with tapestries or painted cloths, but so far as can now be seen, not by any permanent decorations.

The Tee and its enclosures have been thrown down, though some fragments of them are still seen lying on the surface of the mound,—quite sufficient, apparently to justify its restoration, as shown in Plate II. Even, however, if no fragments remained, there could be no doubt but that a Tee once adorned the summit of the monument, and that it must have been very similar to the one here represented. It is probably quite correct to assert that no Dagoba ever was erected without this indispensable adjunct, and from the numerous representations we have of it, both at Sanchi and Amravati, and in other places, we can have little doubt as to its general appearance. Its dimensions are given by the diameter of the platform on the top, irrespective of other evidence.

SANCHI. PLATE III.

FIG. 1.

FIG. 2.

FIG. 3.

FIG. 4.

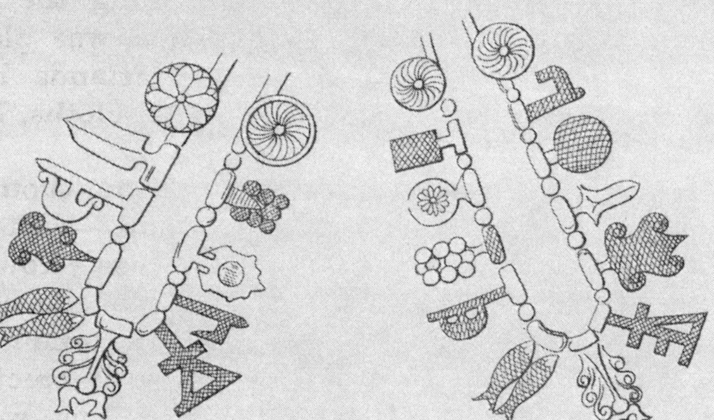

FIG. 5.

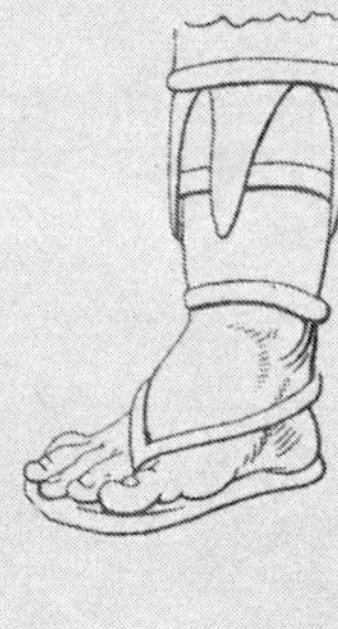

FIG. 7.

FIG. 6.

FIG. 8.

DETAILS FROM SCULPTURES

SANCHI. PLATE VI.

NORTHERN VIEW OF TOPE.

SANCHI. PLATE V.

EASTERN VIEW OF TOPE.

SANCHI. PLATE VI.

RUINS OF SOUTHERN GATEWAY.

SOUTHERN GATEWAY,
FRONT ELEVATION.

W. Griggs, Photo-Lith.

SCALE OF FEET.

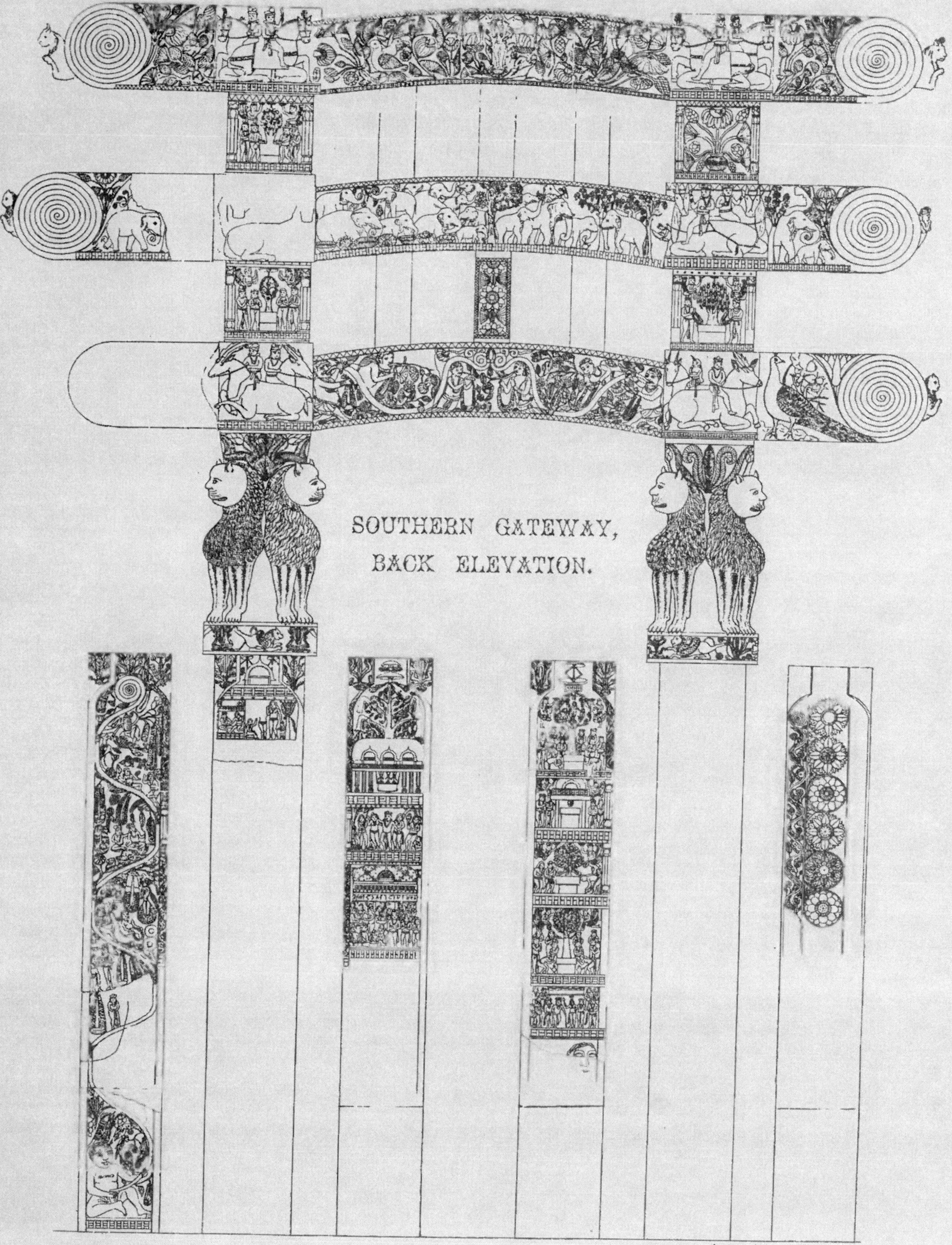

W Griggs Photo-Lith

FRONT VIEW OF NORTHERN GATEWAY.

REAR VIEW OF NORTHERN GATEWAY.

PLATES VI., VII., AND VIII.

SOUTHERN GATEWAY.

FOR the reasons above given, page 101, there seems no reason for doubting that the Southern is the first Gateway that was added to the rail at Sanchi, and consequently the one with which our descriptions should commence.

When Captain Fell visited the place in 1819, it was then entirely prostrate and lying on the ground apparently in the exact position in which it was photographed by Lieut. Waterhouse, as shown in Plate VI. The upper beam is that represented lying in front with the Śâtakarṇi inscription on the central dagoba. The two other beams, with fragments of the Lion capitals, are strewn on the ground behind this, and among them the Lion capital of the Lât, probably of the age of Aśoka,[1] from which the capitals of the Gateway seem to be copies. Behind these is seen the rail itself which is tolerably perfect in this part; and behind that again the masonry of the Tope.

The two lithographs, Plates VII. and VIII., which are reduced copies of Lieut. Cole's drawings, explain the arrangement of the subjects, and their general appearance with singular clearness. The top rail is that shown in the photograph just described, and represents the alternate worship of Dagobas and Trees, with two sacred or Royal Horses on the two wing blocks. On the middle beam is represented the worship of a Dagoba, first by flying figures,[2] and on the right hand by a Râja in a chariot with all his suite behind him; on the left hand by a Nâga people, four men having five-headed snake hoods, and all the women having single-headed snakes at their backs.

On the lower beam is the siege and bringing home of the relics; represented more in detail, Plate XXXVIII., Fig. 1.

On the left-hand pillar we have the worship of the Wheel by people in the ordinary costume of Hindus; and below that two processional scenes. On the right-hand pillar two representations of Tree Worship, both with the usual angels and flying figures, but the upper and more important by a Nâga Râja and his women, the lower by laymen. This distinction in the juxtaposition of the Nâga people with their snake hoods and the Hindus, whoever they were, who had not this adjunct, is curious

---

[1] It is represented more in detail, Plate XXXIX., Fig. 1.

[2] Both General Cunningham and Colonel Maisey call these figures Kinnaras. If I am rightly informed, however, that term is properly applied only to a flying figure with a horse's head. Garuḍa is probably the correct name to apply to them. There is danger, if this name is used, that these Buddhist figures may be confounded with the Garuḍa of the Mahâbhârata, the celebrated son of Vinatâ, and the dreaded enemy of all the Nâga race. Perhaps Devas might be used. These are the first of the Buddhist hierarchy, and at least in one instance are represented as acting as here shown. "When Bosat was about to arrive at that place—" the Bo-tree at Buddh Gya—all the Dévas of the world of forms first hung on the Tree silken banners and " streamers."—See J. R. A. S., XX. p. 157. But on the whole I am inclined to believe that Garuḍa is the term that would be employed by a Buddhist, and, this being the case, it is generally applied here.

and interesting, and one we will find runs throughout the sculptures both here and at Amravati. When we have gone through the whole we shall be in a better position to point out who each were, but even then it will require more local ethnological knowledge than we now possess before we can speak on the subject with certainty.

On the back of the Gateway, the upper beam is occupied by lotus flowers, in the centre of which stands the goddess Śrî or Devî with her two Elephants pouring water over her head. The same figure, but without the Elephants, occurs in one of the blocks in the front of this Gateway, between the upper and second beams, and occurs at least ten times on these Gateways. If we might trust the representations in such works as Moor's Pantheon, we should without hesitation pronounce this lotus-lady to be Devî the consort of Śiva. The various figures of that deity given in Plates 30 to 39 of that work (*see* Woodcut, page 108), are so nearly identical with what we find at Sanchi, that there could be little doubt about the matter. The principal difference being that the modern Devi, like most Hindu deities, has four arms instead of two; in other respects they are the same. But then comes the question, are these images rightly named? In the Vishṇu Purâṇa we find the following passage: "Then "seated on a full blown lotus and holding a water-lily in her hand, the goddess "Śrî, radiant with beauty, rose from the waves, Gangâ and other holy streams attended "for her ablutions, and the Elephants of the skies, taking up these pure waters in "vases of gold poured them over the goddess, the queen of the universal world. "Thus bathed, attired, and adorned, the goddess in the view of the celestials cast "herself on the breast of Hari."[1]

It is so extremely improbable that there should be any connexion, direct or indirect, between the Buddhist religion and that of Śiva, and on the contrary, so very probable that forms known afterwards as parts of that of Vishṇu should be found in early Buddhist sculptures, that I have no doubt but that the Paurâṇic description is the one on which and which alone reliance must be placed.

On the middle beam we have one of those curious travesties of human worship by animals so common in these sculptures. On the left a Royal Elephant with the chatta and chowrie borne over him, and preceded by his family brings offerings to the sacred Tree; on the left he goes to meet a humbler individual of his race, while one of the younger members bears the spouted pot with which we will afterwards become familiar as indispensable on state occasions.

On the inside of the pillars we have, on the left hand, a scene represented on a larger scale Plate XXX., and on the right hand, three forms of Tree Worship. The lower beam and the outside ornaments of the two pillars are graceful examples of the conventional decorations which are frequent at Sanchi, as everywhere else in Indian art, mixed, in this instance, as in other sculptures at Sanchi, with scenes of amorous dalliance we hardly expect to find on Buddhist monuments.[2]

---

1 Wilson's Vishṇu Purâṇa, 9th edition, p. 76.

2 If I had a voice in the matter I would have recommended that this, or portions of this gateway, should have been cast instead of the East Gateway, which was selected by Mr. Cole; besides its artistic interest, being on the ground, it would have cost less, and the same money would have covered also selections from the other gateways. As it is ruined, and never will be replaced on the spot, might not some fragments of it be brought home?

SANCHI. PLATE XA.

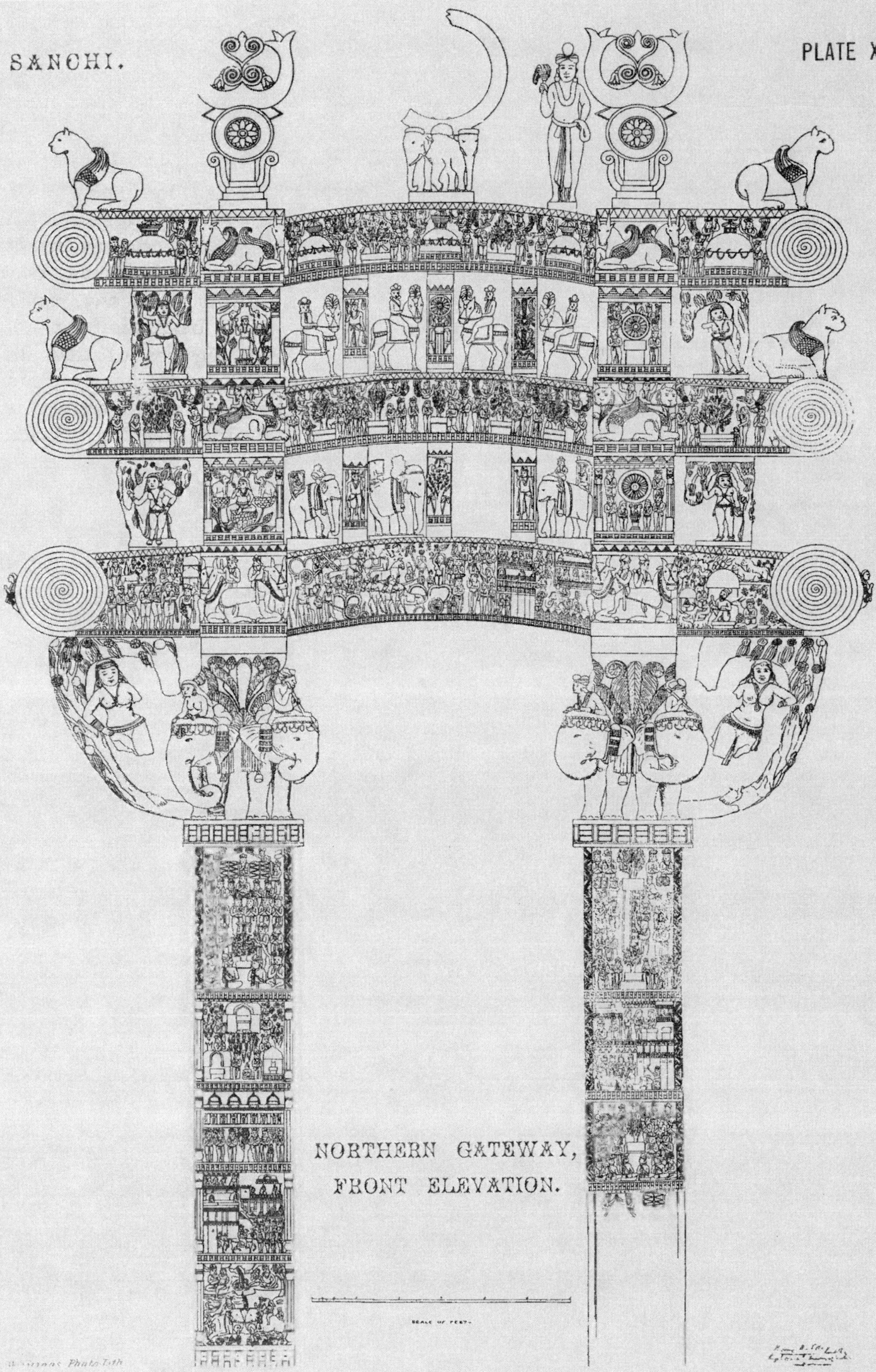

NORTHERN GATEWAY,
FRONT ELEVATION.

FRONTISPIECE AND PLATES IX., X., XA., XI., AND XII.

NORTHERN GATEWAY.

THESE six plates are probably sufficient to convey a clear idea of this, which is not only the most complete, but the largest and grandest of the Sanchi Gateways.[1] Its front, IX. and XA., is the only one that retains in its summit a fragment of the wheel, which once probably surmounted them all in the centre, and its two trisul ornaments.

The upper beam in the front is devoted to alternate Dagoba and Tree Worship. There being five Dagobas and two Trees, each with the flying figures and men in attitudes of worship. The middle beam is devoted to the worship of seven Trees, each of a different species, though what these are has not yet been determined. The lower beam is wholly occupied both in front and rear by the story of the Wassantara Jâtaka, which will be more fully dealt with when describing Plate XXXII., and need not, therefore, be enlarged on here; and there is nothing novel in the two intermediate blocks containing representations of the goddess Śrî, nor of those with the Wheel. But the great brackets which support the outer ends of the lower beam[2] —the horses, men, and elephants in the intermediate panels, the minor female brackets, the winged lions and the tall standing figures on the upper beam—are now found only on this gateway, though probably they were intended, or may indeed have existed on all the others.

On the back of the gateway (Plate X. and Frontispiece) we find, on the upper beam, elephants approaching and bringing offerings to the sacred Tree,—this time apparently a Pepul (Ficus religiosa).

On the middle beam, a scene which it is not very easy to interpret. Mr. Beal considers it the temptation of Buddha "by the ghoulish army of Mâra."[3] I am, I confess, much more inclined to look upon it as a concluding part of the Wassantara Jâtaka. On the left is a sacred tree with its garlands and flying guardians, and below it two children and their parents. The same, or probably the other two children of the Jâtaka, also appear; and next, and lastly, the king seated on his throne with the royal umbrella over his head, but without any emblem of Buddhahood, and to his left a group of grinning figures which I take to represent a masque. Nothing the least like either temptation or an attack appears among them. Some are playing on musical instruments, and all are gaping about them and grinning in a manner that may have been thought very comic in the first century, though it may hardly appear to us in that light now.

On the blocks between the beams in front we find on the left two representations of Śrî, one standing, one seated on a lotus; and on the right two wheels, one on an

---

[1] If only one gateway was to be cast this is undoubtedly the one that ought to have been selected.

[2] One of these figures is represented in Plate III., Fig. 1.

[3] J. R. A. S., N. S., V. p. 177.

altar, one on a Stâmba. On the rear two lotuses in pots, and below another representation of Śrî, and opposite her a Dagoba with the usual accompaniments of worship, and below the capitals, a Dagoba and a Tree being worshipped in like manner.

All the bassi-relievi on the pillars of this gateway have been drawn by Colonel Maisey and are reproduced from his drawings in the lithographs further on, where they will be described as they occur. Their positions relatively to one another will easily be recognized from the elevation and the photographs.

No. 17.

Ornament on outside of left-hand pillar of Northern Gateway.

No. 18.

Ornament on outside of right-hand pillar.

The outside faces of the pillars, which are richer and more elaborate then any other of the series, are reproduced in the annexed two woodcuts. That on the left hand represents the Trisul ornament with its circle below it, supported by a pillar on each side of which are keys or hooks from which garlands or wreaths and emblems are dependent. Two of the last are represented, Plate III., Fig. 4, and many of them will be easily recognized, others require identification by Buddhist authorities, familiar with such symbols at the present day. At the bottom of all an impression of the sacred feet of Buddha.

The other face is more purely ornamental and has less of a religious or emblematic character. The outside is foliage with birds interspersed, and in the centre a conventional tree with groups of figures, two and two, alternately male and female, bearing offerings. In beauty of design these will bear comparison with almost anything of their class, not excepting those of the wonderful loggie of the Vatican, though their execution may fall short of what we see there.[1]

On the top of each of the pillars of this Gateway is an emblem which, in order to avoid hypothesis, I have, throughout this work, styled the Trisul or Trident ornament, and which also occurs, as just mentioned, on the outside of one of the pillars. It apparently occupied a similar position on the summits of all the four gateways, though only now found on the two standing ones.

Between these Trisul ornaments on this Gateway will be observed the fragment of what was once a complete circle representing the Wheel so common on the bas-reliefs of this and the other Gateways.

The question what these emblems were intended to represent is by no means satisfactorily settled. General Cunningham seems to consider the Trisul as representing Dharma or the law;[2] the second object in the Buddhist Triad,—Buddha, Dharma,

---

[1] Both these designs are seen but much less perfectly in the photographs Plates XI. and XII.

[2] Bhilsa Topes, p. 335, ét seqq.

PILLARS OF NORTHERN GATEWAY.

PILLARS OF NORTHERN GATEWAY.

Sanga,[1]—so often repeated, and in which the third term signifies the congregation. If any of the three represented Dharma or the law, it surely, however, ought to be the Wheel. There is no expression so frequent in the lives of Buddha as that representing him as turning the Wheel of the Law; and the Wheel of the Law is so often mentioned as almost to justify us without going further in assuming that the wheels so frequently seen in the sculptures really symbolize the Law.

If so the congregation of the faithful if represented at all, can only be by trees, whose multitude of leaves would be no bad representation of that many-headed entity; and, again, if this should prove to be the case, the Trisul would be the emblem of Buddha himself. Just as the cross is placed on the altar of the Christian churches, on the gables, and everywhere about the building, to signify Christ or Christianity, so this emblem may have been used to signify the founder of the religion at a time when personal representations of him were not known. So far as we at present know no representation of Buddha as an object of worship is found at Sanchi, and very little that would indicate that it was a Buddhist monument, except these emblems; but they are so frequent and so prominent that they must have some very important meaning to the initiated. Besides, however, the appearance of the Trisul ornament on the Gateways it is seen on the standards and arms of the soldiers everywhere. It is found on all or nearly all the old Buddhist coins, and generally may be said to be one of the most favourite emblems of the age. Yet it must be remarked it is never worshipped, as the Wheel emblem is, nor as the Tree or Dagoba are. As an object of worship, it is certainly inferior to those; as an ornament, it occurs more frequently and nearly as prominently.

Perhaps the key to the mystery may, however, probably be found in the annexed diagram from one of the notes by Rémusat on the travels of Fa-Hian.[2] This emblem is also found in China and Thibet, inscribed with Sanskrit letters, which serve further to designate the parts. Thus the lowest marked "a" means the earth; the circle "va" represents water; the triangle "ra" fire; the crescent "ka" stands for the wind; and the cone marked "kha" for ether. General Cunningham,[3] by a different process, makes out that it is compounded of the old Pali letters, meaning the same thing; though in this case it is not quite clear whether the emblem was derived from the letters, or the letters from the emblem.[4] But this is of little consequence, as by any of these processes we arrive at the same conclusion that the Trisul ornament represents the five elements or the material universe.[5]

No. 19.

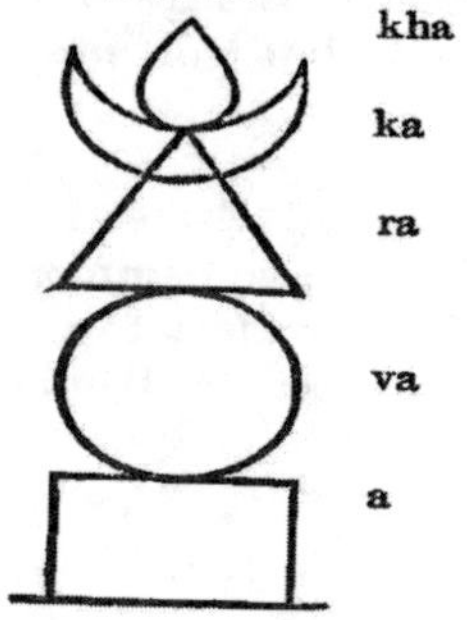

---

[1] See Bhabra inscription. Appendix C.

[2] Foĕ-Kouĕ-Ki, p. 92.

[3] Bhilsa Topes, p. 355.

[4] In the Foĕ-Kouĕ-Ki there is a curious story (chap. xx.) of a king—Prasenajit—"who having a strong "desire to see Buddha, who was then absent in heaven, caused a head of an ox to be sculptured in sandal wood, "in such a manner as to represent the image of Foĕ, and placed it where he had sat." In this form the legend is quite unintelligible; but may not this emblem have been called "the Ox-head emblem" from its similarity to that animal's head, and hence the confusion of ideas?

[5] Mr. Beal's explanation of this diagram (J. R. A. S.; N. S., V. 164) "péche par la base" as the base of the Sanchi Tope is not square, but circular.

Another version of it is given in the Buddh-Gayâ Rail (Woodcut 20), where it looks like a combination of two letters; not exactly the "Mun or Holy" of General Cunningham,[1] but so like it that it seems almost undoubtedly to be made up from some old Pali letters, and, if an epithet of Buddha, would give it all the meaning its position seems to require.[2] One point that seems to give it this meaning more distinctly than anything else here, is its position on the outside of the left-hand pillar of this Gateway, as shown in woodcut No. 17, page 114. It there appears as the head of a pillar composed of Buddhist emblems, rising from the sacred feet, which for reasons to be given hereafter, seem always to indicate the presence of Buddha. The same combination occurs frequently at Amravati[3] with variations, however, as to the intermediate parts, and both there and here would seem to indicate the implied presence of Buddha. There the saint is frequently represented in person, but as at Sanchi he only appears as an historical person, there must have been some emblem by which his presence could be indicated, and this seems to me the only one that will bear that meaning.

No. 20.

Trisul Ornament from Rail at Buddh-Gayâ.

It seems, however, comparatively useless that Europeans should speculate on such subjects, just as a Chinese Buddhist who was ignorant of Christian history might waste his lifetime on trying to find out how the Cross came to represent the founder of our religion, so we may possibly grope for ever in the dark trying to discover a meaning in these symbols which probably any of the initiated could explain to us in a few words.[4]

---

1 Bhilsa Topes, p. 333.

No. 21.

2 It is curiously like the sign of the planet Mercury, or the caduceus of the God of that name; and, if it were not rank heresy even to hint at such a thing, I would venture to suggest that, after all, there may be some connexion between at least the symbolism of the East and West, and that this may extend, in a remote degree, perhaps, to the personages indicated.

3 Plates LXX., LXXI., LXXII., and elsewhere.

4 The Swastica does not, so far as I know, appear at Sanchi, though so common at Amravati, and also so far as we can judge of their age, in the contemporary caves in the Western Ghâts and in Cuttack. Though so common both in India and in Europe in the early centuries of Christianity, its meaning has never yet been satisfactorily explained. Burnouf in the "Lotus de la bonne Loi" merely translates it "signe de benediction ou de bonne augure."

FRONT VIEW OF EASTERN GATEWAY.

REAR VIEW OF EASTERN GATEWAY.

SANCHI. PLATE XV.

2

3

4

SCULPTURES ON EASTERN GATEWAY.

PILLARS OF EASTERN GATEWAY.

PLATES XIII., XIV., XV., XVI.[1]

Eastern Gateway.

If the sequence established above (p. 101) is correct, the eastern is the third gateway that was added to the Sanchi Rail in the first century of our era, and though neither the most perfect nor the most beautiful, it is still full of interest.

The top beam in front is devoted to alternate Tree and Dagoba Worship, five of the latter and two of the former being honoured by equal ceremonies. On the next beam, the upper one, in Plate XV., a procession in which two led horses appear as the principal objects, leaves the city or palace, whose architecture is curiously detailed, and passing under a gateway with a single beam approaches a sacred Tree. Beyond this the same, or two other horses, with the royal umbrella over them, approach the sacred feet of Buddha, which seems in this instance to be the principal object of worship, or one at least as coëqual with the Tree that occupies the centre.

On the lower beam,—the second one in Plate XV.,—the case is different; there the Tree—apparently the Ficus religiosa—is undoubtedly the principal object of worship. It is approached on the left by ten adults and two children bearing offerings. They are accompanied by four men bearing standards with streamers and surmounted by emblems, and behind them a band of twelve musicians playing on conches, fifes, drums, and other instruments so frequently met with in these sculptures. On the other side a prince, in the ordinary costume of the Hindus, descends from his elephant and is being led by his son toward the sacred Tree. Behind him is his chariot drawn by two horses, and around him, are all the insignia of rank and all the accompaniments of Eastern state.

On the blocks between the beams are two representations of the goddess Śrî, in both instances seated on a lotus, and with her two elephants pouring water over her. On the other two are a sacred Tree and a Wheel emblem.

The back of this gateway is one of the most remarkable illustrations of the deification of animal nature that occurs in these sculptures. The top beam is wholly occupied by sacred Trees. Seven of these are represented as standing each behind its altar, and honoured by men and flying figures, and each of a different species.

The central beam,—the third in Plate XV.,—is devoted to what is intended to be a representation of all the animal creation coming to do honour to the sacred Tree. Among them we easily recognize lions, buffalos, deer, and pigeons, as correctly represented as the ability of the artist admitted; but besides these we have a gigantic

[1] The Eastern Gateway being the one selected for casting, no drawings of its sculptures were made by Lieut. Cole's native assistants. We have consequently no lithographic elevation of it, as of the other four. The following account is compiled from the casts themselves and from photographs made from these casts after their arrival in this country.

bird that looks like a Dodo. We have sheep with human faces, and lions with dog's heads and eagle's beaks, and last, not least, we have the great five-headed Nâga coming himself to do honour to the sacred Tree.

The lower beam,—the lowest in Plate XV.,—is devoted to a singular, though not so unexpected a representation of the devotion of animal nature. It is wholly occupied by elephants bringing offerings and performing worship to the sacred Dagoba which occupies the centre. In Hiouen-Thsang's travels we have a description of precisely such a scene as this. He relates that a party of Bhikshus or priests who went to visit the Râma Grâma Stûpa, saw a troup of elephants going and coming. Some, mowed the grass with their teeth, others watered the place with their trunks. All brought rare flowers, and all together rendered homage to the Stûpa.[1] It by no means follows that the Dagoba here represented is that at Râma Grâma, but the action is the same, and may have been traditionally related of fifty other places.

The sculptures on the pillars of the Gateway were all drawn by Colonel Maisey, and will be found described further on when speaking of the lithographs made from his drawings. The one thing he has not drawn is the outer face of the right-hand pillar (Plate XVI.). This represents a building in seven storeys, or rather perhaps four buildings, three of which are two storeys each, the lower storey having pillars architecturally very like those at Kârlâ and in the early Western Caves; the upper finishing with a roof. Each storey is divided laterally into three compartments, in the right hand one of which is a band of six female musicians playing on harps, tomtoms, and other familiar instruments; and in the two other compartments two kings, each seated under umbrellas of state and with six female attendants. Though this is repeated twelve times over, there seems nothing to enable us to discriminate between the one and the other, or to say whether twelve, or six, or two kings are intended to be represented. In the upper compartment of all they are represented as drinking together. In the lowest there are some variations that might help us, but the sculpture is so much defaced that it is impossible to feel sure what they really amount to.

The conventional ornaments, which in this as in all the other Gateways, form the external ornaments to the pillars, are bolder, but it must be added, coarser than those of either of the gateways described above, and show certainly a progress, perhaps it may be called a decadence of style.[2]

---

[1] Vie et Voyages par Hoeï-li, p. 128. Si-Yü-Ki, I. 325.

[2] When in 1847 I published my work entitled "Picturesque Illustrations of Indian Architecture," I engraved a view of this Gateway as the frontispiece from a drawing in the possession of the Royal Asiatic Society. I never learnt by whom that drawing was made, but, from some circumstances, I fancy it must have been taken about 1830. At that time both the Trisul ornaments on the top were standing and the pedestal for the Wheel in the centre, besides many other details which have since disappeared. The Gateways have suffered more during the forty years that have elapsed since they were discovered by the English than they did during the previous eighteen centuries!

SANCHI. PLATE XVII.

RUINS OF WESTERN GATEWAY.

SANCHI.

PLATE XVIII.

WESTERN GATEWAY,
FRONT ELEVATION.

W. Griggs, Photo Lith.

SANCHI. PLATE XIX.

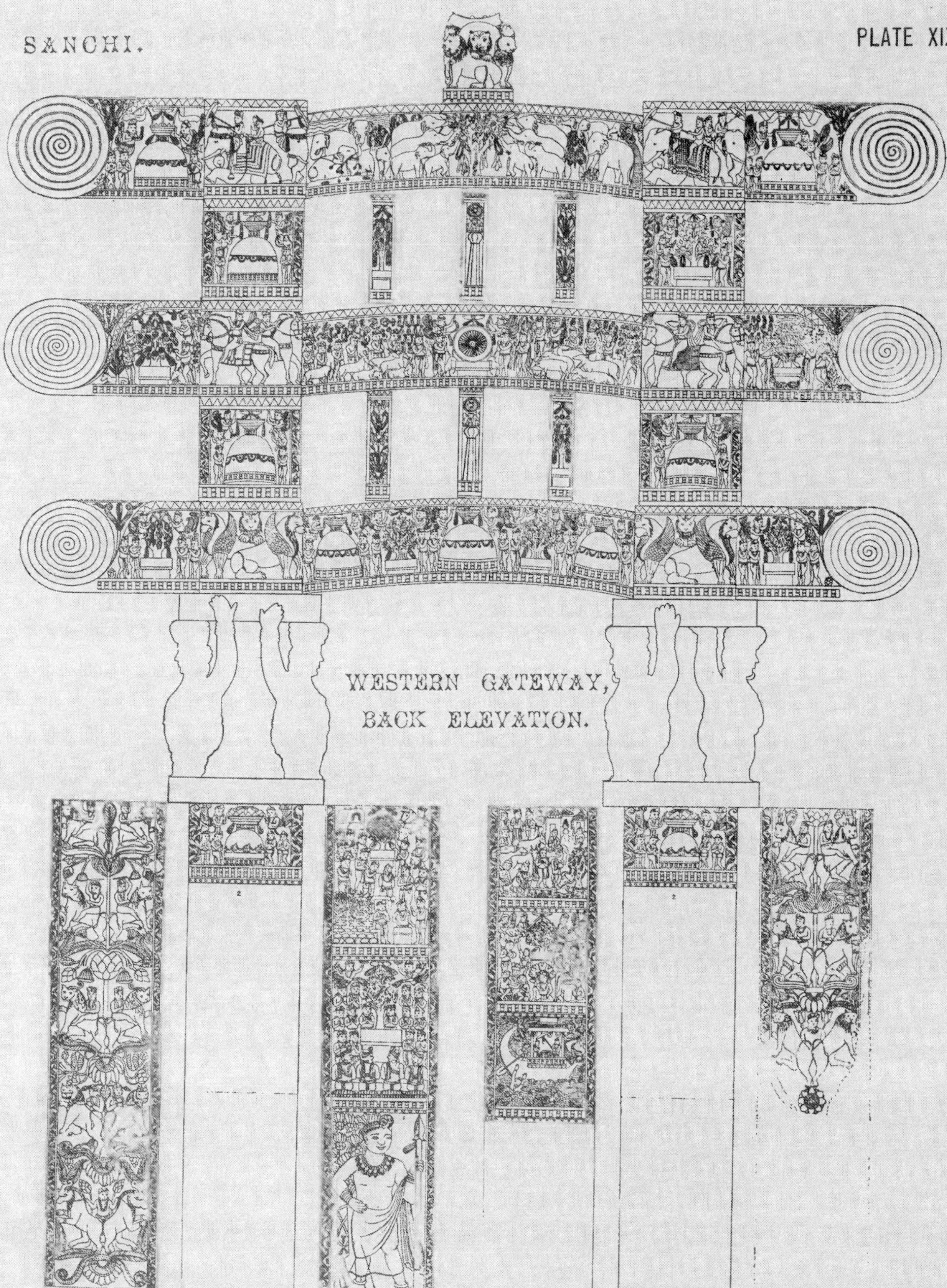

WESTERN GATEWAY,
BACK ELEVATION.

W. Griggs Photo-Lith

PLATES XVII., XVIII. AND XIX.

WESTERN GATEWAY.

THE more it is looked on the more evident it becomes that the western is the last gateway added to the Sanchi Tope. There is a progress in its sculptures, and more so in its decorative details that takes us nearer to the Amravati Tope than any of the others.

The scene represented on the top rail in front is one to which it is difficult to give a name, though it occurs again at Amravati (Plate LVIII. and possibly LXVI.). In the centre is the sacred Tree in its temple and behind its altar. On the left a procession advances towards it with banners and musical instruments, but without arms. On the right an armed host fly in the utmost confusion, elephants, chariots, and horsemen, mixed together, and treading on the fallen and wounded. That it means to represent the destruction of those who on some occasion attempted the desecration of the sacred Tree hardly admits of doubt, but what tree and what occasion is not so clear. Hiouen-Thsang tells us that "the Brahmans and the heretics "attempted over and over again to destroy the tree that grew from the toothpick "which Buddha threw in the ground,"[1] but that it flourished nevertheless to this day. It may be this or some other famous attempt to destroy a sacred Tree which was defeated by the prayers of the faithful which is here recorded, but only a Buddhist can say which.

The right-hand extensions and the centre of the intermediate rail are wholly occupied by a triumphal procession approaching the city gates which it enters to the left, and beyond this on the left-hand extension is the garden palace of the king, evidently outside the city walls. The king himself is represented sitting, with his legs down, on a very solid chair or throne, beneath which is the spouted pot which is so invariably an accompaniment of royalty. In front is the queen seated on a morah; behind her an attendant is pouring wine into her cup, and the harem with its inhabitants finishes the picture.

The lower beam looks like a continuation of the same procession, but here we have a distinct motive for the action. The principal figure in the centre mounted on an elephant bears a relic-casket on his head, and either he, or more probably it, is treated with royal honours. He approaches a sacred Tree with its altar, and the procession enters what may be a temple.

If the two represent the same action the upper beam represents the victorious army returning to the presence of the king. The lower the same army depositing its precious casket in the temple, and it is possible that both may refer to the event commemorated on the front of the South Gateway (p. 111, and in describing

[1] Hoeï-li, p. 123. Si-Yü-Ki, I. p. 292.

Plate XXXVIII. Fig. 1), where a siege is undertaken, and successfully, for the recovery of some relics. As, however, there is nothing warlike in those that take part in the second display, they may refer to different events. With our very limited knowledge of Buddhist history before the Christian era, it is impossible now to give either a name or date to the event here depicted.

The back of this gateway is as usual devoted more to religious observances. The centre of the upper beam is devoted to elephants bringing offerings, and hanging garlands on a sacred Tree, and seems almost like a continuation of the scene on the lowest beam of the Eastern Gateway, but this time it is even more impossible to say what the tree is which is here represented.

On the extensions are two Dagobas, but this time with human and heavenly worshippers, no animals being present.

On the central beam the Wheel is the object of adoration by a mixed company of men and deer in addition to the usual flying figures; and on the extensions two trees are honoured in the usual manner.

The lower beam is devoted to the alternate worship of Trees and Dagobas, four of the former and three of the latter, but without anything to distinguish them from the numerous representations of the same subjects mentioned above.

On the blocks between the beams in front, we find two trees and one wheel honoured as usual, and one representation of the lotus-goddess Śrî with the two elephants pouring water over her; and on the back three Dagobas and one Tree with the usual accompaniments.

As all the bassi-relievi on the pillars of this gateway were drawn by Colonel Maisey, and are represented in the lithographs further on, they will be described in succession as they occur. But the two external faces, which like all the others are conventionally ornamented, are interesting, first, because like the dwarf capitals they differ from the three other gateways, but more because they have a strong affinity to a class of ornament we find currently at Amravati two or three centuries later. There is of course a considerable difference between the ornamentation of the outside of the pillars shown in Plate XIX. and that exhibited in Plates LXXV., LXXXVIII., and XCVIII., further on, but it is just such a difference as we should expect three centuries to produce, and is so far confirmatory of the supposition that this was the last and the nearest to Amravati of the Sanchi gateways.

This gateway fell only a few years ago in consequence, apparently, of the clumsy digging into the tope of some nameless amateurs, who overwhelmed it with the rubbish they threw down from the tope itself.

SANCHI.

PLATE XX.

GATEWAY. SMALL TOPE.

GATEWAY OF SMALL TOPE,
FRONT ELEVATION.

PLATES XX. AND XXI.

Gateway of Small Tope.

Though very much smaller, this gateway is almost of equal interest with those of the Great Tope. It is situated on the south side of the mound, to which it is attached, which is a further confirmation of the idea that the southern is the oldest of those belonging to the Great Tope. From the similarity of its style, and especially of the capitals of its pillars, it probably is of the same age as the western or most modern of those of the Great Tope. It being so, however, by no means involves a similar date for the Tope itself. It may originally have had a wooden gate, and so, in fact, may the Great Tope, till these were replaced by the erection, we now find. Or it may be that originally the Tope had no such ornaments, though I think this unlikely, and cannot believe that the stone gateways are really the first examples of this class of ornament.

The subjects of the sculptures do not differ materially from those of its great rival. On the top beam we have three trees, the centre one a pepul, the other two of a kind very frequently repeated, but which it is difficult to name. There is the royal chatta over them, and garlands hung on their branches, but no flying figures, and the men with joined hands, instead of turning towards the object to be adored, look straight to the front; this is a peculiarity, however, of all the figures on the gateway which distinguishes it from the others.

On the intermediate beam the central tree is replaced by a Dagoba, with the usual flying figures, and the women are worshipping and bringing offerings. On the lowest beam is one of those scenes which may be historical, but to which we cannot yet give a name. In the centre is a pavilion situated in the forest, beneath whose roof is a seated figure, apparently addressing a congregation. This may possibly be either Sariputra or Mogalana, whose relics the Tope contains; or it may be the Tathâgata himself. I am myself very much inclined to the latter idea. The two flying figures above indicate the presence of some person of more than usual importance, but he has none of the insignia of royalty about him, and must consequently be considered as a private individual, important only in Buddhist estimation. To this theory it may be objected that he has none of the characteristics by which Buddha is usually distinguished. It must, however, be borne in mind that in no instance at Sanchi do we find the curly head, the ascetic robe, or the cross-legged attitude with which we are familiar. This is the nearest approach to these things that we find either here or anywhere else at this age, but if, as I believe, this is the last gateway erected at Sanchi it may date in the beginning of the second century, and thus the approach to modern forms becomes more probable; still we must go on to Amravati, or at least one or two centuries in advance of Sanchi, before these things become usual and apparent. In the Caves at Ajanta even after that time there are scenes painted on the walls which are very similar to this, but at the same time so undoubtedly representing Buddha preaching, that it seems most probable that this represents the same subject. On either side of the central group there are two male figures with enormous five-headed snake hoods, each with two female attendants; and these are, no doubt, the persons who are being preached at by the figure in the centre.

On the blocks between the beams we have the usual figure of Śrî with her lotuses and elephants; both on back and front, two dagobas, two wheels, and one tree.

The sculptures on the backs of the beams are without historical interest; they are wreaths of flowers, principally lotuses, with figures of boys and animals intermixed. Some of these blocks are seen lying on the foreground, Plate XX., and are certainly remarkable for their elegance.

On the pillars are three trees, two wheels, and one dagoba honoured as they usually are, but, as is invariably the case on this gateway, with the men standing looking to the front.

One curious nursery scene is portrayed on the outside of the right-hand pillar, but the drawing is too indistinct for much to be made of it. There are three children represented, but nothing that serves to identify them with any family we are acquainted with from these bassi-relievi. It is probably the family of the donor of the Gateway, or of the pillar on which it is sculptured, that is here introduced, as was so frequently done in mediæval pictures in Europe.

Colonel Maisey, in his MS. notes, describes the volutes of the lower beam as formed of snakes, and the portion over the pillars as men slaying monsters, half elephant half snake. The drawings made for Lieut. Cole do not, it must be confessed, quite bear out this description. They show, however, that the volutes are differently formed from any of the others, and more like snakes, while I am inclined to depend more for accuracy on the thoroughly educated eye of an artist like Colonel Maisey rather than that of the native draftsmen employed on the last expedition.

SANCHI, PLATE XXII.

CHAITYA HALL.

RUINS OF VIHARA.

PLATES XXII. AND XXIII.

CHAITYA AND VIHARA.

As before mentioned (p. 88), the ruins (marked Q in Plate .I.) are the only remains of a structural Chaitya Hall that have yet been discovered standing in India. But, judging from its style, it must be considerably more modern than any of the buildings just described. As will be seen from the plan, it consists of a nave with six pillars on each side, and measuring internally 29 feet north and south, by 19 feet 4 inches. Beyond this is a choir 27 feet by 19 feet, surrounded by a wall 4 feet thick, though at present only about 2 feet high; but the photograph reveals to us the fact that the last pillar was evidently built into a wall to its whole height. "In the centre," Colonel Maisey says, "of the curved end is a mass of débris "which seems to have been the remains of a Chaitya, or relic shrine, "such as is seen in the Buddhist Caves." "Round the exterior of "the circular part," he adds, "are traces of masonry at some distance."

No. 22.

PLAN OF CHAITYA HALL.
Scale, 30 ft. to 1 in.

There can be no doubt but that this is just such a hall as we meet so frequently at Kârlâ, Ajanta, and elsewhere. It must originally have had a wooden roof, of a form it would not be difficult to restore, and the general appearance of which may be judged of from the representation of one—probably, it must be confessed, of an older date,—already given, p. 88. Like the example represented in that woodcut, this one was surrounded by an aisle, but whether entirely free, or supported by wooden pillars, is not quite clear. The fact of its internal pillars being of stone and of the slender masonic shape shown in the photograph, proves it to be much more modern than the Cave at Kârlâ or the oldest at Ajanta, which it is nearly certain date from about or before the Christian era. These, though in the rock, retain in every feature their original wooden constructive form. Here, where wooden pillars would have been admissible, stone takes their place. This could hardly have happened before the fourth or fifth century. It may be more modern than even that date.

It would be extremely interesting, if it could be ascertained by excavations what the width and form of the outer aisle were in this example, as enabling us to understand what is now obscure in those cut in the rock. In all those the ornamental pillars extend on each side of the nave, as here, to nearly where the Dagoba stands—as we would express it, to the entrance of the choir. The apse is in all the older rock-cut examples surrounded by plain octagonal shafts without base or capitals, but why this should be so has hitherto always been a mystery. If, however, it was the custom, as in this instance, to enclose the choir by a solid wall in a structural Chaitya, it is evident that such a form could not be adopted in the rock, as in this case the circumambient aisle would thus have been absolutely dark. In structural examples the aisle could easily have been lighted from the exterior; indeed, it probably was an open colonnade. The plain pillars in the rock may thus have been intended to reproduce the solid wall of the structural example. Possibly that part was ornamented with frescoes in structural Chaityas, and may have been hung with tapestries on state and festival occasions in those excavated in the rock.

Vihara.

The photograph — Plate XXIII.— represents in like manner almost the only standing remains of one of the Vihâras or Monasteries which when Buddhism was flourishing, were to be found in every part of India. From its plan (marked L in Plate I.) and details it is, however, evidently much more modern than even the Chaitya hall last described. The central cell is a feature not found in the Caves before the sixth or seventh century, and this one has so Hindu-like an aspect that it is impossible not to suspect that it may be very modern. There were apparently only three cells on each side, one 12 feet by 8, the other two 8 feet square. These open into a verandah, at one end of which is a figure of Buddha seated crossed-legged and similar to another which occupies the central sanctuary. Colonel Maisey's drawing of the last of these is reproduced in Plate XLI. Its style would tend to the impression that it at least belongs to the latest date of Buddhist art in India. Four statues of Buddha, very similar in style and design to this one, stand within the Rail of the great Tope opposite to each of the four entrances. They are all, however, evidently so modern that they have no connexion whatever with the original design, and may have been added as late as the eighth or even the tenth century of our era.

No. 23.

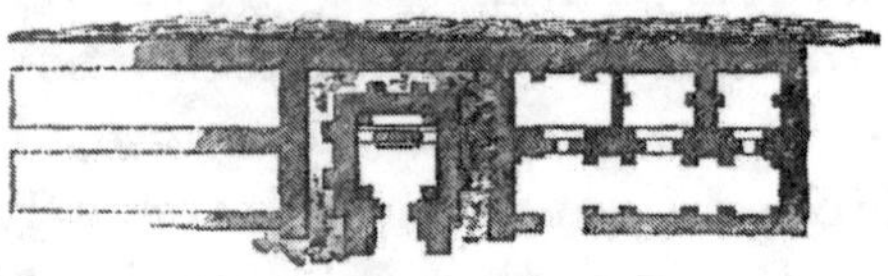

Vihara at Sanchi.
Scale, 50 feet to 1 inch.

The great Vihâra (marked N in Plate I.) seems to have been situated exactly opposite to the eastern entrance of the great Tope, but it is now so completely ruined that its plan can hardly be made out, and no details of architecture are standing from which its character or age could be determined. The spot, however, is interesting as this probably is the site of the Mahâ Chaitya, erected by Aśoka's Queen, and in which Mahindo resided (B.C. 250) before proceeding on his mission to Ceylon.[1]

[1] Vide ante, p. 99.

SANCHI.

PLATE XXIV.

FIG 1.

NAGAS

FIG 2.

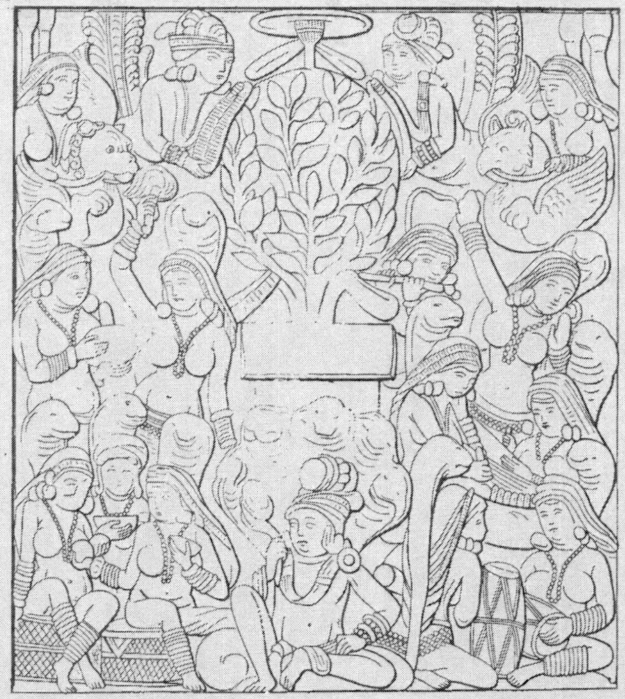

FIG 3.

Lt. COL MAISEY, DEL.

W. GRIGGS, LITH. INDIA MUSEUM

WASSANTARA, JATAKA.

PLATE XXIV.

THIS Plate is one of the most interesting of the whole series, and may in fact be considered as a key to all that follows. The upper relievi (Figs. 1 and 2) are representations of the same subject, but the first is from the southern or most ancient gateway, the other from the western is most modern,[1] and there may consequently be nearly a century between them. In both the sacred Tree occupies the place of honour, behind an altar, and with the royal chatta above it. On either side two celestial figures bear garlands to hang on its branches. In the right-hand figure two of these are mounted on griffins of a curiously Assyrian character.

In front of the altar is seated the Nâga Râja, with the great five-hooded snake behind his head. In the left-hand figure he is apparently accompanied by four of his wives, and one male and one female attendant. In the right-hand figure three of his wives on his right hand are eating and drinking, while one attendant bears a chowrie and the other holds the wine vessel in her hand. On his left six female musicians play on flutes, harps, and tomtoms, and all of these have a single-headed snake at the back of their heads.[2]

Who then were the people here represented, and what is the meaning of this strange symbolism? We will be in a better position to answer these questions when we are further advanced in the work; but it may in the meanwhile be remarked that it is not the Serpent that seems to be honoured in these pictures. The Tree occupies the place of honour and the Serpent looks more like the guardian angel, the protecting "numen" of the Râja and his people; but still, unless the Serpent were considered as a supreme and powerful being elsewhere, he would hardly be selected to perform the function he is here represented as fulfilling.

It is almost as difficult to determine whether these people are the all-powerful Nâgas who rule the clouds and bring rain and send tempests, and who dwelt in the bowels of the earth ten thousand fathoms deep, or whether they are only the chiefs of the Nâga Vansas, the royal races, who assumed the serpent as their symbol, and claimed descent from the demigod. In so far as the sculptures at Sanchi are concerned it seems that the latter is the more probable hypothesis. There is no example there of men worshipping the Serpent direct, nor, except in one instance (Plate XXXII.) of its being represented alone and not simply as an accompaniment of mankind. For the present, at least, it will be as well to consider these, and other similar representations we shall meet with further on, as mortals of the Nâga races accompanied by their protecting deity, but in other respects as coëqual with the other Râjas and people who figure in these bassi-relievi. Fig. 3 of this

---

[1] An allowance must be made for the difference of drawing. Fig. 2 is from Col. Maisey's exquisite pencil; Fig. 1 was drawn by Lieut. Cole's assistant, and though perfectly truthful is painfully inartistic.

[2] If anyone will observe the way the snake attaches itself to the back of the left-hand drummer girl, they will understand how the *two* snakes grew out of the shoulders of Zohák. Some such representation of him must have existed in the time of Firdúsi: hence the fable.

Plate is the most important bas-relief of the Sanchi series. It contains the concluding portions of the story of King Wassantara, which is the best known and most esteemed of all the Buddhist legends, and generally known as the "Almsgiving Jâtaka."[1]

This Jâtaka is translated at length by Spence Hardy in his Manual of Buddhism (p. 116, et seqq.). A précis of it is also given by Mr. Beal in the Journal of the Royal Asiatic Society (N. S., Vol. V., p. 170), and as this is sufficiently clear and distinct for our purpose, it is given here at length :—

"In former times, in a city called Jayaturá, reigned a king called Sanda or Sanja; his principal queen was called Phusatí, and their son was called Wessantara, so named from the street in which his mother was passing at the time of his birth. [There is a very curious similarity between this name and Wessanagara, the old Besnagar, close to Sânchi; vide ante, p. 99.] From the moment he could speak he gave proof that his disposition was most charitable. [Compare the Chinese Shen-chi, 'the charitable one' (Song-yun, p. 194).] When arrived at the proper age he married Madrí-déwí, the daughter of the King of Chetiya. [Compare, again, the singular coincidence in the account of Mahânâma : 'Asôka, when sent to be Governor of Ujjeni, tarried at Chaityagiri, and there married Devî, the daughter the of chief.'] They had a son Jáliya, and a daughter Krishnájiná. At this time there was a famine in Kálinga from the want of rain; but the king, having heard that Wessantara had a white elephant that had the power to cause rain, sent eight of his Brahmans to request it. Wessantara at once gave it up, on which he was banished from the kingdom to the rock Wanka-giri. His wife, Madri-déwí, refused to forsake him, on which all their treasures were collected and given away in charity to the mendicants, and they with their two children, retired into banishment. The nobles then brought a chariot, and Madrí-déwí, taking her daughter in her arms, and her son by his hand, entered it. Two Brahmans followed them, and requested the gift of the horses that drew the chariot. Without hesitation they were given, but Sekra, observing what was taking place, sent four Dewas under the disguise of horses, that yoked themselves to the chariot and drew it. Again, another Brahman cried, 'Sir, I am old, sick, and wearied, give me your chariot.' The chariot was readily given up. The Prince then carried his son, and the Princess his daughter, and so set off on their journey to Wanka-giri. Wiswakarmma had prepared for them two Pansals (leafy huts). Here they dwelt with their children in the garb of ascetics. At length an aged Brahman, called Jujaka, set out to ask the gift of the two children, as slaves. Wessantara, in the absence of his wife, resolved to give up the children, who had fled away and hid themselves. He went forth and called them back and delivered them to the Brahman. The children, however, seeing the Brahman stumble and fall as he went down the hill, ran away and came back to their father; the father again gave them up, and the Brahman, tying their hands together, drove them along with a stick, beating them as they went. At length, when Madrí-déwí was about to return home, Sekra sent four Dewas to assume the form of wild beasts, to delay her return. When Sekra perceived that Wessantara had given away the children, he assumed the appearance of an aged Brahman, and went to the rock. Wessantara asked, 'Why have you come?' to which he replied, 'I have come to receive the Princess as my slave.' On this he gave her up also. As the result, both Madrí-déwí and the children were restored to Wessantara, and all returned safe and sound to Jayaturá."

Turning from this narrative to central portions of the lower beam of the northern gateway (Plate XA.) we see the King and Queen riding on an elephant accompanied by their children on a smaller one, and meeting the seven deputies—not eight as in the printed legends—who came to seek relief from a calamity only too familiar to us at the present day—a famine in Orissa.

A little further on, towards the left, the prince and princess are represented as about to mount their chariot in order to proceed to the wilderness. The two children are first seen standing in the gateway and then in the chariot, but besides these there are two smaller children not mentioned in the Jâtaka, but who play an important part in the sculpture. They evidently are not the same, for their age is

[1] As mentioned in the Preface, I am indebted to Mr. Beal for this identification. I knew the story, and had Upham's illustration of it, Plates IV. and V. of his History of Buddhism; but even now I am puzzled to identify the one with the other, and can take little blame to myself that I did not recognize the ancient legend from its modern form.

different, and though the Hindu sculptor saw no incongruity in repeating the same figures several times over in the same bas-relief, it is easy to recognize them as the same from their size or features, but those two standing in front of the chariot are smaller and younger. To the left again we see a man holding up the pole of the chariot, after the horses had been taken away by the Brahman, to whom they were given, and above this, turning towards the right, the four horses provided by Sekra are being harnessed, and we see indications of the approach to the forest.

On the back of this beam, a little way from the end on the upper line, the prince and princess having assumed the dress of ascetics, embrace one another on reaching their destination. Further on the prince gathers fruits, and the unfortunate princess bears a heavy burden on her head, and carries something also in her hand; between them a boy, apparently an attendant, is shooting game. Still further to the right and on the same upper line they are tranquilly seated conversing in front of their pansals among wild beasts on either hand, and their children are feeding the wild deer with flowers. On the extreme right the prince with his fire pot is either preparing the evening meal, or offering a sacrifice, more probably the former; and this concludes that part of the story, which may be called the life in the forest.

In the centre on the lower edge of the beam the prince gives his children to the Brahman Jujaka, who in the next scene beats them with a stick; and in the last scene he pours water on the hands of Indra disguised as a Brahman to confirm the gift he is making him, of his loving wife, the beautiful Madrî Devî.

Having thus insured his eventual attainment of Buddhahood by his unbounded liberality, the penance closes; and they meet the king, their father, coming from Jayaturâ to bring them back to spend the rest of their days in happiness; but in this scene, as everywhere else, we have four children, the two Jâliya and Krishnajinâ, have grown during their residence in the wilderness, and are those apparently on the left-hand elephant, but the two younger ones follow on another elephant towards the right.

It only now remains to notice the sculpture or the projection, which seems to represent episodes in the same story, but which are not mentioned in any edition of the Jâtaka now before us. That on the right on the front of the gateway represents a hermit in his pansala in the forest surrounded by wild beasts, and attended by two neophytes. Whether it represents Wessantara in some previous state or some other Bôdhisatwa is not clear, but it seems certainly connected some way or other with the main story.

On the corresponding projection on the left-hand we have the four children, one in arms, with their nurses and attendants, but it is very difficult to guess what may be the action it is intended to represent.

On the right-hand projection, on the back of the gateway, the prince and princess are seated in their garden by the side of a pond. The two elder children are seated likewise under a tree in the centre, and the two younger with their attendants to the right; the youngest being still in arms. On the left projection is the palace at Jayaturâ with the two children standing in front of the external gateway.

If I am correct in identifying the sculptures on the back of the intermediate beam as a continuation of the same Jâtaka (supra, p. 113), and from the presence of the four children I have no doubt that is so, the whole of the upper part of this gateway may be said to be devoted to the story of King Wessantara. It thus becomes not only the most extensive, but the most important of all the Sanchi sculptures.

It is important historically inasmuch as it is a pictorial representation of one of the most important Buddhist scriptures, at least four centuries earlier than any written edition of the same legend, and settles to a great extent the question of the antiquity of these Jâtakas. Whatever we may think of the fables and miracles with which the Lalita Vistara and other works have obscured and perverted the life of Buddha himself, here at least we have evidence that the story of King Wessantara as it is now told in Ceylon, did exist with very slight variations in the first century after Christ.

It is important locally, as there is reason to believe, that the neighbourhood of Sanchi was the scene of the events here portrayed. About six miles from the Tope there is a city called Besnagar or Besnagari, in General Cunningham's map, which looks so like a modern contraction of Wessanagara, which was apparently the name of the street or place through which his mother was passing when he was born, and from which circumstance he received his name,[1] and the Chetya-giri of the Mahawansa (supra, p. 99) and of the legend are evidently the same place and almost undoubtedly apply to this locality.[2]

If this is so we may go a step further and assume that the Sanchi Tope was actually erected to commemorate some event in the life of that Bôdhisatwa; where he lived or died, or where he performed some of his celebrated acts of charity; and its being the reputed scene of the most celebrated of the Jâtakas, may have led to its being considered so sacred a locality by the Buddhists, though never visited by Tathâgata himself.

---

[1] Manual of Buddhism, p. 116.

[2] I am quite aware that Sung-Yun (Beal's translation, p. 194) seems to place these localities somewhere in the Punjab, but there is a looseness in the way in which these sacred localities are shifted about in Buddhist legends that renders their determination very difficult (vide J. R. A. S., vol. VI., N. S., p. 232); but in the meanwhile we may safely select one determined probably by Aśoka, certainly in the first century of our era, rather than one vaguely hinted at by a Chinese pilgrim in the sixth century.

FIG. 1

FIG. 2

FIG. 3.

Lt COL. MAISEY DEL. W. GRIGGS, LITH.

TREE WORSHIP.

PLATE XXV.

WHATEVER doubt may exist as to the extent to which the Hindus intend at Sanchi to honour the Serpent, or to represent the Serpent as honouring them, there is none whatever as to the reverence they everywhere are represented as paying to Trees. These alternate with the Dagobas on the architraves as the two principal objects of worship, but taking also the representations on the pillars into account, the Tree is certainly the chief emblem of the divinity in the place.

Fig. 1, of this Plate is one of several subjects to which it is difficult to attach any distinct meaning or story. In the centre is a tree of a different species from any we have yet met with; and two men in Hindu costume, one on either hand, seem to be offering worship to it. In addition to this, however, there are two small shrines or temples, each with what appears to be an altar in front. That in the centre above has no worshippers. The one on the left below is encircled apparently with a wall of rude stones; that on the right by the usual Rail. Men in Hindu costume seem to be offering prayers to both these temples—are they tombs?—and between them a child is seated cross-legged, in the attitude we usually associate with Buddha. This bas-relief is in front of the left-hand pillar of the Northern Gateway (Plate XA.), a little higher than Fig. 2, which is the lowest of three bas-reliefs which ornament the inner face of this pillar.

The tree in Fig. 2 is of a different species from that represented in Fig. 3, though it occurs in both the upper corners of Fig. 1. There, it does not appear as a sacred tree at all. In this bas-relief it stands behind an altar, and has garlands pendent from its branches, but no ennobling Chatta surmounts it. Notwithstanding this, one male and eleven female figures are certainly worshipping it, and one woman presenting an offering.

That represented as the principal subject (Fig. 3) of this Plate, may be considered as a typical example. It occurs in front of the left-hand pillar of the Eastern Gateway (Plate XVI.).[1] The tree itself is the Pipal (*Ficus religiosa*), the true Bo-tree of the present Buddha. A temple has been built around it, and it is represented as growing out of its windows. Above the tree is the ennobling Chatta, and on either hand Garuḍas or Devas bearing offerings. Below, on each hand, two male worshippers in the ordinary costume of Hindu laymen.[2]

In front of the tree, on an altar, is the emblem which I have ventured to call the Trisul or Trident from its similarity to that instrument, when afterwards represented in the hands of Śiva. It has been described above in speaking of the Northern

---

[1] The drawing from which the lithograph is taken is as correct as Col. Maisey's drawings usually are; but the cast of this gateway at South Kensington shows that the drawing was never completely finished. The other Trees, here only indicated, are sculptured in detail.

[2] The inscription, according to Cunningham, p. 263, reads "The pillar gift of Nâgapriya Achavada, the "Śreshṭhî or Chief of the weavers."

Gateway, and it is difficult to understand its presence here unless it is intended to signify Buddha or sacred to Buddha, in the same manner as the cross on a Christian altar means, not the wood, but is an emblem of him who was crucified upon it.

It would be interesting if the species of this tree could be determined, as according to Buddhist tradition each of the twenty-four successive Buddhas of the present "Kappo" had a different Bo-tree.[1] Their names, in Pali, are all recorded, and could, no doubt, be identified with known trees, and many of them with those represented in these sculptures. This is evidently a flowering tree (Champa?), and occurs more frequently than any other, except the "Religiosa," which we know to be the Bo-tree of the present Buddha.[2]

The women in the bas-relief all wear the enormous chignon which ladies in these days seem to have considered a sufficient substitute for all other dress. In this instance, however, their costume is not quite so open to this objection as is usually the case either here or at Amravati.

---

[1] Turnour's Mahawanso, p. xxxii.

[2] I have been unfortunate in not being able to procure from any competent Indian botanist the assistance requisite to enable me to determine the species of the various trees represented in these bas-reliefs. There is difficulty attending it, no doubt, as the representations are to a considerable extent conventionalized; but still artists who could draw animals so well, that in no instance can a mistake be made as to which is intended, could also draw trees so as to enable them to be identified. The subject, however, is neither pressing nor very important, and can be done hereafter. There are, I think, only six or seven species altogether, and there can be very little doubt as to one or two of these. Ward, in his Hindu Mythology (3d edition, vol. I. 263), enumerates the following trees as considered sacred and worshipped by the followers of Vishṇu:—the Pipal and the Banyan, *Ficus religiosa* and *Indica;* the Vukoolu, *Mimusops elengi;* the Huritukee, *Terminalia citrina;* the Amalakee, *Phillanthus emblica;* and the Nimbu, *Melia azodaracta.* Except the Banyan, all these will, I believe, be found in our bassi-relievi.

No. 24.

Tree Worshipped from Rail at Buddh-Gayâ.

The annexed woodcut from the Buddh-Gayâ rail represents a tree as being worshipped, which is undoubtedly intended for a Pine of some sort. It is so like the pines represented on the slabs from Kuyunjik in the British Museum, that there can hardly be any mistake about this. The three leafed tree behind the flying figure seems intended for a Plantain.

SANCHI. PLATE XXVI.

FIG. I.

FIG. 2.

Lt. COL. MAISEY DEL. W. GRIGGS, LITH.

TREE WORSHIP.

PLATE XXVI.

The two bas-reliefs represented in Plate XXVI. occur the one over the other on the inner face of the right-hand pillar of the Northern Gateway; Fig. 2 is, however, on the pillar above instead of below Fig. 1 (Plate XI.). Both are representations of Tree Worship, but the one which is the uppermost on the pillar is remarkable because the two principal devotees are monkeys. Two men in the ordinary costumes stand behind them, with their hands joined in the attitude of prayer, and beside them two females with offerings in their hands. In front of the altar, behind which the Tree stands, are two other Hindu females, with a child between them, kneeling in deep devotion. Of the two monkeys, one is making an offering to the Tree, the other is in ecstasies.

In describing the back of the Eastern Gate, we have already seen all the beasts of the field (not monkeys) hastening to do honour to the sacred Tree, but here we have monkeys mixed with men, or rather preferred to them; as the men stand back, while the monkeys present their offerings, they are really the principal worshippers. All this may have arisen partly from the tenderness for animal life and kindness to all created beings that Buddhism always inculcated; partly from the doctrine of metempsychosis, which was always an essential part of the faith; but something may in this instance be due to local tradition. It was in the forest of Daṇḍaka, certainly not far from Sanchi, that Râma met with Hanumân, the godlike monkey, who played so important a part in the subsequent records of the Râmâyaṇa. If monkeys could fight in Hindu tradition side by side with men, why in Buddhist times should they not pray with them?

The sacred Tree, in this instance, appears to be the *Ficus religiosa*, but two other trees are represented, which occur frequently in the bas-reliefs. The one with the large fruit appears intended for a species of Jack (*Artocarpus integrifolius*), the other a flowering tree, which has not yet been identified.

The other bas-relief (Fig. 1) represents a Hindu Râja, known to be so by his Chatta and followers, and the chowrie borne as usual by his female attendants, who is doing honour to the Tree, to which two of the females, more fully clad than usual, are presenting wreaths. Above, two Garuḍas or flying figures, bearing offerings, are seen full length. This is one of the few instances in these bas-reliefs in which these figures are seen complete, so that all their features may be distinguished. Their feet, wings, and tails are those of birds; their heads and bodies are those of human beings, but always, as far as can be made out, males, which may be an objection to the name of Harpy, which would otherwise seem a name that might be appropriate. These in classical representations were always apparently females, and of an odious nature. Here they are always represented as heavenly messengers, and bringing offerings. As Garudas are always represented as the fifth in rank among the eight heavenly beings[1] in the Buddhist pantheon, that name is probably the one the Buddhists would themselves employ.

Above the tree on the right is another figure very common in these sculptures, but seldom seen so completely as in this instance, though even here we are left in doubt whether the head and fore part of a winged lion here represented is all, or whether he had any hinder part at all. Even in that case he would be better off than our cherubs, but I do not feel sure that it was not only the exigencies of space that induced the sculptor to omit his hind legs. Winged lions complete in all their parts are among the most common objects both at Sanchi and Amravati; but they, like their brethren in Assyria, are always represented on the ground, and never as bearing human beings through the air. These offering bearers may be a variety of the class, though all deriving their origin from the same stock. The representations at Sanchi are, of course, very much more modern than those in Assyria, but it is not clear that the Indian form may not be of an original stock as old or older than the Assyrian.

[1] In the Lalita-Vistara (Foucaux), p. 250, et passim, they are enumerated as les Dieux ou Devas, les Nâgas, les Yakchas, les Gandharbas, les Assouras, les Garuḍas, les Kinnaras, et les Mahôragas.

SANCHI. PLATE XXVII.

FIG, 1.

FIG, 2.

FIG, 3.

LT COL. MAISEY DEL.

W. GRIGGS, LITH. INDIA MUSEUM.

TREE WORSHIP.

PLATE XXVII.

On Plate XXVII. are engraved three forms of Tree Worship, which have been reduced to a smaller scale than usual, as they do not present any great features of novelty, but are interesting as indicating some of its forms. Fig. 1 represents eighteen men in the ordinary costume of Hindus, some sitting, some standing, doing homage to a Pipal tree with an altar in front of it, surmounted by a Chatta and attended by Garudas. It is from the inner face of the right-hand pillar of the Western Gateway (Plate XIX.).

Fig. 2 is immediately above it on the same Gateway, and presents a somewhat more varied form of the worship. Below are three men, one standing in a gateway, in front of an altar, to which their attention seems to be turned, but without any apparent connexion with the group immediately above them. In the middle of the picture are three men, three women, and a child, who also seem bent on doing honour to the Tree. Above these, on the left hand, are five women, apparently of inferior rank to those in the centre of the picture, while on the right hand of the Tree we have a lion, an elephant, a boar, an ox, a horse, and a sheep. Among these latter is a round, very jolly human face, with large ears, and evidently intended to represent a giant or ogre, or some of those semi-human beings so common in Eastern story. The interesting part of the bas-relief is that these animals evidently rank with the females opposite, and join with the men in doing honour to the holy Tree. In the lower part of the picture a Plantain tree is plainly distinguishable, and above that the tree I have ventured to suggest may be a Jack, with the flowering tree that occurs in several of the previous bas-reliefs.

The third bas-relief on this Plate is one which it is extremely difficult to make out, not that there is anything new in the form or in the objects worshipped, but that owing to the imperfect knowledge of perspective possessed by the artist, it is extremely puzzling to suggest what the stone work between the two trees is intended to represent. It looks at first sight like a stair with a rail on either hand, but it does not lead to any terrace or building, and the object for which it was designed, or why the two similar trees should be planted at each end, is by no means clear.[1]

In other respects the sculpture presents no novelty—men, women, and children, with drums and musical instruments, are assembled to do honour to the Trees. The upper one seems to be a Pipal, evidently the same as that in Fig. 2. The lower bears some fruit or flower, but so does that in Fig. 1, which from the form of

---

[1] Mr. Beal (J. R. A. S., N. S., V. p. 181) suggests that it represents the beautiful ladder by which Buddha descended from the Triyastriñshas heaven. I confess I do not see this, for this heavenly ladder, according to Hiouen-Thsang's description, was triple; that in the middle of gold, on the left of crystal, and on the right of silver (Si-Yü-Ki, I. p. 238). This certainly is not a ladder whatever it may be, and all the figures seem to be ordinary mortals in the usual attitudes of adoration, and these objects seem to be the two trees joined by a masonry rail of some sort.

its leaves is intended to be a Pipal (*Ficus religiosa*). In this instance, however, neither of the trees are surmounted by the usual umbrella, nor are they hung with garlands, nor do any flying figures approach to do them honour. They have altars in front of them, but no other sign of their being sacred.

One other thing that distinguishes this bas-relief from most of the others is that on either hand of the lower tree there is a group of a man with his wife and their little daughter in attitudes of prayer. They, however, though in the foreground, are only about half the height of the figures in the centre, though, as far as costume is concerned, they seem to be of the same race. The principal figure in the composition is evidently the lowest figure next the rail on the left of the picture, but he has no emblem of royalty or sanctity about him, nor do the others appear to pay him any attention. On the whole I am afraid this bas-relief must be put aside as one of those for which no satisfactory explanation has yet been suggested; but taken together these three figures may be taken as fairly representing the most popular form of adoration at Sanchi.

This sculpture is from the outward face of the right-hand pillar of the Northern Gateway at the top (Plate XA. and XII.).

The preceding—with one other example on the next Plate XXVIII. Fig. 2—exhaust the illustrations of Tree Worship, in so far as they have been drawn by Colonel Maisey from bas-reliefs exclusively devoted to the subject on the pillars of the Sanchi Gateways. These Plates are far, however, from conveying an adequate idea of the extreme frequency of such illustrations, though they may represent nearly all the forms in which it is found. As explained above (p. 105), the Tree is, generally speaking, the most usual and the most important object of worship represented in the sculptures at Sanchi Tope. Next after this comes the Dagoba, but neither so important nor so frequent. It may be suggested that this is owing to the great Tope being there itself to be worshipped, and that its mimic representation was therefore not needed. A careful study, however, of the sculptures renders this explanation hardly tenable. It can scarcely be doubted but the sculptures are intended to represent the creed, and the whole creed, of the people who erected the Gateways, and the relative importance of each part of the faith. It is probable, therefore, that the frequency or prominence of any object sculptured in these Gateways may fairly be assumed as representing its relative importance.

FIG. 1

FIG. 2

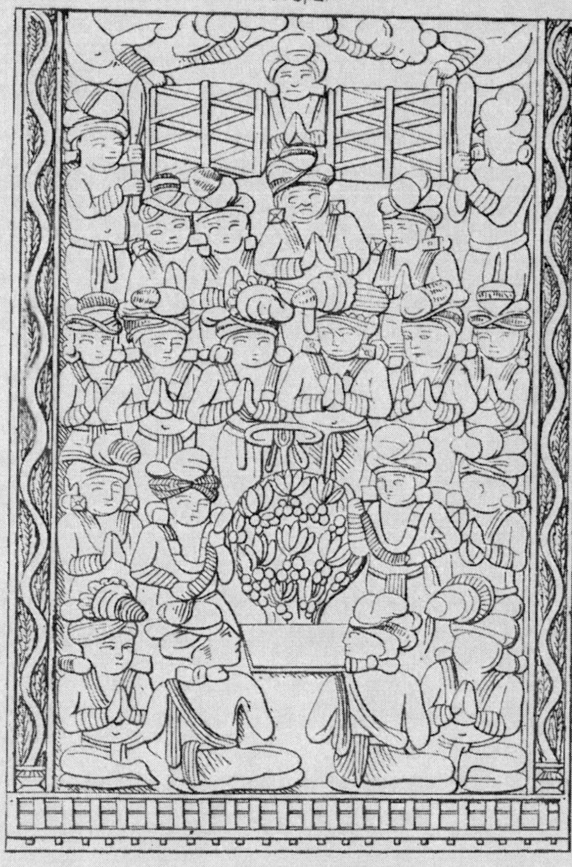

FIG. 3

LT COL. MAISEY DEL. W. GRIGGS, LITH.

TREE AND DAGOBA WORSHIP.

PLATE XXVIII.

Of the three subjects in this Plate, the one (Fig. 2) in the upper corner on the right hand is wholly devoted to Tree Worship, and is not very dissimilar from that represented in the last Plate, except that there is only one tree instead of two, and that here the tree has the umbrella, the flying figures, and other usual accompaniments. The central portion of the lowest bas-relief (Fig. 3) is devoted to the same form of worship, but in conjunction with that of the Dagoba. The upper one on the left hand is wholly devoted to the last form. The two first-named conclude, for the present, our illustrations of Tree Worship at Sanchi, and the pictures in this Plate serve to introduce the form next in importance.

In Fig. 2, twenty-one men, with two flying figures, Garuḍas or Devas, or by whatever name we choose to call them, are assembled to do honour to the Tree, which in this instance is the flowering tree with reversed leaves, frequently alluded to above. The head-dresses of the men are more than usually exaggerated in this bas-relief, and so are the drums which two men are beating with clubs.

In the lower bas-relief (Fig. 3) two men and two Garudas are doing honour to the Tree, in this instance the *Ficus religiosa,* and here treated as equal to the Dagoba, and alternating with it throughout.[1]

With the one exception of that represented in Fig. 1 of this Plate, the typical form of all the Dagobas in the sculptures at Sanchi is that shown in the lower figure (No. 3). The dome is represented as a little higher than a hemisphere, and adorned by a wreath of flowers hung on pegs prepared for the purpose. The lower part is surrounded by a Rail, apparently detached, as in the case of the great Tope, and the summit is always surmounted by a Tee of the usual form. Above this is an umbrella, sometimes with flags, and almost always with two or more wreaths dependent from its angles. Garuḍas almost invariably hover around it, and offer garlands or baskets containing some objects it is impossible to distinguish.

When we come to describe the representations of Topes at Amravati, it will be seen what immense progress had been made in decorating these objects during the three centuries that followed the erection of the Sanchi Gateways. If, however, we compare the Sanchi Dagobas with those found in the Caves of Kârlâ, or the earliest at Ajanta, it will be seen that they are nearly identical. As it has always been assumed, though on perfectly independent grounds, that these Cave Dagobas dated from about the Christian era, this is another confirmation of the date above assumed for the Sanchi portals.

The exceptional Dagoba represented in Fig. 1. of this Plate is the upper bas-relief on the inside of the right-hand pillar of the Northern Gateway (Plate XI.). It is very much taller than any of the others, and is surrounded by three Rails. The upper one of these, possibly the two upper, are attached. They may be merely

---

[1] The upper (Fig. 2) is from the right-hand pillar of the Northern Gateway at top (Plate XI.). The lower (Fig. 3) is from one of the beams or architraves of the same gate.

ornamental like those in the Topes in Afghanistan. The lower is certainly detached, and two figures are standing within it with offerings in their hands. This lower enclosure is entered by a gateway, apparently of wood, but evidently the prototype of the Sanchi portals. The Tee is surmounted by three umbrellas, with their dependent garlands, and on each side are two Garudas or flying figures bringing offerings.

The most interesting point with reference to this bas-relief is, that the people who are represented in the foreground are not the Hindus, who appear in all the other sculptures, but an entirely different race, and who are seen at Sanchi only in this bas-relief. They are all shaven, generally have their heads bare, and the hair bound by a small fillet. Their hair also is peculiar, being short and curly, like a negro's, or as that of Buddha is represented to be in more modern times. Their costume is a tunic with sleeves, fitting tightly to the neck, and reaching below the knees,[1] being unlike the kilt and cloak of the Ascetics or the dhotî of the Hindu, and their boots or sandals (Fig. 5. Plate III.) are also quite different from any seen elsewhere. Their musical instruments are also new to us. The Roman double pipe replaces the flute. The drum is differently formed, and the trumpets are of a kind seen nowhere else in the sculptures, but are almost identical with those represented on the arch at Orange and elsewhere by the Romans as belonging to the Celts or their barbarian enemies whoever they were. Their banner alone, with its "stars and stripes," or rather stars and Union Jack combined, is like what we shall afterwards meet, but this may be local and peculiar to Sanchi.

Who are the people here represented? Their costume would indicate the inhabitants of a northern, or at least a colder climate. Their woolly hair points to a southern, unless it may be that some people with close curly hair did at this time inhabit Afghanistan or some of the countries near it. It has ever been one of the puzzles of Buddhism that the founder of the religion should always have been represented in sculpture with woolly hair like that of a negro. That the Prince Siddhârtha had flowing locks is certain, but how and when the change took place is the difficulty. If we could tell who the people here represented are, it might solve the problem. They probably were the first that made statues of Buddha, and may have endowed him with their own crisp locks. The impression left on my mind is, that they are inhabitants of the Cabul valley, not only from their costume and the tallness of their Tope, but because of their general resemblance to some sculptures found at Taḳ-i-Bahaï, north of Peshawar. They have no women with them, which is unfortunate, as their costume might afford some useful indications, but the circumstance of their absence shows that they were strangers. Some further light will be thrown on the subject before we are done; at present it had perhaps better be left undetermined. But from an ethnographic point of view it is probably the most important and interesting of all the Sanchi sculptures.

---

[1] Arrian (XVI.), quoting apparently from Nearchus, describes the Hindus as wearing tunics (κίθων) of cotton reaching to the knees. The kiton cannot, according to the usual interpretation of the word, be applied either to the kilt of the Ascetics or the dhotî of the Hindus, but might be applied properly to this garment. The context, however, makes it more likely that a kilt was meant, because he adds, "They also wear veils, which "cover their heads and a greater part of their shoulders." If they wore the sleeved tunic represented in this sculpture, such a garment would be superfluous.

FIG. I.

FIG. 2.

LT COL. MAISEY DEL. W GRIGGS, LITH.

FIRE TEMPLE, AND WHEEL WORSHIP.

PLATE XXIX.

The wheel represented in the lower picture of this Plate is among the most common emblems both at Sanchi and Amravati, as already mentioned in speaking of the Northern Gateway (p. 114), it crowned the centre of all the four Gateways, though only a fragment of it occurs now on the Northern one (Plates IX. and X.). My impression is that all the pillars surmounted by lions in front of the Caves, as at Kârlâ, supported originally a wheel in metal,[1] and probably some of the Stambhas or pillars in front of the Gateways, both here and at Amravati, were crowned by this emblem. After the Tree and the Dagoba, it ranks third among the objects to be worshipped. In the Lalita-Vistara it is described as one of the seven precious things indispensable to a Chakravarti Râja. "The King," it goes on to say, "whose fore-"head has received the royal consecration, having thrown his mantle over one "shoulder, and placed his right knee on the ground, with his right hand pushes "the divine wheel, saying, 'Turn, venerable and divine treasure of the wheel, with "'the Law, but not without the Law.'"[2] The expression that at Benares Buddha began to turn the Wheel of the Law, and afterwards that he did so at various other places, is one of the most common phrases in Buddhist scripture; and both from these expressions and the relative positions it occupies in the sculptures, it hardly appears doubtful that this emblem represents Dharma, the second member of the Buddhist Triad. Of this, however, we shall be better able to form an opinion when the Amravati sculptures have been described. In the meanwhile, to avoid all theory, it will be convenient simply to describe it as the Chakra or the Wheel, leaving its meaning to be determined hereafter.

In this instance, from the central beam of the Western Gateway (Plate XIX.), as generally at Sanchi, it has thirty-two spokes. It was surmounted by a Chatta with garlands and ministered to by Garuḍas. It stands on an altar, on each side of which is a deer in act of adoration, but whether the rest of the herd on the right hand are to be considered as worshippers or not, is more difficult to determine. Their presence here seems to be an allusion to one of the eight signs which distinguish the incarnation of Buddha. Of these the seventh is "Turning the Wheel of the Law in the park of deer."[3] This deer park is especially famous in Buddhist legends. It was visited and carefully described by Hiouen-Thsang.[4] Among other things he mentions, "In the centre of the chapel (Chaitya) is a statue of Buddha in copper, "of the exact dimensions of Tathâgata, whom it represents turning the Wheel of the "Law." The place is now known as Sarnath, north of Benares, and a celebrated Dagoba now standing there is the best known Buddhist monument in India. In Buddhist times it was always known as the Mṛigadâva or Deer park, and renowned as the place where Śâkya Muni first and principally taught. The presence of the

[1] Foĕ-Kouĕ-Ki, XX. 171.
[2] Lalita-Vistara, translated by Foucaux, III. 15.
[3] J. R. A. S., XX. p. 140.
[4] Voyage, I. p. 132.

deer here, and the flowering trees and shrubs, seem almost certainly intended to indicate this spot, and the wheel is either meant to represent the one that Buddha turned, or is at least symbolical of his preaching.

The eight men who are represented as worshipping seem all of equal rank, and there were as many more ranged on the other side. They are all dressed as Hindus, and all have their hands joined in the attitude of prayer.

The upper figure in this plate is one whose meaning can only be guessed at by some one intimately acquainted with Buddhist legends, and the conventional modes of interpreting them. Mr. Beal thinks he has discovered the subject in the legend of Dîpânkara Buddha, which he has consequently translated and published, in the last number of the Journal of the Royal Asiatic Society. It is there narrated, "that "from the wick of his lamp he caused the appearance of a city to proceed and fix "itself in space. The city was four-square, 5,000 yôjanas each way—30,000 miles.— "After 3,000 years he thought thus, 'I must convert the people of Jambudwîpa by "'some spiritual manifestation.' The then people saw the city emit from its four "walls very fierce flames, bright and burning hot. The great fear filled their breasts "and they congregated together, and spake thus, 'Alas, alas! see how yonder abode "'is burning in flames, surely it will, soon be entirely destroyed,' and they pray "to be allowed to assist in extinguishing the flames. Just then they saw Devas, "Nâgas, Yakshas, Gandharvas, those who were men and not men (Kinnaras) come "forth from the city and cry out why do these flames burn so. Then suddenly "before the place there appeared three porchways, one of gold, another of silver, and "a third of crystal. From out of these Dîpânkara Buddha issued to convert all "Jambudwîpa."

There is so much in this narrative that illustates the sculpture that it seems probable that Mr. Beal may be right in his identification, but if this is so the legend, as we now have it, must have been very much altered from what it was in the first century. This is not a burning city in mid-air, but a burning mountain, and with no inhabitants to excite pity, but the human-faced rams and dog-headed figures we are already familiar with from Plate XV., and hardly deserve the names given them in the text. The doorway too, with an altar in front, looks much more like a rock-cut temple than a city gate, and altogether the whole is so unlike the minute accuracy of the sculptures representing the Wessantara Jâtaka, that I would feel inclined to pause before laying too much stress upon it; but, as I have no better conjecture to offer, it may be allowed for the present, at least, to stand.

FIG. 1

FIG. 2

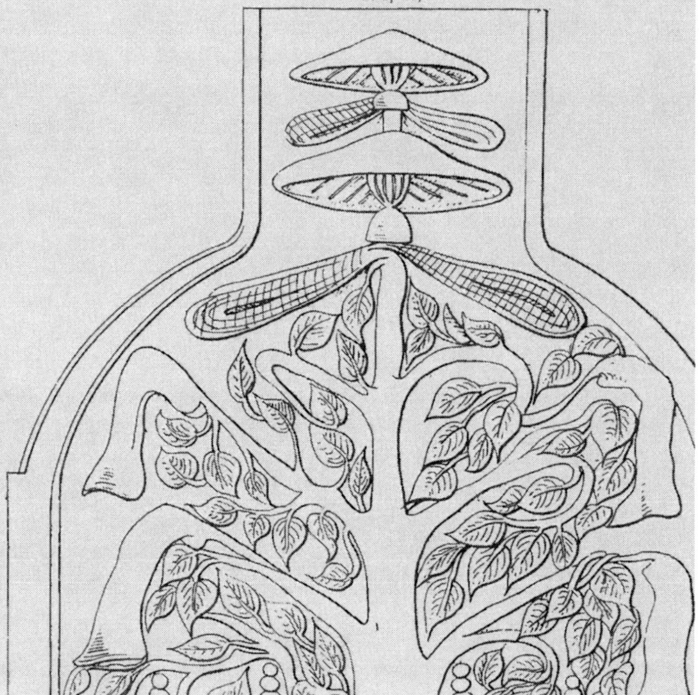

LT COL. MAISEY DEL.

W. GRIGGS, LITH. INDIA MUS.

PILLAR SOUTHERN GATEWAY.

PLATE XXX.

THIS Plate represents in two parts one face of one of the fallen pillars of the Southern Gateway. The right-hand figure is the upper half, that on the left the lower part of the same pillar, as shown in their relative positions in Plate XVI. As with the knowledge we now possess we are enabled with almost absolute certainty to determine that this is the oldest of the Sanchi Gateways, it is more than probable that the historical events portrayed in its sculptures have a direct reference to the history of the monument, and I cannot help believing that this, which is the only strictly historical representation on the pillars, may have a close connexion with the bas-relief representing a siege which occupies the whole of the lower beam of this Gateway. As will be seen further on when describing Colonel Maisey's drawing of this siege (Plate XXXIII.), the main object for which it was undertaken, was the acquisition or recovery of some relics; this event may have established the reputation of Sanchi as a Buddhist shrine, and either the king represented in this Plate or the Nâga Râja depicted, Plate XXIV. Fig. 1, may be the hero of the war. As, however, I can detect no snake hoods in the battle scenes it most probably was the former.

The sculptures in the upper part represent first the sacred Tree, with two umbrellas and garlands above, and on each side are objects which appear to be intended as representations of flags. From the form of its leaves we are able to recognize the tree itself as the Pipal or *Ficus religiosa*. Below this is a building with pillars alternately plain and octagonal, and with pot bases very similar to those found in the cave at Kârlâ.[1] On the altar in this building stands the "Trisul" emblem three times repeated. If I am correct in my belief that it represents Buddha in the Buddhist religion, it here is simply the emblem of the triune divinity of the Buddhist faith.[2]

The lower part of the pillar is occupied by two bas-reliefs of a more domestic character, but still certainly historical. In the upper one of these a Hindu Râja is attended by six females, two of whom support him with their arms. Let us hope he is not tipsy! but the next female carries a vessel which in all similar sculptures we have reason to believe may contain wine, or some intoxicating drink, and she has a cup in her hand. The seated figure on the right holds apparently a cake. On the left, one female bears the Chatta of state, the other is seated with her back turned to the spectators. The expression of the king's face is certainly that of a man who is more or less intoxicated.

The lowest bas-relief is more complicated and difficult of explanation. In the centre, on a tray, rests something which is certainly the principal object in the

---

1 History of Architecture, II. 487.

2 General Cunningham suggests (Bhilsa Topes, p. 359) that this afterwards became the emblem of Juggernath, with his brother and sister. In this suggestion I entirely agree, but the transformation took place at a period long subsequent to that we are now engaged upon. The more I look at it the more do I become convinced that Vishṇuism is only very corrupt Buddhism.

scene, but what is by no means clear. It may be a relic. Whatever it is, we know by the Chatta held over it, and the Chaori-bearer behind, that it is what is here honoured. In front a man's head lies on the ground, severed from its body. On the right are six Hindus, in attitudes of adoration, and on the left a female singer, by no means remarkable for her personal charms, is singing to the accompaniment of a drum. Four or five men in front seem to be charmed with her performance. Behind her, between the pillars, is a figure with a singularly calm and pleasing expression of countenance, and with a head-dress we have not before met with. Owing to the position in which this figure is placed, it is difficult to determine whether it represents a male or a female, and where all are shaven there is no sign on the face. From the necklace of pearls round the neck, it probably was intended for the Queen.

It is not, however, on her or on any of the figures in the foreground that the interest of the scene centres; if we could tell to whom the head belonged, it would add to our knowledge of Indian history, and also afford us a new impression with regard to Buddhist action. Their published histories are singularly reticent as to wars and beheadings, but these sculptures, and the paintings at Ajanta[1] would lead us to suppose they were little better than their neighbours in this respect.

The inscription is, unfortunately, only a fragment and unintelligible;[2] but even if made out, would only tell us probably who presented the sculpture to the Tope.[3]

The architecture of the palace or pavillion in which the lower scene takes place is so well made out on the bas-relief, that it would not be difficult to restore it. It is of course wholly of wood, but of a very ornamental character.

---

[1] In a copy of one of these frescoes now hanging in one of the passages of the India Office, a lady outdoes Herodias' daughter by presenting to one of the attendants of Buddha a charger with three human heads in it.

[2] Cunningham, Bhilsa Topes, p. 264.

[3] Is it possible that the explanation of this bas-relief is to be found in the following extract from the Vishṇu Purana (Wilson's translation, page 471): "Devabhúti the last Sunga prince being addicted to immoral "practices, his minister, the Kánwa, named Vasudeva, will murder him and usurp his kingdom." This event happened about the year 78 B.C., and is therefore not an unlikely one to be recorded in the Sanchi Gateways.

As this Devabhúti was the king who at least commenced the great Cave at Kârlâ, the finest and among the earliest of Chaitya Caves in India (J. B. B. R. A. S., V. 153), we know that he must have been an enthusiastic Buddhist, but should be sorry to learn that he was addicted to drinking!

FIG. 1.

FIG. 2.

COL. MAISEY DEL. W. GRIGGS, LITH.

BOAT SCENES.

PLATE XXXI.

THE upper bas-relief in this Plate is one to which it is extremely difficult to attach a name. It occurs on the inner side of the right-hand pillar of the Western Gateway (Plate XIX.) at the bottom, and certainly represents the triumphal conveyance of some relics across a lake or river, but what lake or what relics they may be there seems nothing to show, nor on what occasion the procession took place. If it represents a periodical festival it still would be interesting to know where it took place, but if it is the bringing home of some particular relic on some special occasion it would be still more so; but without an inscription—and none exists—it is difficult to see how we are ever to find out.

Boats not unlike this one in design may still be seen opposite the Ghâts at Benares on festal occasions, or on the lakes at Udaipur,[1] or wherever a Hindu palace has a lake attached to it; but in so far as I have seen, not with a winged lion's head like this. On the present occasion the boat bears a relic casket, over which the royal umbrella is raised, and beside which the Chaori-bearer stands. The scene is in a freshwater lake, in which the lotus and other such plants abound, and around the boat are numerous figures with garlands in their hands, swimming and disporting themselves, supported on mussucks or inflated skins. It is not easy to make out whether those in the water are males or females; from their bangles and armlets most probably the latter.

The lower picture from the front of the left-hand pillar of the Eastern Gateway (Plates XV. and XVI.), is in its externals in strange contrast with the one just described. Instead of a festal barge we have a rude canoe made up of rough planks sown together with hemp or bark. In it is seated a venerable old man in the garb of an ascetic, accompanied by two disciples or neophytes, one of whom steers while another rows the boat. In front stand four figures, in a similar costume to those in the boat, whose attention is apparently earnestly directed towards them as if taking leave of those who are departing.

From the lotuses and other flowers the scene is evidently laid in a freshwater river or lake, in which several geese are disporting themselves. One is trying to swallow a fish, and seems in great danger of choking in the operation, while another is in equal danger of being swallowed by an alligator which is issuing from behind a tree or bush for that purpose. On either side of the bas-relief are three trees, six altogether, of the species we are already familiar with from their representation in other bas-reliefs. In one some monkeys are disporting themselves, and gathering apparently the fruit; but only one of them seems to be a sacred tree. That in the lower right-hand corner is hung with garlands, and has an altar in front, which is the usual sign of sanctity, though there are no

---

[1] Tod's Rajasthan, vol. I. 373.

worshippers on this occasion; and in the water between the people in the boat and those on the shore is something floating on the water, to which it is difficult to attach a meaning. My impression is that it is the symbol of an altar, meaning that those in the boat are worthy of worship.

None of the Sanchi bas-reliefs have given rise to more different interpretations than this. General Cunningham considers it to represent "Sakya Muni after the "attainment of Nirwâna, on being wafted over the waters which are said to surround "this transitory world."[1] Colonel Maisey considers it of Mithraic origin, and Mr. Beal leaves it as inexplicable.

The most probable explanation that occurs to me is that it is intended to represent Śâkya Muni passing the Hiranyavati river near Kusinara,[2] before he reached the forest of Sâl Trees, in whose shade it was predestined he was to attain Nirvâna.[3] But another hypothesis is also possible. Fa-hian relates that, "going south-east "12 yôjanas from the place where Buddha arrived at Nirvâṇa, we arrive at the "spot where all the Litchavas desiring to follow Buddha to the scene of his "Nirvâṇa were forbidden to do so. On account of their great affection to Buddha "they were unwilling to go back, on which Buddha caused to appear between them "and him a great and deeply scarped river which they could not cross."[4] This so nearly corresponds with the scene depicted in the bas-relief that it may be an earlier version of the same story. The principal difficulty is that the Litchavas in the legend are described as princes—laymen, at least,—in the bas-relief they are ascetics. Be this as it may I feel convinced that it is some such event that is portrayed in this bas-relief. Nothing certainly can be more mundane and less mystical than the whole scene, and I think we are now justified in considering that Buddha is represented more than once in these bas-reliefs as an ascetic, and if this is so this certainly appears to be one of them.

---

[1] Bhilsa Topes, p. 204.

[2] Spence Hardy, Manual of Buddhism, p. 345. Beal, J. R. A. S., XX. 186.

[3] Hiouen-Thsang, Vie, 130. Si-yu-ki, vol. I. p. 333–345. See also Bigandet, Life of Gaudama, p. 290. It is curious that neither at Sanchi nor Amravati is there any representation of Buddha attaining Nirvâna under the Sâl Trees, though it afterwards became so favourite a subject in the Western Caves, and in Ceylon, Burmah, and indeed in all Buddhist countries. Was it like "the predictive signs," a later invention introduced in the declining age of the faith?

[4] Beal's translation, p. 94.

CONVERSION OF THE KASYAPAS.

PLATE XXXII.

THE two subjects represented in this Plate are considered by Mr. Beal to represent one of the most famous legends of the life of Buddha, known as the Conversion of the Kaśyapas,[1] though the correspondence between the written and sculptured forms of the narrative are by no means in such minute accordance with each other as in the case of the Wassantara Jâtaka. It may be, as I fancy I can perceive in other instances, that all that relates to the founder of the religion has been exaggerated and distorted, while the Jâtakas, which refer only to what passed in previous stages of existence, have been left unaltered.[2]

The story as told by Spence Hardy is as follows :[3]—"Three brothers named Uruwel "Kaśyapa, Gayá Kaśyapa, and Nadi Kaśyapa, dwelt in the Uruwela forest, and gave "out that they were Rahats, and deceived many people, while they lived in great "plenty and splendour. As Buddha wished to bring them all into the paths he "went to the residence of Uruwel and requested permission to remain that night "in the fire hall or temple. Uruwel replied that he had no objection, but that in "the hall there was an immense nayá, the poison of which was most subtle. It "did not hurt him or his brothers, because they were Rahats, but as Gotama was "not a Rahat it would be dangerous for him to enter. Buddha fearlessly entered "the hall that he might repose for the night. The nayá came forth in anger, at "the same time sending forth a poisonous blast. Buddha replied by sending forth "a fiery vapour, as from a burning wisp of straw. The nayá then sent forth a "flame to destroy Buddha, but he made a flame seven times more powerful and "subdued the nayá. The light was perceived by Uruwel, and he said Gotama must "have perished for not taking his advice."

The story is told, with slight variations, by Bigandet.[4] Buddha is there made to request permission to pass the night in the kitchen or cook-room, which being granted, he entered the kitchen, and sitting cross-legged, but keeping his body in an erect position remained as absorbed in contemplation.

If all this is so, it is evident that the figure in the Pansala in front in the upper bas-relief is no less a person than Gotama himself, and the earliest representation of him we have yet met with. The cross-legged attitude of the text had, so far as we yet know, no existence in the first century. But if I am correct in my identification in this and in the last Plate, he is represented as an old man, while the next Plate represents his youth. Assuming this to be so, the three figures on the left of the fire temple are the three Kaśyapas, and the five on the right are the five disciples

---

[1] J. R. A. S., N. S., V. 177, et seqq.

[2] The lithograph has, in this instance, been copied direct from a photograph of a cast of the subject now in the South Kensington Museum.

[3] Manual of Buddhism, p. 188, et seqq.

[4] Life of Gaudama, p. 130, et seqq.

that accompanied Buddha to Benares and attended his preaching in the Deer Garden. The animals in the centre would in that case represent those collected by the people from Anga and Magadha as offerings for Uruwel,[1] and the figures in front may represent the disciples of Kaśyapa flinging their fire-worshipping utensils into the lake.[2]

The only difficulty in all this, for a complete identification of the scene is, that the nayá is throughout represented as only a small poisonous snake, which Buddha having killed, puts into his patta, and presented to Uruwel next morning, which is very unlike the seven-headed god-like snake we see here. But as Nâgas became unfamiliar the text may have been altered.

As his conquest of the guardian snake did not suffice to convert the Kaśyapas, various other miracles were performed, among which the last is thus described:—" On a certain day the Rathees were busy splitting firewood. They got a large log " of wood, on which their united efforts could make no impression. Kaśyapa thought " within himself the great Rahan is gifted with mighty power, let us try him on " this occasion. He desired Gaudama to split the hard log. Gaudama split it in " a moment into 500 pieces. The Rathees then tried to light up the fuel but they " could not succeed. Kaśyapa requested his guest to come to their assistance. In " an instant the 500 pieces were in a blaze."[3]

The success of one man in cleaving the log and the failure of the others, as represented in the lower compartment of this bas-relief, and in like manner the brightness with which some of the fires burn, and the apparent inability of others to light theirs, may probably be all taken as a quaint and simple way of telling the story of this miracle, though it must be confessed the bas-relief might be made to have other interpretations, but taken in conjunction with the subject immediately above it, it may fairly be assumed that the text is an exaggerated edition of a story as simple as that represented in the bas-relief.

In the background of the last sculpture is a circular beehive-like building, surrounded by the usual rail. It can hardly be a Dagoba for it has no Tee, but it may be a tomb. Two shells are represented as lying upon it, and between these two eyes or openings of some sort, but what is by no means clear.

Another point of interest in this sculpture is, that the axes used to split the wood seem to be of stone. At least they are so fixed into their handles as no metal implement probably ever was, but are attached as stone implements were generally to their handles.

---

[1] Manual of Buddhism, p. 190.
[2] Beal, in J. R. A. S., N. S., V. p. 178.
[3] Bigandet, Life of Gaudama, p. 135.

LT COL MAISEY DEL. W. GRIGGS, LITH

BUDDHIST BAS RELIEF.

PLATE XXXIII.

The bas-relief represented on this Plate is one of the most extensive as well as one of the most important of the Sanchi series. It occupies nearly the whole of the inner face of the right-hand pillar of the Eastern Gateway (Plate XIII.). There is only the warder below, and a small subject of Tree Worship above. It is more than usually interesting, also, from its being the only subject at Sanchi which can be ascribed with absolute certainty to Buddhism, as we now know it. There are others, as the two last, for instance, which may be assumed to portray events in the life of Śâkya Muni, but this one certainly is meant as a short biography of the Prince up to the time when he assumed the ascetic garb under the shade of the Bo Tree at Buddh-Gayâ.

The relief is divided into four parts. In the upper we have Mâyâ, the wife of Śuddhodana asleep on the terrace of the palace, dreaming that a white elephant appeared to her, and entered her womb. This dream being interpreted by the Brahmans learned in the Rig-Veda, was considered as announcing the incarnation of him who was to be in future the deliverer of mankind from pain and sorrow.[1] It is, in fact, the form which the Annunciation took in Buddhist legends. It does not, so far as our illustrations go, appear again at Sanchi, but it occurs frequently, as we shall presently see, at Amravati, and is repeated in almost every Buddhist book which alludes to the birth of the great ascetic.

In the lowest compartment of the bas-relief we have the accomplishment of this prophecy. The Prince Siddhârtha, at the age of twenty-nine, at the foot of the Bodhi-druma, or tree of knowledge, at Buddh-Gayâ, in presence of his five disciples, lays aside his robes of state, and prepares to assume the garb of an ascetic, and commence that mission which he accomplished only after fifty-one years of self negation and of missionary labour.[2] During that period, however, he had, as his followers still believe, fully earned the title to which he aspired of the deliverer of mankind from the ills that flesh is heir to.

Of the two intermediate scenes, the upper occurs within the city of Kapilavastu, his father's capital, and does not appear to have any special meaning. Two men on horseback meet two others on elephants, and behind the latter are two loose horses attended apparently by a groom. In the centre is the standard, with the usual Trisul emblem. All this seems to represent a night scene in the city, with the guards going their rounds.

---

[1] Lalita-Vistara, p. 61, et seq.

[2] If this is a correct description of the bas-relief, the legend in the first century of the Christian era differed from that related in the XVIIth and XIXth chapters of the Lalita-Vistara in the eighth or ninth century. According to that authority, Śâkya Muni, after leaving his home, prepared himself for his mission by six years of the austerest penance—so severe that his five disciples could not support it, and left him. When nearly at death's door he recovers, eats what the village maidens bring him, bathes in the river Nairanjanâ, and then attains Buddhahood while seated under the Bodhi-druma, or tree of knowledge at Buddh-Gayâ.

In the central compartment, the Prince Siddhârtha in his chariot issues from the city gate attended by bowmen and elephants. In front of the chariot walks a boy with a curly head, but with no apparent occupation. Before him march seven other boys, two playing on fifes,[1] or rather flutes, and two on drums; two blow into a musical instrument formed of a shell, which is found frequently repeated in these bas-reliefs, though never at Amravati, and one has a smaller class of drum or tambourine.

The city walls and the windows of the houses are crowded with men and women looking at the procession, and all in the costume we have called "Hindu." This extends even to drummer boys, whose curly locks give them an aspect so unlike what is usually met with in India. Was it an artificial fashion, or were they foreigners? These questions have been before alluded to, for if we could answer them, we might be able to say whence Buddha acquired the curly hair with which he is always represented in modern times. Except in the bas-relief (Plate XXVII. Fig. 1.), men are seldom so represented in the Sanchi sculptures, and then only persons in the condition of servants, who sometimes have curly heads, but boys are generally represented with hair in this form. There is no representation of Buddha at Sanchi in the dress of a priest in which he is always afterwards represented; but in the most modern sculptures at Amravati there are several, and in all these he has the short curly locks he always afterwards retained. I cannot help an impression that he acquired the peculiarity in Afghanistan, though still at a loss to account for the presence of a woolly-haired race in that province. If I am correct in assuming that we have three representations of the founder of this religion in the last two plates, it is evident that there is no authority for either the curly hair, the priest's garb, or the cross-legged attitude in the first century of our era. As they are all familiarly known at Amravati, it must be between these two epochs that we must look for their origin.

The trees here are of the usual character, except one above the Bo-tree, which looks like a vine. The architecture is identical with what is found in all these sculptures at Sanchi, and is no doubt a faithful representation of the curiously wooden style of the period; stone being then apparently only used for the foundations of the palaces, or what we would now call engineering works; the gateways themselves showing that they must have been among the earliest attempts at stone architecture of an ornamental character.

---

[1] The fifes we have met with before, and shall frequently have occasion to notice them again in the sequel. Yet, so far as we can learn, the "flauto traverso" or flute breathed into at the side without a mouth-piece, was not known in Europe before the thirteenth century. Is it an Indian invention?

SANCHI.

PLATE XXXIV.

FIG, 1

FIG, 2.

LT COL. MAISEY DEL.

W. GRIGGS, LITH.

PROCESSIONS.

PLATE XXXIV.

THE two processional scenes represented in this Plate are both from the left-hand pillar of the Northern Gateway, one in front, the other on the inside (Plates XI. and XII.). There is nothing at first sight to distinguish these scenes from those on the last Plate, but they are interesting as showing varieties of costume and of instruments which were not so distinctly depicted in the preceding Plates. The architecture of the palace is also here very clearly expressed. It is of wood, but so detailed that there would be little difficulty in restoring the building from this representation. The little square tower or pavilion, with its triangular battlements, which is introduced in the lower picture of the Plate, as well as in Plate XXXIII., though not exactly similar, is probably intended to identify the two as parts of the same palace. The peacock which is seen in both may be introduced for the same purpose. Eating and drinking is going on at a great rate in the palace, and outside one boy bears the large spouted vessel like a teapot, but which probably contained some more exciting beverage than tea. The curly heads are here carefully distinguished from those with flowing hair. This is particularly remarkable in the case of the two boys in front of the Râja on horseback, in the lower bas-relief, but even there is nothing the least Negroid in the faces. So far as features are concerned they seem of the same type, but the distinction as regards the hair is carefully marked.

In the two pictures of this Plate, the Prince, whether on horseback or in his chariot, is easily distinguished by the umbrella borne over his head, but in both he bears in his hand an emblem we have not met with before, nor do we meet with it again. It consists of two balls joined together like a dumb-bell. So far as I know it is not found on coins, nor on any other sculptures, and I am, therefore, quite at a loss to suggest what it may be intended to represent.

These processions are more frequent at Amravati than even here, and as all are nearly of the same type, one cannot help suspecting that they were intended to represent the most popular legend in Buddhist mythological history. In the fourteenth chapter of the Lalita-Vistara, and elsewhere,[1] we are told that whilst the Prince Siddhârtha was in the full enjoyment of all the pleasures of his rank, and of the most perfect domestic happiness with his wife, Gopâ Devî, he one day, while driving in his chariot from the city to his pleasure gardens, met an old, decrepid, grey-haired man feebly stumbling along the road. The sight made a deep impression on the Prince, and he reflected that even his rank could not protect him from decay. Some time afterwards, while proceeding in the same manner, he met a poor man, squalid with disease; and a third time, a corpse. Both these gave rise to similar reflections on the ills that flesh is heir to. A fourth time he met a healthy, well clad, and contented-looking man, wearing the robes of persons dedicated to religion;

---

[1] Foĕ-Kouĕ-Ki, 198, 204, et seqq.

and, satisfied that this was the true career for man, he determined to sacrifice station, wife, family, everything, and devote himself henceforward to the redemption of mankind from the ills they had heretofore been subject to.

These four, which are called the "predictive signs," are singular favourites with the Buddhist legendary artists, and one cannot help suspecting that allusion to them is intended here; but if so, it is the play of Hamlet with the *rôle* of the Prince omitted. In no instance can the man suffering from age, disease, or death be detected, and I cannot believe that sculptors so clever in telling their story, as those who executed these bas-reliefs undoubtedly were, would have omitted what would have made it quite clear what was intended if this really was the subject they proposed to introduce. The initiated may, perhaps, recognize the scene by some mark, but neither at Sanchi nor Amravati is it distinguishable to the unassisted vision of the profane.[1]

These two bas-reliefs are also interesting in showing very distinctly the mode in which the horses were harnessed to the chariot, and the form of the bridles by which they were guided. Arrian tells us that "the Indians have neither saddles "nor bridles like those which the Greeks and Celts made use of, but instead of "bridles they bind a piece of raw bullock's hide round the lower part of the horse's "jaws, to the inner part of which the common people fix spikes of brass or iron, "not very sharp, but the richer ones have them of ivory. Within the horse's "mouth is a piece of iron like a dart, to which the reins are fastened."[2] If this was the mode employed by the Indians in Alexander's time, they seem to have benefitted by their intercourse with the West before the Sanchi sculptures were executed. If any one will compare the head stalls of the bridles represented in the Plate, with Figs. 6, 7, and 8 of Plate III., they will see how perfect the head gear of these horses had become; but the sculptures still leave it uncertain whether the horse was controlled by a bit in his mouth or by pressure on front of his face above his nostrils, as is generally done at Naples at the present day. An examination of the sculptures themselves might settle this point, though neither our drawings nor our photographs suffice for this purpose.

---

[1] It is now generally known that the story of the conversion of Buddha in consequence of his seeing the four predictive signs was introduced to the Christian world in a didactic romance by St. John of Damascus, in the 8th century, which afterwards became so popular, that Gautama himself now figures in the Christian Hierarchy of Rome as St. Josaphat, and few of that brotherhood better deserve that distinction. See Yule's Marco Polo, II. p. 263, and Max Müller in Contemporary Review, July 1870.

[2] Arrian, Indica, chap. XVI.

SANCHI.

PLATE XXXV.

FIG. I.

FIG. 2.

L^T COL. MAISEY DEL. W. GRIGGS, LITH.

SACRED HORSE AND DOMESTIC SCENE.

PLATE XXXV.

THE procession represented in the upper picture of this Plate is of a somewhat different character from those just described. It occurs in the front of the right-hand pillar of the Northern Gateway (Plate XII.). The second form the top. In this bas-relief the principal object is the sacred Horse richly caparisoned, who heads the procession, and towards whom all eyes are turned. Immediately behind him follows the man with the spouted pot, and behind him a chief in his chariot, bearing the umbrella of state, not over himself, but apparently in honour of the Horse. Above him sits a young chief, with two women with Chaoris, but no Chatta, and in a balcony on his left three more women, and in an upper balcony, two others looking out.

It is not easy to determine whether this scene is intended to represent the beginning of an Aśvamedha or of some minor ceremony in which the Horse bore a principal part. The whole, however, looks more like a scene from the Mâhâbhârata than from the Lalita-Vistara, and one is almost tempted to call the man in the chariot Arjuna, and the king in the balcony Yudhishthira. They may, however, be intended for very different personages, and must for the present go without names.

When speaking of the sculptures at Amravati, we shall have frequent occasion to revert to this subject, for the Horse there plays a more important part than he does at Sanchi, so much so as to open a wide door of speculation as to the connexion of this worship with that of the Sun god of the Scythians, in the still more mysterious worship of Poseidon by the Greeks. We learn from Herodotus[1] and others how important Horse worship and Horse sacrifices were considered by the Scythians, and cognate tribes, while we must not forget that both he (vide supra, p. 23) and Diodorus[2] represent the Scythians as born from a woman who was a serpent from the waist downwards. They were essentially a Nâga race, and their worship of the Horse and their Amazonian tendencies all point to similarities between them and the people depicted in these sculptures, which must lead to the most curious ethnographical developments, so soon as they are properly investigated.

I refrain from entering on the subject here, for in the first place it is hardly germane to the main object of the work, but more because to treat of the worship of the Horse, and the importance of the sacrifices in which he was a principal object, would require an investigation nearly as intricate as that of Serpent Worship, and almost as large a work to explain its historical and ethnographical peculiarities. Next after the Serpent the Horse was probably the most important object in that old pre-historic animal-worshipping religion which prevailed among the Turanian races of mankind. After him came the Bull, known in Egypt as Apis, and now in India as Nandi. To complete this work, after the Tree and the Serpent, ought to come the Horse and the Bull. The two last must, however, be left for future

---

[1] I. 216; IV. 61, 72, &c.

[2] II. 43.

explorers in the regions of mythology. The Bull, because he does not occur in our sculptures, and the Horse, because though he appears frequently, it is not with such prominence that it is necessary to do more than notice his presence.

It is much more difficult to fix anything like a definite meaning to the scene represented in the lower figure of the Plate. It no doubt tells a tale sufficiently familiar to those who first looked on the picture, but whether we shall now be able to recover the legend is more than doubtful. There seems no one character in the group sufficiently prominent to enable us to give him a name, and no action sufficiently defined to hang a legend upon.

In the upper left-hand corner four women are engaged in occupations sufficiently familiar to all who have visited the East; one is winnowing the grain, which a second pounds in a mortar, and a third rolls out into chitpattees. A fourth is engaged in the same occupation as the last, or ought to be, but is flirting instead with a man who sits beside her.

Below this group is an altar, with the sacred Chatta over it, under which two boys stand in attitudes of prayer, and around it are grouped buffaloes, oxen, sheep, and goats. Are they being blessed? or are they worshipping? On the right hand stands a man on the edge of a pond, into which a girl is pouring water; he has a wreath[1] (or is it a net?) in one hand and a pole in the other, and beside him another man with his hands joined in an attitude of prayer. Next to him stands a woman with a water-pot under her arm. Above them other men and women, and at the top of the picture a man with a bundle driving two oxen either to field or to market. It seems almost impossible to make a story out of so disconnected a picture as this. It may after all be merely meant to represent the family and the pastoral wealth of the giver of the Gateway, in the same manner as the pictures on the tombs round the Great Pyramid represent similar scenes in ancient Egypt. But whether this or any more recondite meaning should be given to it, it is a curious illustration of costumes, and life and manners in India in the first century of the Christian era.

This bas-relief occurs at the top of the left-hand pillar of the Eastern Gateway on the inner face (Plate XIV.), immediately above the two subjects entitled "The "conversion of the Kaśyapas" represented in Plate XXXII. This juxtaposition has induced Mr. Beal to connect the three together as successive scenes in the same history.[2] It may be so, but I confess I see nothing to establish it. There are no persons in the dress of ascetics in the upper picture, while all the grown up persons in the lower are in that costume. There are no women in the two under compartments, while here they are in a majority; and there seems nothing religious in the action of any parties in this bas-relief. Till something more definite is detected, I would prefer describing it as "a scene in domestic life."

---

[1] A similar object, whatever it may be, is hung on a peg on the upper right-hand corner of the picture.

[2] Journal Royal Asiatic Society, V., N. S., p. 177.

SANCHI. PLATE XXXVI.

FIG. 1.

FIG. 2.

Lt. Col. Maisey del. W. Griggs, Lith.

FOREST SCENE.

PLATE XXXVI.

MR. BEAL is of opinion that Figure 1 of the Plate represents the principal scenes of the Sâma Jâtaka as quoted below,[1] and I am not prepared to say this may not be correct, but if it is so the form of the fable must have been considerably altered since the first century. At Sanchi the king does not kill the boy by accident. He is being deliberately shot by a soldier. The king is standing unarmed at some distance, with his minister beside him, talking to an ascetic accompanied by his two wives or daughters, and consequently not Dakhala, which otherwise we might fancy him to be from the repetition of the same figure occurring sometimes in these bas-reliefs. It is probable that the figures in front of the Pansalas are meant to be represented as blind, not only from their being naked, but also from the monkeys stealing the fruit and pulling the thatch off the roof, with other circumstances. The two figures in the centre do look like a reduplication of the boy and the minister, and it is absolutely necessary it should be so if the Sâma Jâtaka is to be identified at all with this sculpture. Notwithstanding, however, the extraordinary consequences that frequently resulted from the extreme practice of the ascetic virtues by Buddhist saints, it does appear, carrying the doctrine "qui fecit per alium, fecit per se," rather too far, to represent a king abdicating his throne and becoming the slave of two blind hermits, because one of his soldiers had shot an innocent boy!

The dress of the soldiers is worthy of remark. They wear a kilt, and the usual cummerbund or waistband, and cross straps to carry their quivers. Their bows are bows of double flexure, which we usually associate with the Parthians or Amazons, but it is doubtful whether any ethnographic distinction can be founded on this peculiarity.

The scene represented in the lower figure of this Plate may possibly be an early version of one of the most favourite legends of the Buddhist chroniclers. It is mentioned by Fa-Hian,[2] and is narrated at length with the most miraculous accompaniments both in the Ceylonese Atthakathâ[3] and the Tibetan Lalita-Vistara.[4] It is

---

1 This fable is given by Spence Hardy (*Eastern Monachism*, p. 275) in these words, "When Gótama " Bodhisat was born in a former age as Sáma, son of the hermit Dukhula, he rendered every assistance to his " parents, who had become blind when he was 16 years of age. It happened that as he went one day for water " to the river, the king of Benares, Piliyaka, entered the forest to hunt, and as Sáma, after ascending from the " river, was as usual surrounded by deer, the king let fly an arrow which struck Sáma just as he was placing " the vessel to his shoulder. Feeling that he was wounded, . . . he called out, 'Who is it that has shot me?' " and when he learned it was the king, he related his history to the monarch, and said that his greatest grief " arose from the thought that his blind parents would now have no one to support them. When the king " perceived the intensity of his grief, he promised that he would resign his kingdom, and himself become the " slave of his parents. Meantime a Dewi, descending from the Dewa loka, remaining in the air near the king " without being visible, entreated him to go to the Pansal, and minister to the wants of the blind parents of " Sáma. He was obedient and went."

2 Foĕ-Kouĕ-Ki, XXII. p. 198.

3 J. A. S. B., VII. 804.

4 Lalita-Vistara, XII. 147, et seq. See also Cunningham, Bhilsa Topes, p. 219.

briefly this: when the Prince Siddhârtha had reached his sixteenth year, his father sought a wife for him among the daughters of the neighbouring Râjas. All refused, however, because the Prince, though handsome, had not been taught any martial accomplishment, and was therefore incapable of controlling women. To prove his power in this respect, he strung a bow that no one else could string, pierced with his arrows iron targets thicker than those of the Warrior or Minotaur, and at distances which neither Armstrong nor Whitworth could face; and lastly, shot an arrow an inconceivable distance, and where it lighted a spring of water gushed forth, which afterwards Fa-Hian tells us was formed into a fountain for travellers.

The only points of resemblance between the picture and the legend are, that a young warrior is shooting across a river, apparently at a rock, out of which a spring of water is gushing. If this is the Prince Siddhârtha, the man on horseback with the Chatta over his head, must be the Śâkya Daṇḍapâṇi, the father of the lovely Gopâ, and the man seated above his head, talking to the monkey, one of his defeated rivals. Two others are standing behind him. These three may be Ânanda, Devadatta, and Saundaranda.

In the foreground are three warriors armed with bow and sword, and beside them the usual accompaniment of drums and fifes.

The scene in which the action takes place is represented as a wood, inhabited by monkeys, who are gambolling among the trees, or seated in holes in the rocks. Through the picture runs a river, full of fish, and on its further bank two deer are lying. In none of the versions of the legend are we given to understand that the scene of the competition was in a forest; but we must recollect that the oldest written version we possess, which gives the details of the scene, is at least 400 years more modern than the sculpture, and in India far less time is sufficient to overlay the simplest facts with the most preposterous fables. It may, however, be that by representing a forest and a river, as intervening between the place where the prince was standing and the object he was shooting at, the artist intended to convey an idea of distance.[1]

The bas-relief is the upper one on the standing pillar of the Western Gateway on the front face. (Plate XIX.)

---

[1] Mr. Beal is of opinion that this bas-relief represents the Asadrisa Jâtaka, as told by Spence Hardy, Manual of Buddhism, p. 114, but I confess I am unable to agree with him in this. He is not firing at a mango e, and the other features of the picture seem to me to accord better with the legend given above.

SANCHI.

FIG. I.

FIG. 2

LT. COL. MAISEY. DEL. W GRIGGS LITH.

GARDEN SCENE.

PLATE XXXVII.

If the two scenes depicted in this Plate can be considered as anything like a fair representation of Buddhist feeling or Buddhist manners in the first century of our era, they present this faith in a marvellously different aspect from anything we have hitherto been taught to believe. If these had been found on a Palace Gateway, it might have been said that the manners of the Palace were not those of the Temple; but the upper one of these is that carved on the front of the Northern Gateway (Plate XII.). The other is the upper compartment in front of the fallen pillar of the Western Gateway.[1]

In the first we have on the right hand a Hindu gentleman playing on a harp, and singing to a lady who is sitting beside him, with her feet in the water of a fountain, and listening with no unwilling ear to her lover's song.

In the opposite compartment the lady is sitting on the gentleman's knee, and he is drinking something out of a cup which certainly is stronger than water.

In the foreground some ladies are disporting themselves in the water with two elephants, and the whole scene is one of pleasure and sensual enjoyment, the only costume of the ladies, except their chignons, is their bead belt and their bangles, but they have not all of them even this. The men are slightly better clad, but even they have more cloth in their turbans than in any other part of their dresses.

The lower bas-relief is of a very similar character. It is divided practically into four compartments, in each of which two persons, male and female, are seated on couches. Two of these groups are close to the waters of a lake, in which the lotus is shown as growing; two others are on a terrace, in the centre of which a flight of steps leads from the lake. On each of the couches a man and woman are seated in close conversation, to use the mildest term, and all are drinking. Below, or in front of the couch of the couple in the left-hand upper corner, is the wine pot or jar which continually recurs in the lithographs from the first (Plate XXIV.), but nowhere can it be so distinctly surmised that it contains an intoxicating liquid as here.[2]

On the top of the steps, between the two upper couple, stand a man and woman, evidently servants, the woman giggling most unmistakeably, and holding

---

[1] The scene immediately below this on this Gateway is so much defaced that it is difficult to make out what it represents; but from what remains, it seems to have been warmer than that here given.

[2] We ought not to be surprised that drinking should be a favourite indulgence in these days. The Mahâbhârata is full of drinking scenes, and many of its episodes turn on the results of intoxication. Even the gods in those days got drunk on Soma juice; why not poor mortals? In addition to this, we must bear in mind that though the Hindus of the plains are so remarkable for their temperance, all the hill tribes drink joyously to the present day. No ceremony, civil or religious, takes place without drinking and dancing, and the festival generally is brought to a close by all—the men, at least—being so drunk as to be unable to continue it.

her hand to her mouth to prevent an explosion of hilarity, and not without reason. The man, too, turns up his eyes in amazed astonishment.

The arbours under which two of the couples are seated, are curious instances of that sort of summer-house which may be found adorning tea gardens in the neighbourhood of London at the present day.[1]

It is scenes like these that make us hesitate before asserting that there could not possibly be any connexion between Buddhism and the Scandinavian religion. As we shall see in the next Plate, Buddhists could also fight—for a religious purpose, it is true,—but still if Hindus of that faith could fight and drink even to the modified extent to which we find them practised here in the first century after Christ, it requires only a moderate knowledge of political arithmetic to calculate what may have taken place a few centuries earlier. The authors of the Mahâbhârata gloat as joyously over the slaughter of the myriads that lay unburied on the fatal battle field of Kurukshetra after eighteen days fight, as any Scandinavian scald could have done over the deeds of any of Wodin's companions; and if Hindus could then drink and fight, as we have every reason to suppose they did, the gulf between the two religions was not at one time so impassable as it afterwards appears to have become. If we would understand the subject, we must turn from those books which have hitherto been our only sources of information, and look back to a time before the iron of asceticism had eaten into the souls of the followers of Śâkya Muni.

---

[1] Mr. Beal, whose opinion on such subjects is generally so valuable, arrived at the conclusion that these love scenes represent the joys of the Triyastriñshas heaven, and quotes several passages from modern Chinese authors, which show that they at least conceived a future state as full of sensual delights, as the Mahomedan; and then goes on to quote several passages from more ancient authorities which promise this heaven to believers, but without mentioning its sensual pleasures, in so far at least as the quotations go (J. R. A. S., N. S., V. p. 181). But, assuming that all this can be reconciled, I cannot see any signs by which these representations can be distinguished from the ordinary mundane scenes around them. There are no flying or celestial figures of any sort, and no peculiarities of divine existence, and when we compare these with similar representations of similar scenes in the frescoes at Ajanta, and trace them on till we reach their development in Vishnuism, I think it must be admitted that they are of the earth earthy, and have no touch of the celestial about them.

SANCHI,

PLATE XXXVIII.

FIG. 1.

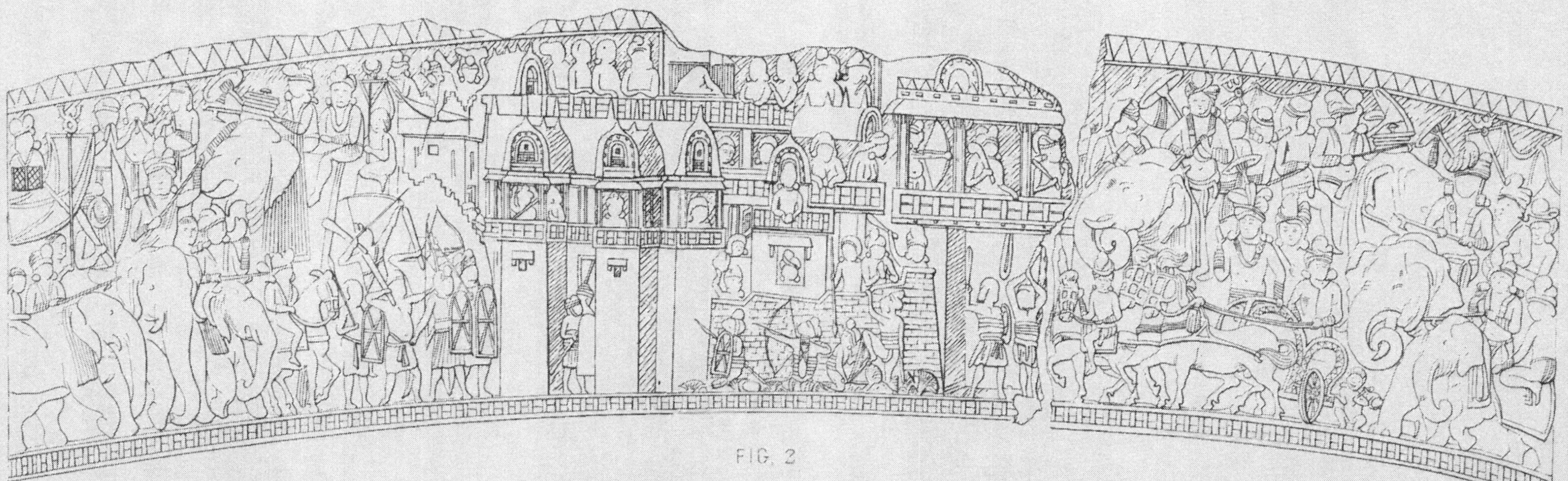

FIG. 2.

Lt. Col. Maisey del. W. Griggs. Lith.

SIEGE AND RECOVERY OF THE RELICS.

PLATE XXXVIII.

From love to war the transition in the history of most nations is easy and direct, but we hardly expect to meet either in the annals of Buddhism. It is not difficult, however, to see from the upper bas-relief in this Plate taken from the fallen fragments of the Southern Gateway what was the cause of the war thereon depicted. It represents a siege, but on either side an elephant is escaping, bearing a relic casket on his head, and that casket shaded by the sacred Chatta, denoting its importance. It is impossible to say, of course, what these relics are, or what the city that is besieged, but it is at least curious that the caskets are almost perfect pictures of those which contain the relics of Śâriputra and Moggalâna, which were deposited in the neighbouring Topes close at hand. Nothing can be more probable than that the acquisition of these important relics should form the subject of a bas-relief, but we have no record of where they were originally deposited, or whether they were stolen from Sanchi and again recovered, nor by whom they were finally enshrined in the Tope from which they were so lately exhumed.

No. 25.

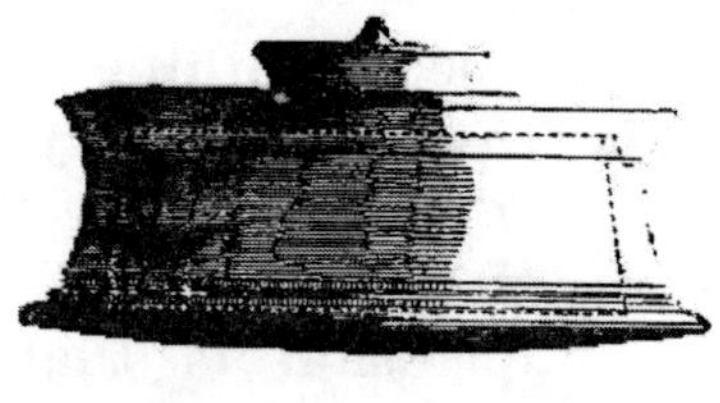

Relic Casket of Śâriputra, from Satdhara Tope.
From a drawing by Colonel Maisey.

No. 26.

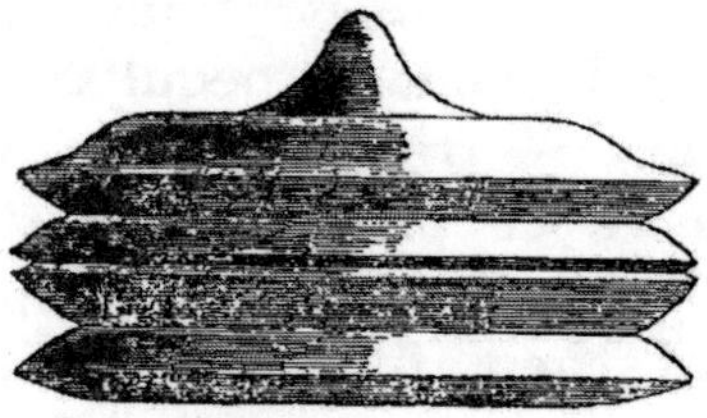

Relic Casket of Moggalâna, from No. 3 Tope.
From a Drawing by Colonel Maisey.

On the right we have three Prinees, or at least three Chattawallahs. The principal of these seems to be the one in the chariot; but none of them are armed, or seem inclined to take any part in the fight. On the left, also we have a chief, without a Chatta on his elephant, with a smaller one in either hand; but he too looks more like a spectator than a sharer in the fight.

In the centre the siege is carried on vigorously. Two men on the right, with the kilt and a breastplate like a Roman soldier, are acting as slingers. A body of archers and spearmen are assaulting a low outwork in the centre, and bowmen and spearmen are storming the gateway, at which two of the assailants seem to have effected an entrance.

The besieged defend themselves with arrows and spears, and throw down large masses of stone on the heads of their assailants; but what seems strange, no engines of war are used,—neither ladders nor battering rams,—nor is any attempt made to set fire to the place. In all these respects the Hindus seem to have been very much behind the stage, in the art of war, which we know from the Nineveh sculptures that the Assyrians reached at a much earlier age.

The lower bas-relief, Fig. 2, has already been partially described in speaking of the Western Gateway. It is a representation on a larger scale of the triumphal procession, depicted on the lowest beam of that gateway, and though distant in time, if we are correct in the date above assigned to the gateway, it looks like the immediate sequel of the events depicted on the Southern Gateway. The relic casket borne on the head of a man seated on an elephant in the centre with the Chatta and Chaori most unmistakeably point it out as the principal object in the procession. There is, however, nothing to indicate whose relics are being thus honoured, nor what the name may be of the city into whose gates the procession is entering. In this part of the procession there is no Royal personage, but there is one above on the central beam, who, with apparently his son in the foreground, are the principal personages there. But there is nothing in either bas-relief that enables us to fix with anything like certainty who these personages are or to what city they are tending.

It seems quite clear that the object of these bas-reliefs is to represent the acquisition or recovery of some important relics by the community at Sanchi, and as the sculptures are the gifts of private individuals, the events depicted probably occurred at some date considerably anterior to that of the sculptures themselves. My impression is that the relics are those of Śâriputra and Moggalâna, and the hero of the triumph, Aśoka himself. But this, in the present state of our knowledge, to say the most of it, is little more than conjecture. Be this as it may, these two bas-reliefs are of great interest, in the first place, as showing the state of the arts in India in the early centuries of the Christian era. They certainly are superior to any of the Assyrian sculptures depicting similar scenes, and can hardly be said to be inferior to contemporary sculptures on Trajan's column or other similar subjects at Rome.

As illustrations of costume, they are also of great value; but perhaps their most curious peculiarity is their being illustrative of a religious Buddhist war! So far as we know, no war was ever undertaken by a Buddhist community for the sake of propagating their faith or extending the area of their religion. But the desire to possess relics seems to have roused passions antithetical to the usual form of their faith, and they fought either to acquire or to recover these most valued treasures, and they triumphed gloriously when they brought back these treasures to the sanctuary, where they reposed till disturbed by the antiquarian curiosity of two Englishmen in 1854!

SANCHI.

PLATE XXXIX.

FIG. 1.

LT COL. MAISEY DEL.

FIG. 2.

W. GRIGGS, LITH.

LION CAPITALS.

PLATES XXXIX., XL., AND XLI.

PLATE XXXIX.

THE lion capital (Fig. 1) in this Plate once adorned a lâṭ that stood immediately in front of the Southern Gateway of the great Tope. From a comparison of the style, and especially of the honeysuckle ornament and the sacred geese of its abacus, with what we find on pillars at Allahabad and Tirhoot, which undoubtedly were erected by Aśoka, we may feel quite confident that this too was erected by him. If this is so, it proves either that the great Tope was erected by that monarch, or that he erected this pillar as an additional ornament to a pre-existing monument. For reasons above given, my conviction is that the Tope was erected by him also, and its date consequently is not far from 250 B.C.

The other capital is that of the fallen Southern Gateway, and seems evidently to be imitated from the older one in its immediate proximity. The honeysuckle ornament has become Indianized, and the execution of the lions is stiff and conventional. It may be suggested that this inferiority may be partly owing to the circumstance that the original lion sculptors came from the north-west—from Bactria—where lions abounded, and that Malwa afforded no models from which the true nature of the animal could be studied. But, on the whole, it seems as probable that they indicate a decay of art from the time when it was first introduced into India under Grecian or rather Bactrian influence, till about the Christian era. Unfortunately we have very little that was executed between these two periods that would enable us to settle this question.

If any of the sculptures of the Caves at Cuttack[1] are as early as Aśoka's time they would throw considerable light on the subject, but their age is still too indefinite to allow of any argument being based upon them. The capitals of these two pillars would certainly justify us in asserting that animal sculpture had declined between the time of Aśoka and the Christian era, but till we have some really authentic example of figure sculpture of the same age it seems premature to express an opinion. Looking forward, it may safely be asserted that the sculptures at Amravati had gained both in power of expression and in delicacy of execution during the three centuries that elapsed between them; and, carrying the series backward three centuries further, we might expect extreme rudeness in Aśoka's time. He, on the other hand, was probably in immediate contact with the Bactrians, and the art may have oscillated backwards and forwards according to the encouragement given it, or the favourable or unfavourable circumstances either of locality or example under which it was practised.

---

[1] J. A. S. B., vol. VII., plates XLII. and XLIV. They will be found described and photographed in the last Appendix at the end of the volume, from casts taken by Mr. Locke in the spring of last year.

It may be observed, *en passant*, that the winged lion on the abacus of Fig. 2 is much more nearly allied to his Assyrian, or rather Persian, prototype than his degenerate descendants at Amravati.

PLATE XL.

The lower group of elephants in Plate XL. is likewise from the Southern Gateway; it is on one of the blocks over the pillars which separate the architraves into parts (Plate XVI.). It is another indication of the greater antiquity of the Southern Gateway, inasmuch as though not a capital itself, it is evidently just such a suggestion as might lead to the design of the elephant capitals of the Northern or Eastern Gateway, one of which is represented in the upper figure of this Plate.

The figure on the elephant in front of the lower one appears to be royal, from the Chatta borne over his head, and to be followed by another elephant, bearing a relic casket on his head, over which the Chatta of state is displayed. The standard which is borne behind him is of the stars and stripes pattern, while that on the upper capital from the Eastern Gateway is the union jack design; both have the Buddhist Trisul emblem, though in the lower one it is partially broken away. The truth and vigour with which the elephants are sculptured in both these groups go far to disturb the theory just hinted at of a general decline of art at the period they were sculptured, and must rather favour the idea that it was in the representation of lions only that the sculptors of Sanchi had broken down.

PLATE XLI.

The lower figure of the Plate represents the capital of the Western Gateway, which is identical in design with those of the smaller or No. 3 Tope (Plate XXI.), and therefore probably of the same age, though, as before stated, there is little doubt that the gateways to which they belong are the most modern of the five here found, though it is difficult to understand how, after executing anything so beautiful as the lion and elephant capitals of the other Gateways, they could perpetrate anything so detestable as these. A desire of novelty may have led to the adoption of the dwarfs, after their introduction on the middle architrave of the Northern Gateway (Plate VII.), or they may have a mythological meaning we fail to detect.

The figure of Buddha (Plate XLI. Fig. 1) from the Vihara is introduced here because it is similar to four figures which now stand against the Tope inside the Rail, and on which it has been attempted to found an argument as to their antiquity. This one, however, has upon it the familiar "Ye dharma hetu" inscription in the Kuṭila characters of the tenth century, and these, with other indications from the locality where it is found, prove that it cannot be earlier than that date. This is, besides, about the date that would be assigned to it from its style, by anyone familiar with Indian sculpture. The others may be earlier, but not by any long period, though without photographs or drawings of them it is impossible to say what their exact age may be.

FIG I.

FIG. 2.

LT COL WISLY DEL. W. GRIGGS. LITH.

ELEPHANT CAPITALS.

SANCHI

PLATE XLI.

FIG. I.

FIG. 2.

LT. COL. MAISEY DEL. W. GRIGGS, LITH.

FIGURES OF BUDDHA AND DWARF CAPITAL.

SANCHI,

PLATE XLII.

FIG, 1.

FIG, 2

FIG, 3.

LT COL. MAISEY DEL.

W. GRIGGS, LITH. INDIA MUSEUM

CHAKRA PILLARS FROM SMALLER TOPES.

FIG. I.

FIG. 2.

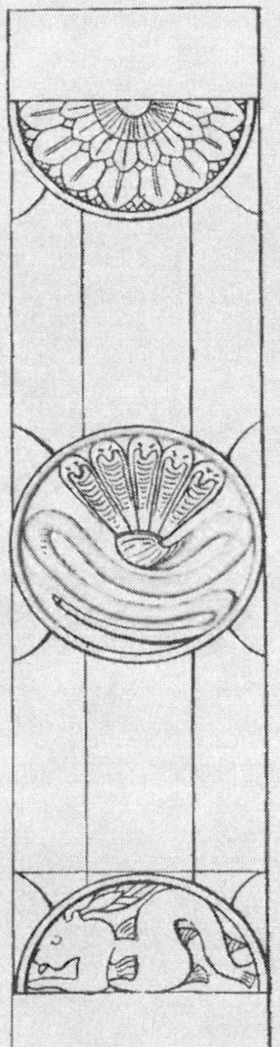

FIG. 3.

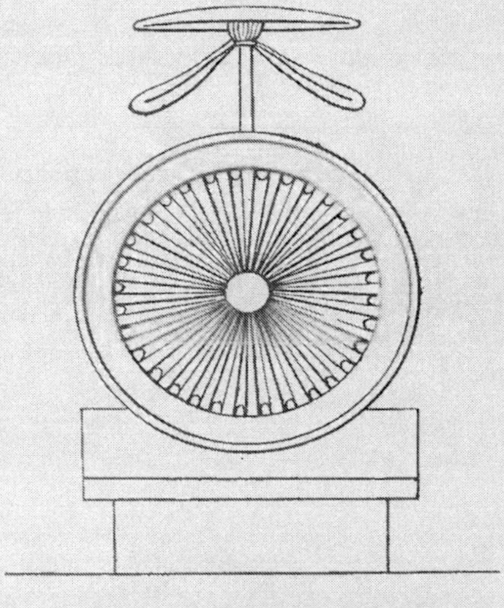

FIG. 4

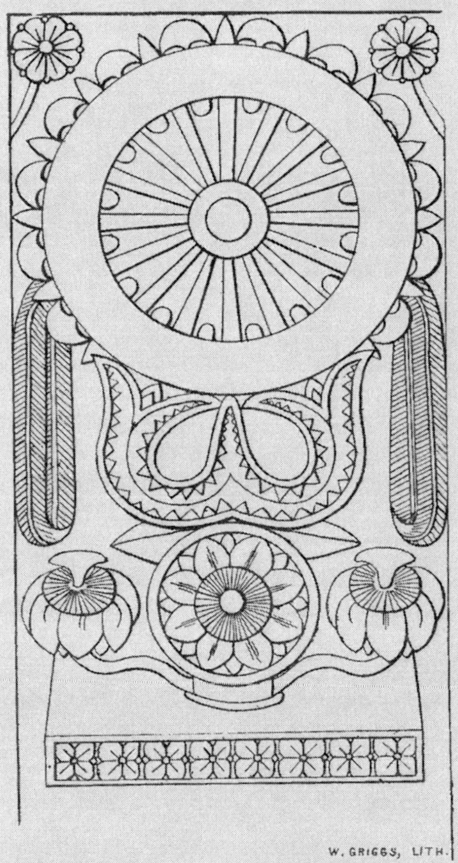

FIG. 5.

LT COL. MAISEY DEL.

W. GRIGGS, LITH.

DETAILS OF SCULPTURE.

PLATES XLII. AND XLIII.

For reasons given above, page 100, it seems probable that the Rail of the smaller Tope (No. 2, in plan, Plate I.), is intermediate in date between that of the Rail of the great Tope and of the Gateways which were added to it in the first century of our era. Were it not, however, for the form of the characters in which its inscriptions are written, there are circumstances which might induce us to assume even a more modern date for its erection. Eventually it may turn out that it is so, but for the present we must be content to assume that it was erected about one century before the Christian era.[1]

There are no bas-reliefs, properly so called, on the Rail, but all the discs on the pillars are sculptured (Figs. 2 and 5, Plate XLIII., are examples) "either with "rosettes, human or animal figures, monsters, emblems, and other objects, very "poorly executed, and, with one or two exceptions, not worth a detailed description." Among these, Colonel Maisey enumerates "elephants, seated female with lotus, bull, "monster with alligator's head and fish's tail, five-headed Nâga, wheel, tortoise,— "emblem of Kâśyapa,—monster half lion half fish, lion, lion with bull in his mouth, "woman riding a male centaur, horseman, female centaur, snake, canopied female "figure mounted on human-headed animal, bird-killing snake, &c." "The angle "pillars of the entrance," he adds, "are rather more decorated, and some of them "of very superior execution." Two of these are represented in Plate XLII. Figs. 1 and 2. The first represents the sacred Wheel adorned with garlands, and standing on a pillar, surmounted by four elephants; three only are shown, of course; and on one side a woman offering a lotus bud, on the other a man in the attitude of prayer. No. 2 is very similar, except that there are two lions and two elephants on the top of the pillar, and no human figures. Both these wheels are adorned externally by objects like hatchets, but which I have no doubt are meant for the Trisul emblem so frequently alluded to above.

Fig. 3, in Plate XLII., is a representation of a similar object from the Gateway of the small Tope No. 3 (Plate XXI.). It is hardly distinguishable in design from the other two, except that it is more crowded with figures, and Garuḍas or Devas bringing offerings, which apparently do not occur at No. 2 Tope. There is also an attempt at perspective in the capital, and on the whole it looks more modern, but how much it is impossible to say.

PLATE XLIII.

Fig. 1 in this Plate is from one of the gate pillars of No. 2 Tope, and represents two men apparently turning the wheel and two women in attitudes of devotion. Is this the original of the prayer wheel of the Thibetans? Fig. 4 is a combination

[1] Whatever its age may ultimately be determined to be it seems quite certain that the great rail at Buddh-Gayâ was erected cotemporaneously.

often met with of the Wheel with the Trisul emblem. If I am not mistaken, it means Buddha and the Law, or it may be the Law of Buddha. Fig. 3 on this Plate is a similar combination of a wheel on an altar, with the ennobling Chatta over it. Figs. 2 and 5 have already been described. The first is one of the pillars of No. 2 Tope, the second a rosette, which replaces the five-headed Nâga on another of these pillars.

One of the most interesting points connected with these wheel pillars is, that they almost exactly reproduce the pillars that stand in front of the Caves at Kârlâ and Salsette; not only is their architectural form identical, but the four lions which surmount them are the same, and my impression is that the Kârlâ pillar once supported a metal wheel, which has now disappeared; but be this as it may, if we are correct in assigning the Kârlâ Cave to the first century B.C.—which I see no reason for doubting—it is a satisfactory confirmation of the date to find identically the same architectural forms at Sanchi at the same period.

At Amravati, three or four centuries later, the wheel pillars became even more important, and also infinitely more elaborate, and are among the most prominent ornaments of that building.

In Fa-Hian's travels (A.D. 400) we have a description of two pillars, 70 feet high, which adorned the entrance of the Jetavana monastery, outside the gates of Śrâvastî, the old capital of Kośala in Oude, in the time of Śâkya Muni. One of these was surmounted by a wheel, the other by an ox.[1] So at least he says; but Hiouen-Thsang corrects him. When he saw the pillars, more than 200 years afterwards, he calls the ox an elephant, which is much more likely; but the wheel had been replaced by a Dagoba[2]—a very common form. If the wheel was of metal, it may have been stolen during the reign of some Brahmanical king.

It is curious that we almost lose sight of Tree Worship in the sculptures of these smaller Topes, though it forms so prominent a feature in those of the great one. It does occur in No. 3 (see Plate XXI.), but in a very subordinate manner, and I can find no trace of it in Colonel Maisey's descriptions of No. 2 Tope. I do not, however, know that any argument can be based on this. Tree Worship certainly did prevail long before they were erected; but their preference for the Serpent and neglect of the Tree is worthy of attention, and may hereafter lead to some interesting conclusions.

---

1 Foĕ-Kouĕ-Ki, p. 171.

2 Si-Yü-Ki, I. p. 296. It is curious, however, to remark that even he was mistaken at Sankissa, where he describes an elephant on the top of a pillar as a lion, when it was an elephant with only his trunk broken off. It was drawn by General Cunningham, and is engraved from his drawing in my History of Architecture, Woodcut, 970.

SANCHI.

PLATE XLIV.

FIG. 3

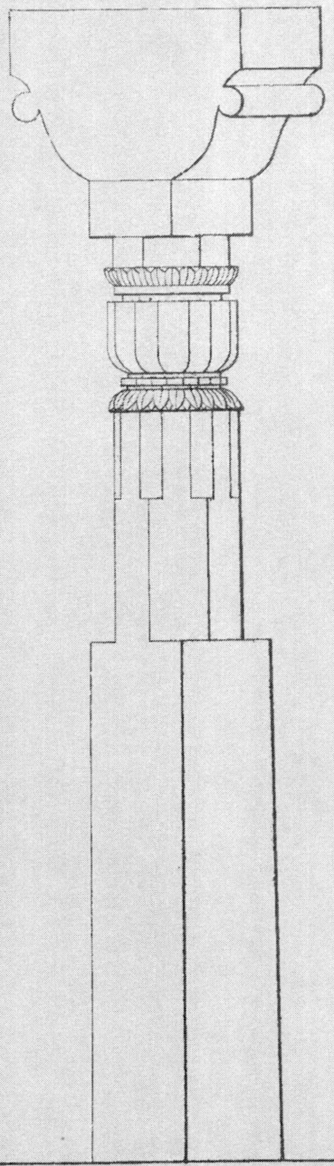

FIG. 1

FIG. 2.

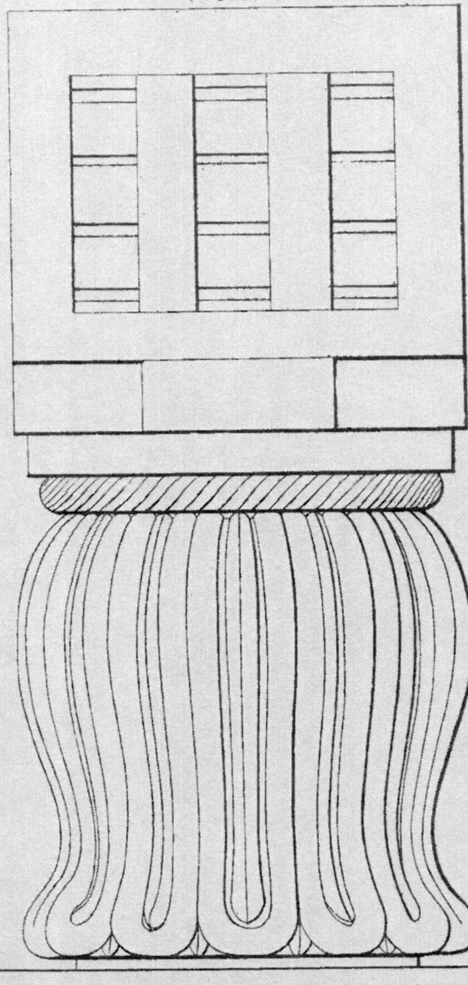

FIG. 4

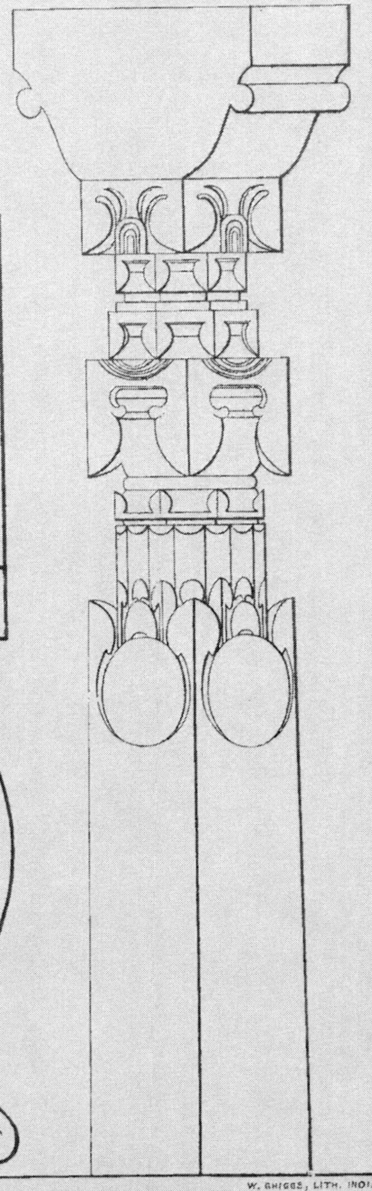

LT COL. MAISEY DEL.

W. GRIGGS, LITH. INDIA MUSEUM

ARCHITECTURAL DETAILS.

FIG I.

LT COL. MAISEY DEL.

FIG. 2.

W. BRIGGS, LITH

NAGA CAPITALS.

PLATES XLIV. AND XLV.

THE statue and capital (Figs. 1 and 2) represented on Plate XLIV. were found lying near the North Gateway, with only a fragment of the shaft that once supported them, the rest having probably been used for sugar mills long ago. The execution of the statue is so extremely good that it would be interesting to fix its date, if possible; but there is no inscription and no indication on the spot to enable us to do so directly. There is, however, at Erun, not far away, a pillar bearing a Gupta inscription, with a capital and statue so nearly identical with this, that the probability is that they may be of about the same age. If I am correct in the date, I assign to the Guptas A.D. 318 to 490; this would place the statue with its pillar in the fourth or fifth century, which, from its style, I am inclined to think is by no means an unlikely date. What adds to this probability is the knowledge that Chandragupta was a benefactor to the Tope at Sanchi. His inscription is seen on the Rail, Plate VIII., and will be found translated in the Journal of the Bengal Asiatic Society, vol. VI. p. 455, and is just such as would lead us to expect some additions to the fane by him about the year 400.

The rays round the head, the absence of a Chatta, or anything indicating kingly state, render it possible that it is intended as a statue of Buddha; in that case one of the earliest known. There are no statues of the great founder of this religion either at Kârlâ nor the early Caves of Ajanta, and I fancy we must come down nearly to the age of Buddha-Ghoso, A.D. 410, before free standing statues were carved in his honour. But we know too little as yet to express any distinct opinion on such a subject. It is also possible that it may represent one of the Gupta kings, or perhaps it is only some other benefactor to the shrine.

The two pillars, Figs. 3 and 4, are from the portico to the Chaitya hall, photographed, Plate XXII. They are very elegant examples of Hindu architecture. Colonel Maisey suggests that the portico may have been added afterwards, and that this may account for their more modern aspect. Applying to them the same test as to the capital and statue, it would seem that they too belong to the Gupta age. If at least the fragments of architecture which are found at Erun belong to the fifth century, which I see no reason to doubt, these must also certainly be ascribed to the same date. It would be extremely interesting if this could be established, for we have no other structural remains in Central India which are known to belong to that age, and the gap so formed is one it would be most desirable to fill up.

The two Nâga shrouded statues represented in Plate XLV. are found in the immediate neighbourhood of Sanchi—No. 1 at the village of Ferozepore, the other on the Nagore hill, not far off. They are both probably more modern than the Topes or their sculptures, and, like the statue in the last Plate, may date from the time of the Guptas. Fig. 2 is evidently the most modern of the two. Neither are remarkable as examples of sculpture, but are curious as exemplifying the belief in the efficacy of the protecting hood of the Nâga.

Our lithographed illustrations began with a representation of this snake hood on Plate XXIV., which is nearly as old as the Christian era. They terminate with it here, at a period probably as late as the sixth or seventh century. After this period it seems to have faded out of use as applied to mortals, but to have been appropriated either to the Jaina Tírthankars, or to some of the forms of Vishṇu. It is the common accompaniment of the image of that god even to the present day.

Although it died out in India, the custom still exists elsewhere. In Nepaul, for instance, when it was desired to do honour to one of the late kings, a statue of him was placed on the top of a tall pillar, exactly as is done here; and a cobra, standing on his tail, is represented as spreading his protecting hood over his sacred-head.

All this, as well as many other things advanced in the preceding pages, will be much more clear and intelligible when we have described the sculptures at Amravati. The two together form a nearly complete illustration of the arts and architecture of India during the first five centuries of the Christian era; but Amravati is scarcely intelligible without Sanchi, and the contrary is equally the case. Many things which the older and simpler forms leave obscure, become clear when they are read by the light of the more modern gloss. We have hitherto been wholly dependent on the rock-cut examples for all we know on the subject, and they, as before explained, are rude, from the nature of the material in which they are carved, and imperfect from the exigencies of their situation. These two Topes supply their deficiencies, and when the sculptures at Amravati have been described, we shall have a tolerably clear conception of the earliest forms of lithic art in the peninsula of Hindostan.[1]

---

[1] All the emblems which adorn these Gateways, and which are alluded to in the preceding descriptions, are found with more or less distinctness on the coins of the period. In the annexed example, for instance, Woodcut No. 27, borrowed from Mr. Thomas's paper in the 1st vol. New Series of the Journal of the Royal Asiatic Society, we have nearly all of them.

No. 27.

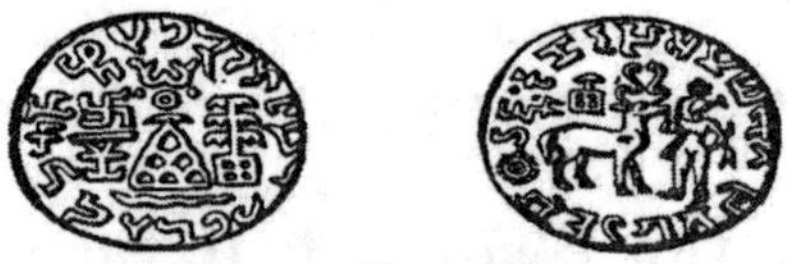

Coin of Kraṇanda.

In the centre of the left-hand figure is the conventional representation of a Dagoba surmounted by a Chatta, and above this the circle, and over that the Trisul. If the interpretation suggested in the Woodcut, No. 19, is correct, these symbolize water and air. On the right of the Dagoba is the Tree, very similar in form to the Persian example, Woodcut, page 12, and in the field on the left the swastica, and below it an emblem which is found in the necklace, Plate III. Fig. 4. It may be an altar. Below the Dagoba is seen the Serpent, which is hardly ever omitted from these early coins, and often occupies a more prominent place than he does here. On the other face of the coin the field is occupied by a conventional representation of a deer, attended by a female as lightly clad as those in the bas-reliefs generally are. Over the deer what seems intended as repetition of the Tree emblem, or it may be only the symbol of a sacred enclosure with the ennobling Chatta over it.

The inscription on the two faces of the coin, in old Pali and in Aryan characters, reads, "This is the "coin of the great king, the king Kraṇanda, the brother of Amogha." On the strength of the name, and other indications, Mr. Thomas ascribes this coin to one of the nine Nandas who reigned before 325 B.C. My own impression is that it is more modern, probably subsequent to Aśoka, but certainly anterior to the sculptures of the Sanchi Gateways.

THE TOPE AT AMRAVATI.

CHAPTER I.

UNLIKE that at Sanchi, the Tope at Amravati has been so completely destroyed that a traveller might ride over the mounds in which it is buried without suspecting what they covered, any more than those who, before the discoveries of Botta and Layard, looked on the mounds of Assyria, guessed what treasures of antiquity were concealed beneath their green slopes. In some respects it is fortunate that it is so, for so soon as a slab is uncovered, either by the monsoon rains or an accidental excavation, it is taken away to be used as a door-step, or more frequently to be burned for lime by the incurious natives. The consequence of this is, that nothing of the central building probably now remains on the spot, and hardly anything of the inner enclosure; but of the outer Rail there may still be enough to enable us to complete our restoration of it, and to fill up many of the lacunæ which the imperfect materials now available have left in our descriptions.

Although two of the Gateways at Sanchi have fallen, two others are still standing, almost quite perfect; and a quadrant of the Rail is entire, and so is the bulk of the Tope itself. We have consequently no difficulty in assigning their proper place to all the fragments of sculpture, nor any in comprehending the general appearance or form of the building. At Amravati the case is widely different. It is probable that many of the slabs which Colonel Mackenzie first saw in 1797, and afterwards drew in 1816–18, were then *in situ*, but he has left no written description of his excavations,[1] and it is only in the rarest possible instances that he has written in pencil on his drawings such brief indications as "inner circle" or "outer circle." Beyond this, there is no explanation of his plan. The slabs recovered by Sir Walter Elliot, which form the bulk of the available materials, had all been removed probably in the twelfth or thirteenth century from their original site, and built into a little chapel of which they formed the walls, so nothing was to be learned from them. The task, however, is by no means so difficult as it at first sight appears. First, there are numerous analogies with other buildings which are evident at a glance; but the circumstance that rendered the restoration most easy

[1] The late Professor Wilson, who had long charge of the Mackenzie MSS., and knew more about them than anyone else, says, in his Ariana Antiqua, p. 32, "I have not found any description of it (the Tope at Amravati) "amongst his papers, but from a few brief memoranda it appears to have been visited by him repeatedly, and in "1816 to have been measured and surveyed."

arose from the practice common to Indian architects of repeating everywhere representations of their main buildings as ornaments to the various parts of it. These, as will afterwards be explained, not only suggest the form, but confirm the restoration in a most satisfactory manner.

The Amravati Tope first attracted the attention of Colonel Mackenzie when on a tour of duty in the district in the year 1797. It seems that some two or three years previous to his visit, the Râjah of Chintapilly, attracted by the sanctity of a temple dedicated to Śiva, under the title of Amareśvara,[1] determined to erect a city on the spot, and on looking for building materials for his new capital, opened this and several other mounds in the neighbourhood, and also utilized the walls of the old city of Durnacotta or Dharaṇikoṭṭa, which stood about half a mile to the westward of the site of the new city.[2] Many of the antiquities perished in the process, and large quantities of the stones were used by the Râja in building his new temples and palaces, but several sculptured slabs still remained *in situ*. These attracted the Colonel's attention so strongly that he subsequently communicated an account of them to the Asiatic Society of Bengal,[3] and afterwards returned to the spot in 1816. Being now Surveyor-General of Madras he employed all the means at his disposal during the two following years to the elucidation of the principal temple, which he now styles Dîpaldinna, and translates as meaning "Hill of Lights." The results of his labours are careful plans of the building and maps of the surrounding country, together with eighty very carefully-finished drawings of the sculptures. These were made by his assistants, Messrs. Hamilton, Newman, and Burke, and are unsurpassed for accuracy and beauty of finish by any drawings of their class that were ever executed in India. Three copies were made of all these drawings. One was sent to the Asiatic Society of Calcutta, another was deposited in Madras, and the third sent home to the Court of Directors, in whose library it still remains. As no text or description accompanies these drawings, they have attracted but little attention, probably because of this deficiency, and the consequent difficulty of understanding the form of the monument or the position of the fragments.

At the same time Colonel Mackenzie sent several specimens of the sculptures to the three museums just mentioned, and they have remained their principal ornaments to this day. But, except an attempt to translate two of the inscriptions, which appeared in Prinsep's Journal in 1837,[4] very little notice seems to have been taken of them.[5]

Fortunately, however, when Mr., now Sir Walter Elliot, was Commissioner in Guntur, in 1840, he determined to follow up what Colonel Mackenzie had so well

---

[1] Hence the full-length name of the place is Amareśvarapuram, city of the immortal God. Anglice, Amresbury?

[2] These and many other historical particulars in this paper are gleaned from two letters communicated by Colonel Mackenzie to Mr. Buckingham, published by him in the "Calcutta Journal," in March 1822. They were afterwards reprinted in "Allen's Asiatic Journal," in May 1823, and as the latter publication is generally accessible while the former is not, all my references to these letters will be taken from it.

[3] See Asiatic Researches, vol. IX. p. 272, et seq.

[4] Journal Asiatic Society, Bengal, vol. VI. p. 218.

[5] In 1855 I published a plan of the building in my Handbook of Architecture, hoping to attract attention to it, but I was not then aware of what Sir Walter Elliot had done, nor had I discovered any key to the mystery. Except the inscription just mentioned, it was, I believe, the first and only attempt made to utilize Colonel Mackenzie's materials.

begun. He excavated a portion of the monument which had not before been touched, and sent down to Madras a large collection of the sculptures, where they lay exposed to the sun and rain for fourteen years,[1] till they were ultimately sent home to this country about the year 1856. Unfortunately they arrived here in the troublous times of the Indian Mutiny, and just in the interval between the death of the old East India Company and the establishment of the new Indian Council. There was no proper place for their reception, and the greater part of them were consequently stowed away in the coach-house of Fife House, where they remained buried under rubbish of all sorts till accidentally I heard of their existence in January 1867. With the zealous co-operation of Dr. Forbes Watson and the officers of his establishment, I had them all brought out into the open air and photographed to a scale of one-twelfth the real size and this was done so exactly that the photographs can be fitted together almost as well as the real stones could be. With these materials I set to work to restore the building; but though I had considerable knowledge of similar buildings, both older and more modern, I should not have succeeded but for the circumstance just mentioned, that among the sculptures themselves there are numerous miniature representations of the building itself and of its different parts, quite sufficiently correctly drawn to be recognized. With all these aids I believe I can now assign the true place and use to at least nine-tenths of the 160 fragments the Indian Museum possesses, and feel very little doubt that I might be able to recognize the position of all; but the process is slow and difficult, and requires more time and study than perhaps the value of the additional information now to be obtained would justify.

The position of the Amravati Tope will be easily understood from the map (Plate XLVI.). It is situated on the right or south bank of the Kistnah river, about sixty miles from its mouth, and nearly opposite to its junction to the Moony Air river. The Tope itself stands about half a mile to the eastward of the old town of Durnacotta, or Dharanikoṭṭa — the magic city—and unfortunately in the middle of the modern town of Amravati, to which circumstance it owes its destruction. To the westward of the town, a little more distant, is another mound, called Cootchtippa, which has not yet been explored; and to the south a third, called Nuckadeverdinna, which was dug up, and the materials used in building the new town. To the westward of the old town, near the Cootchtippa mound, are a great number of those rude circles of stone which were the burying-places of at least some of the inhabitants of the old city. A still greater number of these, however, are found at a distance of between four and five miles to the south-eastward, where they cover the roots of the hills in great numbers.[2] They range apparently from 24 to 32 feet in diameter, and when dug into have always yielded cinerary urns, burnt bones, and other indications of being burying-places. One of these has already been given from Colonel Mackenzie's work (Woodcut, No. 8), where several of

---

[1] Selections from the Madras Records, 2nd series, vol. XXXIX. p. 195.

[2] In the map they are called "Circular Tumuli." This they certainly are not, as they are not raised in the centre. They are literally stone circles, but as the map is a fac-simile, I have thought it better to alter nothing. I have also generally retained the spelling of the map, though it certainly is not in all instances correct.

those at Amravati are drawn. They are, however, all alike in character, not only here, but, so far as I can ascertain, are to be found all over the south of India as far as Cape Comorin.

We are still very far indeed from any such knowledge of the modes of sepulture among the aborigines, as to be able to speak regarding them with anything like certainty. Ample materials, however, exist in India, and so soon as anyone will take the trouble to collect and classify them, we shall from their graves be able to discriminate between the different races, and assign to each its proper locality with a precision now entirely wanting to such researches. Nothing of the sort can of course be attempted here, but one curious feature may be alluded to, as it has not yet been suspected by European antiquaries; it is, that these rude megalithic monuments are of all ages; some no doubt of extreme antiquity, but many others of quite recent date; many, in fact, have been erected within the limits of this century, and it is not possible, either from their design or their form, to distinguish between those which are really old and those which are quite modern.[1] In the meanwhile, however, I may be allowed to state that, to my mind, it does not appear doubtful but that the great Rail of the Amravati Tope is only a sublimation of these primitive models, though we are still unable to trace the various steps by which so wonderful a transformation took place.

Besides these antiquities in the immediate vicinity of the town, we learn from a note by Col. Mackenzie that there is a very extensive excavation near Datchapully, forty miles westward, covered with sculpture in a most masterly style, and another on the road leading from the river to the pagoda of Srichallum, ten miles further on. There is also a four-storied cavern at Oondavully in Guntur, mentioned further on (p. 168), and another series in the Ellore districts, at a place called Jilkaragoodum. All these, however, are quite unknown to Europeans, though, if carefully examined, they would probably prove as interesting as the better known Caves of Western India.[2]

---

[1] In my work on "Rude Stone Monuments" I tried to utilise such materials as were then available to describe and classify these Indian sepulchres. Since this work was published, about a year ago, I have obtained a good deal of additional information, all confirmatory of the conclusion I had arrived at, and which, with some further additions, may make this history as clear to others as it is to myself.

[2] The following curious memorandum, in a clerk's handwriting, is pasted into one of Colonel Mackenzie's volumes with some pencil marks of his own. I fancy it belongs to 1798, though that date on it is erased. Speaking of the Amravati sculptures, he says, "The most curious and most complete is to be found further on "(from the Dipaldinna) close to the outside walls of the Pagoda enclosure, on the south, and going towards "the river. Here is a small Pagoda of the Lingam, formed by three rough stones or slabs set on end and "covered on the top by another placed transversely" (exactly like Kits Coty House, as shown by a little sketch on the margin). "On this stone is represented the escalade of a fort, a figure ascending a ladder, another "from a turret on the walls shooting an arrow. Before the gate of the place a figure with a round shield "prostrating himself before a chief seated on an elephant, and followed by others on horses, bullocks, &c. The "whole forms a group in a very different style from anything observed anywhere else in this country; and as the "attitudes, profiles, &c., differ from the common Hindu style, a correct drawing would be desirable."

This apparently was never made, and the slab is not in the Museum collection. The description reads almost as if intended for the Sanchi (Plate XXXVIII.), but the scaling ladder is an addition to the siege materiel there represented.

CHAPTER II.

History of Monument.

Before attempting to fix the date of the Amravati Tope it will be well to try and ascertain whether the building can be identified with any temple or place mentioned in any works bearing on the subject. Fortunately this can be done with almost absolute certainty, as there seems no doubt but that it is the Avaraçilâ Sangharâmâ mentioned by Hiouen-Thsang,[1] and also the Temple of the Diamond Sands mentioned in the Tooth-Relic traditions.[2] As the former, however, is by far the most important, we will dwell on it only in the first instance.

After describing his journey from Kośala and his arrival in the kingdom of Danakachêka,[3] he adds, "A l'est de la capitale on a construit sur une montagne le "couvent Pourvaçila Samghârâma et à l'ouest de la ville on a élevé sur le côté "opposé de la montagne le couvent Avaraçilâ Samghârâma. Le premier roi de ce "royaume le construisit en faveur de Buddha, il creusa la vallée et y pratiqua "un chemin fit ouvrir les flancs de la montagne et eleva des pavillons." A little further on it is said, "A une petite distance au sud de la ville il y a un enorme "rocher," or as the Si-Yü-Ki expresses it, "une grande caverne de montagne," where Bhâvavivêka dwelt waiting till Mâitrêya Bôdhisatwa dissipated his doubts.

When the first edition of this work was published all this was mysterious enough. The one thing that seemed clear was, that the Amravati Tope was the Avaraçilâ Sanghârâma. But it was unfortunately situated close to the *east* side of the town of Durnacotta, and no possible site for the Pourvaçilâ monastery had then been discovered. Worse than this, neither in Colonel Mackenzie's nor in any other maps could anything like the "enorme rocher" be found. It was in fact one of those puzzles that had to be left for further research to solve. This has now fortunately been done in a report addressed to Government by the late J. A. C. Boswell, officiating collector of the district, and by some photographs by Captain Ross Thompson, which are now before me. From these we learn that to the eastward of Bezwarra, there is a high hill, on the top of which a white building may be seen in the photograph, occupying no doubt the site of the Pourvaçilâ convent. To the west of the town is a high mountain full of caves, abutting on the river; and seventeen miles beyond that to the westward, the Amravati Tope or Avaraçilâ Sanghârâma. But the most remarkable feature is, that immediately south of the town is a singular isolated rock or hill, "along whose base and sides," says Mr. Boswell, "there are the remains of

---

[1] Vie de Hiouen-Thsang by Hoëi-li, p. 188, and Si-Yü-Ki, II. p. 110 et seq.

[2] Vide infra, p.

[3] A full description of this route will be found in an article I have written in the J. R. A. S., vol. VI. p. to which the reader is referred.

" a considerable number of rock caves and temples, evidently of Buddhist origin. " There is a rock temple of two storeys close to the village which has been recently " utilized as a granary." " In various places the figures of elephants and other " animals, in the Buddhist style of representation, are to be seen depicted. At one " place there is a Mantapam cut out of the rock, and supported by stone pillars, " more solitary cells, and lastly a rock temple in four storeys of considerable pro- " portions." It may be added, that neither was the report written nor the photographs taken with the smallest idea of proving any theory; but their united testimony proves, almost beyond the shadow of a doubt, Bezwarra or some city on its site was the capital of Danakacheka when Hiouen-Thsang visited the place in 640, and the Amravati Tope to have been the Avaraçilâ Sanghârâma which he describes.

The topographical difficulty being thus satisfactorily settled, it now only remains to try to fix the date to which the Amravati sculptures belong in so far as that is possible with the materials now available.

In the present state of our knowledge this cannot be done with absolute certainty; first, because none of the inscriptions bear dates, nor with one doubtful exception,[1] do any contain names that can be recognized as those of historical personages; next, no history or reliable tradition mentions the place by name, with either a date or the founder's name attached to it. A considerable degree of vagueness also prevails, and always must, because the buildings are not all of one age, but certainly extended through one, it may be through two or even three centuries. Notwithstanding all this, their date may, I believe, be fixed with fair approximate certainty, quite sufficient for our present purposes.

As in all true styles, but more especially in India, the first and safest test of age is the style of architecture. Take, for instance, Gothic architecture; when once the true chronometric scale was ascertained by Britton and Rickman, no other argument was allowed to prevail, and the most distinct historical assertions were put aside whenever the evidence of style was found to contradict them. Even inscriptions, especially in India, must make way for this class of evidence. They may have been added afterwards. Their dates may be incorrect, and very frequently it is difficult to ascertain from which of the numerous eras which perplex the Indian student they ought to be calculated from.[2]

Owing to the circumstance of India being divided into numerous distinct nationalities, and the local circumstances being sometimes so various, it cannot be said that the chronometric scale for all the styles of Indian architecture has yet been definitively settled, still it is so nearly ascertained that no better test of age exists,

---

[1] This is the name of the Andhra king Yajnaśrí, read doubtfully on a fragment of an inscription copied by Colonel Mackenzie and reproduced, Plate XCIX. No. IX. This king was most probably the Yue-gnai of the Chinese, who we learn from Des Guignes was a zealous Buddhist, and is stated to have sent ambassadors to China in the year 408. If it really is this king who is mentioned in the inscription, his date would perfectly accord with all we learn from other circumstances. In Appendix F. his date from Hindu sources is fixed at 394, but may be moved a few years either way, as additional information comes to light. His coins and those of Gotamiputra are said to have been found in quantities in and about Amravati.

[2] Witness, for instance, the innumerable controversies still unsettled with regard to the dates or eras of the mediæval Gupta or Ballabhi kings. In fact without corroborative evidence no inscription anterior at least to the sixth or seventh century of our era can be accepted as fixing the date of any building in any part of India.

and in all cases its evidence must be accepted as conclusive unless good cause can be shown to the contrary. Bearing this in mind, when we compare the rail of the Great Tope at Sanchi or even that of No. 2 Tope with the outer rail at Amravati we feel at once that we have passed into another age altogether. The same is true if we compare the sculptures of the gateways at Sanchi with those of the Amravati enclosure. The progress is immense, and it evidently belongs to a totally different age, although we cannot now trace all the steps by which this progress was achieved. There are, however, indications in the western caves which show it must have been slow, and that centuries must have elapsed between the erection of the two monuments.

The difference of age is even more striking when we come to consider the wonderful progress that had been made in developing the ritual forms of the religion of Buddhism in the interval between the two monuments. At Sanchi Buddha is nowhere distinguished from those by whom he is surrounded. There is no glory round his head, no sacred garb, no conventional attitude. Our knowledge of history or tradition may enable us to recognize him, but the sculptor affords us no assistance. In like manner we have no shaven priests at Sanchi, and nothing that would induce us to believe that at that period the priesthood were separated from the laity. At Amravati all this is different. When Śâkya Muni appears as Prince Siddhârtha he has a glory round his head; when he had attained Buddhahood he is always clothed in that conventual robe by which he can be recognized to the present day in all Buddhist countries. The attitudes, either standing preaching or seated in contemplation, or expounding, or cross-legged with the soles of his feet turned upwards, are all found at Amravati exactly as we find them now with the slightest possible variation. The shaven priests too, with their conventional robes, are those exactly which may be seen in China or Ceylon at the present day, and altogether we feel that in the interval between the Gateways at Sanchi and the great Rail at Amravati the religion has passed from its primitive—semi-secular—form into that later priestly development which it retains to this day; to use Buddhist terms, from the simple Hînayâna to the complicated Mahâyâna, analogous to the change from Evangelical Christianity to the complicated Catholicism of the middle ages. Judging from the analogy of the Christian religion, which ran so nearly parallel a course during its whole existence, and from what we know of its subsequent career, such a revolution as this must have taken centuries to effect. Without other indications it is of course difficult to assign even approximate figures to the impressions we derive from the progressive changes in art and religion; but as both the traditions and such scraps of history as are available all point to a period of about three centuries between the two buildings, this is so consonant with what we observe that we may safely adopt it. It might have been more, it certainly cannot be less.

If, however, we cannot at present fix the initial date for the beginning of the buildings at Amravati, there seems no difficulty with regard to a final date before which they must have been erected. Hiouen-Thsang, in describing the Avaraçila monastery, uses the following terms, from which I quote at length because of the many interesting points the description contains:—"Un ancien roi de ce royaume "l'avait construit en l'honneur du Bouddha et y avait déployé toute la magnificence "des palais de Ta-hia (de la Bactriane). Les bois touffus dont il était entouré, et "une multitude des fontaines jaillissantes, en faisaient un séjour enchanteur. Ce "couvent était protégé par les esprits du ciel, et les sages et les saints aimaient "à s'y promener et à y habiter. Pendant l'espace des mille ans qui ont suivi le "Nirvâṇa du Bouddha, on voyait constamment un millier de laïques et de religieux "qui venaient ensemble y passer le temps de la retraite pendant la saison des pluies. "Mille ans après (le 'Nirvâṇa') les hommes du siècle et les sages vinrent y demeurer "ensemble. Mais depuis une centaine d'années les esprits des montagnes ont "changé de sentiments et font éclater sans cesse leur violence et leur colère. Les "voyageurs justement effrayés n'osent plus aller dans ce couvent. C'est pour cela "qu'aujourd'hui il est complétement désert, et l'on n'y voit plus ni religieux ni "novices."[1]

I am afraid that very little reliance can be placed on the 1,000 years twice mentioned in the passage quoted above from Hiouen-Thsang as an indication of the true date. First, because he is evidently speaking loosely and in round numbers; but more because we cannot feel sure when he placed the Nirvâṇa. If we assume the Ceylonese date (543 B.C.), which we now know to be the correct one, it would place the period of prosperity 457 A.D., which would accord perfectly with what we gather from other circumstances. Although, however, this indication may not be of much value, it seems evident from this passage that about the middle of the sixth century Buddhism had suffered such a blow as to prevent any such work as this being undertaken. From what our author says of what he saw in Kalinga on the one hand and Djourya[2] on the other, it is evident that, in the century before his visit, war, pestilence, and famine had swept over the three Kalingas, and nearly obliterated the original population. We know, too, that in the neighbouring province of Orissa the Keśari family, worshippers of Śiva, had raised themselves before that time (A.D. 473) on the ruins of the Buddhist dynasty;[3] and we also know that in the year 605 the Châlukyas conquered Venga,[4] the country in which Dharanikoṭṭa was situated, and they were neither Buddhists nor Snake worshippers. From all these circumstances it may, therefore, fairly be assumed that it was at some time before the middle of the sixth century, or before 550 A.D. at all events, that all the buildings around the Tope had been completed and were deserted.

If we can thus fix, at least approximatively, the period before which our buildings must have been finished, we can with equal probability ascertain the date when they were commenced. In the first place, we find that Colonel Mackenzie collected a considerable number of coins about "Durnacotta." Some of these were Roman, others of the Bactrian Kadphises type,[5] showing that the place was probably of some importance about the Christian era; but as none of these were found in the Tope

---

[1] Histoire de Hiouen-Thsang, 188.
[2] Ibid. p. 185 and 189; and Si-Yü-Ki, vol. II. p. 116.
[3] Stirling's Account of Cuttack, Asiatic Researches, vol. XV. p. 264.
[4] Journal R. A. S., N. S., vol. I. p. 254.
[5] Asiatic Researches, vol. XVII. pp. 561 and 582, Plate II. Fig. 29, c. 41.

itself, they have no direct bearing on our investigation. Those coins which were found in the Tope were all of lead, but their date not having yet been ascertained they at present afford us no assistance in our inquiry.[1] Among the slabs, however, from the Tope, sent home by Colonel Mackenzie, there is one which bears directly on this point. It is photographed in Plate LXXVIII., Figs. 2 and 3. The sculpture on the front is of the age of the inner Rail, probably the fifth century, but on the back of the same slab is a bas-relief evidently of about the same age as those of the Sanchi Tope. This confirms the evidence we acquire from the coins that a city and buildings did exist here as early as the Christian era, but proves at the same time that none of the buildings we now find there are so early. Some centuries must have elapsed between the times when the sculptures on the back and front of that slab were executed.

Colonel Mackenzie also collected a number of traditions referring to a Mokunti Maharaja[2] who, among the Hindus on the spot, is the reputed builder of the Tope,[3] and curiously enough among his own manuscripts there is one which places a Mokunti Raja exactly where we want him, if looking for a founder of the central building, which, from the evidence of the architecture, seems almost certainly to date from about the year 200, which is the date given to this king in that document.[4] On examination, however, these traditions are found to refer either to Rudra Deva of Warangal (A.D. 1132), or more probably to Pratâpa Rudra of Orissa (A.D. 1503), and have, consequently, no bearing on the date of the monument. They are all of Brahmanical origin, and Benares is the scene of action, but like most Pauranic traditions they are foolish and fabulous in the extreme, and refer to a persecution, when the last feeble remnants of the Bauddhas, here called Jainas, were finally expelled from India. It would be curious to find Buddhists in India as late as the beginning of the sixteenth century; but though this has little reference to our present inquiry, we must bear in mind that the inscription translated by Mr. Prinsep and Sir Walter Elliot's excavations, prove that Amravati was a temple of the Buddhists at least as late as the twelfth or thirteenth century. My impression is that the Tooth relic again visited the place in 1187, but of this hereafter[5]

---

[1] Asiatic Journal, vol. XV. p. 471. Madras Journal, vol. XIX. p. 220, et seqq.

[2] On the spot it is called the Doop Mogaśâla of Mokunti Maharaja. Mogaśâla, in the Telinga language, signifies a court for public affairs, and the distribution of justice. "Doop" is Hindostani for sun, or rather sunshine; translated into architectural language this would be "Hypethral Basilica." This would perhaps be the best term that could be applied to it; but it involves a theory it is as well to avoid at present. See Asiatic Journal, vol. XV. p. 469.

[3] Asiatic Journal, vol. XV. p. 470, et seq. Wilson's Catalogue of Mackenzie's MSS., vol. I. p. cxxiv., and Taylor in Madras Selections, Second Series, No. XXXIX. p. 229, et seq.

[4] Madras Journal, No. 19, April 1838, p. 352.

[5] It is to be regretted that the Daladâvansa has not been completely translated, for it appears that in the twelfth or thirteenth century the tooth relic was taken back to India at a time apparently when (1187) a Kîrti Nissanga, a prince of Kalinga, was one of the many Indian princes who held sway in Ceylon. It is said to have been conveyed to the banks of the Ganges (Upham's History of Buddhism, p. 32), but as Landresse suggests (Foĕ-Kouĕ-Ki, p. 345) this more probably was the Godavery, or, in other words, the Kistnah. From some particulars furnished me by Sir Walter Elliot, it seems that the part of the monument he dug into was a chapel formed of old slabs arranged unsymmetrically by some prince about that time, so as to form a chapel for some unexplained purpose. It may have been to receive this relic. The inscription translated by Prinsep (J. A. S. B., vol. VI. p. 218) shows that Buddhism was flourishing at Amravati in—say the twelfth century. Altogether

Turning to the monument itself, we find upon it a great number of inscriptions, and my friend General Cunningham has kindly undertaken to investigate this branch of the subject. The result of his labours will be found in Appendix E. Unfortunately they merely record that the pillar, or bas-relief, or object on which they are found, is the gift of some piously-disposed persons whose names are given; but these names, with one doubtful exception, are, unluckily for our purpose, all unknown to fame. At present, therefore, it is only from the form of the characters that the inscriptions aid in ascertaining the date of the monument. Generally this may be described as the Gupta alphabet, as used either immediately before or after A.D. 318. No trace of the Lât character occurs, though that was used in a modified form at Sanchi on the northern limits of the province certainly after the Christian era.[1] The inscriptions in which the form of the letters most closely resembles that found at Amravati are those of the Kanheri and Nasick Caves. If Dr. Stevenson[2] is right in ascribing these to the first half of the fourth century, and I see no reason to doubt his correctness in this respect, this evidence, "valeat quantum," would assign to the Amravati Tope the same epoch.

The evidence derived from the architecture of these Caves confirms this attribution to the fullest possible extent. Two drawings have already been given (Woodcuts 11 and 12), and more will appear in the sequel, but meanwhile, if I am correct in ascribing the Nasick Cave to Gotamiputra (A.D. 309) and the Kanheri Cave to the age of Buddhaghosa (A.D. 410), this evidence, as far as it goes, would fix the erection of the great Rail at Amravati within the limits of the fourth century.

A good deal has yet to be accomplished before this branch of the investigation can be said to be complete; but everything that has yet been brought to light tends to confirm the assumption that the extreme elaboration of ornament which placed sculptured discs on the intermediate bars, as well as on the pillars of Buddhist rails, was not introduced before the third century, and every building where it is found must consequently be dated subsequent to the year 200 at the earliest. In so far, therefore, as either palæographic or architectural evidence is concerned, the great Rail belongs to the fourth century. The central building, as will afterwards appear, is older, and the inner Rail more modern.

Notwithstanding all this, there is so much of Greek or rather Bactrian art in the architectural details of the Amravati Tope, that the first inference is that it must be nearer to the Christian era than the form of the inscriptions would lead us to suppose. On the other hand, we do not know how long the classical influence

---

nothing would surprise me less than to find that the Tooth relic sojourned here for seventy-six years before its recovery by the Ceylonese, about 1314 of our era. The materials exist for settling this question, but they have not yet been made available.

[1] Cunningham, Bhilsa Topes, p. 264, Plate XIX. In his Ancient Geography of India, p. 541, General Cunningham disputes this, but I refer the reader to his own Plate XIX., Figures 177 and 191, where the two characters are written by himself. There is not one letter in the one which is not easily recognisable from the other. The difference is about the same as exists between the type used for the first edition of Shakespeare and the latest. There are differences, of course, but the alphabet is the same. In his haste to find fault he apparently overlooked my use of the word "modified."

[2] J. B. B. R. A. S., vol. V. p. 39, et seq.

prevailed, and how much it may have been nourished by intercommunication with the West. Down at least to the age of Constantine, probably to that of Justinian, Rome seems to have maintained its intercourse with India, and we must pause before we draw a line as to the time when classical feeling may have ceased to exert an influence on Indian art. Certainly, in this instance, the expression of Hiouen-Thsang, that this Tope was ornamented with all the art of the palaces of Bactria, is borne out to the fullest extent; but there seems no reason to suppose that this classical influence may not have endured till the break down of the Roman Empire, or rather the Byzantine, in the sixth century, though at that time it practically ceased.[1]

The one point which it seems necessary to insist upon at this stage of the inquiry is the strong Bactrian influence which is manifested in all the details of the monument. As has been explained, the sculptures, with scarcely an exception, refer to a Nâga people and to a Nâga worship; and since, as pointed out above, p. 44, Taxila and Cashmere were the head-quarters of that faith at this age, that circumstance alone would almost suffice to indicate the north-west as the source from which we must expect information regarding its origin. But, again, how long did the Bactro-Parthian kingdom exist? and how long did it continue to influence the politics and arts of India Proper? These are questions to which no very definite answer can be given in the present state of our knowledge; my own impression is that the influence continued to a much later date than has hitherto generally been supposed; but there is nothing in this Bactrian influence sufficiently definite to enable us to found on it any argument as to the date of the Amravati Tope.

Although, therefore, it must be confessed that neither these classical influences nor the Mackenzie traditions seem to throw any steady light on our subject, the information collected by Mr. Stirling; and published in his invaluable history of Cuttack, does seem to bear on its origin.

The following extracts from his memoirs[2] are those which seem most to the point:—"In the reign of Bajra Nath Deo the Yavanas are said to invade the "country in great numbers from Babul Des—explained to mean Iran and Cabul— "but are finally driven back." "In the reign of Huns or Hangsha Deo (query, "Hushka) the Yavanas again invade in great force from Cashmere, and many bloody "battles ensue." In the reign of Bhoja, the Yavanas from Sindhu Des invade the country in great force, but are driven back. Then follows Vikramâditya. If therefore, the dates are to be depended upon, these invasions took place before the Christian era. Other Yavana invasions occur in the next four reigns; but the most important of all occurred in the reign of Subhan Deo, who ascended the throne 318 (the year of the Ballabhi era). In the ninth year of his reign a Yavana, Rakta Bâhu, invades the country by sea, and conquers it. The king escapes with the image of Juggernath, which he buries under a ber tree, and flies farther into the jungle, where he dies. His son succeeds to the title, but is murdered by the

---

[1] India and Rome, by O. de B. Priaulx. London, 1873. Reinaud, Relations Politique et Commerciale de l'Empire Roman avec l'Asie Orientale. Journal Asiatique, 1863.

[2] Asiatic Researches, vol. XV. p. 254, et seq. J. A. S. B., vol. VI. p. 756, et seq.

invaders. "A Yavana dynasty then ruled over Orissa for a space of 146 years, or "down to A.D. 473." If these dates are to be depended upon,—and I see no reason for doubting their general correctness,—the period of the supremacy of this Yavana dynasty in Orissa exactly coincides with the dates which from other circumstances I would ascribe to the principal buildings at Amravati. No Stirling has yet visited Guntur, and we cannot therefore assert it, but it seems more than probable that the foreigners who conquered the northern, would also take possession of the southern Kalingas.

This account of this last invasion, being derived from Brahmanical sources, would hardly help us much; but, fortunately, we have two Buddhist accounts of the same transaction, which are much more complete and detailed, and which do, I fancy, throw great light on our researches. The first is contained in the Daladâvansa, partially translated by the Hon. G. Turnour, and published in the J. A. S. B. vol. VI. p. 856, et seq.; the other is abstracted by Colonel Low from the Siamese Phrâ Pat'hom, and published in the same journal, vol. XVII. part II. p. 82, et seqq. Unfortunately, neither work has been completely translated, and the extracts having been made with reference to other objects, do not give us all the information we want. The following abridgment of the story will, however, suffice for present purposes:—

The left canine tooth of Buddha had been preserved in Dantapura,[1] the capital of Kalinga, probably at or near the spot where the celebrated temple of Juggernâth

[1] It is not easy to feel certain about the position of Dantapura—the tooth city,—but, assuming the Brahmanical and Buddhist accounts to refer to the same transaction, which I see no reason for doubting, the following facts seem to fix it with tolerable certainty at or near Puri.

It certainly was in Orissa, and could not have been so far south as the Godavery, as General Cunningham supposes (Ancient Geography of India, p. 517), because of its intimate relation with the Magadha dynasty at Patna, and there is no proof whatever that their power ever extended to Rajahmehendry.

It was on the sea coast. As according to the Brahmanical account the invasion was discovered from the dung of the horses and elephants floating on shore from the ships, and the Chilkea lake was the result of the invaders' anger (A. S., XV. p. 264).

It was not on the banks of a river, for the prince fled from the city, and "proceeding to the southward "crossed a great river and buried the relic in a sandbank of that river," evidently at some distance from the town (J. A. S. B., VI. p. 866).

When they return, dig up the relic, and embark for Ceylon, it is from the port of Talamita, which is either Tamralipti or Tcharitripura, both ports on the Hugli, Satgaon or Tumluk (J. A. S. B., VI. p. 866). Had Dantapura been situated on the banks of the Godavery, they would have embarked from some place at or near its mouth, probably Coringa or Musilipatam.

The tradition places the Diamond Sands half way between the port of embarkation and Ceylon. They are close to Rajahmehendry if they are to be identified with the site north of Amravati, which I see no reason for doubting (J. A. S. B., XVII., Pt. II., p. 86); but they are just half way between the Hugli and Ceylon, and this indication again points to some locality at least as far north as Puri.

A new light has lately been thrown on this matter by a paper by Mr. St. John, in the Phœnix, a new monthly periodical. In describing Thatone, which certainly was the original seat of Buddhism in Burmah, he says, "Somewhere about this date (318) Mahla (Hêmâ-mâla) daughter of the king of Kahlaneka (Kalinga) a town "on the east coast of India, arrived with a Buddhist relic" (vol. II. p. 182). Thatone or That'hun was the Suverna Bhumi of the Hindus, the Aurea Chersonesus of the Greeks, and a city of such importance in ancient times that Aśoka sent there the missionaries, Sôna and Uttarô, to convert the people (Mahawanso, 71), and at the period of which we are speaking was so important as the entrepôt between India and Cambodia and China, that there is no improbability of its inhabitants having taken part in an expedition to steal the tooth relic from its resting place. But they hardly could have done unless the place where it was deposited was on the sea coast, and accessible to ships, as Stirling's account above quoted would lead us to suppose it was.

Lastly, when the tooth relic was at Pataliputta, "a Nighanta moved by envy remarked, 'Dewo the Awatârâ

now stands, for 800 years, when Gûhaśivo, the king, early in the fourth century, was converted to Buddhism from the Brahmanical faith, which he had professed up to that time. With the zeal of a convert he dismissed and persecuted the Brahmans, who had hitherto enjoyed his favour. They repaired to Pâtaliputra (Patna) to complain of this to the paramount sovereign, here called Pâṇḍu, but who, as it appears from the context, most probably was the Gotamiputra of the Śâtkarṇi dynasty. He orders Gûhaśivo to repair to his court, bringing the relic with him. It is then subjected to every sort of trial. It is smashed on .an anvil, thrown into the gutter, and everything conceivable done to destroy or dishonour it. It comes triumphantly out of all its trials. The king is converted, and finally devotes himself to a religious life.

While all this is going on, a râjâ—it is not quite clear whence he came [1]—named Khîrâdhâro, attacks the capital, in order to possess himself of the wonder-working relic. He was defeated and killed in battle, and Gûhaśivo returned, it is said, with the sacred tooth to his capital. Some time afterwards the nephews of Khîrâdhâro, allying themselves with other kings, march against Gûhaśivo. He, though seeing that resistance is hopeless, prepares for defence; but, before going to the combat, he enjoins on his daughter Hêmâ Mâla, as she is called in the Daladâwansa, or Hema-Chala, as her name is spelt by Colonel Low, who was married to a prince of Oujein, called Danta Kumâra, that in the event of his falling, they should take the relic, and escaping by sea, convey it to Mahâsena, king of Ceylon, who had been for some time negotiating for its purchase.[2]

" 'of Wishno in the character of Râmâ and other forms has already taken place. If this human bone is not part of " 'his body, whence these miraculous powers?' " "The Titthya impostors chanting forth the praise in every " possible form of Wishno sprinkled it (the relic) with the holy water. The relic did not, however, move from " its position" (J. A. S. B., VI. p. 862). The whole transaction showing how intimate the connexion was between the two religions was at that time, and how likely it was that the worship of Jugganath should succeed to that of Buddha in one of his most famous shrines.

More might be adduced, but the above is probably sufficient to show that Dantapura was situated either at Puri or some place very near it, and that this struggle for the tooth relic, in about the year 318, excited not only all India and Ceylon, but extended across the Bay of Bengal to the neighbourhood of Martaban, and probably even further east; but centered, if I mistake not, at Amravati.

[1] J. A. S. B., VI. p. 865, Gen. Cunningham following Col. Forbes Leslie, makes him king of Śrâvastî (Report for 1862–3, p. 40), but I prefer the much more trustworthy testimony of Turnour, who says (loc. sup. cit.) "I can find no authority for assigning Sawattipura to be the capital." My impression is that the conqueror came from the eastward, probably Arakan. If nominal similarities were not the most deceitful things in the world, I would remark that it is here that Ptolemy places the Kirrhadæ, but I should be sorry to rely on this.

[2] Some years ago Dr. Bird opened a small Tope in front of the Kanheri Caves in Salsette. In it he found a copper plate recording that a canine tooth of Buddha had been deposited there. The plate is dated in the year 245. From the expression "Samvat" being used, Dr. Stevenson (J. B. B. R. A. S., vol. V. p. 13) assumes that it must be from the era of Vikramâditya. I believe, however, it is correct to assert that no Buddhist inscription is dated from the era of the hated opponent of their religion. If, on the other hand, we assume the era of Śâlivâhana, it brings the date to almost the exact time—A.D. 323—of these events on the east coast; and though it is not directly stated in the inscription, it seems that the tooth was deposited there by Gotamiputra, the very king who played so important a part in the narrative just recorded, and what is more it seems extremely probable that the Kanheri tooth was, or was supposed to be, the identical one which performed so many miracles in Pâtaliputra.

This might seem paradoxical had not the same thing happened to the same relic in similar circumstances more than twelve centuries afterwards. When the Portuguese conquered Ceylon, Constantine de Braganza seized the Daladâ and conveyed it to Goa. The king of Pegu sent an embassy after it, and offered any amount of

The prince and princess fly from the city before its fall, bury the relic in the sand, in the same manner as the image of Juggernath is said to have been concealed in the Brahmanical account, and, afterwards returning, the princess conceals it in her hair, and escaping to the coast, they take ship at Talamita, apparently Tamralipi, either Satgaon or Tamluk, and sail for Ceylon. Half-way between the place of embarkation and Ceylon they are shipwrecked, at a place called the Diamond Sands.[1] From the context I do not think there can be much hesitation in fixing this locality on the banks of the Kistnah. First, from its position half-way;[2] next, because here only, so far as I know, are there diamond[3] mines near the coast; but more because, as will be abundantly proved by the sequel, it was the residence of the Nâga Râja.

The Nâga Râja steals the relic from the princess when she is asleep, but he is forced by the power of a Thero, from the Himalaya, to restore it, and the wanderers again embark, and after various adventures reach Ceylon in the year 312.[4] Mahâsena had been dead nine years, but the fugitives are received with open arms by Meghavarna,[5] the reigning sovereign; a brick and mortar Chaitya is made, and the relic brought by the prince and princess enshrined with great solemnity.—(Colonel Low, p. 86.)

The narrative then proceeds:—"Three years had passed away, when the king "of Lankâ perceived from an ancient prophecy that in seven years from that date "a certain king, Dhammâśoka Raja, would erect a temple on the Diamond Sands; "and he likewise recollected that there were two Donas of relics of Buddha still "concealed in the country of Nâga Raja. He therefore directed a holy person to

---

ransom for it. But the bigotry of the priesthood was proof against any such temptation. The tooth was consumed by fire in presence of the Archbishop and all the notables, and the ashes cast into the sea. The result was peculiar. The Ceylonese pretended that the one so destroyed was a counterfeit. A true one was discovered and sold to the king of Pegu, and as soon as he was gone and had paid for it, another true one was found concealed in Ceylon, and is probably the crocodile's tooth that is now so honoured in that country. To complete the parallelism, both the Burmese and the Concani teeth have disappeared, and only their empty Chaityas remain. The Ceylonese tooth still remains with the oldest pedigree of any such relic that the world possesses.

The particulars of this second great attempt to destroy the Daladâ will be found well stated in Sir E. Tennent's Ceylon, vol. II. p. 199. Translations of the original authorities are there given also.

[1] *Dinne* means sand bank in Telugu. This may be the origin of the name Dîpal-dinne, which certainly does not mean "Hill of Lights." Can Dîpal, by any synonym, be assumed to mean diamond?

[2] The Siamese, as Colonel Low points out, wishing to make their own country the scene of these events, have lengthened the periods of the voyage preposterously. They make it three months from Cuttack to the Diamond Sands, and three more from thence to Ceylon. J. A. S. B., vol. XVII. pt. II., pp. 86, 87.

[3] One of the objects of Colonel Mackenzie's surveys was to mark the diamond mines in the locality. He plots the diamond district as extending to about eight miles north of Amravati, but it seems there are no mines elsewhere. Their position is marked on the map, Plate XLVI. There is also a wonderful account of the the diamonds in this district, and the mode of obtaining them in Marco Polo, Book III. chap. XIX. (Yule's edition, II. p. 395), and the diamond mines of Golconda have been famous in all times. There are no diamonds found on the eastern shore of the Bay of Bengal, but Col. Low and his authorities, seem sometimes to have got confused between the "golden" and "diamond" sands. It may safely be said we now know certainly the position of both.

[4] It does not seem quite clear how far the Ceylonese dates are to be relied upon as quite correct about this time. Avowedly there is an error to the extent of at least sixty years in the date their annals assign to Aśoka. This has subsequently been adjusted, to some extent, by Mr. Turnour, but not, so far as I can judge, in such a manner as to inspire entire confidence. My impression is that the dates in the fourth century are all from ten to fifteen years too early.

[5] Is not this the Varâja of the Western Cave Inscriptions?—J. B. B. R. A. S., vol. V. p. 42.

"go and bring these relics." The Nâga Râja's brother swallows the relics, and flies to Meru, but they are taken from him and brought back. "Soon after this Nâga "Râja arrived (in Ceylon), in the form of a handsome youth, and solicited a few "relics from his majesty, which were bestowed upon him accordingly."

His majesty now ordered a golden ship to be made. It was one cubit long and one span broad. The relics were put into a golden cup; this was placed in a vase, and the whole put into the golden ship. A wooden ship was next built, having a breadth of beam of seven long cubits.

Danta Kumâra and Hemamalâ being desirous of revisiting their country, the king of Lankâ sent with them ambassadors to one of the five[1] kings who now ruled there, requesting him to show them every attention. The vessel reached the Diamond Sands in five months, and the prince and princess went on shore, accompanied by the priests. An account is then given of the building of the temple, and the mode in which the relics were placed. The vessel now set sail for Dantapura, which it reached in little more than three months. The ambassadors of the king of Lankâ landed with the prince and princess. They were treated with much distinction, and remained in the country.

After this follows a third tradition which Colonel Low treats as if referring to another king and to different circumstances, but, both from the name he bore and the whole of the circumstances mentioned in the context, seems undoubtedly to have been the same person. In the legend he is called Dhammâśoka[2] and ruled the country of Arvadi, apparently Avanti (Ougein) with strict justice, but is forced by a famine to emigrate with his followers, amounting to 31,000 able-bodied men. The wanderers proceeded southward for seven months. After various adventures they reach a place where water and fish were abundant. Next day the king mounted his horse and reached the Diamond Sands. Here he meets the Nâga Râja, builds a Chaitya, and founds a city.

"Dhammâśoka reigned here quietly for seven years, but mortified and unhappy "because he could not reach the relics. His Majesty accordingly offered a high "reward to any one who should find the relics and disinhume them. But this proved "of no avail. It so happened that, in the dilemma, a Putra or son of the king of "Róm or Roum, named Kâkabhâsa, who happened to be trading to the country of "Takkhasilâ, encountered a violent storm. He had 500 souls on board, who, suppli- "cating the gods, were rescued from death. The ship, with much difficulty, reached "close to the Diamond Sands, and observing signs of population cast anchor with "a view to refit."

The Prince of Róm[3] assists the Nâga Râja to recover the hidden treasure, and to build a wonderful nine-storied Chaitya over it, many particulars of which are

---

[1] Those who, according to the Daladâvansa, had combined with the nephews of Khîrâdhâro and conquered the country.

[2] This is evidently a title, though from the similarity of the name Colonel Low confounds him with the great Aśoka, and places him 321 B.C.

[3] It would be absurd to found any serious theory on the mention of the name of Rome, if it stood alone and unsupported. The circumstance mentioned in the narrative of the strangers being white men, and coming by sea, is a small confirmation that the people here mentioned were really Europeans. My impression, however,

given; but as they are too long to extract, and either are imaginary or do not refer to the particular building we are engaged upon, it is hardly necessary to quote them here. These quotations might be multiplied to almost any extent; but enough has probably been adduced to show that, in the beginning of the fourth century—about the time when the struggle for the tooth relic was convulsing all India—Buddhist tradition points most distinctly to the Diamond Sands, on the banks of the Kistnah, as the place where a great temple was being built. The kingdom of the Nâga Râja certainly was there; and so far as can be judged from every indication as to the locality, if it was not at or near Amravati, it could not possibly have been far from the spot.

Though all this tends to confirm the idea that the building referred to is the Amravati Tope, the inference rises almost to certainty when we come to examine the sculptures with which it is adorned. In one bas-relief a ship is represented with two persons on board, bearing relics, and is being welcomed by a Nâga king on approaching the shore. In another an ark, in the form of a ship, like that described above, is being borne in state on men's shoulders; and in numerous scenes there are conferences between the Nâga king and a prince or king accompanied by a lady, neither of whom nor any of whose suite are Nâgas. Of course these may represent other similar scenes which have happened to other people; but a careful examination of the whole presents so many points of coincidence that I hardly think they can be accidental. One point which the sculptures undoubtedly reveal is that Amravati was the capital, or, at least, the residence of the Nâga Râja. In all the sculptures which do not relate to the life of Buddha, and in many of these, the Nâga king appears with his hood of a seven-headed snake, and all his women have also single snakes at the back of their heads. As will be presently shown, Nâga worship almost supersedes Buddhism in the religious representations, so much so, indeed, that it is sometimes difficult to say to which religion the temple is dedicated.

It may be quite true that no single part of this evidence is sufficient to prove the case, but, taking the whole of it together, I think it must be admitted to be sufficient to justify the presumption that the beginning of the fourth century was the great building epoch at Amravati. When all the evidence about to be advanced in describing the Plates is added to what has been adduced, few, I fancy, will be inclined to doubt but that the two great Rails at Amravati are part of the Temple at the Diamond Sands, which, according to the Ceylonese computation, was commenced in the year 322. Judging from the elaboration of the outer Rail, it may have taken fifty years to complete. If this be so, the date of its completion may be about the year 370 or 380 of our era, and the principal part of the building

---

is that few who are familiar with the arts of Rome in Constantine's time, and who will take the trouble to master these Amravati sculptures, can fail to perceive many points of affinity between them. The circular medallions of the arch of Constantine—such as belong to his time—and the general tone of the art of his age so closely resemble what we find here, that the coincidence can hardly be accidental. The conviction that the study of these sculptures has forced in my mind is, that there was much more intercommunication between the East and West during the whole period from Alexander to Justinian, than is generally supposed, and that the intercourse was especially frequent and influential in the middle period, between Augustus and Constantine.

may thus have remained complete for 150 or 200 years after that time, before it was deserted, as mentioned by Hiouen-Thsang. From evidence which will be brought forward hereafter, it would appear that the central building or Tope itself is at least a century older than the great Rail, and that the inner or smaller Rail is at least as much more modern, so that, like our own cathedrals, the erection of this Tope may have lasted for two or three centuries, or say from 200 to 500 A.D. Even beyond this, however, there are reasons for believing—as will be shown in describing Plate LXXXIII.—that a building of importance existed here as early as the Christian era, or contemporaneously with the gates at Sanchi. On the other hand, we know for certain that it was afterwards repaired and used for Buddhist purposes as late as the twelfth or thirteenth centuries; but the particulars of this restoration are less interesting, and further explorations on the spot are necessary before they can be made intelligible. All this, however, will be clearer and more easily intelligible when we have gone through the description of the 54 Plates, which are devoted to the illustration of the architecture and sculptures of the Amravati Tope.

PLATE XLVI.

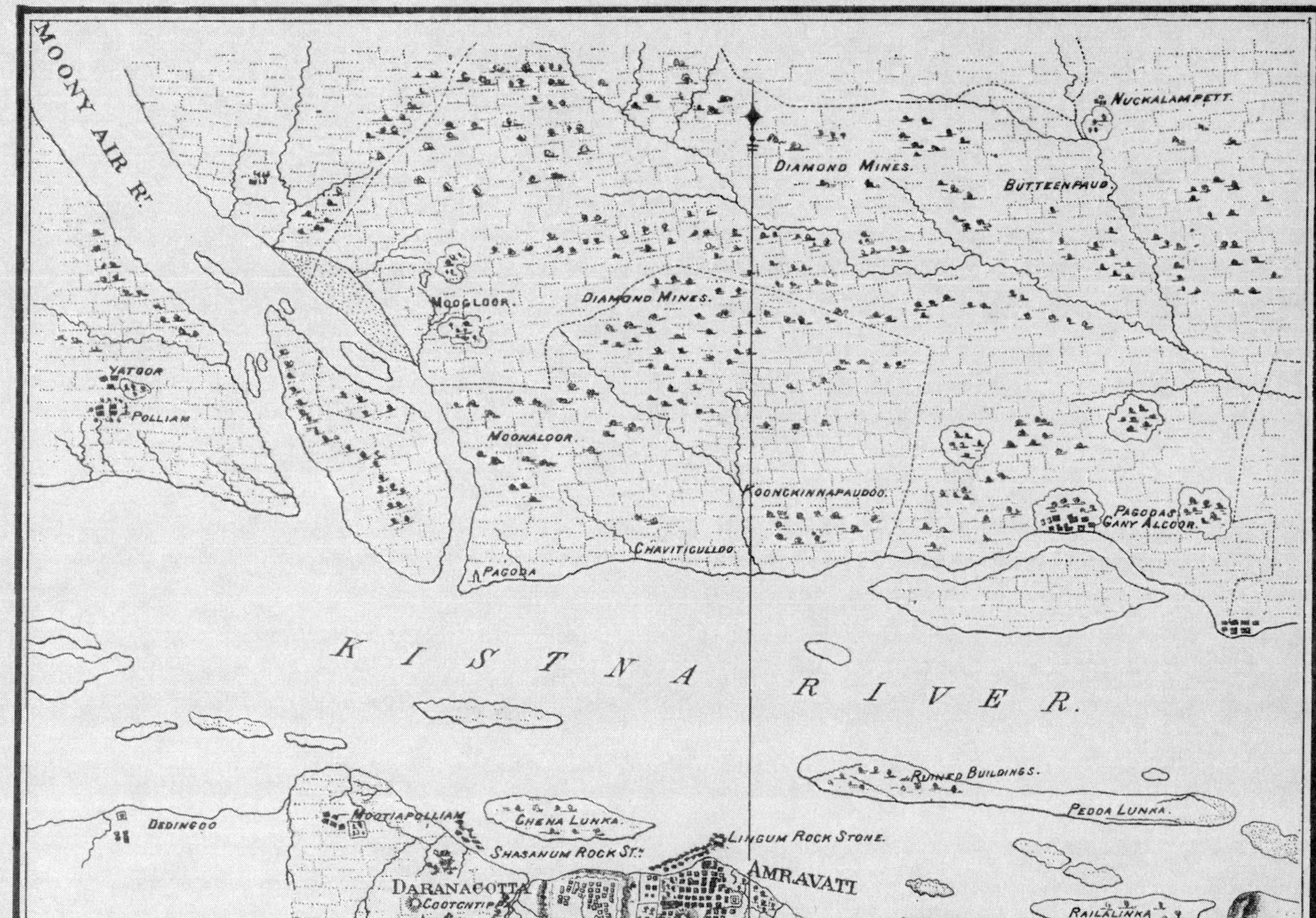

W. GRIGGS LITH.

INDIA MUSEUM

MAP OF AMRAVATI IN GUNTOOR
& OF PURTYALL & THE DIAMOND MINES
WITH THE VILLAGES ADJACENT REDUCED FROM THE ORIGINAL SURVEY.
IN 1816.

SCALE OF 1 MILE TO AN INCH.

FURLONGS.

Plate II.

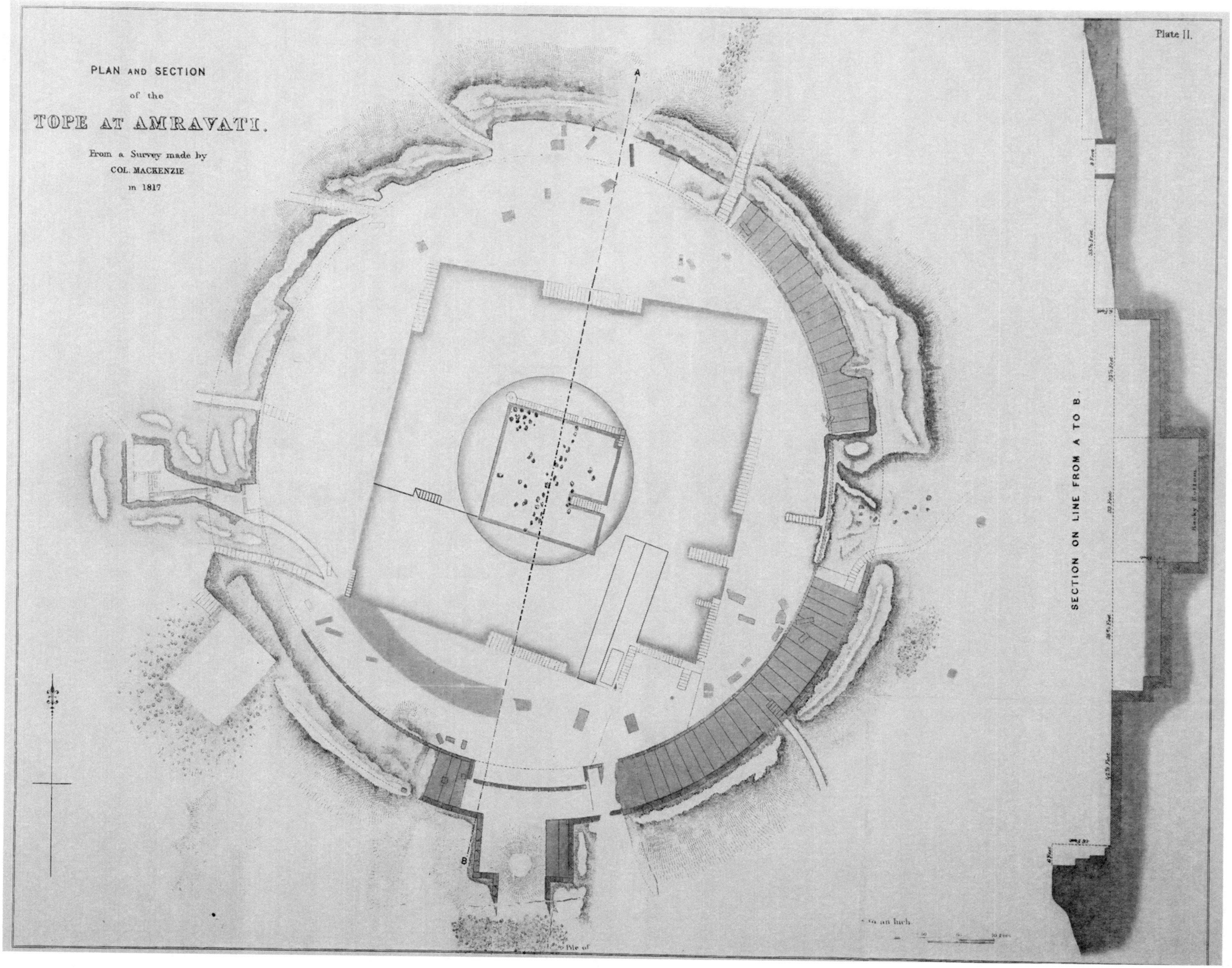
PLAN AND SECTION
of the
TOPE AT AMRAVATI.
From a Survey made by
COL. MACKENZIE
in 1817
A
B
SECTION ON LINE FROM A TO B.
Rocky Bottom

DESCRIPTION OF THE PLATES.

AMRAVATI TOPE.

PLATES XLVI. AND XLVII.

PLATE XLVI. is copied literally from the survey of the locality made by Colonel Mackenzie in 1816–17, and suffices to explain the exact relative position of the different antiquities already alluded to (page 164). In order to prevent any appearance of adjusting it to suit any theory, the spelling has been retained as found in the original map, though it differs occasionally from that adopted in the text.

The ramparts of the old town of Durnacotta will be observed to the westward of the modern town of Amravati, and the site of the several mounds of Dipaldinna, Nuckadeverdinna, and Cootchitippa are also plainly marked. One cluster, though the smallest, of the circular tumuli or stone circles, is close to the old town to the westward; but by far the most numerous groups are gathered round the bases of the hills in the right-hand lower corner of the map, where they are described as existing in hundreds. The diamond mines are all on the left bank of the river, opposite the town.

Plate XLVII. is likewise copied literally from a drawing in the Mackenzie Collection,[1] and represents the monument as it existed in 1816–17. At that time the slabs coloured dark red were either standing or were lying in such a position that their original site could be identified; and the paving stones of the procession path, coloured pink, were also *in situ*.

The central building had at that time entirely disappeared, the materials having been utilized by the Râja in building the new town.[2] Having cleared it away, he was induced to dig deeper in search of treasure, which is always supposed to be buried in these mounds; and having made a great hole in this pursuit, he afterwards determined to make use of it by forming it into a water tank. This, as will be seen from the plan and section, was not complete at the time it was abandoned, the Râja having ruined himself by extravagance some time before Colonel Mackenzie's second visit. In the process of excavation the earth had fortunately been thrown on to the path and rails, so as to protect them to a certain extent; and those slabs

---

[1] A reduction of it to the scale of 100 feet to 1 inch was published by me in the Handbook of Architecture (Woodcut 9), in 1855.

[2] "The whole of the inner circle has been dug up, and the stones removed for building purposes. They have been chiefly applied to the repair of Pagodas, and a great many were put to form a flight of steps to the square tank of Shivagunga."—Colonel Mackenzie, in Asiatic Journal, p. 469.

which had not been carried away were thus partially protected till some were excavated by the Colonel.[1] Sir Walter Elliot's explorations were apparently wholly confined to the northern side of the Western Gateway, where a mound of earth concealed the modern chapel, the walls of which furnished nine-tenths of the slabs now in the India Museum.

All that the Râja discovered to reward his search was a small relic casket, which is now in the Madras Museum.[2] It was apparently similar to those found at Sanchi, but has no inscription and is of no intrinsic value.

The dimensions of the Tope, as shown in the plan, and recorded by Colonel Mackenzie, are 195 feet[3] for the inside diameter of the outer circle, and 165 feet for that of the inner. The procession path is paved with slabs 13 feet long, and the inner rail is 2 feet in width. Each of the four Gateways projected about 30 feet beyond the outer rail; but all are so ruined that the dimensions cannot be ascertained with exactness.

The only addition I have made to the plan is the yellow circle in the centre. This is the site and I believe the dimensions of the enclosing Rail of the central Dagoba. For reasons which will be given when describing Plates XCIII. to XCVIII., it would appear that it did not exceed 30 feet in diameter; and if this were so, it seems nearly certain that other buildings occupied the rest of the enclosure; but as it is nearly certain that all these were erected in wood it is in vain now to hope to find any remains of them. A nine-storied pagoda has already been alluded to (p. 177); and my conviction is that, besides this, there must have been a Vihâra or residence, a Chaitya hall, a Dharmaśâlâ, and other conventual buildings. These, or the greater part of them, must have existed prior to 322; and it was to enclose and unite them that the great Rail was erected. Nothing is so common as such an arrangement as this in the Madras territory. In nine cases out of ten, in their greatest temples, the sanctuary itself is relatively less important, as compared with its surroundings, than this 30 feet Dagoba is to its rails and the other buildings; so that there is at least no *à priori* improbability in the arrangement.[4]

---

[1] "In the present state of the mound it is impossible to form any conjecture whether there was any or what sort of building standing in the centre, or for what purpose it was intended."—Asiatic Journal, vol. XV. p. 469.

[2] The following extract from a letter of 12th June 1867, from Sir Walter Elliot, contains all the information available on this subject:—"They found in the centre of the mound a stone casket, with a lid, on opening "which a crystal box was found, containing a small pearl, some gold leaf, and other things of no value. The "Raja sent the relics to his tosha khanah, and there they remained. At a later period I succeeded in securing "them for Government, and they are now in the Museum at Madras."

[3] By a curious coincidence this is exactly twice the diameter of the outer circle at Stonehenge. There the inner diameter of the outer circle is exactly 100 Roman feet, or 97/6 feet English. The outer rail in the Indian example is rather more than 14 feet high; that at Stonehenge is, as nearly as it can be now measured 15/6. These coincidences may be accidental, but though at first sight so different, it does not appear to me doubtful but that they are both simulated sepulchres—cenotaphs—relic shrines, or whatever they may be called, and are utterances of the same primæval faith. What does not appear to admit of doubt is, that they were being erected simultaneously—the western one to commemorate a martyrdom, the eastern to perpetuate the memory of the visit or enshrinement of a relic.

[4] So convinced am I of the correctness of the view, that I had prepared a drawing purporting to be a bird's eye view of the Tope, with all these arrangements, and intended it should form the frontispiece to this work. On second thoughts I abandoned the idea. All the other Plates in the work are absolute facts; this would have been said to have involved theories.

AMRAVATI.

PLATE XLVIII.

ELEVATION OF EXTERNAL FACE OF OUTER ENCLOSURE.

SCALE 1-3RD OF 1 INCH TO 1 FOOT.

ELEVATION OF INTERNAL FACE OF OUTER ENCLOSURE.

SCALE 1-3RD OF 1 INCH TO 1 FOOT.

PLATES XLVIII. AND XLIX.

When I was first furnished with a complete set of Photographs of the Amravati marbles in the India Museum, I confess that the task of arranging them or of finding out to what parts of the building each belonged, seemed hopeless enough. By degrees, as I became familiar with them, I perceived that they might be classified in three great groups. First, I perceived that in one portion the figures were very much larger than the others, the sculpture coarser, and they had the Sanchi form of Rail as an ornament. These, I afterwards made out, belonged to the central building, and they are found arranged in Plates XCIII. to XCVIII. Once their general characteristics are perceived, there is no difficulty in recognizing them either in the marble or in Colonel Mackenzie's drawings.

A second group consisted of marbles diametrically opposed in style to these. The figures were the smallest, the carving the most delicate, and the ornamentation more elaborate than in any of the others. They were in fact more like ivory carvings than things to be executed in stone. These I discovered belonged to the inner Rail. They will be found in Plates LXXV. to LXXXV.

There only then remained the principal group, which there was no difficulty in recognising as fragments of the great outer Rail. They occupy Plates XLVIII. to LXXIV. There only then remained a few fragments, Plates LXXXVI. to XCII., which were of no architectural importance, and may have been placed anywhere. Once this assortment was completed, there was no great difficulty in restoring the great Rail. Many of the pillars were entire for their whole height, and some where sculptured both on the back and front; so that, with a little familiarity, that distinction could be easily recognised. In addition to this, each was furnished at the sides with three lentil-shaped mortices, like those at Sanchi, as shown in the frontispiece and in Woodcuts 9 and 10. Some also of the intermediate discs still retained their flanges, which fitted into these mortices, though the greater number had been trimmed into circles, apparently for convenience of carriage. There could, however, be no mistake as to their position. The upper Rail was easily recognised by the rounded and weather-worn top, but the animal frieze at the bottom of Plate XLVIII. for a long time puzzled me. Eventually, however, I found fragments which represented the Rail in its complete state. Such, for instance, as Figs. 1. and 2., Plate LXXXVIII., represent the external appearance of the Rail with minute accuracy. They have the waving roll at top, the Zoöphorus at bottom, the octagonal pillars, with one central disc and two half discs at top and bottom; and their intermediate Rails with their circular discs and the open spaces between.[1] With these aids and the sculptures themselves, as I became familiar with them, the task became easy, and the restorations were made which are shown on a reduced scale in

[1] Compare these with Woodcuts 11 and 12 from Nasick and Kanheri.

Plates XLVIII. and XLIX., and so perfectly do all the parts fit together that I do not think there can be any doubt as to their correctness.

Plate XLVIII. represents the outer face of the great Rail, and is plainer than the inner face, as shown in the next Plate. This was an arrangement singularly consistent with good taste and architectural propriety, as it is evident that those who wished to study the sculptures could do it with more facility in the quiet and seclusion of the interior than from the outside. The only additional ornament on the exterior was the lower animal frieze, which forms a base to the whole. As that was raised two feet above the level of the country outside, something was necessary to hide its external face, while it would be difficult to design anything more elegant or better adapted to its purpose than this frieze of animals. This was not wanted internally, as the pillars there rose from the paving stones of the procession path.

Plate XLIX., Fig. 1, represents the inner face of six pillars of the great Rail, with their intermediate discs and the upper frieze; the whole, as will be observed, were elaborately covered with sculptures. The lower range of sculpture is omitted, as it apparently represented on the outside the height of the solid pavement in the interior. Fig. 2 represents a portion of a frieze of the same dimensions, but from a different part, probably one of the gateways or projections.

There were apparently twenty-four pillars in each quadrant, and eight at least in each Gateway, say 112 to 120 in all. This involves 230 to 240 central discs, all of which were sculptured; and as each of these contains from twenty to thirty figures at least, there must have been in them alone from 6,000 to 7,000 figures. If we add to these the continuous frieze above and the sculptures above and below the discs on the pillars, there probably were not less than 120 to 140 figures, for each intercolumniation, say 12,000 to 14,000 in all. The inner Rail contains probably even a greater number of figures than this, but they are so small as more to resemble ivory carving; but except, perhaps, the great frieze at Nakhon Vat,[1] there is not, perhaps, even in India, and certainly not in any other part of the world, a storied page of sculpture equal in extent to what this must have been when complete. If not quite it must have been nearly perfect, in all probability less than a century ago, or at all events it appears as if none of its sculpture had been removed or utilized at that time.

---

[1] History of Architecture, vol. II. p. 713, et seqq.

ELEVATION OF THE EXTERNAL FACES OF TWO PILLARS OF OUTER ENCLOSURE.

SCALE 1 INCH TO 1 FOOT.

ELEVATION OF THE EXTERNAL FACES OF TWO PILLARS OF OUTER ENCLOSURE.

SCALE 1 INCH TO 1 FOOT.

ELEVATION OF THE EXTERNAL FACES OF TWO PILLARS OF OUTER ENCLOSURE.
SCALE 1 INCH TO 1 FOOT.

ELEVATION OF THE EXTERNAL FACES OF TWO PILLARS OF SMALLER RAIL.
SCALE 1 INCH TO 1 FOOT.

PLATES L. TO LV.

THESE six Plates contain all the fragments belonging to the outer face of the great Rail which exist in the India House collection—with the exception of the friezes (Plates LVI., LVII.),—and are all photographed to the same scale, 1 inch to 1 foot.

The left-hand pillar (Plate L.) is dedicated to the five-headed Nâga, who occupies the place of honour in front; on either side of him is a female figure bearing offerings, and standing on two reptilian monsters, apparently dead. Above are elephants worshipping the Dagoba. On the right-hand pillar the Dagoba occupies the principal position, crowned by eleven Chattas, and guarded by two three-headed serpents whose bodies are entwined around it. On either side a male and a female figure are represented in attitudes of ecstatic devotion; and beyond, on the outside faces of the octagon, a man in Hindu costume and his wife on each side, approaching the Dagoba, bearing offerings apparently of flowers.[1] Above are elephants and winged lions worshipping the Tree.

On both these pillars, on the octagonal compartment below the central disc, are Gaṇa or dwarfs, playing and laughing and throwing themselves into grotesque attitudes.

The left-hand pillar in Plate LI. is so much weather-worn that it is extremely difficult to make out what the story of the sculptures may be. In the upper compartment two figures appear to be upholding a tray, on which a relic or some precious object is placed; and six other figures, floating in the air, appear as worshipping the object, whatever it may be. In the lower compartment two men seem to be seizing something that is descending to them from what might be called a shoot or vessel of some sort.[2] The story evidently refers to some relic or gift received miraculously below, and exalted and worshipped above, but what the precious object may be there is nothing to show.

The three following pillars (Plates LI. to LII.) contain no novelty, but are interesting as exhibiting the endless variety of detail with which these pillars are executed, and the grotesque form of the dwarfs with whom they are adorned. The drum, it will be observed, is here beaten with two crooked sticks; at Sanchi only one was employed.

The two pillars (Plate LIII.) belong to a somewhat smaller Rail, and the patterns upon them are of a purer and less exuberant style of art. Possibly they may be older, but hardly materially so; and I am clearly of opinion that they are only parts of the great outer Rail, perhaps the old part, or perhaps some detached portion or projection. Both are inscribed. The inscription on the left-hand pillar, according to General Cunningham, is to the effect that the pillar on which

[1] Mr. Beal (J. R. A. S., VI., N. S., p. 394) considers this to represent the favourite legend of Bhadrâ's offering. I confess I cannot see the relevance of his remarks, and must leave it to my readers to determine whether he or I am right in this respect; the three-headed serpents twined round the dagoba seem to me fatal to this identification.

[2] There is a drawing of this pillar in the Mackenzie Collection, Plate XXXI., but it does not help us to an explanation of the meaning.

it is engraved was the pious gift of a householder—whose name is partly obliterated—together with his wife and son. The other inscription, on the right-hand pillar, is longer, but to the same effect. It records the pious gift of two pillars by Tunulauraka the householder, son of Pusili, together with other members of his family.[1]

I have before had occasion to point out (page 92) the similarity that exists between the arrangements of the Rail in front of the Gotamiputra Cave at Nasick and that at Amravati. The coincidence becomes even more striking when we compare the pillars in this Plate with one from the same Cave, represented in the annexed woodcut (No. 28). The central circle and the two half-circles at top and bottom are as like as the difference of material would allow; and the lotus buds used to fill up the angles in both examples are nearly identical. It seems to me impossible that the two can differ much in age; and if I am correct in assigning the beginning of the fourth century to the Cave, we cannot be far wrong in assuming that the Rail was erected within a few decades of it either way.

No. 28.

PILASTER IN NASSICK CAVE.
From a Drawing by E. W. West.

Plates LIV. and LV. contain nine of the intermediate discs of the great Rail, as seen from the outer side. The three upper ones in Plate LV. belong to the smaller Rail last described, and fortunately have not been trimmed, like some of the larger ones, so that the flanges by which they were inserted into the pillars can still be observed. The other six, with the six in the centre of the pillars just described, and the eight half discs on the pillar, are sufficient to exemplify the usual form of these ornaments. Every one is different, though all have a general resemblance, and display an exuberance of fancy for such details not probably to be found in any classical or mediæval monument of its class.

In one other point they are interesting as exhibiting a classical tendency, more than any other details at Amravati. They forcibly recall the expression of Hiouen-Thsang, "that the Avaraçila Sanghârâma was ornamented with all the art of the palaces of Bactria,"—an expression the more remarkable because our traveller does not apply it to any other building he saw in India, and we do not know any one in that country where so much classical feeling prevails.[2] The ornament is the wạter-leaf of the classical artists, and might be used now on the ceiling of any modern classical hall without anyone detecting that its details were borrowed from any building east of the Euphrates.

---

[1] See Appendix E., Nos. IV. and XV.

[2] Supra, p. 170.

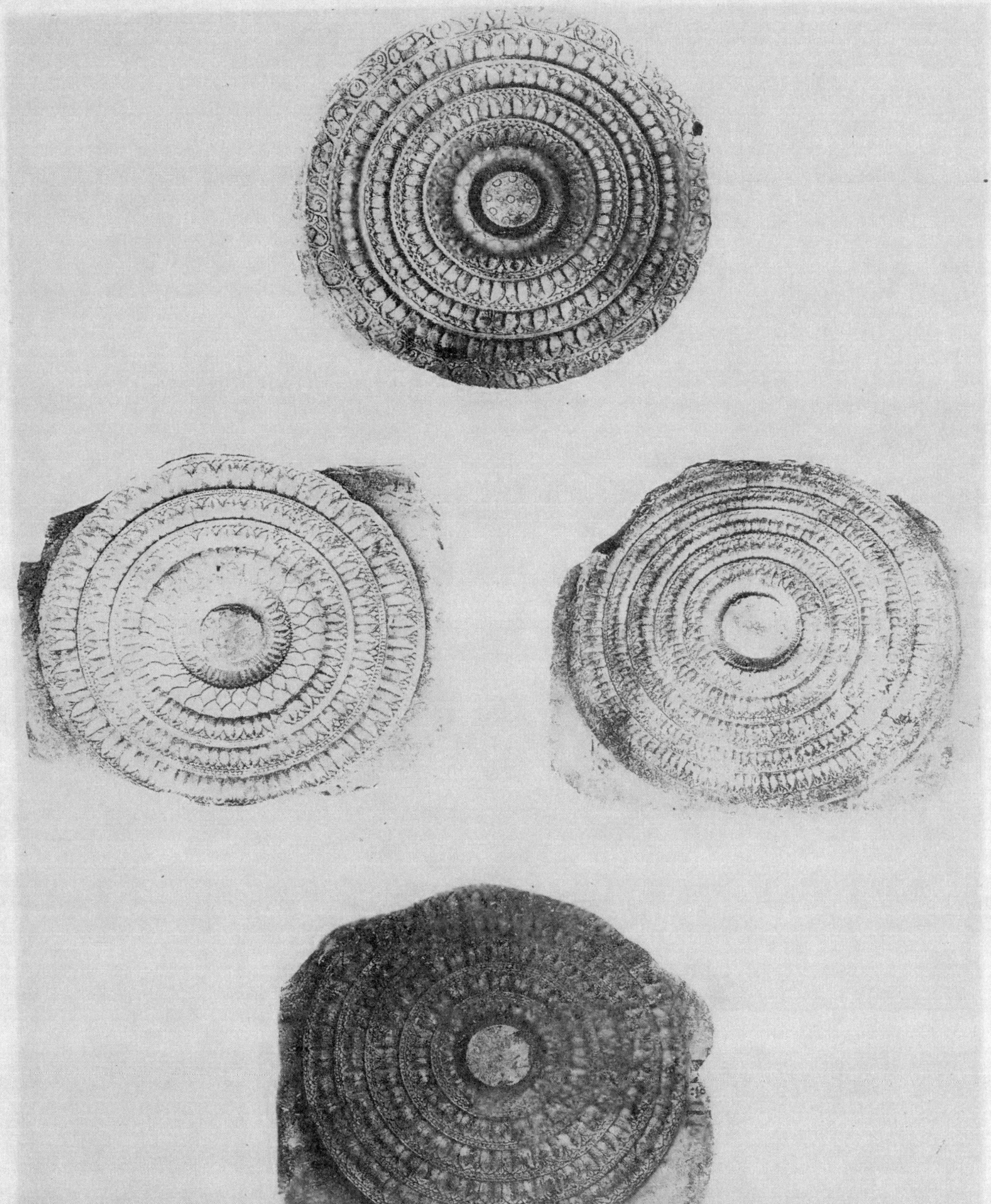

DISCS ON INTERMEDIATE RAILS OF OUTER ENCLOSURE.

SCALE 1 INCH TO 1 FOOT.

AMRAVATI. PLATE LV.

DISCS ON INTERMEDIATE RAILS.

SCALE 1 INCH TO 1 FOOT.

1

2

3

FRAGMENTS OF INTERNAL FRIEZES OF OUTER ENCLOSURE.

SCALE 1 INCH TO 1 FOOT.

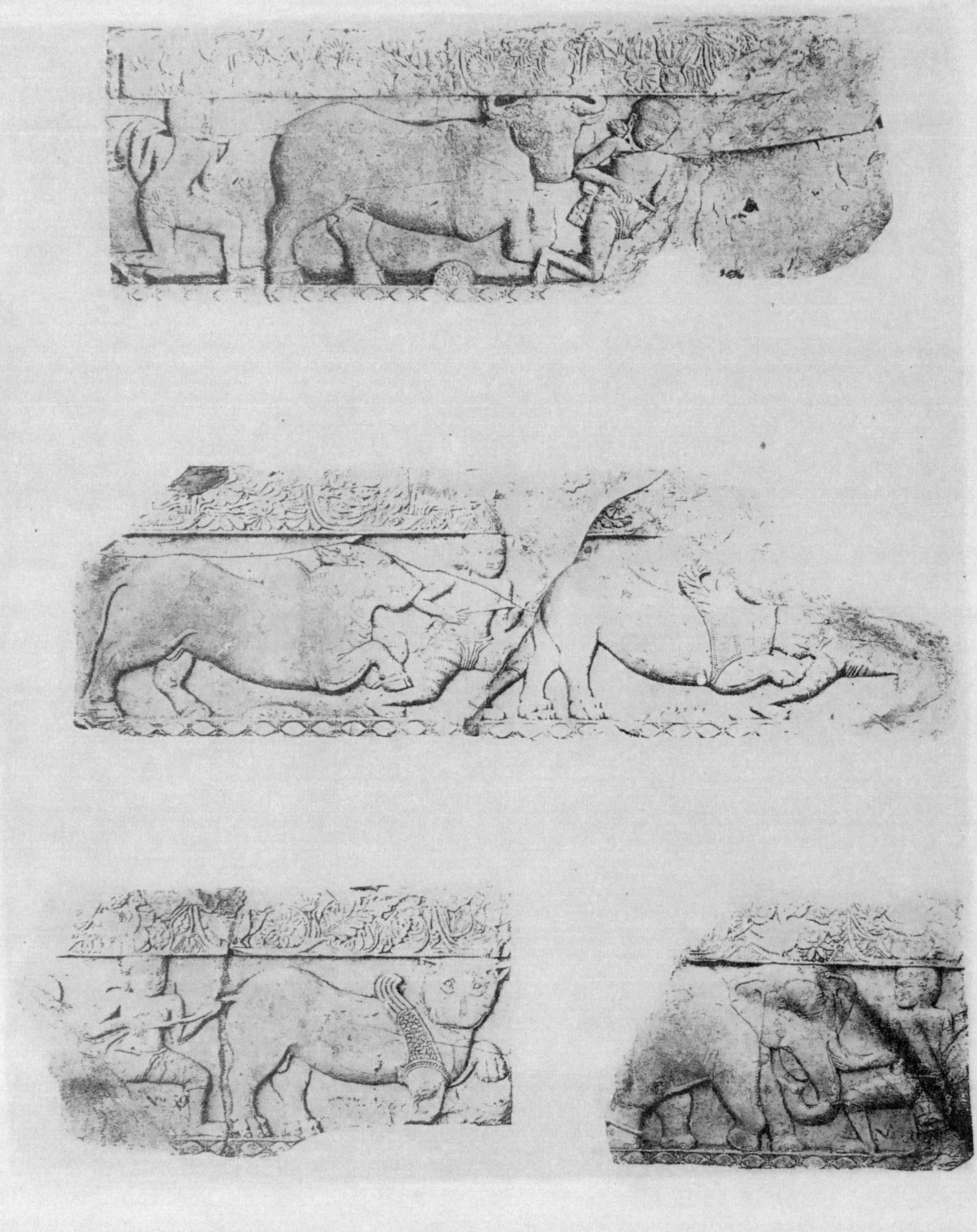

FRAGMENTS OF PLINTH OF OUTER ENCLOSURE.

SCALE 1 INCH TO 1 FOOT.

PLATES LVI. AND LVII.

THE upper external frieze of the great Rail, Plate LVI., is in many respects one of the most pleasing parts of the design. Nothing can well be better, as an architectural ornament than the wavy flow of the long roll, borne by animated figures, and interspersed with emblems appropriate to the dedication of the Tope.

The three fragments in this Plate, it will be observed, are all of different depth though of the same design, and must therefore have belonged to different parts of the great Rail. Either it was that the deepest were used to eke out the height of the small Rail (Plate LIII.), and so make it range with those parts having taller pillars, or there was one quadrant or some part which had a Rail of a smaller proportion altogether. As we have no information where each fragment was found, it is impossible to say which theory is the true one, either is equally probable, such irregularities being very usual in all Hindu buildings.

Like the last-described features, it seems to be of Bactrian origin. Something at least very like it occurs among the sculptures at Jamâlgiri near Peshawer,[1] and there so mixed with classical details as to make it appear much more ancient. Similar forms are still used, I am told, in Burmah. On the occasion of the funeral of the late High Priest at Rangoon, long rolls, made as lightly as possible of paper, and bound round with rags and coloured decorations, were borne by men on each side of the procession in precisely the same manner as here represented, and probably the same practice will be found elsewhere when looked for. At Amravati the roll is not only most elaborately, but also very tastefully, ornamented, and so interspersed with emblems as to give it all the variety requisite for architectural embellishment. These are generally, of course, the emblems with which we are already familiar, such as the Tree,[2] the Wheel, and the Dagoba, but in the centre of the upper left-hand fragment an ornament is introduced which is new to me, in so far as India is concerned, but is found on the mystic representations of Diana of the Ephesians.[3]

By far the most curious, however, of the episodes introduced into this frieze is that on the right hand of the upper portion. It represents Garuḍa, the bird of Vishṇu, the dreaded enemy of the Nâgas in all ages, holding in his beak, evidently

---

[1] One slab of this frieze was destroyed in the fire at the Crystal Palace in December 1866. A very imperfect representation of it will be found, J. A. S. B., XXI. 606.

[2] The following is a curious instance of the irradicability of local forms, even long after the religion to which they belonged may have perished. At the present day, during the festival of Navarâtrî, in honour of Śiva as Amareshwar, the immortal lord, on the third night a brazen tree is carried round the town in procession; on the fifth night a ten-headed serpent in brass. At the close of the festival the worshippers go in great pomp to a tree called Shemmu Veerchum, where the god is made to exercise in shooting an arrow at the sacred tree, followed by a discharge of fire-arms in the air, which closes the ceremony. In the festival called Śiva Mahârâtrî, the procession to the same tree is the culminating point, to which all previous arrangements are subordinate, and thus the festival closes.—See Asiatic Journal, vol. XV. pp. 472, 473.

[3] There is a statue of the Ephesian Diana in the Museum at Naples, which has been frequently engraved, which is covered with figures like these. A representation of it will be found in Falkener's Ephesus, p. 286.

for the purpose of destroying it, a five-headed Nâga. It is difficult to guess what this can mean in a temple where the Nâga is honoured almost as the chief god, and where everything is at least so mixed up with the honour of this many-headed divinity. It is interesting, however, as it is just one of those incidental allusions which, when a sufficient number of them are collected together, may enable us to trace the affiliation of Indian religions, and to decide as to their affinities. In the present instance it is another of the indications of the connexion between Buddhism and Vishṇuism so often alluded to in these pages.

The lower frieze, Plate LVII., is not remarkable in a mythological point of view, but curious as a piece of playful fancy, and in perfect keeping with the frolics of the Gaṇa or dwarfs, which are next to it in position. The leading idea throughout the frieze is the humorous one of boys holding on by the tails of animals in a state of greater or less excitement, which they are evidently incapable of controlling.

In the upper figure a boy has got hold of the tail of a bull, very fairly executed, but not so well as the galloping humped animal next below it in the Plate. The latter is as perfect a representation of a bull of purely Indian breed as can probably be found in any Indian sculpture, and the action also is free and animated in an unusual degree. The two-winged lions who follow are by no means so commendable as works of art, but they are curious as lineal descendants of those discovered by Botta and Layard at Nineveh. They are, however, considerably further removed from those prototypes than those which adorn the gates at Sanchi (Plate VII. or Plate XXXIX.), and which still retain many features in common with their Assyrian ancestors.[1]

The elephant in the last figure shows the same perfect appreciation of the characteristic features of that animal as is done in all the representations of the elephant, both here and at Sanchi. The boy in this instance has got hold of his tusk,—the comic element of the representation, as just remarked, consisting apparently in the absurdity of a boy controlling the largest of animals by such means, or of holding a lion or bull by their tails.

---

[1] At the great Pagoda at Rangoon winged lions with human heads guard all the portals leading to the enclosure in which it stands. As may be supposed, from the distance of time and place, they are very different looking animals from their prototypes, but, nevertheless, I do not think it admits of a doubt but that they, and a great deal of the architecture of Burmah, were derived from the banks of the Euphrates or Tigris.—See my History of Architecture, II. p. 518.

PLATE LVIII.[1]

THE sculptures on Plate LVIII. are wholly devoted to Tree Worship. In the central circle some circular object is placed on the altar in front of the Tree, to which the attention of the bystanders seems to be especially directed. Two men on either hand are making offerings to it, or adding offerings to one already made, and two kneeling figures in the foreground seem trying to catch what may overflow from the right-hand man's offering, which seems to be a liquid presented in a jar. Behind him is a yoke of oxen, indicating that he is a stranger arrived for the purpose of worship. Below the altar are impressions of Buddha's feet.

There can be very little doubt but that the upper relief represents a celebrated miracle performed by Buddha in the Jetawana Monastery at Śrâvasti. On a certain day he proclaimed that he would perform a miracle under a mango tree. The Tirttakas in consequence bought up all the trees in the place, for the purpose of destroying them; but, a gardener having presented him with some fruit he set the stone of a mango in the ground. "In a moment the earth clove, a sprout appeared, "and a tree arose." "It was 300 cubits in circumference and laden with blossoms "and the richest fruit."[2] On the left of the tree the King of Kośala and the inhabitants of the city are seen coming to worship. On the right the unbelievers fly, but at the same time expressing their astonishment at what they see.

If I am correct in this identification it seems hardly doubtful that the feet in front of the tree must be taken as symbolizing the presence of Buddha. According to the legend he performed the miracle, yet there is no one here represented who can be for one moment assumed to be intended for that august personage; but if this is so, it opens our eyes to a fact that I think the study of these sculptures forces upon us, which is, that the sacred feet are intended to symbolize the bodily presence of Buddha, wherever they are found. It may consequently be assumed that he was present in the scenes depicted in the upper and middle bas-reliefs on this pillar, but was not present in the lower. The figure on the left with the umbrella over his head was, in this case, the hero of that event whatever it may have been.

Something of the same action is repeated in the lowest bas-relief on the pillar. Four women on the left and four dwarfs on the right are worshipping the Tree. On the right stands the king or prince, with the umbrella of state borne over his head, in front of another Tree, with a kneeling figure in front of the altar. On the right a man on an elephant pursues or flies with a horseman. His horse has fallen on his knees, and he is being knocked on the head by a dwarf with a mallet.

---

[1] Of the two great pillars of the outer Rail represented in this Plate, that on the left hand was considered as the most beautiful in the Elliot Collection. It was in consequence selected for the honour of being exhibited, and was attached to the outer wall of the India Museum at Fife House. The result has, however, been unfortunate. The frost of our winters has so destroyed the surface of the stone that it has in many cases peeled off to such an extent that it is now difficult to trace the design, and the whole is in a degraded and perishing condition.

[2] Spence Hardy, Manual of Buddhism, p. 296. There is a curious resemblance between this miracle and the Mango tree trick as now performed by Indian jugglers, making of course allowance for the exaggeration that disfigures all Buddhist narratives as we now have them.

The incident here portrayed is the same as occurs on the upper beam of the Western Gateway at Sanchi, and is repeated at Amravati in the pillar Plate LXVI., and probably in other places. From its being repeated these three times at least, it evidently was a favourite legend with the Buddhists in the early centuries of the Christian era. It represents an attack on the sacred Tree by an armed force, defeated by the prayers or intercession of the faithful. Without further information, however, it is hardly probable that we shall be able to identify either who the discomfitted actors are in this scene, or what the particular tree is, or on what occasion the attack was made. My own impression is, that it represents the attack made by heretics and Brahmans, on the celebrated Tooth-brush Tree at Vâisaka as related by Hiouen Thsang, vol. I. p. 292.

The two lower bas-reliefs on the right-hand pillar of this Plate are devoted to the same subject. In the centre a number of women—there are no men—are performing various acts of devotion, and bringing offerings to the sacred Tree. The scene is laid in the centre of a village, the huts of which are seen both above and on either hand. In the lower one all the actors are men. Two in the centre present pieces of cloth or garments to the Tree, and those in the side compartments seem also to be bringing scarfs or similar objects.

The sacred feet are seen in the lower bas-relief and, if we are right in our interpretation of their symbolizing the presence of Buddha, the offerings may be considered as made to him personally. In the central relief as there are no feet, it is the Tree, and the Tree only, to which worship seems to be directed.

The upper sculpture is of a different nature. In the centre a flight of Hansas or sacred geese are winging their way across what appears to be a lake, between two trees. A hand issues from the right-hand tree, with two circular objects in it, and the geese under it look as if falling dead on the shore, but it may be they are only flying downwards. On the sand are five impressions of the sacred feet,—there were probably originally eight,—and two birds, apparently peacocks, are somewhat indistinctly seen strutting on the sand. I have met with no legend that explains all the incidents depicted in the bas-relief, but it seems probable that it is an early form of a Jâtaka, still found in Ceylon. "The royal Hansa assembled all his subjects " in an extensive plain, that his daughter might choose a husband from among " them. She chose the peacock, at which the vain bird was so elated that he raised " his tail, and made such a display as to disgust the king, who in consequence " broke off the match."[1] If this is the legend, all that can be said is that what is here represented must be an earlier form.[2] On the left hand are several women presenting flowers in pots, and on the right the Nâga Râjâ with his seven-headed snake hood, and behind him his three wives, over each of whose heads may be seen the single-headed snake, which always marks them.[3]

---

[1] Upham's Historical Books of Ceylon, vol. III. p. 289.

[2] There is another legend quoted by Schiefner (Transactions of the St. Petersburg Academy, 1851, p. 238) from a Thibetan life of Buddha, which may be the one referred to. Devadatta, it is there related, wounded a goose, which fell into the garden of the Bodisattwa. He extracted the arrow, and having cured the wound let it go. It was claimed, however, by the sportsman, and hence arose a serious quarrel. A tree figures as the most important feature in this legend, which may be that one on the left hand; but no hand from another tree, and no peacocks. On the whole the probability seems to be that there was an older legend which is here represented, and which was afterwards broken up into numerous fragments.

[3] The inscription, will be found in Appendix E., Nos. XVII. and XIV. They merely record the names of the donors.

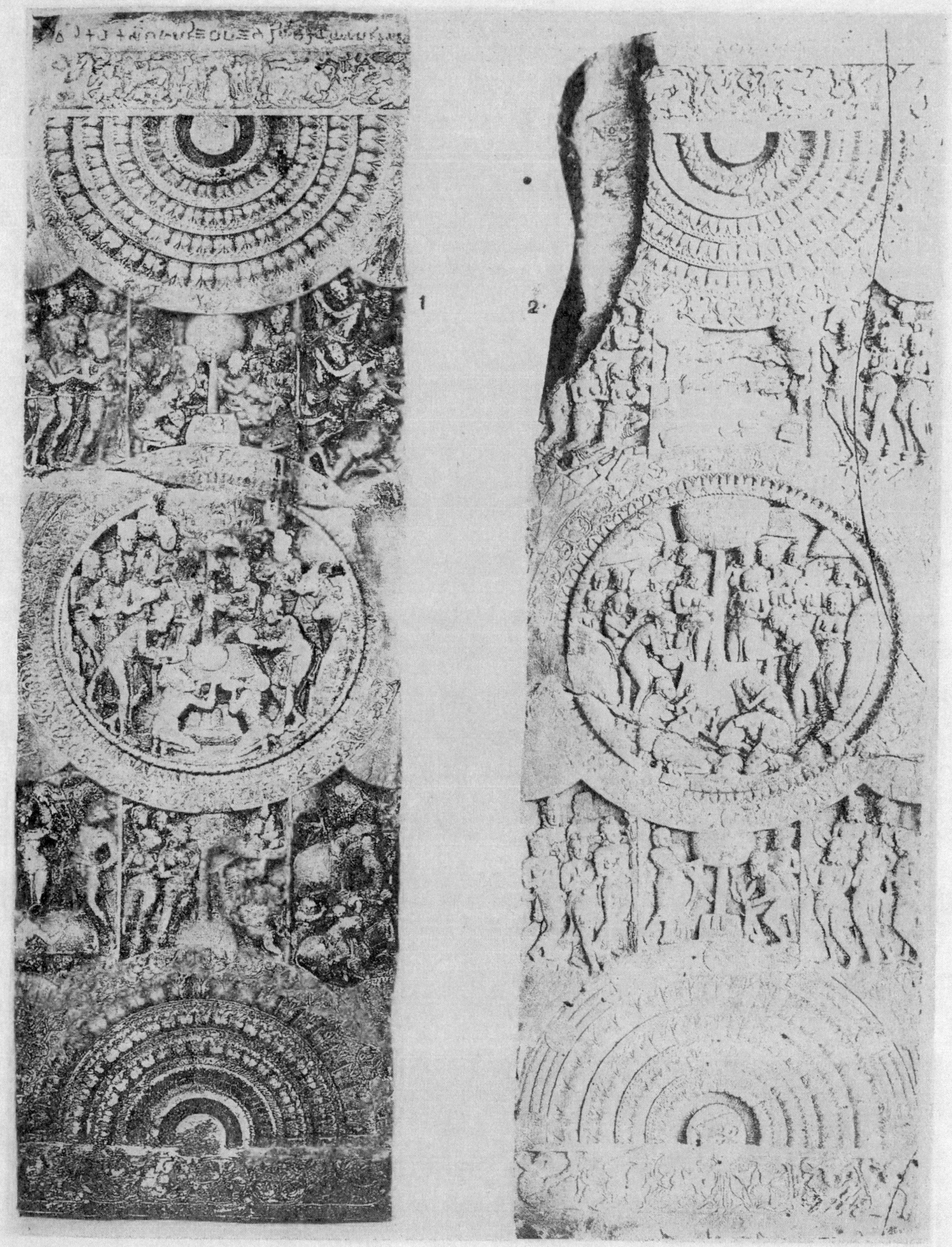

ELEVATION OF INTERNAL FACES OF TWO PILLARS OF OUTER ENCLOSURE.

Scale 1 Inch to 1 Foot.

ELEVATION OF INTERNAL FACES OF TWO PILLARS OF OUTER ENCLOSURE.
SCALE 1 INCH TO 1 FOOT.

PLATE LIX.

THERE is no difficulty in recognizing the principal figure in the two central circles of the pillars in Plate LIX. In the first it is the Prince Siddhârtha riding[1] forth from the city gate, with all the insignia of his rank. The umbrella of state is borne over his head; Chaori bearers attend on either hand, and music and dancing precede him. The glory round his head marks him as the elect—the future regenerator of the world. This is the first time we meet with this distinguishing mark, as there are no glories at Sanchi, though they are found commonly behind the heads of saints in the Peshawer sculptures.

As in the processional scenes at Sanchi (ante p. 147), we naturally look here for something that might indicate this as representing one of the predictive signs of the more modern Buddhist legends. Nothing, however, of the sort can be detected here, nor, so far as I know, in any of the sculptures of either the Sanchi or Amravati Topes.

In the circle of the right-hand picture we have the same individual after he had attained Buddhahood, in the robes in which he is always represented after apparently the second or third century of our era. On his right a woman, more fully clothed than any other woman in these sculptures, presents a boy to him, who catches hold of his garment as if entreating him to come with him. The boy's toys are seen in the foreground. It hardly seems doubtful but that this represents Yaśodharâ and her son Râhula entreating the great ascetic to return home to them, and re-occupy the position due to his rank and his duties as a prince and a father.

The figures around Buddha are his disciples, among whom will be remarked in the foreground a hump-backed woman (Kubja), who frequently reappears in the sculptures.

The lower bas-reliefs on both these pillars seem to continue the subjects represented in the principal circles. In the centre of the left-hand pillar we have Siddhârtha with the glory round his head; one man kissing his feet, and others in reverential attitudes; and beside him "the Horse," to whom we shall frequently have occasion to revert hereafter. On the left of this a man bearing a relic in a tray; the same as seen in Plate LI., whatever it may be. Below him is a Nâga Râjâ in a kneeling attitude. On the right is the worship of the Chakra or Wheel, with the usual accompaniments, and two antelopes in the foreground. Evidently the same scene as that represented at Sanchi, Plate XXIX., but in this instance with a throne in front of the Wheel, and a relic or cushion on it.

The story told in the lower bas-relief of the right-hand pillar is easily made out. A prince is seated on a couch, surrounded by his attendants, and a boy with a bow

---

[1] It is worthy of remark that at Sanchi the prince is always in his chariot, at Amravati on horseback. There is only one chariot in all the sculptures at Amravati, Plate LXXXVI., and the subject of that bas-relief is singularly connected with Sanchi.

seems to ask him to join in the chase or some martial exercise. In the central compartment he resists the temptations of the daughters of Mâra, or some other bevy of females, who wish to take possession of him;[1] and in the third, having assumed the priestly robes, teaches a multitude under a Bo Tree. It looks at first sight as if intended for an epitome of the life of Buddha, but it may be doubted whether he is really the person intended here, as in none of the three compartments has he a glory round his head, and it is hardly probable that in the same pillar he would be represented with and without this accompaniment. It may be some Bodhisattwa, but on the whole I am inclined to believe that it may represent scenes in the life of Râhula, who seems certainly to be the hero of the central bas-relief; and if this is so nothing can be more natural than that his story should be continued on the same pillar. This prince, according to the legend, at the age of twenty, assumed the garb of a priest and shortly after, by his father's teaching rose to the rank of a Rahat.[2] It will be observed that the old woman who appears behind the boy in the central picture re-appears in the left-hand lower picture. Is she the mother of Yaśodara?

The two upper bas-reliefs are too completely destroyed for their subjects to be made out. We can just see in the central bas-relief of the left-hand pillar that some person or object is being worshipped by women in the usual attitude, and on the right-hand pillar that Buddha himself is seated in the usual cross-legged attitude, and being worshipped by his followers. We can, however, restore with tolerable certainty the upper representation on the left of the left-hand pillar by comparing it with the left-hand pillar, Plate LI., or Plate LXXIII., Fig. 2. The man whose legs only appear, almost certainly bore a tray on his head, on which stood a cup or some similar object, and the others are reverencing it, whatever it may have been.

It will be observed the representation of Buddha here is very far in advance of anything found on the Gateways at Sanchi, and much more nearly resembling the modern representations found everywhere. The whole of the scenes, indeed, represented on these two pillars, show a progress, which not only in style but in fullness of legendary detail, which must have required the 300 years that elapsed between the execution of the two monuments.

---

[1] This scene occurs again more in detail, Plate LXIII., where it will be more especially referred to.

[2] Bigandet, Burmese Legend of Buddha, p. 229, Journal Amer. Orient. Soc. III. 69. His having entered the priesthood by no means precludes his having succeeded to the throne of Kapilavastu on the death of his grandfather. In Burmah, at the present day, nothing is so common as for members of the upper classes to become priests. Some remain so, but many more resume their civil status after three or four years' probation. A young Burmese gentleman looks on entering the priesthood very much as an undergraduate in one of our semimonastic colleges at Oxford or Cambridge regards his wearing a surplice in chapel. Many in our country remain in the priesthood, but as many return to civil life.

PLATE LX.

The palace scenes portrayed on the two pillars in this Plate are among the most elegant of the Amravati sculptures, and interesting as pictures of life in India during the fourth century, though it is not easy to affix any particular story to the scenes they represent. Still, as the seated figure in the upper part of the central circle of the right-hand pillar has a glory round his head, we cannot refuse to recognise him as the Prince Siddhârtha; and if so, the scenes represent the Harem at Kapilavastu, which he deserted to devote himself to save his fellow creatures from sin and death.

In front of him, two of the ladies of the Harem are playing at Pachîsî, or drafts, or some such game, while others are looking on; and in front of them a very graceful figure is dancing, while another plays on the flute, a third on a guitar, and one on a drum. Others are listening or applauding, and one child (is it the infant Râhula?) appears in the foreground.

In the lower bas-relief a Prince is seated on a couch, probably the same as in the upper bas-relief though he has no glory behind his head, in conference with a Nâga Râjâ, and in front of them two women are seated, most probably their wives. On the left are the Nâga Râjâ's people. On the right the country people are bringing presents of cattle, fruit, &c., to the seated Râjâs, while one is feeding or making an offering to a tame snake that lives in a curiously constructed cell in the left-hand corner of the bas-relief.

The head of the principal figure of the circle of the left-hand pillar is so completely destroyed that we cannot now know whether he had a nimbus round his head or not, nor consequently whether he is the same as the person represented on the right-hand pillar. Most probably he is. The object of the sculpture is to represent the entertainment of two distinguished guests. They are seated on a dais, on the King's right hand, with a table in front of each. The major domo stands between the Raja and his guests, and presents something to the nearest; while a girl in front offers apparently something to drink. In front of her, with his back to the spectators, is a man seated in one of those square-backed chairs which are common in these sculptures. The Queen sits on the Raja's left, in a chair of another and more elegant pattern, but extremely like the modern chairs we now use. To those familiar with Indian habits at the present day, few things are more curious than the fact that all dignitaries in these sculptures are always seated on chairs or sofas, like Europeans; never on the ground or on cushions cross-legged, as is the universal practice now-a-days. The only difference seems to be that the seat of the chair or throne must always have been made wide enough for the sitter to put up one leg on it, as this seems to have been the fashionable attitude.

In the central picture some of the women are seated on stools, some on chairs; but in both the circular bas-reliefs, as in the lower one on the left hand of the left-hand pillar, the Raja is seated on a throne with a square back, ornamented with lions' heads.

In the centre of the foreground of the circular bas-relief of the left-hand pillar, is a child attended by two women, one old and one very much younger. This would seem to connect the two bas-reliefs as representing the same persons, and if that is so, it scarcely admits of doubt but that the principal figure in both is intended for the Prince Siddhârtha, and the child in that case must be his son Râhula.

The lower bas-relief under the central circle on this pillar is one of the most curious and interesting of the Amravati sculptures. It represents the legend of King Sivi who, to redeem the life of a pigeon which had claimed his protection, offered to the falcon that was pursuing it an equivalent weight of his own flesh cut from his right thigh. The story goes on to relate that the dove, which was an incarnation of Agni, went on increasing in weight supernaturally to such an extent that in order to counterpoise it he was obliged to cut off, and throw all his flesh into the scales, and then his whole body, when Indra who was personified by the falcon acknowledged his goodness and the greatness of his self-sacrifice.

The Sivi Jâtaka has not been translated, but I learn from Herr Fausböll that this is not the form of the story there related, and the particulars given above are taken from the Mahâbhârata where the story is told twice over with very slight variations.[1] It is also alluded to by Fa-hian who, enumerating the sacrifices of Bodhisatwa, says, "he mangled his flesh to deliver a dove from the hawk,"[2] and it certainly was a favourite legend of the early Buddhists. I do not detect it at Sanchi, but it occurs twice at least again at Amravati, Plate LXXXII. and Plate LXXXIII., probably also in LXXXI. It occurs also in the sculptures at Boro Buddor in Java, and I have no doubt will be found elsewhere when looked for.

The Gateway in this last bas-relief is curious, as almost literally reproducing those at Sanchi. There are at Amravati at least a dozen representations of the same thing, all nearly though not exactly alike, but all evidently intended to represent a wooden erection, such as it can hardly be doubted suggested those at Sanchi. Though these are in stone, this material did not at once supersede the wooden form which continued to be employed long afterwards in India, and is to be found everywhere at the present day in China.

---

[1] Fauche's Translation, vol. III. p. 547 et seqq., and vol. IV. p. 253 et seqq. For these two references I am indebted to my friend Mr. Childers of the India Office Library.

[2] Beal's translation, p. 156.

ELEVATION OF INTERNAL FACES OF TWO PILLARS OF OUTER ENCLOSURE.

SCALE 1 INCH TO 1 FOOT.

ELEVATION OF TWO PILLARS OF OUTER ENCLOSURE.

Scale 1 Inch to 1 Foot.

PLATE LXI.

There does not seem to be any sign or symbol by which we can attach a name to any of the actors in the scenes portrayed in the principal circle of the right-hand portion of Plate LXI., though it is easy to describe the action. It is evidently a disputation held between two men, one of whom, of superior rank, sits in the middle of the picture, and lays down the law in an authoritative manner. The other, on a lower seat, is evidently represented as beaten in argument. Between the two disputants sits an old man with something like a book on his lap, the arbiter in the contest, and behind him an attendant apparently with refreshments. Another man is standing in a gateway of the Sanchi type, and turning to listen. The rest of the audience are all women, ten of them are there as listeners only, an eleventh bears a fan, and a twelfth food. This presence of women in such scenes as these is one of the remarkable features of the sculptures, both here and at Sanchi. Not only do they take part in every action almost without exception, but seem almost as important as the male actors. Certainly the idea of a veiled or Purdah woman had not occurred to the Hindus when these sculptures were executed.

In the lower bas-relief the king or prince issues from one of these Sanchi portals, followed by his wife, to meet or feed a body of mendicant friars or monks. It is the first appearance of these noted priests in these sculptures, and is the more remarkable as there are several other instances in which they appear at Amravati, but, as before mentioned, no trace of them is to be found at Sanchi. The absence of priests is the more remarkable, because if we were to believe Buddhist books, they flocked in thousands and tens of thousands from all parts of India to attend the great convocations held five or six centuries before these sculptures were commenced.[1]

---

[1] In the Mahawanso there is a curious enumeration (page 171) of the priests who are said to have attended at the dedication of the Ruanwelli dagoba at Anuradhapura, 157 B.C. As, however, the Mahawanso was compiled or reduced to its present form by Buddhaghosa (A.D. 408), it may be taken rather as belonging to the fourth or to the beginning of the fifth century; and though no doubt a gross exaggeration, may be fairly understood as indicating the relative importance of Buddhism in the various countries of India at the time when the Amravati buildings were in course of erection.

Indagutto, from Râjagaha (Rajagriha) - - - - -	brought	8,000	theros.
Dhammasêno, from Isipattana Temple, near Benares - - - - -	,,	12,000	,,
Piyadassi, from the Jêtovihâra Śrâvastî - - - - - -	,,	60,000	,,
Buddharakkito, from Wesâli (on the Gunduk) - - - - -	,,	18,000	,,
Dhammarakkito, from Kôsambia (Kâlinjar) - - - - - -	,,	30,000	,,
The same thero from Ujjêni (Ougein) - - - - - -	,,	40,000	,,
Mittinno, from the Aśoka Temple Pupphapura (Patna) - - -	,,	100,000	,,
Rettinno, from Kasmîra (Kashmere) - - - - - - -	,,	280,000	,,
Mahadêwo, from Pullawabhago - - - - - - -	,,	1,460,000	,,
Dhammarakkito, from Alasada (Alexandria), capital of the Yona country (Cabul)	,,	30,000	,,
Uttaro, from the Uttania Temple, in the wilderness of Winjha - -	,,	60,000	,,
Chittagutto, from the Bôdhimando (Gayâ) - - - - - -	,,	30,000	,,
Chandagutto, from Wanawaso country - - - - - -	,,	80,000	,,
Sûriagutto, from the Kêlâso Vihâra - - - - - - -	,,	96,000	,,

The story of the left-hand pillar is perhaps more graphically told than almost any other on these pillars. A king is seated on his throne, to whom a messenger with clasped hands brings intelligence or solicits orders. In front of him a part of the army is seen defending the walls of the citadel, and on the left hand the moveable force is sallying from the city gate. In front the infantry, in attitudes of great excitement, are seen advancing to the fight, and the rear is brought up by horsemen and elephants, all remarkably well drawn and foreshortened. In the foreground one of the enemy falls on his knees to beg pardon and mercy.

If the lower part of the pillar had been preserved, we might have seen the result of this sally. It no doubt was successful, and as women appear in the fragments that remain the whole ended probably in triumph.

According to the Lalita-Vistara[1] and other Indian works, a perfect army always consists of four arms, elephants and horsemen, chariots and infantry. Three of these are represented here, but strange to say the chariots are absent, as they always are at Amravati, though, as before remarked, they are so prominent at Sanchi. This probably is owing to some local peculiarity which could only be discovered on the spot. It can hardly be that they had gone out of fashion, because in the great temple of Nakon Vat, in Cambodia, built probably eight centuries after Amravati,[2] chariots are everywhere used by the chiefs in war, and with wheels as perfect and as light as could be made now by a London coach-builder. Those who know how much civilization is involved in a perfect wheel will acquire a higher estimate of the stage reached by the Snake-worshippers there, from these mechanical appliances, than even from their sculptures themselves.

Taken altogether, this pillar, both in its decorations and its sculptures, is one of the most elegant at Amravati, and it would consequently be extremely interesting if its inscription told us something of its story. All, however, we gather from it is that the pillar was the gift of three men and their three wives.[3]

It is so much narrower than the others just described, that it evidently did not form one of the regular pillars of the outer Rail, but as it is the same height and the circles are the same distance from centre to centre, it probably belonged to one of the projecting Gateways, either as an angle column, or on some return where narrower pillars only could be introduced.

Except a few of the last, all these can be identified, and their modern names are given. Pallawabhago, from its importance and its position between Kashmere and Kabul, can hardly represent any other country than the Punjab.

The two last have not been identified, but I cannot help fancying that the name Winjha is no other than Vengi, or the country in which Amravati is situated, though the fact must not be overlooked that in the 19th chapter of the Mahawanso, Winjha (Vindhya ?) is applied to some place near the Ganges between Patna and the sea. Nothing, however, is so common as duplicate names in India, and as Amravati then existed it must have been represented, or at all events it was known to Buddhaghoso, and could hardly have been omitted.

It will be observed there is no mention of Dravida, nor any hint of any Buddhist establishment south of the Nerbudda, unless the Uttania Temple really is the Pali synonym for Amravati. Had there been any Buddhist establishments in the south they, being so much nearer Ceylon, could not fail to have been represented at this great gathering.

[1] See also the Nîti-sâra, or Elements of Polity, by Kâmandaki. Calcutta, 1861, ch. 19.

[2] See History of Architecture, by the Author, vol. II. p. 713, et seqq.

[3] See Appendix E., No. XIII.

PLATE LXII.

THE two circular bas-reliefs represented in this Plate are the two most perfect of their class in the collection, and have consequently been photographed to a larger scale in order to make their details more easily visible. The upper one Colonel Mackenzie considered as the most elegant of the Amravati sculptures,[1] an opinion in which he probably was not far wrong. It is somewhat weather-worn, however, now, and was very seriously damaged on its return from the late French Exhibition.

The action is simple. A casket containing a relic is placed on the throne under an elaborate canopy, and is being worshipped by the Nâga Râjâ and his people. The Nâga Râjâ stands in the centre, with the seven-headed snake hood over him, and the two attendants on either hand, with Chaoris, have also the same canopy. It is not easy to see whether the two men with their hands clasped over their heads are Nâgas also, but the probability is that they are. None of the men behind him have the snake hood, but the twelve females in the foreground have all of them a single snake on the back of their heads. The whole is, however, arranged so much more elegantly than at Sanchi (Plate XXIV.), that it is not offensive, and the snakes would not, indeed, be noticed unless attention was directed to them. The two standing female figures on either hand are singularly elegant, especially the one buying the wreath to present to the relic,—or at least she was before her visit to Paris.

It is probably in vain to inquire what the relic is that is enclosed in this casket. If the conjectures hazarded above with regard to the visit of the Tooth relic to this place have any foundation, it is by no means impossible that the famed Deladâ may be contained within, and is here exposed temporarily on the throne to be worshipped by the Nâga Râjâ and his people.[2]

Both the throne and the canopy or umbrella over it are singularly rich and elegant specimens of the furniture of the period. Such thrones frequently occur, but no such canopy in any other of the sculptures.

The lower circle contains no peg on which it will, I fear, be possible to hang a story. It is simply this, two Hindu

No. 29.

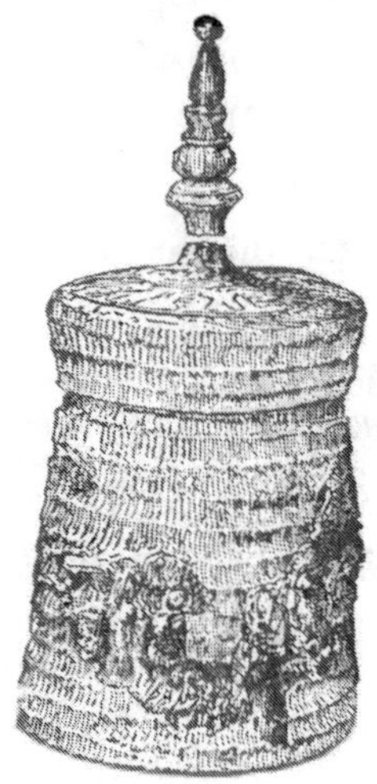

RELIC CASKET FROM MANIKYALA.

[1] From a pencil note in his handwriting on the drawing of this sculpture in his book.

[2] In the Tope at Manikyala, opened by General Ventura, a casket was found, of which the annexed is a representation. It contained only fragments of amber in a brown liquid, but the inscription not yet having been satisfactorily made out, we are ignorant to whom it belonged. See Thomas, Edition of Prinsep, vol. I. p. 97, et seqq., and Professor Dowson, in vol. XX. p. 244, J. R. A. S. It probably belongs to a date not far distant from the Christian era. The casket represented in Woodcut No. 14, p. 95, is, perhaps, even more like the one worshipped by the Nâga Râjâ in this bas-relief. It, too, was found in a Tope at Manikyala, and, to judge from the coins that were found with it, should be of about the same age. Its form, however, and other circumstances, incline me to think it may be more modern.

gentlemen,—they are not Rajas, as they have no umbrellas of state borne over them,—not much burdened with clothing, are seated on a sofa of modern form, listening to a concert of music, which is being performed by a number of women in the foreground. Eighteen women seem to be engaged in the performance. Three are playing on harps, three or four on drums, some on flutes, one is blowing a horn, and others are performing on instruments, the nature of which it is not easy to make out. One woman, with her back to the spectator, standing in the centre, appears to be the leader, and is beating time with her hands. In front of her, with one foot on a stool or drum, is the *prima donna*, accompanying her voice with a harp. She has short curly hair, and, like all the musicians, rather a sharp Roman nose, extremely unlike the men or any other of their women. It will also be observed, she alone of all the women has no bangles on her ancles, though she has on her wrists. Besides the eighteen performers wo others of the same race will be observed on the right of the circle: one with her ɑands joined is addressing the principal Queen, while another lower down seems to covet the bead belt of a girl she is talking to. Whoever these performers are they are a class we have not met before, nor do we, so far as I can make out, meet them again. They are very unlike all the other people represented in the sculptures, and very easily distinguishable from those of a different race in this bas-relief. The latter have all rather flat noses, and a more Tartar-like cast of features than are generally seen in these sculptures. Are they Gonds? The performers, on the contrary, have singularly sharp features and prominent Roman noses, and seem to have curly heads, but nothing in the least approaching the Negro type in any way. Are they Gypsies?

Besides the musicians and the gentlemen on the sofa, there are three ladies of rank, two on the right and one on the left of the picture, who are accommodated with chairs. Their principal articles of dress are their bangles and their bead belt below their waists.[1] There are two little girls in the foreground, and about twenty others, who seem to be the attendants on inmates of the Harem.

One other point requires notice. Below the sofa are two things that look like jars or pots, and if they are vessels, evidently containing some drink for the refreshment of those seated upon it. The same thing was observed at Sanchi (Plate XXX. and XXXVII.). There it certainly contained some intoxicating fluid. I am afraid that in this instance also they contain something stronger than water, unless indeed they are the supports of the sofa which is a possible, but hardly a probable, solution of their presence.

---

[1] "On the east of the Chanda district (the Gond district nearest Amravati) the men wear no covering for their heads or the upper part of their bodies. The women deck themselves with thirty to forty beads, to which some add a necklace of pendent bells. Bangles of zinc adorn their wrists, and a chain of the same metal is suspended from the hair, and attached to a large boss stuck in the ear. But the greatest peculiarity connected with their costume is the practice that prevails, in more remote districts, of the women wearing no clothes at all; instead of which they fasten with a string passing round their waists a bunch of leafy twigs to cover them before and behind." Barring the twigs, which seem to be a modern innovation, nothing can more correctly describe the costumes of the sculptures than the above extract from Mr. Hislop's paper on the Gonds, edited by Sir R. Temple, p. 8.

INTERNAL FACE OF TWO DISCS ON INTERMEDIATE RAILS OF OUTER ENCLOSURE.

SCALE 1 INCH 3-4TH TO 1 FOOT.

AMRAVATI.

PLATE LXIII.

1

2

3

DISCS ON INTERNAL FACE OF INTERMEDIATE RAILS OF OUTER ENCLOSURE.

SCALE 1 INCH TO 1 FOOT.

PLATE LXIII.

The three circles represented in this Plate are the only other intermediate sculptured circles in the Indian Museum. All three are so much damaged and weather-worn that it is extremely difficult to make out their details, and to feel certain about their story. The subject of the upper one is clearly a temptation scene, and is a more detailed representation of the central bas-relief on the lower compartment of the right-hand pillar (Plate LIX.). A man in great wrath drives from him a number of females, some of whom are in the act of asking favours; some are laughing, some going quietly away, but others have tumbled down, and are being apparently trampled upon. The first impression is, that this is meant to represent the temptation to which Buddha was subjected by the Apsaras, the daughters of Mâra, as described at length in the Lalita-Vistara.[1] In every respect it would answer for this legend but for the attitude of the main figure. The nearly perfected Buddha replied calmly to all their seductions, that he had conquered all the passions, and that love of women had long since ceased to influence him. He looked on them as mere illusions, and their power was gone. It was by calmness and dignity that he repulsed them. This figure is in violent action. He holds a stick—it may be a bow—in his hand, and seems in wrath. All this is so unlike Buddhism that we must probably look elsewhere for a solution of the myth, though it may only be an earlier form of it than that found in the Lalita-Vistara. It might be suggested that the face of the principal and only male figure being destroyed, we mistake the action; but the representation on Plate LIX. negatives this hypothesis. There the face and the figure are complete, and in that instance they can hardly be assumed to be identical with those of the principal figure in the central circle above them. On the whole I am inclined to believe rather that Râhula is the hero of the scene, but the Lalita-Vistara and our other usual authorities on Buddhist tradition, are so singularly silent with regard to him or his connexion with his father's preaching, that I do not know where to look for elucidations. Some one more familiar with Buddhist legends than I can pretend to be, may probably suggest an interpretation.

Though the upper part is broken off, this is one of the few circles that have not been trimmed. It retains the flanges by which it was fitted into the pillars nearly entire.

The middle circle is entire though weather-worn. It represents a Hindu chief. He has the Chaori, but no umbrella, and is followed by one of his wives on the left hand. Two others are on the right, worshipping a throne, or a circular object placed on one. It is extremely difficult to feel certain what the object may be, though we shall frequently meet with it again in these sculptures; generally however, there are two of them. Most probably it is a measure called a Droṇa, or

[1] Lalita-Vistara, p. 306, et seqq.

Dona, and contains a relic or relics, but it may also possibly be only a cushion, though in that case it is difficult to understand what the object is which the people are represented as worshipping. There is no other object in this bas-relief which can be considered an idol. Two men like shaven priests stand behind the throne, with their hands joined in the attitude of prayer, and behind them nine women, also worshipping. Several women in the foreground are in attitudes of violent devotion, one has fallen, in her ecstasies, quite on her back. This circle also retains a portion of its flanges.

The third or lowest circle in this Plate refers to some legend to which it probably will not be easy to give a name. It may be wholly local. A Raja, with the umbrella of state over his head, stands in a very easy and graceful attitude, leaning on his horse, which issues from the portal of the palace led by a groom in very complete clothing. The Raja is addressing or being addressed by an old lady seated on a couch or easy chair on his right. She is surrounded by her handmaidens, some of whom in the foreground seem to be busy preparing wreaths, while one is taking something out of a box. In front of the hero a number of objects are spread out on a tray or table. They look like lotus flowers, but they may be refreshments of some sort.

At the time the bas-relief was sculptured everyone of course could recognise who the old lady was, and who her son, as easily as we can name at once the Virgin Mary or her Son in any picture of the Italian school, but without some symbol it is as difficult to do so with these Buddhist sculptures. Just as in our modern exhibitions it frequently is impossible to guess what subject any particular picture is intended to represent, without referring to the catalogue, which in this instance we do not happen to possess. It will be observed that the Trisul ornament surmounts the Gateway in the background precisely as at Sanchi. The pillars had, apparently, lion capitals; but the sculpture is too much worn to feel sure of this.

It is to be regretted that a greater number of these circles have not been rescued. Originally there must have been 100 or 120 at least, and judging from the interest of five which the Museum possesses, the whole, when complete, must have formed a very complete picture-bible of Buddhist tradition, as understood at the time they were executed. They are so light and so easily handled, however, that it is to be feared the greater number have been carried away, and either built into walls as ornaments, or what is more probable, burnt for lime.

PLATE LXIV.

THE photographs on Plate LXIV. represent the only two fragments of the inner face of the frieze of the great Rail which have reached this country. This is to be regretted, as the sculpture is singularly spirited, and a bas-relief 130 feet long, which each quadrant must have possessed when complete, could hardly have failed to tell a story and to give a distinct idea of the arts of the age in which it was executed. As it is, we must content ourselves with two fragments, each only a little more than 8 feet long—17 feet out of 500—and the lower one so much weather-worn as to lose very much of the spirit it originally possessed.

In the upper fragment we have on the left hand a prince seated on a throne inside a city, surrounded by a host of admirers doing him homage; and above, two of his wives looking out of a window. Next we have a procession, with elephants and horsemen, issuing from the city gates, escorting what appears to be the principal object of the ceremonial. From the ruined and worn state of the stone it is not easy to feel sure what this is intended to represent. The lower part of it is certainly an ark or palankeen, shaped like a boat, and borne on the shoulders of men with short curly hair. The upper part may be intended to represent four figures seated in the ark, under a canopy, or if, as I fancy, it is meant to represent a ship, this may be a rude way of depicting the sails and equipment. The boat-like form forcibly recalls the golden ship which the King of Ceylon ordered to convey the relics to the Diamond Sands. It is too big, if the scale is to be depended upon, for the golden ship, and too small for the wooden one, but as the whole representation is conventional, it seems difficult to escape the conviction that it is intended to represent the identical relic vessel mentioned in the legend, and if this is so it becomes a most satisfactory confirmation of the conjectures hazarded above,—proving, it appears to me incontestably that they were not without foundation. As the procession approaches him, the Raja, who is easily recognised in the centre of the picture from the Chatta borne over him, descends from his elephant and proceeds on foot to the sacred Bo-tree, in front of which, and under whose shade the throne is placed for the reception of the relics.

There is another representation in Plate LXXXIV. of a procession bearing what is apparently the same or at least a similar object. In that Plate there are certainly two persons seated in front, and three more inside the litter, or whatever it may be and they seem bringing a number of presents which are depicted in front. Taking the two together I see nothing in the representation to militate against the idea that this bas-relief may represent Danta Kumâra and Hemamalâ bringing the relics from Ceylon, as recorded above, page 177.

It is not clear whether the space within the gateway of the Sanchi type is to be considered as a separate picture, and that the cushion-like ornament at the back of the chair is meant to be represented as already containing the relics or only prepared for their reception. A number of persons are represented as already worshipping either the object on the throne or the tree behind it. Beyond the tree on the right there is a division where a new subject certainly begins.

There is a very legible inscription on this frieze, but unfortunately it is imperfect at the beginning, and what remains only records that the bas-relief is the gift of the five daughters of Maditi, with their sons and two slaves, whose names are given.[1]

The lower sculpture represents a procession issuing in like manner from the city gate, and proceeding to a Dagoba with all the accompaniments with which we shall presently become so familiar.

There is the Tee, the five steles or pillars on each face, the Rail with its four projecting Gateways, each with two lions, and on the front of the Dagoba the seven-headed Nâga in the principal place usually occupied by Buddha himself, showing that at Amravati at least the two were considered interchangeable and entitled to equal honour.

Beyond the Dagoba, to the right, are three separate subjects, first, seven men in the usual Hindu costume, listening to a man in priestly robes who is preaching, with three other monks standing behind him. The head of the principal figure is unfortunately broken off, so we cannot be sure who is intended. It may be Buddha himself. In the next division five men are listening to a seated priest expounding, and accompanied by four others of his order. Above them, there is a sacred tree in a square enclosure. The last scene represents the Raja, or Hindu chief, pouring water from the mysterious spouted vessel on the hands of a priest, probably confirming a grant. Behind him are some fragments which seem to represent a monastery. The fragments of marble would, however, require to be very carefully fitted together before they could be reproduced by photography. They are certainly parts of this bas-relief, and when put together may be of some interest.

No women appear on either of these bas-reliefs, except the two in each fragment looking out of the windows on the extreme left of each.

Though so much injured as to make it a little difficult to judge correctly, I look on these two fragments of the frieze, with the left-hand pillar in Plate XLI., as the masterpieces of Amravati art. They certainly are more spirited and tell their story more distinctly than any others of those which have been brought to this country.

---

[1] See Appendix E., No. I.

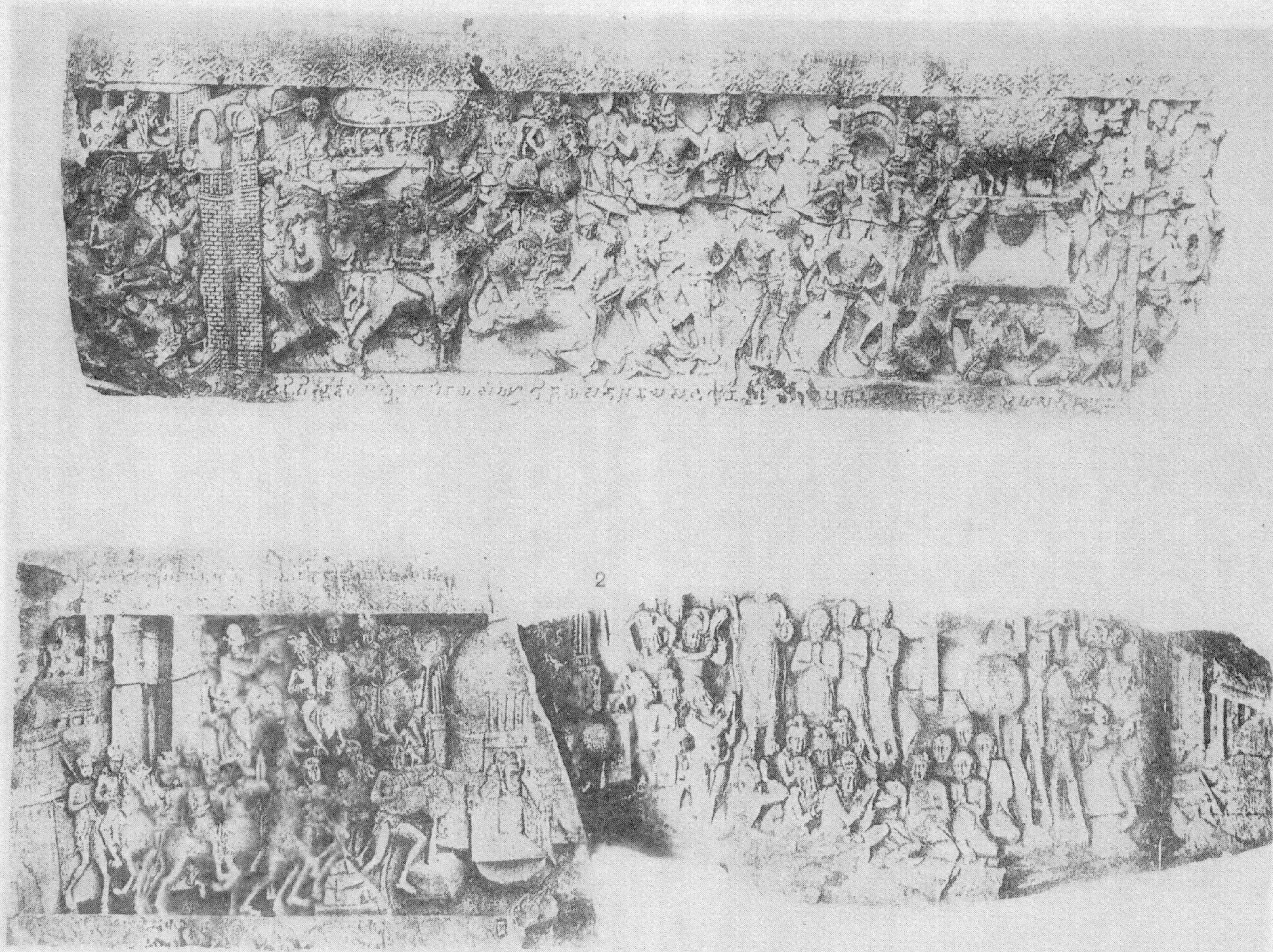

FRAGMENTS OF EXTERNAL FRIEZE OF OUTER ENCLOSURE.
SCALE 1 INCH TO 1 FOOT.

3

FRAGMENTS OF INTERNAL FRIEZES OF OUTER ENCLOSURE.

SCALE 1 INCH TO 1 FOOT.

PLATE LXV.

THIS Plate contains three fragments of friezes similar in dimensions to that described in the last Plate, but certainly not parts of the same continuous decoration. The first, on the left hand at the top, is not only different in style, but is three inches less in depth, and must therefore have belonged to some other part of the building. Fig. 2 may be part of another quadrant; its depth is exactly 2 feet, like the others in the last Plate. Fig. 3 I fancy must have belonged to one of the returns of the Gateways. It is a complete picture in itself, and if it belonged to the outer Rail, could only have been placed in some such detached position.

Fig. 1, besides its inferior style, is dreadfully weather-worn, so that it is difficult to make out the subject. In the first compartment we have a Hindu Raja, with his teapot, pouring water on the hand of a man who carries a parasol, and he is accompanied by another man who likewise carries his own umbrella. Between these figures stands a dwarf, bearing a tray on his head, either to support the spouted vessel when not in use, or to catch the drops of the liquid if they are precious. My impression is, however, that generally speaking the spouted vessel contains most probably water. In the next compartment we have a covered cart drawn by two bullocks, remarkable as being one of the few wheeled carriages at Amravati. The Hindu in the cart meets a man with a parasol, and above him a man with a bangy follows one with a parasol, who is apparently welcomed by a tall figure with two children. In the third compartment three seated figures receive a deputation bearing offerings. Is it possible that these men with the parasols are Chinese, and the subject of the bas-relief the reception of an embassy from China? We know that Fa-hian visited India from China in 399[1] and travelled in search of Buddhist books and traditions over a great part of India, though he did not reach Amravati. Yadjna Śrí, however, a king whose coins are found frequently at this place, and whose name appears—doubtfully—in one of the Amravati inscriptions (see page 168) sent an embassy to China about the year 408. From its style it is evident that this is among the most modern pieces of sculpture at Amravati, and certainly executed after the dates just quoted. There is, therefore, no *à priori* improbability, and on the whole I am very much inclined to believe that this is the true interpretation of the subject.

Fig. 2 represents in its first compartment the worship of the Dagoba, with its usual accompaniments, and on the right one of those Harem scenes to which it seems impossible at present to attach a name. A noble—he has no emblem of royalty—pats under the chin a lady who is seated on the same sofa as himself. She apparently has a glory round her head, which he has not. It is not, however, Mâyâ, for she died seven days after giving birth to her illustrious son, and I do not know any other female who would be so honoured. Perhaps, however, it is not a glory

[1] Foĕ-Kouĕ-Ki, translated by Rémusat and others, Paris, 1836.

after all, but something borne by one of the attendants behind. The attendants both before and behind seem to be bringing refreshments, and the chief seems to hold something eatable in his hand. The two ladies seated on chairs in the foreground are, or ought to be, the wives of the principal figure. They certainly are so in other bas-reliefs, though this would make it still more difficult to understand who the lady on the sofa can be. The figures are all elegant, and the sculpture of the best class of those at Amravati.

Whatever may be the difficulty with the two others, there is none whatever in identifying the subjects of the lower bas-relief. In the first compartment Śuddhodana, the father of Buddha, is seated on his throne. In the centre, on his right, sits Mâyâ, this time certainly with a glory behind her head. On his left stands his prime minister, and further on are four seated guests.

The central compartment depicts the well-known legend of the birth of Buddha. When Mâyâ felt her time approaching, she left the city for the beautiful Lumbinî garden, and gave birth to the future prophet, standing and holding on to a branch of a tree.[1] Behind her stands her mother-in-law, distinguished by her umbrella, and beside her four men or gods hold a long cloth, which they are prepared to wrap round her. The infant was delivered from her left side. The cradle is prepared in front, and the gods look on and worship above.

The third compartment represents the Prince Siddhârtha seated on a couch under a gorgeous canopy, with a glory behind his head. On the same couch is seated Gopâ, his first wife. In front one woman is playing on a harp, another on a flute. Two in front of them are either listening or singing, and one is playing with a little girl.

All these subjects occur frequently again in the sculptures of the Amravati Tope, and are almost as common in Buddhist iconography as the Nativity, or the Virgin and Child, are among Christian pictures. The mode of treatment varies, however, in all, but excepting that it is somewhat weather-worn, this is one of the clearest and best I am acquainted with.

In both this one, and in No. 2 above, it will be observed that the different groups are cleverly divided from one another by walls, with ornamented ends towards the spectators; these separate without interrupting the action of the piece.

---

[1] The Lalita-Vistara calls the tree a Pipal, "*Ficus religiosa*," p. 86. Others say it was an Aśoka, "*Jonesia Asoka*." In the bas-relief it looks like a Pipal.

ELEVATION OF INTERNAL FACE OF PILLARS OF OUTER ENCLOSURE.

W. GRIGGS, LITH. INDIA MUSEUM.

3 Feet. 1 Inch

ELEVATION OF INTERNAL FACE OF A PILLAR OF OUTER ENCLOSURE.

ELEVATION OF INTERNAL FACE OF A PILLAR OF OUTER ENCLOSURE.

PLATE LXXIV.

THIS bas-relief[1] is the pendant to that represented in the photographs, Plate LXV , Fig. 3. It is indeed earlier in Buddhist chronology, as that represented the birth of Buddha, this only the annunciation. It is divided into three compartments. In the first sits Śuddhodana, the father of Buddha, surrounded by the gentlemen of his court. There are no ladies present, which is unusual.

In the central division, Buddha, symbolized by the white Elephant, descends from the Heaven Tûshita, borne by celestial dwarfs and surrounded by Devatâs. An umbrella of state is borne before him, and music and dancing accompany him. In the third division, Mâyâ is represented asleep on her couch. Four men guard the four angles of her bed, and her women stand or sit on either side. She dreams she sees the white Elephant descend from Heaven and enter her womb. As this same subject has already been presented in Plate LXV., and will occur again, it is not necessary to describe it more particularly here. It is evidently as great a favourite with the Buddhists as the Annunciation is with early Christian painters.

The preceding twenty-six Plates may be sufficient to convey a correct impression of the form of the great outer enclosure of the Amravati Tope, and of the mode in which it was decorated; but in extent they can hardly be considered as representing more than a tenth or a twelfth of the whole. Even supposing that some of the subjects may have been repeated in different quadrants of the Rail, still the whole conveys a marvellous impression of the fertility of invention and patient labour with which the Indians in all ages decorated their religious edifices. There are temples both in India and in Cambodia which equal Amravati in this respect, but in none of these, so far as I am aware, is the art so dramatic, or the story told with such distinctness or such elegance, when looked at from an outside point of view.

It would be extremely interesting if any ancient traveller had left us even an indication of what such a monument was intended by its founders to express; none such, I fear, exists. Yet when Fa-Hian visited Ceylon in the year 410, he describes the preparation made for the great annual festival in honour of the celebrated Tooth relic; on which occasion it was conveyed in procession, from Anurâdhapura to Mehentele, a distance of about six miles. After the preliminary ceremonies, he goes on to say "The king next causes to be placed on both sides of the road, representations of the "500 bodily forms which Bôdhisatwa assumed during his successive births. For "instance, his birth as Sutana, his appearance as a bright flash of light, his birth as "the king of the Elephants, and as an antelope. These figures are all beautifully "painted in divers colours, and have a very life-like appearance."[2] I have

[1] The slab from which this drawing was made was presented by Colonel Mackenzie to the Museum of the Asiatic Society of Bengal, where it now is. It was engraved for M. Foucaux's Translation of the Lalita-Vistara, Plates III. to VI.

[2] Beal's Translation, p. 157. Foĕ-Kouĕ-Ki, p. 335.

already had occasion to remark[1] that the Ceylonese mode of making Rails seemed to depend on some such arrangement. Instead of a continuous stone screen, as at Sanchi or at Amravati, they consist of stone posts adapted to hang tapestries or pictures upon, and I fancy that this pictorial display described by Fa-Hian is the counterpart of what we see in stone on the banks of the Kistnah. The Amravati Rail may have been in progress while Fa-Hian was in Ceylon, and both displays were, if I mistake not, got up in honour of the sacred Tooth.

The sculptures of the Amravati Rail were at one time painted, and traces of colour may still be detected in the recesses of the sculptures. When this was the case, the difference between the temporary decoration along the path through which the Tooth was borne in triumph in Ceylon, and the permanent procession path at Amravati, would not be so great in appearance.

We must wait, however, till all the Rails known to exist in India are published before these and many other points can be settled in a satisfactory manner.

Perhaps the most interesting point, regarding it at least for our present purposes, is that it is a purely original and Buddhist form of art. It hardly seems doubtful but that the unhewn circles of stones that exist at Amravati and all over the western world are the rude originals out of which it grew, first into such a circular enclosure as we find at Stonehenge, then into such a Rail as we find at Sanchi, and lastly into such a screen as this. It is the blossoming of a long series of attempts which probably would have for ever remained rude in the hands of the western nations, but which Indian taste fashioned into beauty, as we see it here.

Besides its history, however, and its originality, this outer Rail at Amravati is to be admired for its elegance and appropriateness. I do not know of any architectural form which, in such a climate, is or could be more beautiful than this. The sculptures on the walls of a temple could not be so well lighted or so well displayed, and to a certain extent must always be subordinated to the architecture. Here the two are perfectly in accord, helping one another, and as the "temenos" enclosing a sacred spot, and uniting without hiding a group of sacred buildings, I do not know where to look for anything combining so many excellencies of design as this encircling screen of the great Temple of the Diamond Sands.

---

[1] Supra, p. 93.

PLATES LXVI., LXVII., AND LXVIII.

PLATE LXVI.

THIS Plate, lithographed from a drawing in the Mackenzie Collection, represents one of the angle pillars of the great Rail. The tall pillar, with three full and two half circles, is introduced as an angle piece terminating the curved part, and commencing the straight projection of one of the Gateways.[1]

The subject of the central circle, though much broken, is either Buddha or some Buddhist preacher addressing men and women who occupy the foreground, and listen in attitudes of adoration; while higher up floating figures, Devas or Devatâs, attend and bring offerings.

The three bas-reliefs in the octagon part below seem at first sight similar in subject to those described above in speaking of Plate LVIII., though on closer inspection the differences are so great that they can hardly be referred to the same event. On the left a chief, seated on a throne, is listening to the animated eloquence of a warrior, who seems addressing a youth seated cross-legged on the ground. The result of this speech is seen in the central compartment. The Prince,—he is certainly not the occupant of the throne in the first compartment,—sallies forth on his elephant, but unarmed, and accompanied by two of his women. His army accompany him in the foreground, and a floating figure above offers a wreath. In the third compartment the enemy fly, apparently without striking a blow!

As the head of the principal figure in the central circle is broken off, we cannot feel sure that it represents Buddha himself. If it is he, this bas-relief ought to refer to some legend of his youth. If it is one of the Bôdhisattwas, which is possible, it is to him that the event depicted must be referred.

It will be observed that two of the unarmed spectators, probably peasants, who occupy the right hand compartment have the close curly hair which afterwards became so characteristic of Buddha himself.

PLATE LXVII.

It will not be necessary to say anything here about the mutilated circle in this Plate, as another representation of the same subject will be found further on in Plate LXXIII., where it occurs on an intermediate Rail and is complete.

In the lower bas-relief we have in the centre a Saint or Bôdhisattwa seated expounding. From his being accompanied by a horse, it most probably is intended to represent Avalokiteśwara. One man is embracing his foot, but the principal personage is presenting a cloth.

---

[1] Compare it with woodcut No. 28, page 186.

On the left we have the worship of an emblem. It recurs frequently further on, so we shall have to refer to it again and again, and it will be better to defer what we have to say regarding it till we meet with a more prominent example, merely remarking that here the Trisul emblem is placed on a tall pillar, from each side of which issues what appears to be flames. At the bottom are the sacred feet on the Lotus. To the right of the pillar is the Nâga Râjâ with his wife. On the left a saint with a glory, or at least a circle behind his head, either supported by two birds somewhat like pigeons, or adorned by these figures. Behind him is a Nâga woman, and above them four women bearing pots on their heads.

On the right-hand side are seven women, looking at the gambols of dwarfs and grotesque figures in front of the sacred Tree. Unfortunately, however, it is impossible in our present state of knowledge to give a name to any of the figures, unless it be to the one in the centre.

PLATE LXVIII.

This pillar, though very much dilapidated and badly drawn, is of considerable interest, first, as a means of comparison with Plate XXXI., representing a similar scene at Sanchi, and secondly, because it may possibly represent the arrival of the relics, in charge of Danta Kumâra, from Ceylon. The upper circle is too much mutilated to be deciphered; but in the centre of the lower compartment we have a boat or ship, in which is one man paddling. In front a man in the garb of a priest, with his hands joined, worshipping a relic or rather two relic bundles or Droṇas, placed on a throne, below which the sacred feet are seen. Above these is the same Trisul emblem as was seen in the last Plate. If I am correct in my conjecture this would simply mean relics of Buddha, whether or not they were coming from Ceylon.

Below, the Nâga Râjâ is welcoming the arrival, accompanied apparently by two women and a man. In the right-hand compartment a chief bears himself the canopy of state, evidently in honour of the relics, and his wife stands behind in the act of worshipping.

That these represent relics arriving by water at Amravati seems nearly certain, but whether they are those mentioned at page 176 or some others, must for the present I fear be matter for conjecture. My own impressions are entirely in favour of the Ceylonese relics being those here depicted, but the destruction of the upper part of the pillar and the fracture of the sides deprives us of the means of determining the point. I may also add that, notwithstanding the general fidelity of the drawings made for Colonel Mackenzie, it would be satisfactory, in a difficult and important case like this, to see the slab itself. It is thus especially unfortunate that, as hinted above, this should be one of the least carefully drawn of the whole series.

4 FEET 7.5 INCHES.

W. GRIGGS, LITH. INDIA MUSEUM.

6 FEET 8.9 INCHES.

ELEVATION OF INTERNAL FACE OF A PILLAR OF OUTER ENCLOSURE.

ELEVATION OF INTERNAL FACE OF A PILLAR OF OUTER ENCLOSURE.

PLATES LXIX. AND LXX.

THE central circle in Plate LXIX. represents the reception of a Princess and Prince by some one, very important from his size, who stands under a canopy with his hands joined. The princess presents a piece of cloth, on which is the impression of two feet. If any dependence can be placed on the story in the Râja Taranginî,[1] this would indicate that the strangers came from Ceylon, and consequently they probably were Hemamalâ and Danta Kumâra. If the person receiving them were the Nâga Râjâ, I should consider this as nearly certain. Unfortunately, his head is so defaced that it is impossible to be sure; but as none of his women have snakes at the back of their heads it is most probable that he was not a Nâga. It may, however, represent the reception of the same persons in Ceylon; and there are peculiarities about the head-dresses of the women which would lead to the belief that we have got among a new people.

The story of the lower bas-relief is not difficult to make out, though, without knowing who the principal person in the central bas-relief may be, it is not easy to give a name to the principal parties concerned. On the right "a gay and a gallant knight"—a Raja on horsebank attended as his body-guard—comes to court a maiden, who sits in a tall round-backed chair on the left. Between the two in the centre sits the stern father with his two wives, with the ladies of his household disporting themselves in front and attending on him behind. One of the attendants of the expectant bride is getting a garland out of a box, and others are ready with refreshments, while the principal ladiesmaid reports to her mistress the arrival of the Prince, and describes his person. The shields and helmets of the Prince's attendants are worthy of remark, as they are unlike any others we have hitherto met with in these sculptures.

PLATE LXX.

This is one of the most interesting, in a religious or ritualistic point of view, of the whole series of pillars at Amravati. In the central circle we have a throne, on which are placed two objects I have ventured to call Dronas of relics, though it is possible they may be only cushions after all. At the back is the Trisul emblem on a pillar beneath the sacred Tree, and the sacred feet are in front. The same emblem, but without the throne or the Tree, occurs in the right-hand lower bas-

---

1 Mihira Kula, King of Cashmere, made war on Ceylon because the cloth of Sinhala was stamped with a golden foot as the seal of the monarch. (It means evidently the feet of Buddha, as used everywhere.) His wife, wearing a jacket of Sinhala cloth, the impression came off on her bosom, and the king, indignant that the mark of anyone's foot should appear on the bosom of his wife, invaded Ceylon, and forced him in future to stamp his cloth with the golden Sun.—Asiatic Researches, XV. 28. Mihira Kula, it should, however, be observed, lived before the time of these events (his date was probably 200 A.D.), but cloths with the sacred feet stamped upon them are by no means uncommon in the Amravati sculptures, where no reference to Ceylon can be intended.

relief, and in both instances it is worshipped by shaven priests in the robes of the priesthood of the present day.

The diffi lty here is to know what this flaming pillar represents. I have above suggested (p. 189), that the pillar with the Trisul at the summit and the feet at the base, as seen at Sanchi (Woodcut 17), is practically an emblem of Buddha or Buddhism, but unless this pillar is what is represented in the Linga-purâṇa, I do not know what it is. The primitive Linga, it is there said, is a pillar of radiance in which Maheśwara (Śiva) is present. "The appearance of the great fiery Linga takes place in the interval "of a creation to separate Vishṇu and Brahma." "Upon the Linga the sacred "monosyllable Om is visible."[1] Whether the Sivites borrowed this from the Buddhists or vice versâ, I cannot help thinking this is the emblem common to both.

In the left-hand lower bas-relief three beardless and three bearded ascetics are worshipping a five-headed serpent on either side of whose neck are the sacred feet in a pansala or hut, the emblem—if I am not mistaken—of the presence of Buddha.

In the centre a relic—what, it is not easy to say—is exposed on a throne with the feet in front and the Trisul behind it. It is worshipped by five bearded ascetics and four beardless men, who may or may not be of the same class.

Besides its ritualistic importance, this bas-relief is historically important in showing the progress made in the development of the religion, and more especially of the religious orders, in the interval that elapsed between the building of the Sanchi and Amravati Topes. The emblems here introduced, are, most of them, unknown at Sanchi, at least in their present forms, and the priesthood here represented are entirely new, having certainly sprung up in the meanwhile.

---

[1] Introduction to Wilson's Translation of the Vishṇu Purâṇa, p. xliii.

AMRAVATI.

PLATE LXXI.

FIG. 1.

FIG. 2.

INTERNAL FACE OF TWO DISCS ON INTERMEDIATE RAILS OF OUTER ENCLOSURE.

PLATES LXXI. AND LXXII. FIG. 2.

THESE three circles from the intermediate Rails of the outer enclosure are lithographed in fac-simile from drawings in the Mackenzie Collection, and represent the Trisul emblem in various combinations. It is a little unfortunate that no stone with this emblem upon it in this combination has reached this country, because, though we may feel great confidence in Colonel Mackenzie's draughtsmen, it might aid us in understanding this emblem if we could touch the real stone, and feel whether that flame-like emanation on each side of the pillars was really intended to represent fire, or what it really was. Flame occurs several times in the sculptures at Sanchi; and if this emblem was found there in that form, it would be easy to say what was intended; but flame does not occur anywhere at Amravati in an unmistakeable manner, and it is impossible therefore to say how far it may have been conventionalized. I can only, therefore, state it as my conviction as on the previous page that flame is here intended.

The upper part of circle Fig. 1, Plate LXXI., is unfortunately destroyed, and we cannot, therefore, feel sure how the emblem terminated, but all the rest of the arrangements are easily intelligible. Both in this and in Fig. 2 the cushion-like object, which I have called a "Droṇa of relics," is placed on the throne, and below it are the impressions of the sacred feet. If indeed these bundles do not contain relics, it is very difficult to guess what they are. We have already seen undoubted relics enthroned and worshipped as these are, Plates LXII. and LXX. And if not for this purpose, why is the throne introduced here? The emblems with the feet are found in Plates LXVII., LXX., and LXXII., and seem complete in themselves, but where the throne is introduced, it must be for some purpose and I can conceive no other than this. The throne itself would hardly be an object of worship, and if that which is placed on it is not so, why is it here? Besides this, cushions are a most unlikely accompaniment of thrones in hot climates, and cannot be detected anywhere as mere seats in these sculptures.

In the upper circle, on the right-hand side, is a group of Buddhist priests in their yellow robes worshipping. In front there are two supple women in attitudes of adoration, who occur so frequently in these sculptures, and on the left a chief in the ordinary Hindu costume presents his little son to the emblem. Around him are the women of his family.

In the lower circle the same structural arrangements occur up to the Trisul, but the whole is surmounted by the Chakra or Wheel, which, as above suggested, I believe to be the emblem of Dharma or the Law. Here all the worshippers are men. It is, in fact, one of the very few scenes in these sculptures from which women are entirely excluded. Whether it was considered that the study of the Law was not appropriate for women, or from whatever motive, the fact of all the worshippers being of one sex and of one race is exceptional. The only other peculiarity worthy of remark is the introduction of two antelopes, one on each side of the throne.

Fig. 2, Plate LXXII., represents the Trisul ornament, not on a throne, but behind an altar. The sacred feet are there, but no relics. The principal worshippers in the upper compartment are two men with seven-headed snake hoods, and two women with single snakes. The Chaori bearers and other attendants have not this appendage.

In the centre of the bas-relief sits the principal personage, with a nine-headed snake hood, between two of his wives, and beyond, on the edge of the circle on either hand, is a female figure standing, and holding on to the branches of two trees. A girl attends on each, one of whom has a snakc at the back of her head, the other has not. In front are three musicians with snakes, and on their right a lady without a snake seems to require the assistance of a girl with a snake. Whether she is tipsy or merely faint is not clear. There is a pot on a table behind her that looks suspicious.

This distinction between people with snakes and those without is most curious and perplexing. After the most attentive study I have been unable to detect any characteristic either of feature or costume by which the races can be distinguished, beyond the possession or absence of this strange adjunct. That those with snakes are the Nâga people we read of, can hardly be doubted. The snake seems their tutelary genius, watching over, perhaps inspiring them; but whether they borrowed this strange emblem from the natives of the country, or brought it with them from the north-west, are questions we are hardly yet in a position to answer satisfactorily.

To revert, however, to the Trisul. It will be observed that in all the six representations of it in these three Plates the central limb terminates in a point. In this it differs essentially from thosc which crown the Gateways at Sanchi, though it agrees generally with the form found on the coins and elsewhere. At Sanchi (Plates VI. to IX.) it will be observed that a shield-like emblem is introduced between the outer horns. This is represented in the necklace of emblems (Fig. 4, Plate III.), the fourth from the top on the outside of the left-hand string, and the fifth on the opposite one. It occurs above the Swastika on the great Khaṇḍagiri inscription,[1] and is found by itself painted on the pillars of some of the oldest of the Western Caves. If the diagram, page 115, is to be taken as an explanation of the compound emblem, it represents Ether, and is here omitted. The crescent there meant Air, the triangle Fire, the circle Water, and the square block Earth. As nothing the least resembling the triangle is found in any of these emblems, this would favour the idea that flames were really meant in these representations. All this, however, is so hypothetical that I would willingly refrain from entering upon it if I knew where to look for information elsewhere. Surely there must be Buddhist books that treat of emblems; but as both General Cunningham and Colonel Maisey whose attention was turned to the subject in India, are quite at sea regarding them, I fear the requisite explanations are not easily accessible.

---

[1] J. A. S. B., vol. VI. plate LVIII.

AMRAVATI. **PLATE LXXII.**

FIG. 1.

FIG. 2.

INTERNAL FACE OF TWO DISCS ON INTERMEDIATE RAILS OF OUTER ENCLOSURE.

PLATE LXXV.

THE inner Rail of the Amravati Tope that bounded the procession path on the side next the centre, was richer and more elaborately carved than the great outer Rail, though inferior both in dimensions and in architectural design. It was, in the first place, only half its height, or 6 feet above the path, as compared with 12 feet on the other side. It had, however, some metallic finishing on the top, which is now lost, and must have added not only to its height but to its architectural effect. The holes by which the metal cornice was fastened to the marble still remain, but no trace of the metal itself; and I have failed to detect any representation of this inner Rail from which it might be restored. My impression is that it must have been a range of Trisuls, not unlike fleurs-de-lys; but this is only a guess.

A portion of this Rail is restored in Plate LXXV., from fragments that undoubtedly belong to it, and its vertical dimensions and arrangements are certain, so far as it goes; but I cannot feel certain how far the Dagobas were apart, nor whether the other parts were arranged exactly as I have placed them. The arrangements probably varied in parts, but could not have been very different from what is here suggested.

My impression is that there were twelve representations of the Dagoba in each quadrant, and that they were spaced about 10 feet apart from the centre, and that the same representations were repeated four times, or once in each quadrant. My reason for this supposition is, that in the Elliot and Mackenzie Collections we have thirty different representations of Dagobas, of which twenty-seven or twenty-eight certainly belonged to this Rail, and the principal emblem on the front of each is repeated as follows:—

Buddha seated on the Nâga, with hood - -	3	times.
Ditto, without Nâga - - - - -	3	,,
Ditto, standing preaching - - - -	4	,,
Ditto, with Horse - - - - -	1	,,
The Chakra or Wheel emblem occurs - -	4	,,
The Horse - - - - - -	3	,,
The Feet enfolded in the Nâga - - -	3	,,
The Tree - - - - - -	1	,,
The Relic Casket - - - - -	1	,,
The Nâga Râjâ, with attendants - - -	1	,,
The great five-headed Nâga alone - - -	6	,,
	30	,,

It is with reference to the last alone I am in doubt. Some of the Nâga Dagobas do undoubtedly belong to this Rail; others in the Mackenzie Collection may not. It is a little difficult to judge from the drawings; from the sculptures it is always easy to determine to which Rail any bas-relief belonged, or whether it formed part of the decoration of some other building.

Looking at the above list, it will be seen that some subjects are repeated four times, several thrice, others, it is true, only once, and we miss one subject to make up the twelve. Still, considering how small a portion of the Rail we have, and that the subjects were not selected, but picked up by accident, the inference seems fair that there may have been twelve subjects, and each was repeated four times.[1]

Whether the Chakras with their pillars, or the steles terminating in Dagobas, were placed exactly as shown in the restoration, must for the present be an open question, but one not of much importance. The frieze was certainly arranged as shown, but alas its metal crowning ornament is gone and cannot be restored. All these parts are repeated in the following Plates, where they will be again referred to. The central object has not been repeated, being too much damaged to be of much artistic importance; but it is one of the most interesting fragments of the Rail, and if it was repeated, as I suppose, in each quadrant, it would be interesting if another copy could be found. It contains the whole creed of Amravati. At the bottom we have the throne, with the relic Droṇa; behind that the Tree. In the central compartment the Wheel with garlands, upon or behind the throne, and men worshipping; and the whole crowned by the Dagoba with its Rail, its five steles, its lions, and the five-headed Nâga in the place of honour. The worshippers, both terrestrial and celestial, have been so defaced as to be hardly perceptible in the photograph, though plain enough in the marble. We miss both Buddha and the Trisul, except around the Wheel; but otherwise this one sculpture contains a fair epitome of the religious faith to which this gorgeous monument was dedicated.

This inner circle has been so ruined that it is difficult to make out now where the entrances were, by which access through it to the interior was obtained. Judging from what we find at Sanchi and elsewhere, we may feel certain it could not be direct. Care was taken to hide from those outside what was passing in the interior, so as to add mystery to sanctity. My conviction would be, that the entrance was past the ends of the small advanced segment shown in front of the Southern Gateway, were it not that Colonel Mackenzie's plan (Plate XLVII.) shows two slabs placed there, blocking the passage. I do not, however, gather from his descriptions that all the stones marked red were actually standing *in situ* when he was there, but only that they were found lying about, and that their places could be recognized. Joining the two segments, as shown in the plan, is just such a suggestion as an over-clever draughtsman would make; but if so, it is a mistake I am afraid there is now no means of rectifying. All I know of the subject would lead me to suppose that they did not exist there, and that the seven detached stones originally stood alone in the centre of the procession path and unconnected with the rest of the Rail.

---

1. If this theory is correct, the two standing Buddhas in the restoration in this Plate would not have appeared in the same quadrant. Unfortunately, they are the only two slabs in the collection which are perfect and of moderate width, so as to fit my scale.

1

2

3

ELEVATIONS OF PORTIONS OF INNER ENCLOSURE.

SCALE 1 INCH TO 1 FOOT.

PLATE LXXII. Fig. 1, and PLATE LXXIII.

With the upper circle in Plate LXXII. we return to one of those domestic scenes which it is easy enough to understand, though it is so difficult to assign names to the principal actors.

Above, a Raja, with two females behind him, is seated on an elephant in a boat, being apparently ferried across a stream—the Kistnah? Two of the females who accompany him jump on shore the moment the boat reaches land, and embrace two other females who seem awaiting their arrival. The Raja's ladies are easily distinguishable by their allowing their long back hair to hang loose behind them. Those who receive them have a roll, something like a comb, at the back of their heads.

In the foreground a lady is seated, with her attendants; on the left, as usual, are the musicians, and above them are two "dames d'honneur." On the right of the lady in the foreground one attendant offers her something apparently to eat, and another something to drink out of a small pot slung on her arm.

The story seems simply to be, that a certain Raja, whose name we cannot guess, comes across the river to demand the hand of the fair lady in the foreground, but beyond that we cannot at present go.

The story of the bas-relief, Fig. 1, Plate LXXIII., is likewise simple enough, except perhaps the name of the principal figure. From the glory round his head, however, he is either Śuddhodana or his son Siddhârtha, before he became Buddha. If the upper part of the bas-relief were complete, we might speak with certainty, but from what we see I fancy it more likely to be the king than his son.

Whichever it is, he is represented seated on the throne between his two principal wives on high-backed chairs,[1] and surrounded by the ladies of his court, some seated, some standing in pairs, but all collected to witness a wild dance performed by six men in the centre. The left, as usual, is occupied by the musicians, who are all women, and the dancers are certainly exerting themselves in a manner quite unknown in the east in modern times, and which could hardly be surpassed in the ballet of a modern opera house. No religious significance seems to be attached to the ceremony. It appears to be only an amusement of the palace.

This cannot be said of the lower circle, Fig. 2 of Plate LXXIII. Here five men in the centre dance wildly while upholding a tray, on which is a cup, possibly the begging dish of some Bodhisatwa. It may even be supposed to be that of Buddha himself. Seventeen men, with various head-dresses, though in the same Hindu

[1] It will be observed that here as everywhere else throughout these sculptures, where any persons are seated on thrones or chairs they are invariably without cushions. Had they sat on cushions, which in a hot climate is most unlikely, we could hardly fail to perceive them.

costume, dance wildly in front of these three. The women dance in the background, and behind the tray, in the centre, is seen the head of the principal personage of the ceremony, among the ladies and gentlemen of his court. He has no emblem, so it is impossible to say what his rank may be.

There can be little doubt but that this sculpture is intended to represent a great religious ceremony, on the occasion of the public display of a much-valued relic.[1] The wildness with which the men dance in these two sculptures is very unlike anything we are accustomed to in India at the present day among the Hindus. All the hill tribes, however, from Beerbhoom westward, to the extreme limits of Gondwana, are passionately addicted to dancing. The young men and women of the villages meet on all festal occasions, and at certain seasons of the year dance all the night through, and with as much zest and as violent action as any Celtic Highlander could display.[2] We must never overlook the fact that these sculptures do not represent the Aryans—at least certainly not in their purity—but the aborigines, or tribes of very mixed blood, and dancing with them was a passion. I am afraid drinking was so also.

As before remarked, this bas-relief is an exact reproduction of the central circle of the pillar, Plate LXVII., except that there a man with a seven-headed snake hood appears among the performers. From this circumstance, and others to be mentioned further on, I am inclined to believe that if we had the whole Rail we should find the same subjects repeated possibly as often as four times, once in each quadrant, and with very little variation. This I think is almost certainly the case with the inner Rail, but this is the only instance of a duplicate which I have yet found belonging to the outer enclosure.

---

[1] Fa-Hian mentions having seen the begging dish of Buddha in Afghanistan, and also "un vase où Foĕ a craché ; il est de pierre et de la même couleur que le pot de Foĕ" (page 27), and he describes the honours paid to them and to other relics which he saw, but he does not mention dances as part of the ceremonies. According to the usually received tradition, the form of the pot here displayed is not that of the begging dish of a priest, but it may be his spittoon !

[2] Campbell's Ethnology, J. A. S. B., Special Report, 1866, page 182, et seq., and the Government Reports on the Central Provinces, passim.

AMRAVATI.

PLATE LXXIII.

FIG. 1.

FIG. 2.

INTERNAL FACE OF TWO DISCS ON INTERMEDIATE RAILS OF OUTER ENCLOSURE.

PORTION OF INTERNAL FACE OF FRIEZE OF OUTER ENCLOSURE.

AMRAVATI. PLATE LXXV.

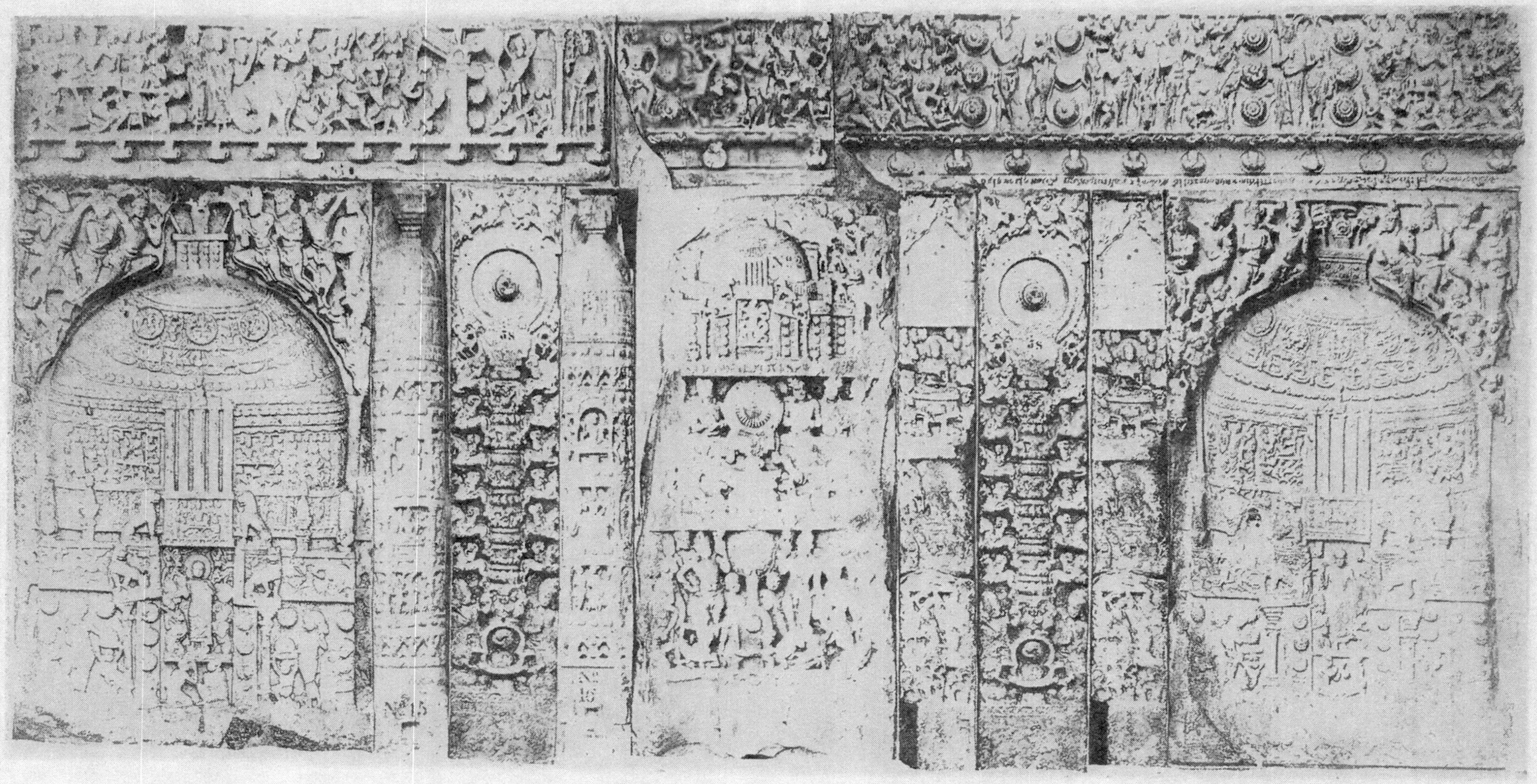

RESTORATION OF A PORTION OF INNER ENCLOSURE.

SCALE

1 2 3 4 5 6 FT.

ELEVATION OF A PORTION OF INNER ENCLOSURE.

SCALE.

1 2 3 4 FT.

PLATES LXXVI. AND LXXVII.

THESE two Plates represent the two most perfect Dagobas from the inner Rail which are now in the India House Collection. They were sent home by Colonel Mackenzie, and were among the principal ornaments of the old museum in Leadenhall Street, which they reached about the year 1820. It is probable that other slabs of the same description exist in the museums at Calcutta and Madras. As their details are so minute the two here represented have been photographed to twice the scale of the others, or 2 inches to 1 foot.

For reasons to be given hereafter, when describing the central building, I believe these Dagobas to be free copies, "mutatis mutandis," of one which existed in the centre of the circle, and which, having become pre-eminent for some reason or other, in the fourth century, these Rails were erected to enclose it; but whether this is admitted or not, they are interesting as showing how Dagobas were ornamented, or how at least the Buddhists thought they ought to be ornamented, in the fifth century, which is the time at which this enclosure was most probably erected. If we compare the very plain Rail at Sanchi with the very elaborately sculptured enclosure at Amravati, we ought to expect the same progress towards elaboration in the Dagobas themselves. Even if we assume that the older Dagoba was as little ornamented as it now appears, or as plain as those sculptured on its gateways represent the Dagobas of the first century to have been, it seems natural to expect from comparison with the Rails, that in the fourth century the Dagobas may have been as richly sculptured as these representations would lead us to expect they were. The progress, however, is so great that it seems impossible it could have been effected in less than three centuries of time. A shorter period certainly would not suffice.

All these sculptures represent the Dagobas as surrounded by a Rail four discs in height, whereas the great Rail has only three. The Rail in these representations is surmounted by a frieze, sometimes of animals, sometimes of the great rolls depicted in Plate LVI. Inside the Rail, and to the same height, the Dagoba is perpendicular, and ornamented by pilasters, between which are the usual stambhas, terminating upwards in the Dagoba, the Wheel, the Serpent, or the Tree, as the case may be. Above this are two rows of sculptures, divided into panels, the lower generally single figures or emblems, but sometimes also groups; the upper always historical groups, generally three on each quadrant. Among these it is not difficult to recognise many of the scenes described above. For instance, on each side of the five steles in Plate LXXVII. we recognise the subjects already depicted in Plates LXII. and LXV., and others may be made out. The central right-hand upper panel in Plate LXXVI. represents a battle scene, which ought not to appear on a Buddhist monument, but seems the same as that on the small pillar, Plate LXI. The medallions, also, higher up on the dome, all contain subjects which are repeated over and over again elsewhere.

One of the remarkable peculiarities of these sculptured Dagobas is the five steles which occur over the principal figure in each face, twenty in all. What they symbolize it is difficult to say. It may be the five Buddhas of the present Kalpa, or the five Dhyâni Buddhas, or the five Elements. Everything in Buddhism seems to go by fives. Generally the central stele is crowned by a Dagoba, and on their lower parts are represented Wheels, Trees, Dagobas, and other emblems, sometimes singly, sometimes in pairs; in Plate LXXVII., by an inscription recording the donation.[1]

Inside the Rail are generally four other pillars or lâṭs, bearing figures or emblems.

The dome is always surmounted by a Tee with an umbrella and flags, and when the slab is perfect, floating figures, but without wings or griffins to ride upon, as is generally the case at Sanchi, are always represented as worshipping the Tee. That they are intended as celestial beings is certain, and this being so, perhaps the best name to give them is Devas or Devatâs.

As before mentioned, the principal figure is generally varied. On Plate LXXVI. it is Buddha seated on the folds of a great Nâga, with an inner hood of seven and an outer of fourteen heads, with the usual worshipping figures. In Plate LXXVII. it is Buddha standing with his right hand raised. The worshipping figures on his left are Nâgas, on his right a man and woman in the usual Hindu costume.

Outside the Rail a man or a woman on either side of the entrance is always represented either as purchasing offerings from persons who are selling them, or are bringing offerings, generally borne on the heads of dwarfs. On either side of the entrance is always placed a vase,[2] which will be alluded to hereafter.

All this is practically new to Indian antiquaries. Hitherto our ideas regarding structural Dagobas have been derived from the present appearance of those at Sanchi or Manikyala, or from the very imperfect representations we possess of those in Afghanistan, and these are all, now at least, plain or nearly so. The one which it seems was intended to have been as richly ornamented as these was that at Sârnâth; but it was left incomplete, probably at the great revolution which took place in the middle of the eighth century. Had it been completed it would have been even more elaborately decorated than those at Amravati. The Dagobas in Caves hardly help us in this respect; they probably were painted, and the colours having perished, there is nothing left from which to form an opinion. Those in Ceylon, too, are in much too ruinous a state to aid in this inquiry, so that these representations on the inner Rail are really the only authentic documents we have, and they thus become in this respect invaluable.

---

[1] Appendix E., No. VIII.

[2] One which belonged to the central building is shown on Plate XCVI. It is photographed to the usual scale.

ELEVATIONS OF PORTIONS OF INNER ENCLOSURE.

SCALE 1 INCH TO 1 FOOT.

PLATES LXXXIII. AND LXXXIV.

PLATE LXXXIII.

THE lithographs in this Plate represent two other portions of the frieze of the inner Rail from Colonel Mackenzie's drawings. The upper one, Fig. 1, is a repetition of the legend of King Śivi, above twice referred to (vide ante, p. 194). On the right the king holds the rescued bird in his hand; in the central compartment, for the left is broken off, he is stepping into the scale, while a man in the foreground holds the bird in his hand. If we possessed the left-hand compartment we should in all probability have the flesh-cutting scene, and the bas-relief ought, probably, to be read from left to right.[1]

In the lower bas-relief, Fig. 2, on the left hand, are four priests worshipping the Trisul, with the flaming column, the throne, and the Droṇa, and the feet, as in Plates LXVIII., LXXI., and LXXII. In the next compartment a palanquin or litter, borne on men's shoulders, with an accompanying crowd; and beyond this to the right, in the small compartment, two figures, male and female, which it is almost impossible to identify, and between them one of the most essentially Nâga groups of the series. The sacred feet on a lotus are shielded by a five-headed Nâga, and worshipped by three men, one of whom has a seven-headed Nâga behind his head, the two others appearing with three heads, while the women apparently have not any. On the right hand Buddha, in the conventional robes and attitude in which he is represented at the present day, is expounding to a congregation of women. The right-hand compartment is broken off.

PLATE LXXXIV.

Figs. 2 and 3 of Plate LXXXIV. represent two other portions of the frieze of the inner Rail. From the style of sculpture and the arrangement of the lotus discs, they evidently belong to a different part of the Rail from those previously quoted, and have all the appearance of being the most modern of the sculptures at Amravati. From their character I should guess that they might belong to the sixth century, but, as something of this appearance may be due to the draughtsmen, this indication must not be implicitly relied upon.

The figure seated on the couch between his two wives in Fig. 2 is probably the same as is depicted in Plate LXXIII. Fig. 1. The interest of the story evidently hangs on the three old women in the foreground, whoever they may be.

In Fig. 3 we have Buddha represented in the usual attitudes in which he appears in all sculpture subsequent to the fourth or fifth century, but in which he hardly appears before that time.

---

[1] The long inscription on Fig. 1 will be found in Appendix E. No. II. It is unfortunately only known to us from a transcript by Colonel Mackenzie's draughtsman, who did not know the character. It can, however, be made out tolerably satisfactorily.

Fig. 1 is also of an inferior character as a piece of sculpture, but is curious as representing what appears to be a kind of litter borne on men's shoulders, in which five persons are seated. Two men only are represented as carrying it, though it must have required at least a dozen. It is introduced here not because of its beauty, but because it may serve to illustrate a somewhat similar representation in Plate LXIV. Fig. 1. and in LXXXIII. If, however, it is only a litter or palanquin, this would seem to militate against the idea expressed when describing the first named Plate, that it was the boat-shaped ark bearing relics from Ceylon; but taken together with Plate LXVIII. I cannot help believing they all refer either to the arrival of the Tooth relic at this place, or to the return of the prince and princess from Ceylon with the relics which were presented to them by the king of that country to compensate the Nâga Râjâ for the loss of the Tooth.[1] In this last Plate the difficulty of ascertaining what this action may represent is very much augmented by the fact that the marble is only a fragment, and we do not see to whom or towards what object the procession is tending. So far as can be made out, the persons in the litter are bringing as presents, inter alia, those objects—jewels or relics—which are displayed in front of them, to some person or shrine that was depicted in the front part now broken off; and it may be that Danta Kumâra and Hemamalâ were thus borne on their return to Dhanakacheka. At present, however, I am afraid the materials do not exist for determining this question.

---

[1] It is not quite clear, but it seems probable from a statement in the Mahawanso, p. 116, that the branch of the Bo Tree was landed at Amravati on its way from Gâya to Ceylon, and worshipped there for seven days. It certainly was "with the consent of the chief priestess (Sanghamitta) conveyed to the settlement of the Nâgas, "and for seven days innumerable offerings having been made by the Nâga Râjâ, they themselves bringing it back, "replaced it in the vessel!" If Amravati was the country of the Nâgas, which it seems difficult to doubt, this certainly would seem to have been the case.

ELEVATION OF A PORTION OF INNER ENCLOSURE.

SCALE: 1 2 3 4 FT.

1

2

3

ELEVATIONS OF PORTIONS OF INNER ENCLOSURE.

SCALE 1 INCH TO 1 FOOT.

PLATE LXXVIII.

THE upper figure in this Plate is the only slab belonging to this Rail representing the Nâga in the place of honour on the Dagoba.[1] But there are among the drawings in the Mackenzie Collection six others similar to this, with merely such variations of detail as occur in all these representations. Generally speaking, the Nâga Dagobas are less profusely ornamented with sculpture than those more essentially Buddhistical in their arrangements, but the subjects all belong to the same class. In this one, for instance, we have Mâyâ's dream, the birth of Buddha, and other well-known subjects in the medallions on the dome, and the Wheel, the Tree, the Trisul, and other familiar emblems on the band under the five steles. The Serpent of course occurs there also. The Rail, too, is identical with that of the other Dagobas. The frieze is generally of the roll pattern (Plate LVI.), and there are the four Lions as usual, belonging to each entrance.

What we really do miss, and what seems the characteristic distinction between the two, is the absence of worshippers. As will be observed, the panel under the Nâga is blank. In a more purely Buddhist Dagoba it would have had two or more kneeling or worshipping figures. There are no persons outside the Rail bearing offerings, and there are no historical bas-reliefs. The Nâgas had no history apparently. All this makes it difficult to say whether these purely Nâga Dagobas were worshipped generally or were appropriated to a particular class.[2] My impression is, that at the time these sculptures were executed the Nâga and the Buddha were so mixed up together, and so nearly equal, that it is impossible to draw any distinction between them, either as to the worship or their worshippers.

The two lower photographs in this Plate represent the obverse and reverse of the same slab. The Dagoba itself is the duplicate of that represented in the last Plate, and is so very nearly similar that at first sight they might be mistaken for the same. On close examination, however, the differences are easily detected. The Rail in Plate LXVII. has an animal—this has a roll frieze. The Nâga worshippers are on Buddha's right instead of his left. The position and character of the upper range of bas-reliefs are slightly altered. The subjects of the medallions are changed. In the last Plate the subjects represented in them were Buddha seated, and on either hand the men dancing, and bearing the relic trays on their heads. In this Plate the scenes are the Annunciation and the birth of Buddha. The two may, however, be taken as a fair example of the extent of variation with which the same design was repeated four times, once in each quadrant of the Rail.[3]

---

[1] I, of course, except the central slab in Plate LXXV., and such representations as occur in Plate LXIV., and elsewhere, where the Dagoba with the serpent occurs in conjunction with other objects. Two other Nâga Dagobas will be found, Plate XCI., but belonging to some other part of the building.

[2] In the Mackenzie Collection, Plate XIII., two Hindus are worshipping a Nâga Dagoba; but from their position it is not quite clear that they are worshipping the Nâga.

[3] The reader will of course bear in mind the scale to which the first one is photographed is double that of the present example.

The great interest of this slab, however, resides in the sculptures on the back of it. They are very much larger and ruder than any thing else at Amravati, and so different in design that they must evidently belong to another age than those we have been describing. On the other hand the figures, the tree, even the flying harpy-like figures above, are so nearly identical with what are found at Sanchi (Plates XXIV., XXV., XXVI., XXVII., XXVIII., and XXIX.), but not found elsewhere at Amravati, that we can hardly help ascribing them to the same age; obviously executed by an inferior artist, but still nearly identical.

The question thus arises, Was there an older building at Amravati, contemporary with the Gateways at Sanchi, which was desecrated when the inner Rail was erected, and its slabs used up for the new buildings? Or was it *in situ* when the elaborate sculpture of Fig. 3 was added on the other side of it? Taking all the circumstances of the case into consideration, my impression is that the latter may be the true solution of the difficulty. According to this hypothesis, that which is now the inner Rail was originally the outer Rail of the Tope, sculptured, like Fig. 2, on the inside, but probably plain on its outer face. When the great outer Rail was added in the fourth century, and the procession path carried outside this Rail, then these elaborate sculptures were added to match those of the great outer Rail then being erected. All this is so completely in accordance with what we find being done in Hindu temples in the south of India down to the present day, that I can hardly bring myself to doubt that this was what took place in this instance.

On the other hand, however, it may also be that both these Rails are parts of an entirely new design commenced only in the fourth century, and that this slab belonged to some building which may have been removed in order that it might not interrupt their alignment. Whichever hypothesis we adopt, the conclusion is the same as regards the age of the sculptures on the front and back of the slab. It proves incontestably that there was at Amravati a building as old as the Gateways at Sanchi, if not older. My impression, indeed, is that this sculpture is the most ancient of any represented in this volume. It is so difficult, however, to know what allowance should be made for locality or the personal equation of the artist, that it is impossible to speak positively on such a subject. Be this as it may, the very archaic form of the sculpture on one side of this slab, compared with the elaborate finish of that on the other, is another proof among many of the long period that must have elapsed between the date of the erection of this Tope as compared with that at Sanchi.

As before remarked (page 155) the coins found by Colonel Mackenzie would lead us to suppose that Amravati was a place of importance as early at least as the Christian era; this sculpture, therefore, not only tends to confirm that surmise, but aids us materially in understanding the history of the place.

PLATES LXXIX., LXXX., AND LXXXI.

THESE three Plates contain nine photographs of fragments of the Dagobas of the inner Rail, all to the scale of 1 inch to 1 foot. They are not all the examples which the Museum Collection contains, but they are probably sufficient to illustrate the variety as well as the monotony of these representations.

In Fig. 1, Plate LXXIX., the principal object of worship is the Wheel, but the Nâga appears very prominently on the Dagoba.[1] The same object is repeated in Fig. 3, which, though very much broken, is a better and more perfect piece of sculpture than the other, tending to show, as other circumstances do, that the different quadrants were not all exactly of the same age.

The lowest figure on the left hand of the same Plate contains a form we have not yet met with. The principal object here is a representation of the sacred feet enveloped in the folds of the Nâga, and worshipped by Nâga men and women.

The emblem has unfortunately disappeared from Fig. 1, Plate LXXX. This is to be regretted, as it seems a beautiful fragment, and the two children below the panel in which it ought to appear, betoken something new.

Figs. 2 and 3 of this Plate, and Fig, 3 of Plate LXXXI., instead of the emblems we are usually accustomed to, contain two medallions. The upper, representing the worship of the Horse, the lower Buddha or some Bodhisatwa seated cross-legged, surrounded by listeners or adorers. I cannot help suspecting that it is intended as a representation of Avalokiteśvara, but the sculpture is so small that it is difficult to make out exactly what is intended.

As we have frequently had occasion to remark, the Horse plays an important part in the sculptures at Amravati. It is once represented as honoured at Sanchi (Plate XXXV.), but this form of worship occurs here several times, but nowhere so prominently as in these three Dagobas. (It is to be presumed that there was a fourth.)

It is not easy to say what we are to understand from the prominence of the Horse in such a position as this. Is it an importation from Scythia, brought by immigrants from that country? Is it the Horse of the Sun, or of Poseidon? Is it the Avalokiteśvara of the Thibetan fables? Some one must answer who is more familiar than I am with Eastern mythology. At present it will be sufficient to recall to memory how important a part the Horse sacrifice or Aśwamedha plays in the Mahâbhârata, and in all the mythic history of India. What is still more curious is that the worship of the Horse still seems to linger in remote parts of India. At least in a recent work by Mr. Hislop, missionary at Nagpore, edited by Sir R. Temple, he describes the religion of the Gonds in the following nine words:—"All introduce figures of the horse in their worship." Other instances might no doubt be found if looked for, but the subject is new and unthought of.

---

[1] This slab has been so long exposed on the external wall of Fife House, that it is nearly destroyed, and its details can but with difficulty be made out.

In all these Dagobas in which the Horse occurs, the objects next in importance are the sacred feet. They occur on each side of the five steles under a great umbrella, but what the connexion between the two may be is by no means clear.

The principal representation on the Dagoba, Fig. 1, Plate LXXXI., is a repetition of the scenes depicted in the upper circle, Plate LXII.,—the worship of the relic casket by the Nâga Râjâ; but so far as can be made out, there does not seem to be anything in the other bas-reliefs on this Dagoba which would enable us to identify the relic, or say whence it came. The scenes here depicted, are, most of them at least, those we are already familiar with, as existing on various parts of the great Rail. Indeed, I am inclined to believe, though it is difficult to feel certain from the limited material at our command, that no new subjects are introduced in these Dagobas, but only scenes that may have been repeated four or five times on different parts of thc monument, but the difference of scale makes the recognition sometimes difficult. So far as execution is concerned, this is one of the most delicate as well as onc of the best preserved examples belonging to the series.

The remaining Dagoba, Fig. 2, Plate LXXXI., is the most essentially Buddhist of the whole, using the word in the sense in which we now understand it. Buddha is seated in his usual cross-legged attitude in the place of honour, and reappears in easily recognizable forms in the sculptures above. Yet, if I mistake not, on the very top of the dome, there are the remains of a great Nâga, in a position more prominent than on any other Dagoba of this class.

In all these Dagobas, when sufficiently perfect to enable the emblems to be made out, it appears that the central stele of the five was crowned by a miniature Dagoba. But on the lower part of thc steles (Plate LXXX.), on the left-hand lower corner, there are in the centre a Dagoba, on each side of that the two Wheels, and then two Trees, and in others, a figure adorns the base of each stele, but without any mode by which he or they can be distinguished. Other combinations are found, both on those represented here and on those in the Mackenzie drawings, but all of the same character, and apparently without any important significance.

We shall have occasion to refer again to these miniature Dagobas when speaking of the central one, for the restoration of which they are most important. Even in themselves, however, they are as interesting as any of the slabs at Amravati, and as important as illustrations of the form of Buddhist art in the fourth or fifth century of our era.

ELEVATIONS OF PORTIONS OF INNER ENCLOSURE.

SCALE 1 INCH TO 1 FOOT.

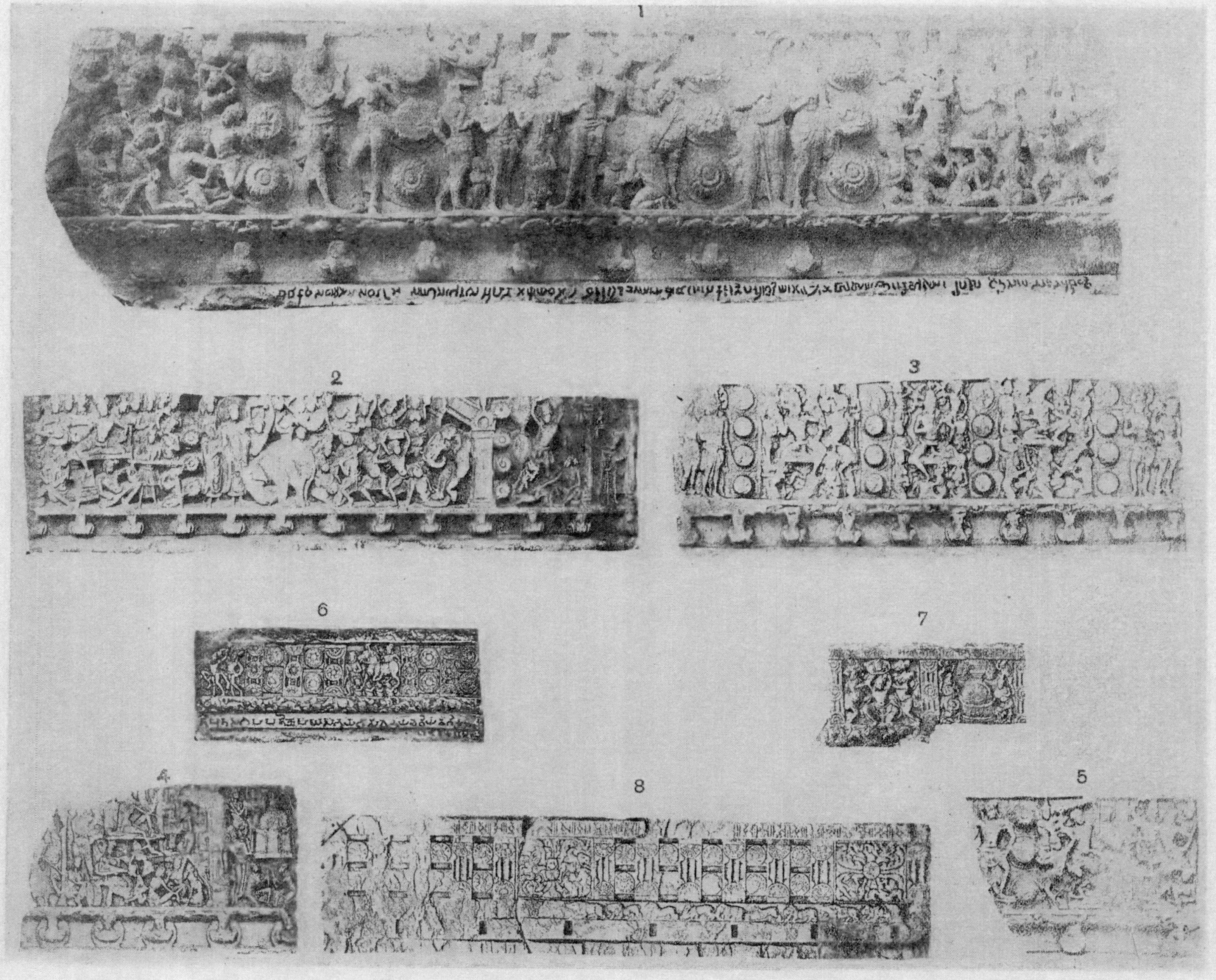

FRAGMENTS OF FRIEZES OF INNER ENCLOSURE.

FIG. 1 ENLARGED SCALE, FIGS. 2 TO 8 1 INCH TO 1 FOOT.

W. BRIGGS LITH.

INDIA MUSEUM

FEMALE FIGURES FORMING PORTION OF INNER ENCLOSURE.

AMRAVATI. PLATE XC.

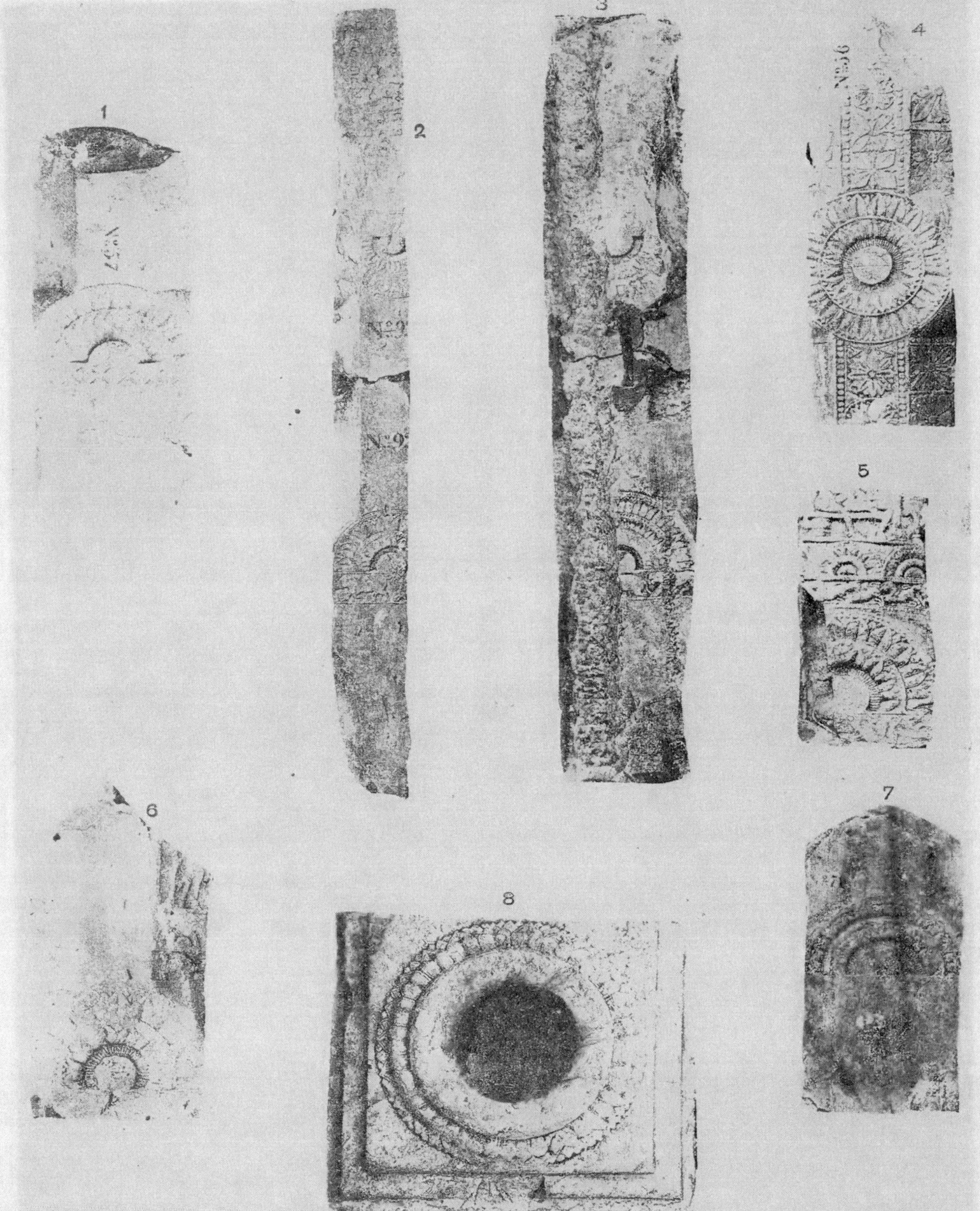

FRAGMENTS OF PILLARS.

SCALE 1 INCH TO 1 FOOT.

PLATE LXXXII.

We have unfortunately very few fragments of the frieze that crowned the inner Rail. Like that of the outer, it seems to have been one of the most elegant as well as interesting parts of the whole. The India Museum contains no specimen of the best quadrant, but one found its way by accident into the British Museum,[1] and is photographed to an enlarged scale in Fig. 1, Plate LXXXII. Two others are represented by drawings in the Mackenzie Collection, and are reproduced in Figs. 1 and 2, Plate LXXXIII. Figs. 6 and 7, Plate LXXXII, belong probably to a different quadrant, and Figs. 2 and 3 on the same Plate are certainly from another part of the enclosure from that represented in the three fragments just enumerated.

The whole frieze was very ingeniously divided into compartments by conventional Rails, with three discs or knobs. The central one is sculptured, but the upper and lower knobs are merely lotus flowers, like those of the great Rail. Between each of these pillars is a small compartment, containing a man and a woman or an object of worship, while the larger compartments always contain an historical subject. I am not aware that any more ingenious or pleasing mode of treating such a sculptural representation is to be found in any other building in any part of the world. Had it been invented when the Sanchi bas-reliefs were carved, there would have been infinitely less difficulty in identifying them, but there the same figures appear four or five times over in the same bas-relief, without any division to mark the different scenes.

In Fig. 1, Plate LXXXII., we have, first on the left, the man bearing the relic on his head, and men, women, and Nâgas following in wild dance (vide ante, Plates LXVII., LXXIII.). In the centre we have Buddha, or rather Prince Siddhârtha, or it may be Avaloketeśvara, with his horse, apparently blessing little children. In the third a Bodhisattwa—he has no glory—expounding to a Nâga people, all of whom have snakes at the back of their heads.

---

[1] The history of this slab is so curious that it may be worth recording. When I was at the Crystal Palace, Monti the sculptor one day asked me to come to his place in Great Marlborough Street to see a piece of Indian sculpture which belonged to a friend of his, and had been left in his charge. I was so struck with its beauty that I got it moulded, and three casts were taken. One was presented to the Crystal Palace, one to the Asiatic Society, and a third to the India Museum. The two first were destroyed in the fire in December 1866; the third luckily was safe. When I became familiar with the Amravati marbles, I at once recognized this slab as belonging to that Tope, and immediately set to work to try and find out what had become of it, but for a long time in vain. One day, however, talking to Mr. Vaux, of the British Museum, about the Amravati discovery, he said, "We have a slab with a Gupta inscription on it in the cellars," and sent a man with me to point it out, when I at once recognized my old friend. It seems an officer of the Museum was getting his hair cut in Great Marlborough Street, when the barber, knowing who his customer was, asked him to look at a piece of marble lying in the back yard. The officer had the good taste to see its value, got a grant from the trustees for 10*l.*, and purchased it. I may mention that there is also in the British Museum a figure from one of the Gates at Sanchi, though how it got there nobody knows. There is nothing from Sanchi in the India Museum. This, therefore, is the only opportunity that exists in this country of comparing the two styles from actual examples.

In the small compartments there is on the left a Hindu man and woman in the usual costume; on the right a man and woman in a costume betokening that they belong to a colder climate; but in order to prevent its being understood that they are represented as in a colder country, a palm tree is introduced between them. Are they Scythians? Do they bring the Horse? The man who kneels in front of it is in the same costume, and the whole may be parts of one story or one symbolism.[1]

It was on the top of the Museum slab that I first perceived the holes into which the crowning metal finish was fixed. From their form and position I would have had little hesitation as to what they were intended for, but the fact that every ridge in the great Serpent temple of Nakhon Vat in Cambodia was originally adorned by a metal ornament, removes at once any doubts that might exist. This inner Rail being apparently the last thing erected, there are no representations of it in any other part of the building, and till one is found the exact form of the ornament must remain doubtful. As before suggested, my impression is that there was a repetition of Trisuls.

Fig. 3 in this Plate is scarcely historical. It only contains figures of the Nâga Râjâ in various attitudes and with various accompaniments. The central compartment in Fig. 2 is the adoration of Buddha by the white elephant and various people bringing apparently offerings, though the stone is so much worn that it is difficult to make out the subject, or what the right-hand compartment is intended to represent. On the left we have another edition of the story of King Sivi. The stone is so worn that the bird cannot be made out, but the attitude of the man in the foreground, and the whole accompaniments are so like the sculpture on the left-hand pillar, Plate LX., that there can hardly be any doubt they represent the same thing.[2]

Fig. 4 is apparently a duplicate of Fig. 2, Plate LXV., but belonging to a smaller Rail.

Figs. 6 and 8 represent portions of two friezes of two smaller Rails, with only two intermediate bars, and with occasional decorations and historical subjects interspersed. In Fig. 6 the only one that can be made out is the adoration of the Horse.

In Fig. 7 we have the same wild excitement displayed on the elevation of the relics as is portrayed in Plates LIX., LXVII., LXXIII., and elsewhere.

---

[1] The inscription on Fig. 1 will be found Appendix E. Fig. XX., and translated in so far as its weather-worn character will allow. It is one of the most interesting of the series, as it records a gift to the Mahâ Chaitya of Danakakata. If this is established, it is a satisfactory confirmation of this being the place described by Hiouen-Thsang as Danakacheka. The long inscription, Fig. 1, will be found in the same Appendix, No. II. It is unfortunately only known from a transcript by Colonel Mackenzie's draughtsman, who did not know the character, but it can be made out tolerably satisfactorily.

[2] The same subject appears to be represented on the right-hand side of the five steles on the Dagoba, Fig. 1, Plate LXXXI.

AMRAVATI.

FIG. 1.

3 Feet 7.5

FIG. 2.

W GRIGGS, LITH

6 Feet 3.8

INDIA MUSEUM.

FRAGMENTS OF FRIEZES OF INNER ENCLOSURE.

AMRAVATI. PLATE LXXXIV

FIG. 1.

FIG. 2.

FIG. 3.

W. GRIGGS. LITH. INDIA MUSEUM

FRAGMENTS OF FRIEZES.

W. GRIGGS, LITH. INDIA MUSEUM.

FRAGMENT OF BAS RELIEF.

PLATES LXXXV. AND LXXXVI.

PLATE LXXXV.

THE two female figures represented in this Plate, with several others, were used as pilasters either at the angles of the inner Rail or in the centre, when it was desirable to separate the subjects into groups. They cannot be said to be pleasing specimens of sculpture, showing all the defects of the style in an exaggerated manner, but they are certainly curious. That on the left bears apparently a torch in her right hand, and behind her head is seen the familiar snake. The figure on the right holds a dagger run through a human head, and in her left another head held up by a handle. Whether these are to be considered as heads severed from human bodies, or as vessels in the form of heads, is by no means clear. If the figure were Durgâ, or any shadowing of her appearance on the stage, we would at one acknowledge them as skulls, but in the absence of the marble itself, we must not speculate too boldly.

The niches in which these figures stand are curious reminiscences of the Sanchi Gateways, but are so similar to several others sculptured in these bas-reliefs that it does not seem possible to refer these figures to a different age, which otherwise, from their inelegance, I would be inclined to suggest might be the case.

PLATE LXXXVI.

The principal interest in this piece of sculpture centres in the figure with the beard in the lower division. Except those represented in Plate LXX. he is the only man with that appendage[1] at Amravati.

From his dress and surroundings he is evidently an ascetic of the same class as those so frequently represented at Sanchi. But he is the only representative of his class here, where it is evident that the shaven monk had superseded the lone hermits in the interval between the ages of the two monuments. From the animals that accompany him he is intended to be represented as a dweller in the woods, and his hermitage is seen behind him—no longer a circular thatched hut, but a well-built square cell. Beside it is a tumulus, on or in a square basement or enclosure, somewhat similar to that represented in Plate XXXII., but evidently in a more advanced style of architecture, and with a pot of flowers at each angle. Still, from the absence of a Tee, it remains uncertain whether we are to consider this as a Dagoba, or a Tomb, or a Temple of some older people, from whom the Buddhists may afterwards have adopted this form for their Dagobas. My own impression is, that the latter is the most likely hypothesis. From the reverential mode in which the women approach him, and the manner in which the man in the chariot brings his gift, it is evident that the bearded man is considered a very holy hermit.

---

[1] The Scythians, in Fig. 1, Plate LXXXII., ought perhaps to be excepted, but they are evidently strangers.

I am afraid, from the style of drawing, that this bas-relief has been entrusted by Colonel Mackenzie to an inferior artist to copy, which is to be regretted, as it is one of the most interesting in the series. So far as can be judged from the style, it is one of the most modern of the whole. The chariot, the hermit, and the square enclosure of the dagoba or tomb do not occur in any other sculpture at Amravati. The altar in front of the Pipal tree is peculiar, so is the mode in which the women dress their hair. Besides all this, it does not seem, either from its style or dimensions, to belong to either of the Rails or to the central building. It probably was part of some later erection, of which no other fragment now remains, but with such evidence as this drawing affords it is not possible to say what that was or when erected.

The head-dress of the Raja in the upper division of this bas-relief is also worthy of remark. We have met with it before, but only rarely in Plate LX. and in Plate LXXXIII. Fig. 1, but is similar to some that are found in the Caves at Badamî, belonging probably to the ninth or tenth century. A similar head-dress is also represented by Colonel Abbott, as found in a fragment of a statue at Mullote, in the Punjab.[1] My impression is, that it is of Persian or rather Yavana origin, and in these sculptures seems to belong to king Śivi or his race.

If this work were wholly devoted to the illustration of the Amravati Tope, and the subject was thought of sufficient importance to justify it, it might have been expedient to have added several others to the lithographs given above, copied from among the eighty-six drawings in Col. Mackenzie's collection. Those selected, however, are those which seem to be the most interesting, as well as the most varied of the series. The others are either of inferior value or duplicates of those here given, or of each other, with only such slight variation in detail, as hardly to warrant their being repeated. It is well, however, that those who wish to master the subject, should bear in mind that only about one-third of the drawings in that collection are given in this work, and that the photographs are far from making up the entire deficiency.

---

[1] J. A. S. B., vol. XVII. Plate IV. Fig. 2.

FRAGMENTS OF SCULPTURE.

SCALE 1 INCH TO 1 FOOT.

PLATES XC., XCI., AND XCII.

PLATE XC. contains seven fragments of other pillars and one base. Two of them, the first and last, have inscriptions, but so faint that it is difficult to make them out. Fig. 2 has an inscription at the top, the letters of which are beautifully legible, but unfortunately it is split down the middle, so as to be utterly unintelligible. It is not easy to say whether these are fragments of the five steles which ornamented each face of the great Dagoba, or whether they were "Stambhas," bearing emblems which may have stood in various places in the enclosure. From their form and style, as well as the minute character of the inscriptions, which could not have been seen at that height, it would seem probable that they may have stood on the ground. On the other hand, however, the position of the inscription on the columns of the Dagoba, Plate LXXVII., would favour the idea that they once occupied a similar position.

PLATE XCI.

Contains four fragments of considerable interest, though it is at present impossible to say what position any of them may have occupied in the buildings within the enclosure.

The first is a Dagoba divided into compartments by pilasters, with double Lion capitals of a curious Persepolitan type, but altogether of considerable elegance. The pillars themselves, however, are of the same form as those used in the Rails, with one central circular disc, and two half circles at top and bottom. The cushion capital also recalls what we find afterwards at Elephanta and Ellora. Between them, in the place of honour, is the five-headed Nâga; on the right the Wheel, and on the left the Tree. With the Dagoba, these form the four principal objects of adoration in this place. Were it not for the very wooden form of the Tee, I fancy this sculpture would be of comparatively modern date. No. 2 is simpler, but certainly more modern. The Nâga here reigns supreme on the Dagoba, without any compeer. The crowd of umbrellas that crown the Tee is a curious ebullition of Hindu fancy.

The upper part of Fig. 3 is so defaced that it is difficult to make out whom it represents. It is probably, however, the same scene as recurs in Plate XCV. Fig. 1. Whatever his name may be, he is a man who possesses two wives, two friends, a horse, and an elephant, and is probably meant to be contrasted with the Raja in the lower compartment of the bas-relief, who is a Chakravarti Râja possessed of the seven precious things which, according to the Lalita-Vistara,[1] constitute human greatness,—the treasure of the Wheel, the treasure of the Elephant, the treasure of

---

[1] Foucaux's Translation, p. 14, and Plate II., where this subject is engraved.

the Horse, the treasure of a Wife, the treasure of a Pearl, the treasure of a Major Domo, and of a counsellor. The sequence is curious but characteristic.

Fig. 4 is another edition of a legend more frequently repeated than almost any other in Buddhist scriptures. As mentioned above, it was with their artists as great a favourite as the Annunciation and Nativity were with Christian painters. In the left upper compartment we have Śuddhodana and his friends, and on the right Mâyâ's dream. The upper part of the slab being injured, his umbrella and her elephant have both disappeared. Below we have on the right the scene in the Lumbini Garden, which immediately preceded the birth of Buddha. It is not quite clear what the fourth compartment is intended to represent, as it is not to be found in any edition of the legend I am acquainted with. It looks as if it were intended that the old woman who appears in the first compartment should announce to the King in his bath the birth of his miraculous son. The cloth she carries in her hands bears the same impression of the sacred feet as that which is wound or to be wound round Mâyâ, in the next compartment.

PLATE XCII.

The upper figure in this Plate once formed part of the frieze of some Rail. It may have been one of the returns of the great Rail, but it is difficult to see, if that is so, where it would fit. It is the now familiar subject, the adoration by men of the Wheel, placed behind the throne on which the cushion or relics are placed, and with the sacred feet in front (compare Plate LXXI. Fig. 2). The inscription upon it merely records that it is the pious gift of Akasavâdi and Samiriti householders.[1]

The three fragments in the centre of this Plate certainly belong to the outer frieze of the great Rail. Fig. 4 shows its commencement. Fig. 5 is a portion of another Rail belonging to some unknown building. It is very carefully executed, and though the "motivo" is the same as the first frieze, still the introduction of the dwarfs and the arrangement of the whole is novel and of great beauty.

[1] Appendix E., No. XVI.

2

3

4

FRAGMENTS OF SCULPTURE OF CENTRAL BUILDING,

SCALE 1 INCH TO 1 FOOT.

AMRAVATI. PLATE LXXXVIII.

FRAGMENTS OF SCULPTURE.

PLATES LXXXVII., LXXXVIII., AND LXXXIX.

THESE three photographic Plates contain representations of various details, some of considerable interest, but which do not belong to either of the Rails, and to which, except the lions, we cannot at present assign any definite position in the building. They are all to the scale of 1 inch to 1 foot.

No. 1. Plate LXXXVII. is a figure of Buddha, as he is usually represented in the fifth and sixth centuries. It is of no especial merit, and probably is among the most modern sculptures of the place, coeval with the fragments of the frieze (Plate LXXXIV.).

Fig. 2 represents a fragment of a frieze of the Trisul emblem, of the best age and very good execution. It did not belong to either of the Rails, nor to any building of which we have now any knowledge.

Fig. 3 represents the sacred feet of Buddha, probably of the same age, and it may be from the same building as the last. In the centre of the soles is the Chakra; above it the Trisul emblem reversed, or it may represent the Chakra supported on the Trisul, with a Swastika on each side. Below the Chakra is the Swastika again, with an ornament like the crux ansata on each side. On the great toe is the Trisul, on each of the others a Swastika. The whole, however, is in such low relief that it is extremely difficult to bring it out in the photograph.[1]

Fig. 4 is the Chakra, with the Swastika and foliage, all of very elegant sculpture.

Fig. 5 is one side of the abacus of a pillar, meant to bear a lion or some other emblem. The representation on it is one we have frequently met with before of two elephants bringing offerings to the Dagoba. This is not only a favourite subject of Indian sculptors, but of Indian legends, and has already been described at length from Hiouen-Thsang's narrative when speaking of the sculptures of the Eastern Gateway at Sanchi, page 118. The same story is also repeated by Fa-Hian.[2]

Fig. 6 represents a seven-headed Nâga of more than ordinary perfection of sculpture.

Figs. 7, 8, and 9,—are architectural fragments of great elegance, but which could not belong to any building we now know. These, with other sculptures in the collection, suffice to prove that there must have been several different edifices within the enclosure, which have been so utterly swept away that it is impossible to say now what they may have been.

PLATE LXXXVIII.

Figs. 1 and 2 in this Plate are curious as being exact elevations of the outer face of the great Rail, used evidently as a frieze to some building in the enclosure. On comparing it with the elevation in Plate XLVIII., it will be seen at once how exactly they tally. The pillars are octagon, with a central complete lotus disc, and

[1] The worship of the sacred feet, or footprints, is one of the favourite forms of Vishṇuism at the present day. At Gayâ the Vishṇu Pud is the principal temple, and wholly devoted to this form. It succeeds Buddhism in its original seat as Juggernath superseded the Tooth relic at Puri.

[2] Foĕ-Kouĕ-Ki, p. 227.

a half-circle at top and bottom. Between the pillars are three Rails, each with a complete foliated disc or circle. Above them is the roll ornament, and below the zoöphorus or animal frieze. With such pictures the restoration, though sometimes puzzling, becomes when done perfectly authentic.

Fig. 3 is made up of fragments of one of those curious columns on which the Chakra is usually placed. A similar one, but much smaller, is shown in Plate LXXV., and another from the Mackenzie Collection is lithographed in Plate XCVIII. Four other representations of similar columns exist in that collection, all differing, but all equally fantastic. They all commence at the bottom, with the throne and the relics upon it. Behind them rises a central column of varied and fantastic design, and on each side are men riding on horses, lions, oxen, giraffes, and human-headed monsters of most varied design. This one, when complete, must have been about 13 feet in height.

On the outside of the pillar of the Western Gateway at Sanchi, Plate XIX., an earlier form of this fantastic ornament will be found. It is interesting as one of the many indications of the progress in style that took place between the two monuments. As the Western Gateway was the last erected at Sanchi the decoration there may be considered the first of its class. It is thin and poor compared with those found at Amravati two or three centuries afterwards.

Figs. 4 and 5 represent two of the lions that adorned the portals of the great Rails. If we may trust the bas-reliefs, there must originally have been four to each Gateway, or sixteen to each Rail.

PLATE LXXXIX.

This Plate represents four faces of a very beautiful octagonal pillar that once stood probably within the enclosure, and supported a statue or an emblem; most probably the former, as all the principal emblems are on its faces. There is the sacred tree in its circular enclosure, and easily distinguished as a Pipal from the form of its leaves. The Wheel, supported on a square pillar,—the Lion-pillar and the Dagoba.

The foliage on three sides is the flowing lotus pattern, executed with great delicacy and elegance. On the side with the wheel, it is different and more complicated, but equally beautiful. It seems, however, that the wheel should always crown a complicated arrangement of this sort, but from what motive we do not now know.

Above the emblems the pillar changed into a polygon of sixteen sides, and may have been as high again—it is now about eight feet high—before terminating with the capital on which the crowning object stood.

The inscription merely records that it is the gift of Hagha of Gadhika, together with his son and daughter. (See Appendix E., No. V.)

DETACHED PILLARS WITH EMBLEMS.

SCALE 1 INCH TO 1 FOOT.

1

2

3

4

FRAGMENTS OF SCULPTURE.

SCALE 1 INCH TO 1 FOOT.

FRAGMENTS OF SCULPTURE.

SCALE 1 INCH TO 1 FOOT.

PLATE XCIII.

Looked at from an architectural point of view, the most difficult question connected with the Amravati Tope was to ascertain whether any building occupied the centre of the enclosure, and if any, whether it was a Dagoba or a Chaitya hall, or a Vihâra or monastery. Owing to the excavation of the tank in the centre of the mound, as mentioned above, absolutely no trace of its foundation remained, and it might as probably have belonged to one as to any other of these classes. *A priori*, both from what Hiouen-Thsang says[1] and the general probabilities of the case, I should have felt inclined to restore it with a Sanghârâma or Buddhist choir, or monastery. But, on looking carefully through the Mackenzie drawings, I soon perceived there existed among them representations of a class of sculpture which certainly did not belong to either of the enclosures; and from some pencil memoranda on the drawings, some of these were identified with the loose stones lying in the centre of the enclosure (Plate XLVII.). In the Elliot Collection, also, there are some twenty fragments, some of which are those drawn by Colonel Mackenzie's assistants, others so exactly in the same style, that it was easy to group them apart. Having got so far, it was not difficult to see that these fragments formed part of a Dagoba similar in design to those of the inner Rail, and which consequently must have formed the central object of the group of buildings.

If anyone will look carefully at any of the Dagobas represented in Plates LXV., LXVI. to LXXIX., he will perceive that the solid part to the height of the Rail is divided into slips by long pilasters, between which are various sculptures, generally hid by the Rail, but terminating upward by a Dagoba, with the three umbrellas on each side, or a Wheel or some such emblem, as in Figs. 1, 3, and 5 of Plate XCIV.

The historical subjects belonging to this group of sculptures were all found to be two-storeyed—if such an expression may be used. The lower group stands on a simple three-barred Rail of the Sanchi type; above them is a flat band, variously ornamented.[2] Besides these, there are a considerable number of fragments, which all terminate upwards by a cornice or battlement of Trisuls, evidently forming the crowning ornament of a wall.

All the principal fragments of this class have been arranged in this manner in Plate XCIII., and, if compared with any of the Dagobas of the inner Rail, it will be seen, I think without doubt, that the one is a copy of the other. There is first the perpendicular part, terminating in the Wheel or Dagoba. Then the two

---

[1] Voyages, 188. Ante, p. 167.

[2] One of the slabs in the India House Collection is sculptured on both sides, from what motive I am unable to guess. The slab is too thin to stand alone, and it could hardly have formed part of any screen or rail. Either it may have been done from some religious motive—by no means so unlikely as would at first sight appear—or it may have been that the first executed design was not approved, and the slab turned round and a second engraved on it.

storeys of sculptured panels; and then the rich cornice, which invariably terminates the whole, up to the springing of the dome.

Arranged in this manner, these fragments make up a wall 22 feet high, and taking the widest of those sculptured on the Rail as our model, this would make the central Dagoba 30 to 35 feet[1] in diameter, and its height, including dome and Tee, about 50 feet.

To those who are not familiar with the architecture of the country where this Tope is situated, it may appear strange that so magnificent an enclosure should have been erected to enshrine so insignificant an object. Such an arrangement is, however, in the south of India rather the rule than the exception. Take, for instance, the great temple at Seringham. The outer enclosure measures more than 2,500 feet each way. Each of its Gateways is 130 feet in width, 100 feet in depth and would, if completed, have risen to 300 feet in height. The inner six enclosures, though less than the outer, are all of great magnificence; but the central building is smaller and less in magnificence than nine-tenths of the village temples in the neighbourhood. The cause of this inversion of the usual rule is easily explained. A village temple becomes famous from some miracle performed by its god, or rich from the endowment of some dying sinner. To pull it down would be desecration, but to add enclosure after enclosure and gateway to gateway was easy, and has happened in nearly all the great temples of Southern India, and did, I fancy, happen at Amravati.

In Egypt, too, something of the same sort occurred at Karnak. The little sanctuary of Orsortasen became there the nucleus of all the subsequent magnificence, and, though overshadowed by the palace of Thothmes and the great hall of Menephthah, it still remained the most venerated, though the smallest of all the erections in that vast enclosure. If this is so, the Central Dagoba was the first erected of all the buildings at Amravati, of which any remains have come down to our day. This indeed we gather from the style which is ruder than that of the great Rail, and very much simpler, and less elaborate than that of the inner Rail. The simple Sanchi-like Rail, which forms a string course through the centre of the building, is also an indication of greater antiquity. Wherever a Rail is represented on the enclosures at Amravati, it is always of a more ornate and more complicated character than that on the central building.

Another test is the form of the characters of the inscriptions. Both General Cunningham and Mr. Thomas are of opinion that those on the central building are the oldest, but cannot, from their limited extent, feel sure how much more ancient they may be. Altogether I fancy it was erected certainly before the year 300 of our era, and was the temple of the Diamond Sands, which figures so prominently in the legends of the Tooth relic, which was carried here in the early part of the fourth century.

---

[1] The yellow circle in the plan, Plate XLVII., which is meant to mark its site, is 50 feet in diameter. It was made so to include a terrace or procession path, with or without a Rail, which I conceive must have surrounded it.

PORTIONS OF FRIEZE OF CENTRAL BUILDING,
SCALE 1 INCH TO 1 FOOT.

that existed before these or any Buddhist books we now possess were reduced to their present legendary form.

Taken altogether the sculptures of these two Topes present a deeply interesting picture of the form which Buddhism had attained to in the early centuries of our era, and as curious as illustrations of the progress that religion made, and the change which took place in it during the three or four centuries through which their execution extends. Neither the catacombs nor the early Byzantine mosaics afford anything like so complete a picture of the early form of the Christian religion. Indeed it would be difficult to find anywhere so complete an illustration of one epoch of one of the most important forms of faith which have hitherto been adopted by mankind, and as such it need hardly be added well worthy of the careful study of all who are interested in such inquiries.

Ethnology.

It is more difficult to speak with anything like precision regarding the ethnology than as to either the architecture or religion displayed in the Topes. This does not arise so much from any want of distinctness in the sculptures as because the countries of Hydrabad and Berar have never yet been scientifically explored. We are almost entirely ignorant regarding the different races who inhabit the vast central plateau of India, on whose outer edge these two Topes were erected, and we neither know whence they came nor when they settled in their present locations. Now that the Nagpore territory has escheated to British rule, there is a prospect of something being done to clear up these difficulties, but the only result hitherto obtained is to show us how much remains to be done, and at the same time what a vast amount of valuable material exists on the spot and is available for the inquiry.

Among the minor races depicted in these sculptures, perhaps the most distinctly marked are those with short curly hair. There are only two men so distinguished at Amravati, and the sculpture on which they are found is of such inferior execution (Plate LXXXIV.) that no argument can well be founded upon it. In Plate LXII., Fig. 2, several women are so distinguished, but no men. At Sanchi the case is different. The drummer boys generally have curly hair, so have the charioteers and menials in many instances, and in one bas-relief (Plate XXVIII.) these curly-headed people seem to be the principal actors. From their costume they seem to come from some colder country, and I have suggested Bactria, though there are no doubt many difficulties in such an attribution. At first sight it might be supposed they came from Africa—Zanzibar—like the Hubschees at present in the Nizam's service, but in the absolute silence of all tradition the difficulties in the way of such a hypothesis are greater than as regards the other. The question has rather a curious interest in an artistic point of view, as there seems little doubt that it was from this people—whoever they were—that Buddha derived the negroid hair by which his statues are always distinguished, and which has given rise to so much speculation. In so far as we now know, sculpture, taught by the Greeks, was practised in the North-west long before it penetrated into India Proper, and it is probable that the earlier statues of Buddha were fabricated there. If this is so it would favour the idea that the curly heads may have belonged to that country.

Even supposing it were possible to locate and name such minor groups as these, the great question would still remain, Who are the people who in the preceding pages have been designated as Hindus? From the appearance of Śâkya Muni, and their being so generally associated with him, I think that there can be very little doubt but that the sculptors meant to represent the inhabitants of the province now known as Upper Bengal, more especially of the districts of Behar, Tirhoot, and Oude, which were assuredly the cradle of Buddhism. At first sight it might appear that a distinction ought to be drawn between the followers of Buddha at Sanchi, and those at Amravati. The figures, especially of the women at the former place, are so much fuller, it may be said coarser, and so much more like what we are accustomed to call Scythians or Tartars, that it might be assumed that they could not belong to the same race. On the whole, however, I am inclined to believe that the difference is more artistic than ethnographic. From the earliest sculptures in the Caves to a late period, there seems to be a tendency to refine and attenuate, and my impression is that this difference is due to that cause.

If this is so, the people who are associated with Buddha in both Topes are the mixed race of Bengal,—a people with a certain infusion of Aryan blood in their veins, but which had become so impure from mixture with that of the aboriginal tribes who existed in Bengal before the Aryan immigration, that the distinctive features of their higher civilization were almost entirely lost. Of this no greater proof could be given than that Buddhism was able to rise on its ruins.

After all, however, the most important ethnographical question that arises from the facts stated in the preceding pages of this work, is the inquiry who the Nâgas were to whom reference has been so frequently made. Although their name, and the narrative of their sufferings, and conversion, crowd the pages of the Mahâbhârata and Mahawanso, and indeed of all Buddhist books, we nowhere acquire from these writings any information as to who the Nâgas were supposed to have been, nor what their personal appearance or characteristics were.

There are one or two hints in Hiouen-Thsang, such for instance as that mentioned on page 48, which might lead us to suspect that they were supposed to have many-headed serpents growing from their shoulders, but nothing to give us to understand that this characteristic was so general as we now know that it was from our knowledge of the sculptures at Sanchi and Amravati.

So far as I know there is only one passage in Indian literature which describes a Nâga as the sculptures represent him. It occurs in the Nâgânanda referred to above, page 64. When the Nâga Śankachûda expostulates with the hero of the drama for his self-sacrifice, he exclaims: "The error is a likely one forsooth! Not to mention "the mark of the Swastika[1] on the breast, are there not the scales on my body? Do "you not count my two tongues as I speak? nor see these three hoods of mine, the "compressed wind hissing through them in my unsupportable anguish? While the "brightness of my gems is distorted by the thick smoke from the fire of my direful "poison?"[2] This is no doubt a correct description of the ideal Nâga, but the curious

[1] This mention of the Swastika as emblem of the Nâga race is curious, the more so as we find it prevalent in Scandinavia, in parts of Britain, in France and Italy—wherever, indeed, we have been able to find traces of Serpent Worship in the western world. Burnouf translates it merely as "signe de bénediction ou de bon augure" (Lotus de la Bonne Loi, App. p. 625), but does not seem to be aware of this connexion.

[2] Nâgânanda, translated by P. Boyd, B.A., p. 84.

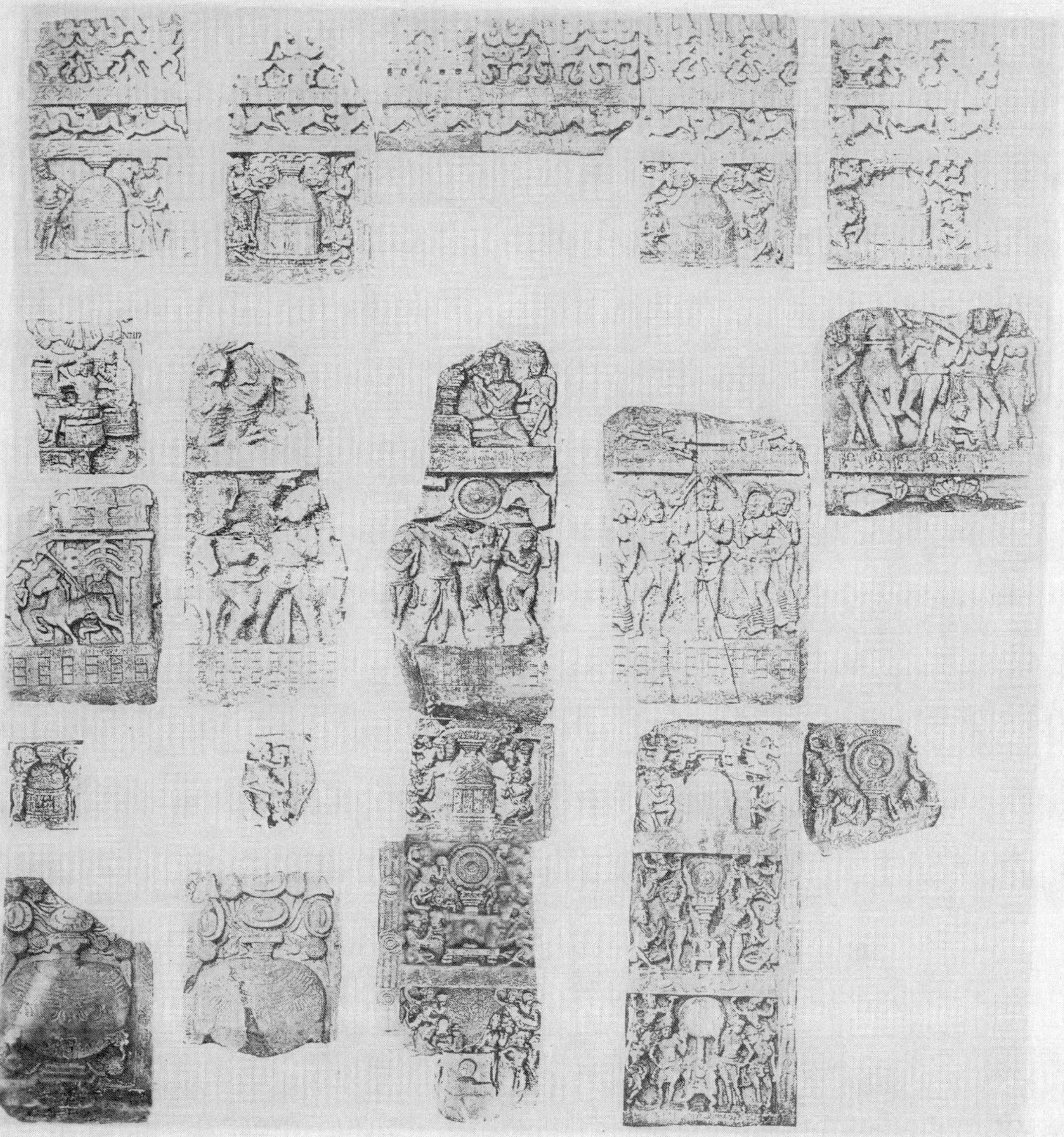

RESTORATION OF A PORTION OF CENTRAL BUILDING.

SCALE. 1 2 3 4 8 FT.

AMRAVATI. PLATE XCIV.

PORTIONS OF SCULPTURE OF CENTRAL BUILDING,

SCALE 1 INCH TO 1 FOOT.

1

2

3

4

PORTIONS OF SCULPTURE OF CENTRAL BUILDING.

SCALE 1 INCH TO 1 FOOT.

PLATES XCIV. TO XCVII.

THERE is very little in the sculptures of the central Tope that calls for any particular remark after what has been said in the preceding pages. The emblems employed in its decoration are those with which we are already familiar. The Throne, with the relics upon it, the Tree, the Wheel, and the Dagoba. In two instances, at least, (Plate XCIV. Fig. 3[1] and Plate XCVII. Fig. 1) the five-headed Serpent is in front of the Dagoba, and in both these instances the worshippers are unmistakeably Hindus, and the same who are worshipping the Wheel and the Tree in the same sculptures.

The Nâga people also occur in at least one instance in the lower part of the bas-relief, Fig. 1, Plate XCVI. The slab was complete when Colonel Mackenzie drew it, but even without that, enough remains of the lower bas-relief to show that it represented one male and three female Nâgas, but who were essentially Buddhists, if we may judge from the seven figures of Buddha,[2] seated cross-legged, which appears immediately over their heads, and the five impressions of the sacred foot that are placed between the snakes' heads.

The Horse, too, forms an important element in the decoration of the central monument. In Plate XCV. Fig. 1, and Plate XCVI. Fig. 1, he may be merely the favourite charger of the man who is leaning against him, but in Plate XCV. Fig. 4. he is introduced in mid air alongside the Wheel as an object of equal reverence; and on a piece of sculpture where the Wheel just above him is the especial object of worship; and in Plate XCVI. Fig. 3, he issues from the portal with the umbrella of state borne over him, the hero of the representation. The same subject is repeated on another slab, Plate XCVIII. Fig. 2, from a drawing in the Mackenzie Collection, but which is easily recognized as belonging to the upper or sculptured part of the central building. The first impulse, on looking at these and on the last-quoted illustrations, is to consider them as representing the commencement of an Aśwamedha, or horse sacrifice; but one of the essentials for that is wanting in both. The story of the Aśwamedha is easily understood. A Raja, who claimed to be lord paramount in India, let loose a steed to wander wherever he listed, and followed close behind him prepared to fight anyone who dared to meddle with the horse, and to release him if anyone took possession of him. If he accomplished this, and brought the steed back in safety, he was acknowledged a Chakravartti Raja. If he failed, the sacrifice did not take place.

In the bas-relief at Sanchi, Plate XXXV. Fig. 1, a Raja is following the steed in his chariot, and that may therefore be the commencement of the Aśwamedha. At

---

[1] This slab has been so long exposed on the outer wall of Fife House that its sculptures are nearly obliterated.

[2] That is, assuming the figures of Buddha to be cöeval; but they have very much the appearance of being added afterwards.

Amravati the challenger is in all instances absent, and it seems difficult to account for this if such a sacrifice were intended. On the whole I am much more inclined to believe that the Horse was an object of reverence, if not exactly of worship, at Amravati, and that those bas-reliefs on the Dagobas (Plates LXXX. and LXXXI.), and those on the central building, as well as those elsewhere, all shadow forth that faith and that only.

I would require that much more attention should be paid to this subject than I can pretend to have done, and also that more materials should be available for the investigation, before any confident opinion could be expressed regarding the real position of the Horse in these sculptures. Meanwhile I may state that the inference I draw from the representations of the Horse in the sculptures is that the reverence paid to him is the counterpart of the worship of the Bull-Nandi by the Śivites. The two sects are and always were the antipodes of each other in India, and each seems to have adopted an animal as their emblem, the Buddhists taking the Horse as theirs. This does not of course preclude the idea of this form of worship being borrowed from Scythia. On the contrary, everything we learn from either Sanchi or Amravati points to the north-west and to countries beyond the Indus as the source whence everything took its origin. What the Buddhists derived from those countries was, however, directly antagonistic to anything which we know that the Aryans either possessed or affected, and must consequently have been derived from some other race. Whether, therefore, we call the people Turanian or Scythian Huns, we come back to the same thing. The Buddhists must have derived the foreign influences from a northern Turanian race, occupying the countries both to the north and to the south of the Himalaya chain. The people, in fact, who were Buddhists in India in former days and are now Buddhists in Thibet. If Śivaism arose among the Dravidians, they were of a different race, and must have come into India by another route, probably across the Lower Indus.

The principal inscription—No. XIX. Appendix E.—merely records that the sculpture on which it is found is the pious gift of Agheya, the pupil of Buddha Rakshita.

AMRAVATI. PLATE XCVIII.

PILASTER INNER ENCLOSURE.

PILASTER CENTRAL BUILDING.

PLATE XCVIII.

THE Wheel pillar represented in Fig. 1 of this Plate eontains no novelty, or anything whieh is not found in those represented in Plates LXXV. and LXXXVIII., but it is more distinct than the first and more eomplete than the last of these, and is eonsequently useful towards understanding one of the most eharaeteristie features of the inner Rail to which it belonged.

The slab, Fig. 2, whieh is also from the Maekenzie Colleetion, is extremely useful towards eompleting the restoration of the eentral building, inasmuch as it carries us direet from the three-barred Rail to the Dagoba frieze. It will be observed in Plate XCIII. there is a hiatus between the upper range of sculptures and the Dagoba, whieh, as far as any evidenee went, might be of any dimensions. In this slab we have the Rail, the two ranges of sculptures, and the erowning Dagobas, all in one slab, and fortunately with the dimensions written upon them, which settles the question.

The upper seulpture is also interesting as illustrating the legend of King Dharma Aśoka, alluded to above, page 177. "After reaehing the Golden Sands, his majesty "had a dream in whieh Devatâs appeared to him and said that underneath the temple "were relies which had been deposited there by order of the king of Lankâ. Next "day the king direeted people to dig into the Chaitya, but the crows, or spirits in "their shape, compelled them to desist.

"It happened that at this time the Nâga with seven heads and as many tails "guarded the Chaitya, but no sooner had the king aceompanied by Mahâ Tuli "(sent by Indra to assist) and a large retinue, approaehed elose to it, than this "mighty snake king was observed to be majestieally disentwining himself from "the huge fold with whieh he had encompassed the relic shrine."[1] As already related, with the assistance of the king of Róm he was eventually successful, and founded a eity, and built a new Chaitya to enshrine the reeovered relics. Was this the temple we now see? and are the relies those so frequently represented in the foregoing Plates?

It is, of eourse, extremely diffieult to arrive at anything like eertainty in such a ease as this, but after what has been said above, I think the history of the Amravati Tope may be made out with very tolerable preeision. First, we have indieations from the eoins eolleeted by Colonel Maekenzie, and also from the slab, Plate LXXVIII., Fig. 2, that buildings did exist on this spot as early as the Christian era, but we have now no means of knowing what they may have been. In the next plaee, judging from the eharacter of the seulptures, as well as from sueh shadowy traditions as exist, it does not seem that any part of the buildings

---

[1] J. A. S. B., XVII. p. 90.

which have been described above, were undertaken till more than a century after the Gateways at Sanchi were completed.

About or after the year 200, however, the central Dagoba may have been commenced with an enclosing Rail, of which, however, nothing has reached this country. Subsequently, in the beginning of the fourth century, either in consequence of the visit of the Tooth relic on its way to Ceylon, or from some other local cause, the place acquired celebrity, and the great outer Rail was commenced, and it may have continued during the remainder of that century before being completed. The sculptures of the inner Rail seem then to have been taken in hand, possibly were not completed till the year 500, after which time decay seems to have set in, and nothing further was done.

All that we know of Indian art is perfectly in accordance with this, and now that we are enabled to study the sculptures at Sanchi we can speak with some confidence on this subject. Before they were known, everything as we traced the history of art backwards seemed to become more and more elegant and perfect. Now that we have got hold of the earliest examples, we find that the art began in rude vigour, but without any of that refinement it afterwards attained. About the fourth century seems to have been the culminating point, and from that period the rock-cut temples, and those at Bhuvaneśwar and elsewhere, carry us on without intermission till we reach such temples as those on Mount Abu, 1032; those around Hullabeed, dating from 1200 to 1300; or those at Kanaruc in 1241. We know that during this period there was no retrocession nor any age of decay which would account for the inferiority of the sculptures of the central building compared with those of the enclosure, on the supposition that these were the more modern of the two.

The architecture, as far as it goes, bears out the same conclusion as the sculpture. At Sanchi it is careless and wooden, the string courses seldom horizontal and occurring at every different level. It is the same in the central building at Amravati, especially in the crowning cornice, Plate XCVII. In the Rails, all afterwards became precise, almost finicking, and that remains a characteristic of Hindu art to the present day. The great Rail on the contrary is set out with very considerable precision, and though extremely ornate there is method and dignity in the arrangement of the parts. When the inner rail was executed the style degenerated into littleness, being elaborate and elegant, but more suited to ivory carving and metal work than to an architectural design; and this remains too much a characteristic of Indian architecture to the present day.

part of the business is, that till he proclaimed it nobody saw it. Certainly Jîmûtavâhana, the hero of the piece, took him for an ordinary mortal, and his mother had not a distinguishing mark. Even Garuḍa, who from his eating a Nâga every day for his lunch, ought to have been tolerably familiar with their characteristics, exclaims, "Both "of you wear the distinctive badge (a red cloth) of victims. Which is really the Nâga "I know not." The fact perhaps is that when men allow their imagination to create new classes of men or animals they cannot long maintain their characters consistently. Be this as it may this description answers accurately to the Nâgas we are now so familiar with from the sculptures at Sanchi and Amravati, but whom we only knew from such passages as this before these representations of them were published.

All this, however, does not help us to answer the question who these Nâgas were, or which of the various races inhabiting India the Buddhist or Hindu authorities intended to designate by that name. Aryans they certainly were not, and nearly as certainly they could not be any of the Dravidian races inhabiting the south of India. We are, therefore, reduced to seeking for them among the Dasyus or various original tribes who peopled India before either of these two great dominant races attempted to colonize it.

The chief difficulty in this case arises from the wideness of their spread. We learn from Hiouen-Thsang that they, or at least a tradition of them, was everywhere prevalent in the Cabul valley, and the Punjab—Cashmere was, we know, par excellence a Nâga country;—and from the Chinese travellers as well as the Mahâbhârata we find evidence of their being spread over the whole length and breadth of the valley of the Ganges. From the sculptures at Sanchi, and the sculptures and traditions at Amravati we know that the latter place was the seat of a Nâga kingdom; and Ceylon and Burmah are said to have been inhabited by Nâgas before their conversion to Buddhism.[1] The question really, therefore, is what tribe or tribes could have been so widely disseminated as to cover all that space of ground?

So far as I have been able to master the subject the answer to this does not seem to me doubtful. Before the advent of the Aryans the whole of the north of India seems to have been occupied by races in a very low state of civilization, whom they called Dasyus. By their superior power and influence they taught all those in the Punjab or the valley of the Ganges to speak languages so nearly akin to the Sanskrit so as to obliterate their individuality. In like manner the Dravidians forced those on the southern side of the Vindhya to speak their tongues,[2] but owing to their isolation among the hills have not been able so completely to obliterate

[1] All these facts have already been stated in the Introduction, pp. 47 et seqq., and the references consequently need not here be repeated.

[2] When the Romans first entered Gaul, in the first century B.C., there is no reason for supposing that any of the inhabitants of that country spoke Latin, or any tongue nearly allied to it. When they left it, four or five centuries afterwards, Latin was the language of the country, and remains so to the present day. The same was the case with Spain, and now all Italy, France, and Spain speak languages so closely allied to one another, and these to Latin, that according to the laws of philology, as hitherto understood, the Celts, Franks, Iberians, Lusitanians, Ligurians, Etruscans, and Basques, and all the various tribes that inhabit those countries, belong to the same race and derive their origin from one branch of the great Aryan family. Wiser councils now prevail, and even Max Müller, the most strenuous advocate of the hard-and-fast philological test, in his opening lecture at the Strasburg University, in autumn last, gave up the whole question, and admitted that language without corroborative evidence was no test of nationality or of affinity of blood between two races.

their national characteristics, and the Gonds and other hill tribes still retain many of their original peculiarities. It is consequently among them that we must look for the nearest approach to the scenes we find depicted at Sanchi and Amravati, and among the Nâga Râjâs of the two Nagpurs [1] for the last historical trace of this once all pervading race. In the north of India at the time we first become acquainted with them through our books, the Nâgas of these regions were so distant in time, that they had been relegated to Majerika and other subterranean or subaqueous abodes; while in central India the Nâga kingdoms were still so recent that there seemed no incongruity in the sculptures representing them as taking part in the affairs of men, and associating as equals with the people of those countries, on the outskirts of which these two monuments are situated. If this is so, the only explanation that occurs to me, of so strange a myth, is, that the Dasyus were a Serpent Worshipping people whom the fertile imaginations of the northern poets converted into a race of Nâgas or snakes, and relegated them to the infernal regions, while in the more backward regions of Central India they still, at the time our Topes were erected, retained a portion of their human attributes, and interfered in the affairs of men.

They, too, if I am not very much mistaken, were the Gentiles who adopted the religion of Śâkya Muni, which was rejected by the Aryan Brahmans to whom it was originally preached, and it was their quietude and their abhorence of caste, so characteristic of a Turanian race, that sustained the Buddhist religion as it was during the thousand years it maintained its supremacy in India.

Be all this as it may, everyone will probably be inclined to admit that the Plates published in this volume are a most important contribution for the elucidation of many of the difficulties connected with Indian ethnography, but the real value of this evidence will never be extracted from them till they are carefully examined by persons on the spot, who have local experience and personal knowledge of the tribes of Central India. When this is done the Topes at Sanchi and Amravati may contribute as much to our knowledge of the ethnography of India in the early centuries of the Christian era as they have certainly done towards completing the history of the architecture and illustrating the religious forms of the faiths of India at that early period of time.

---

[1] Vide supra, p. 65, et seq.

No I – PL, LXIV, FIG, I.

No II, – PL, LXXXIII, FIG I,

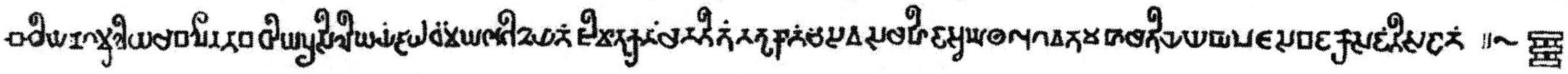

No III, PL, XC FIG 7

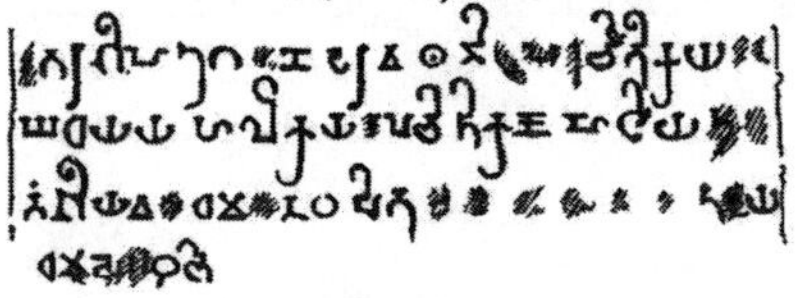

No IV – PL, LIII, FIG 2,

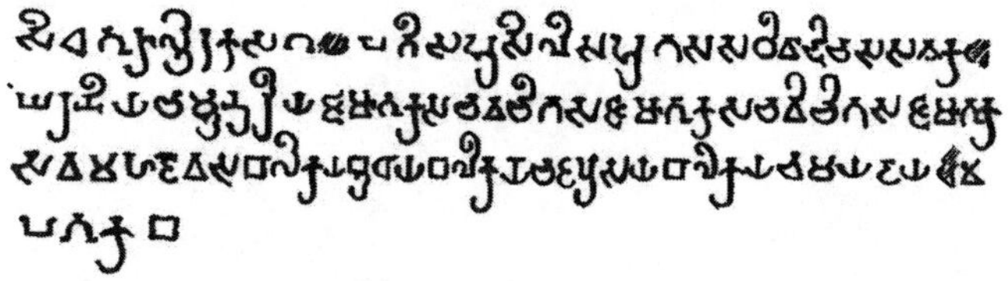

No V – PL, LXXXIX.

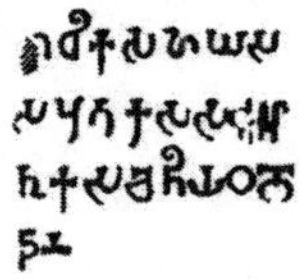

No VI – PL, XC, FIG 2,

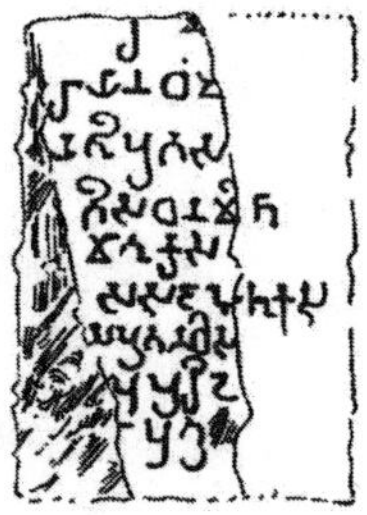

No VII – PL, XC, FIG I,

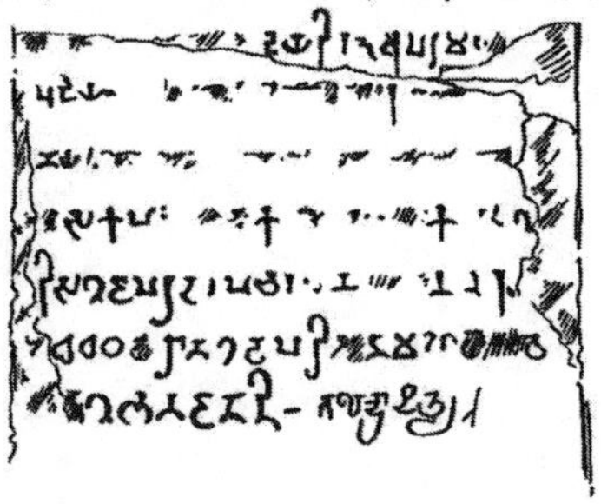

No VIII – PL, LXXVII.,

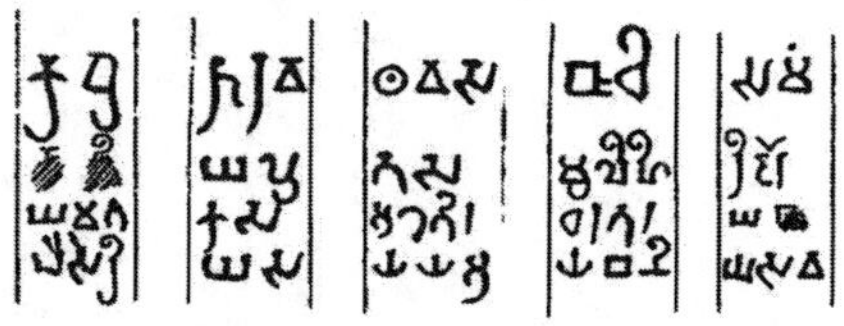

No IX J.A.S. BENGAL, 1837, PL X, MACKENZIE, M.S.

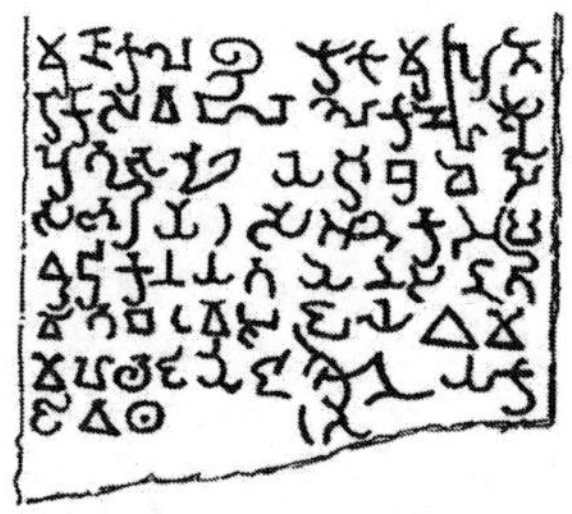

No X. – PL, XCV, FIG 3.

No XI – PL, LXXXII, FIG 6

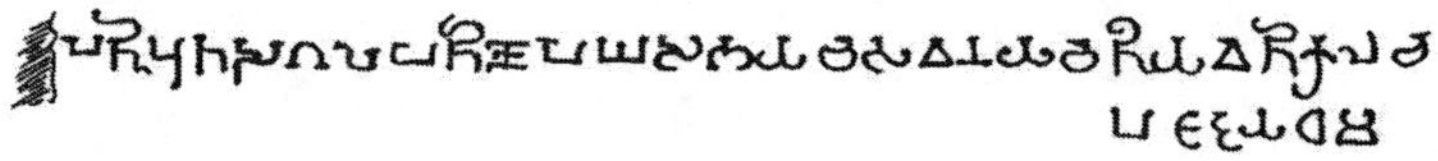

No XII – PL, LXXV,

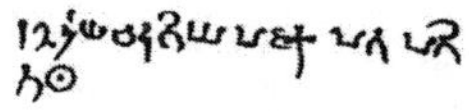

No XIII – PL, LXI. FIG I,

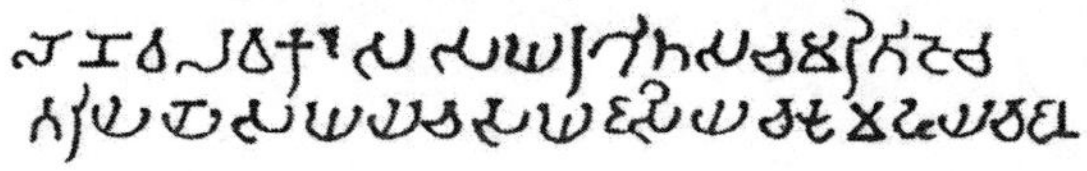

No XIV – PL, LVIII, FIG 2.

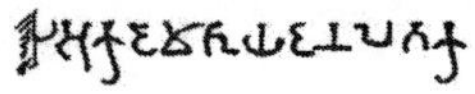

No XV – PL, LIII, FIG, I.

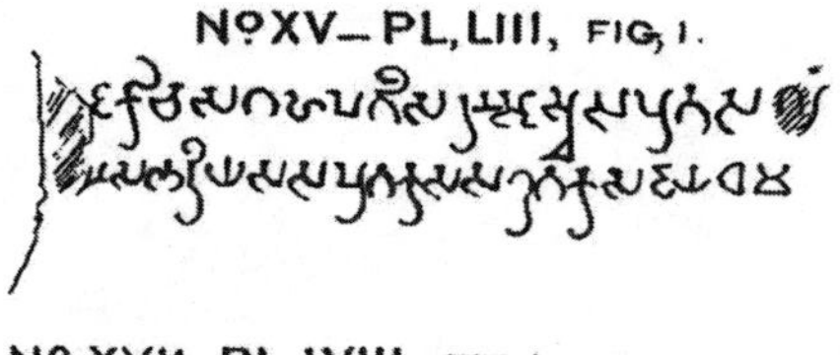

No XVI – PL, XCII, FIG, I.

No XVII – PL, LVIII, FIG, I

No XVIII. PL, LXXXVII, FIG 5.

No XIX – PL, XCV, FIG, 4.

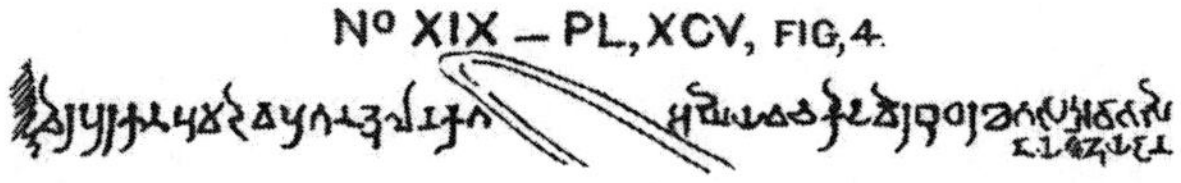

No XX PL, LXXXII, FIG, I.

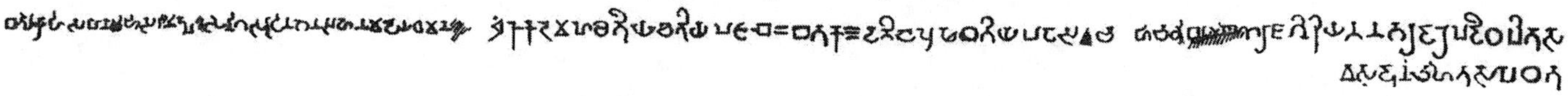

INSCRIPTIONS.

CONCLUSION.

ARCHITECTURE.

THERE are few of the subjects mooted in the previous pages regarding which it would not be easy to say a great deal more than has been said, nor would it have been difficult to find illustrations from other monuments which would have rendered the subject much more complete. It has, however, been thought better, in the first instance at least, to confine the work to the representation of the two monuments named on the title page, with only such introductory matter and descriptions as were requisite to render them intelligible, and to leave their application to a future time and probably to other hands.

In so far as the History of Architecture is concerned, we do not learn much from these Topes that had not previously become known to us from an examination of the rock-cut examples, but there is a great deal in them that confirms what was previously only suspected, while a knowledge of their forms fills up some important gaps which existed in our history of the early styles of Indian art.

Irrespective of this, however, these two Topes are interesting, inasmuch as they are the two oldest structural buildings which, so far as we yet know, are to be found in India in anything like an intelligible state. If the Tope at Sanchi was really erected by Aśoka—and there seems no good reason for doubting that it was so—it is the only one of the 84,000 Stûpas he is traditionally said to have erected of which a vestige now remains, and its Rail is the oldest and simplest in form of all those of which any fragments now exist. Its Gateways, too, are unique, as no other example of such a form is known to exist anywhere in India, though judging from the frequency with which representations of them occur at Amravati, they must have been at one time very common. All those, however, that occur in the bas-reliefs of the Southern Tope seem to have been of wood, and those at Sanchi, though of stone, are very slightly removed in form from their wooden prototypes.

The whole of the superstructure of these gateways is so essentially wooden in construction that we rather feel inclined to wonder how men dared to attempt its erection in stone, and are equally astonished that it should have stood for eighteen centuries nearly uninjured. The pillars, too, are evidently imitations of carved logs. The irregularity in spacing the divisions, the mode in which the dividing string courses stop, without running all round, and the wavyness of the lines, all betray the workmanship of people unfamiliar with the even bedding requisite for stone masonry in such positions, though the irregularity may be rather pleasing in wood carving.

All this is changed when we come to the age of the Great Rail at Amravati. There the architectural details are carved with sharpness and precision. The string courses are horizontal, and the general construction so truly lithic, that it requires some study and some knowledge to detect the wooden forms that still remain. The examples of Rails at Muttra and Buddh Gayâ are probably intermediate between those at Sanchi and Amravati, and when published in detail may perhaps enable us to render our history a little more complete. Enough remains at Gayâ to enable it to be restored with certainty when anyone will take the trouble to do so. That at Muttra is probably too far ruined, but meanwhile, till casts or photographs can be obtained, it is impossible to speak with any certainty regarding them. These four Rails, however, are nearly all that now remains to enable us to write the history of structural architecture in India anterior to the building of the great Bhuvaneśwar temple in 627 A.D., or that at Iwulli in Dharwar in 640 these being probably the two oldest structural temples now existing in India. We may eventually be able to eke out this meagre list by hints borrowed from the Topes in Ceylon and Afghanistan, but they, I fear, are either too modern or too much ruined to be of much service. The real complement to our scant knowledge must be derived from the Caves. We have in Behar some Caves nearly as old as the age of Aśoka, and at Bhâjâ and Kârlâ in the Western Ghats we have others which were excavated certainly before the Christian era. From that time to those at Junir and Nassick there are probably a hundred examples, including those of course at Kanheri, Ajanta, and elsewhere, which may have been executed in the first three or four centuries of the Christian era, and some of those at Cuttack may be as early as those of the western side of India. From this time we have a very numerous series of rock-cut examples at Ajanta, Bang, Kolvi, and Ellora, which illustrate very fully the forms of Buddhist art down to the time when it appears to have gone out of use about the year 750. At one time I thought it might have been carried further down towards more modern times, but recent researches have convinced me that no important architectural work was undertaken by the Buddhists in India after the great revolution which practically terminated their power, and extinguished their religion as a dominant form of faith in the middle of the eighth century of our era.

The fact, however, of our having been obliged hitherto to rely to such an extent on rock-cut examples for our knowledge of the early arts of India, has prevented our being able to ascertain how far the history of sculpture and decorative art has coincided with that of architecture. There is very little sculpture in the early Caves, and what there is, is generally carved in a coarse unsuitable material, and frequently in situations where it is badly lighted and imperfectly seen. It was therefore perfectly open to anyone to argue that these sculptures were not a fair test, and that the Hindus may have been proficient in representations of the human form and in decorative sculpture at a time when their architectural knowledge was still in its infancy.

This entire dependence in rock-cut examples makes it difficult to over estimate the immense advantage to our knowledge of Buddhist art which we derive from the study of the two Topes illustrated in the previous pages. It is true they do not yet supply us with all we want. We do not for instance quite know what the external appearance was of the great Chaitya halls or of the Vihâras. The façades of the former we can easily realize not only from such illustrations as that given above in Woodcut, No. 7, p. 88,[1] but from the actual existence of the original wooden framing in the great Cave at Kârlâ,[2] and other examples in western India. The Vihâras, too, might be restored with fairly approximative certainty from the representations in the Caves; but no study of the Cave art would have given us any information with regard to Dagobas, and their rails and gateways such as we derive from the study of the Topes themselves.

The great and most satisfactory result of this investigation is, that when we come to put all these materials together we now obtain a complete and perfect idea of the Buddhist style of architecture as it existed in India, during the whole period in which that religion flourished in that country. This style took its rise when the religion was adopted as that of the state, under Aśoka, 250 B.C. It died with the revolution that extinguished Buddhism with the fall of Ballabhi in or about 750, and curiously enough it left no successors. The Jains did not adopt it, but inclined more to the Hindu form of art, and no other sect in India preserved any reminiscence of it; while in Burmah, Thibet, China, and other countries where Buddhism still prevails, their architecture differs so essentially from that of India that their affinities are with difficulty recognized. It thus becomes one of the most complete and interesting chapters in the history of architecture. Born from the wood without any parentage among the lithic styles of architecture in other parts of the world, and dying in the height of its perfection without leaving any direct descendants; but during its 1000 years career combining great originality with considerable grandeur, and frequently with great elegance of detail. There may be still some gaps to fill up—some details which require rectification, but for the first time it can now be said that we know the beginning, can follow the career, and can assist at the death of the most important branch of Indian architectural art, and of one well worthy of a place among the other well-known styles of the ancient world.

Religion.

The picture which the sculptures of the Topes at Sanchi and Amravati afford us of the religious faith of the inhabitants of India at the time they were erected is perhaps more novel, and also more interesting, than even the information they afford regarding the arts of the country. Before they were discovered, the only contemporary record we possessed of the early forms of the Buddhist faith was that derived from

---

[1] A drawing of another of these façades from the Buddh-gayâ Rail will be found in the new edition of General Cunningham's report, just received from India (Vol. I. Plate IX. Fig. F.) He, however, quite mistakes the construction by omitting the intermediate blocks. It is perfectly drawn by Kittoe, in the India Office Collection.

[2] The wood framing of this facade, which is without exception the most ancient and most interesting example of its class in India, is, I am sorry to hear, in great danger of falling out of its place from internal decay. I have frequently written to India in hopes something might be done to arrest this, as it would be an irreparable archæological misfortune, and finding the Indian revenues not sufficient to bear this strain, have offered to pay the expense myself. But unfortunately there is no one in authority in the Bombay Presidency who cares two straws about the matter, and we may any day hear of its being too late to avert the ruin that awaits it.

the inscriptions of Aśoka, engraved on pillars at Delhi, Allahabad, and in Tirhoot, &c., and those on the rocks at Orissa, Gujerat, Peshawur, and elsewhere (see Appendix C.). What we find in them is Buddhism without Buddha. Except in the short inscription at Bhabra near Jeypur (App. C.), the founder of the religion is not once mentioned, nor any of his doctrinal formulas. That marvellous tenderness towards everything that has life is strongly inculcated; respect for parents and superiors, mutual kindness and forbearance, and above all, toleration of other faiths, are insisted upon, and many moral doctrines common to Buddhism and other forms of faith; but we scarcely gather whether they emanated from some Solon or Socrates or from Śâkya Muni. The faith was then the rival of that of the Vedas, and affected their purity and absence of all human agency or miraculous manifestations.

At Sanchi, 300 years afterwards, we find the state of affairs altered, but not to any very great extent. Buddha, the great pervading spirit of the universe as we have always hitherto known him, nowhere appears. In his place we have only the Prince who forsook parent, wife, and child, and threw aside his royal state and all worldly advantages, that he might devote his life to the benefit of his suffering fellow men. Or we have the pious ascetic who devoted his life to privation and contemplation that he might attain Buddhahood. But even this is, as it were, only incidentally announced. It requires some knowledge and a great deal of study to detect it. On the other hand the religious observances which the sculptures of Sanchi reveal to us are, that in those days the old ancestral worship of a Turanian people had been refined from reverencing the sepulchres of their forefathers into a veneration for relics and relic shrines, the Dagoba or Tope being among the objects most frequently and most prominently worshipped there. Next to the Dagoba, if not indeed more important, is the worship of the Tree. It occurs twice as frequently, and often in more prominent positions in the sculptures, but against this we must bear in mind the fact, that the great Tope itself was there, and those Gateways were themselves erected to do it honour, so that representations of Topes were not so important as those of Trees which did not otherwise exist.

Next in importance to these, but very much less frequent, is the worship of the Wheel, and next to it the Trisul emblem, though it is very doubtful whether this last ought to be considered as an object of worship at Sanchi, and not merely as an hierogram, expressing a sacred meaning,—most probably as the cross is of Christ, this may be considered an emblem of Buddha himself.

Next to these comes the goddess Śrî or Devî which seems so like a loan from the Hindu Pantheon that we are at a loss to account for her presence on so purely Buddhist a monument, and what is still more curious is that though occurring at least ten times at Sanchi her presence has not yet been detected at Amravati.

The most remarkable circumstance, however, connected with the bas-reliefs at Sanchi is the absence of any apparent segregation of the clergy from the laity. No priests appear anywhere; and though we have palaces, there is no building that can be taken for a monastery. On the other hand, the sculptors revel in depicting regal state. Music and dancing take the place of divine service, and drinking and love-making fill up the time of the Buddhists of those days. Most strange of all, we have war! It is true it may have been undertaken to acquire or recover some valued relic, or for some such Buddhist object, but fighting on a Buddhist monument even for the propagation of the faith is at strange variance with usually received opinions.

When from these we pass on over another three centuries to the time of the sculptures at Amravati, we find a state of affairs much more nearly approaching to the usually received formula of Buddhism. Buddha, the ascetic, occasionally appears in the usual attitudes and the usual costume, but this is the case much more frequently in the more modern than in the older bas-reliefs of this Tope. His statue does not apparently occur among the fragments of the central Dagoba,[1] and rarely on the fragments we possess of the great Rail. On the smaller Rail, however, such representations become frequent, and very similar to what we are accustomed to on the Caves and Buddhist temples after the fifth century.

The actual worship of the Dagoba occurs as a rule only on the central building. It is frequently represented afterwards, and with more elaboration, on the inner Rail, which I take to be the last important addition to the Tope, but it can hardly be said that it is there represented as worshipped by the people of the sculptures, the adoration seems to be addressed to what may be called an idol in the place of honour, in front of the Dagoba. It is more like a frame to contain pictures to be reverenced by the people. The purely abstract symbol of Relic Worship had become a storied page of legendary lore, and, if I read it rightly the picture has to a very great extent obliterated the original idea of the relic shrine.

The Chakra or Wheel, on the contrary, seems to have gone on growing in importance. Nothing at Amravati exceeds the fanciful elaboration of the pillars which support this emblem, and it is introduced so frequently and so prominently that it was evidently considered one of the principal emblems of the faith.

The Trisul emblem seems also to grow in importance as we descend the stream of time. As before mentioned, it does not seem to have been directly worshipped at Sanchi, nor is it so treated in the central building at Amravati, but on the great Rail it occurs several times elevated on what have been called pillars of radiance, and most decidedly as a thing to be worshipped.

On the other hand, Tree Worship maintains nearly the same relative position of importance at Amravati that it did at Sanchi, but with this important qualification. Where the two Topes have anything in common, it is most apparent in those points in which they approach nearest in age. We find, consequently, the Tree Worship most important in the central building, next in the great Rail, but nearly evanescent in the sculptures of the inner Rail. It only occurs once in the place of honour on any Dagoba in our collections, and never on the frieze nor on the wall. The change is so gradual that it can hardly be accidental, and I am on the whole inclined to believe that Tree Worship was to some extent losing its importance before the sculptures at Amravati were complete.

The greatest change that took place between the two epochs seems to have been in the position of the Nâga. As just mentioned, he appears only once at Sanchi as if he were an object of worship in the representation of the conversion of the

[1] I do not feel quite sure about Fig. 1, Plate LXXXVII. It may belong to the central building, but I rather think it was a detached statue.

Kaśyapas, and even that is hardly borne out by the form of the legend as we now have it, but he appears frequently either alone or as spreading his seven-headed hood over some important personage.

At Amravati he occurs certainly ten or twelve[1] times in the place of honour on the Dagoba or on pillars as the principal object to be worshipped. Twice he occurs in a similar position shielding the head of Buddha, thrice protecting the sacred feet, and at least thirty, it may be fifty times spreading his hood over Rajas or persons of importance, exclusive of course of the women with their single snakes, who are always more numerous. There is of course some uncertainty in stating these figures, as we have only so small a portion of the Amravati sculptures at our command, but on the whole I am inclined to think that what we possess is a fair representation of the whole, and if so, it is not too much too assert that the Nâga is the great and ruling idea at Amravati, and seems to have been growing in importance from the oldest buildings there till the time when additions ceased to be made, and the place became deserted.

The conclusion that seems to me to flow inevitably from these premises are, that Tree and Serpent Worship was the primitive faith of the aboriginal casteless Dasyus who inhabited northern India before the advent of the Aryans. Buddha or the early Buddhists seem to have adopted Tree Worship as an innocent form of worship, and their early legends teem with allusions to it, but as the primitive forms of the faith faded, this religion died out and finally disappeared. Serpent Worship, on the contrary, seems to have been entirely rejected by the founder of the new religion, but as the purity of the faith he taught became faint the old superstition cropped up again, and became more and more prominent, till Nâgârjuna, about the Christian era elevated it into the position of an almost coëqual power with that of Buddha himself, and as such we find it portrayed at Amravati.

The Horse is another object which was certainly honoured at Amravati to an extent that we are justified in calling worship; it hardly, however, seems to have been a growing faith, and probably was more prominent in the central building than in subsequent erections, though it appears prominently on the inner Rail.

Another important change is, that at Amravati we have shaven priests, such as we easily recognise and such as we find at the present day on the other side of the Himalayas, or in Ceylon or Burmah.

Music and dancing are still represented at Amravati, though rarely. Drinking hardly occurs, and love is kept in the background. In fact we cannot but feel, in comparing these sculptures, that when we come near the end of the Amravati series we are approaching very nearly to the state of affairs which existed when the Ceylonese and Thibet books were first composed. At Sanchi we were in another and an older world, but by degrees religious forms assumed a state more nearly resembling what we now find. Another century, and the sculptures of the Tope might have served literally as illustrations of the Mahawanso or the Lalita-Vistara. Meanwhile their great interest resides in the fact that they represent a state of affairs

[1] I am forced to state the numbers thus rather vaguely, because I cannot always feel quite sure whether some of the drawings in the Mackenzie Collection may not represent the same sculptures as those of Sir W. Elliot; generally, the difference is easily recognized, but not always.

APPENDIX.

APPENDIX A.

THE following two extracts are taken from a work entitled "Der Ehsten abergläubische Gebräuche Weisen und Gewohnheiten, von Johann Wolfgang Boecler, weiland Pastor zu Kusal in Ehstland und des Consistorii in Reval Assessor. Mit auf die Gegenwart bezüglichen Anmerkungen beleuchtet von Dr. Fr. R. Kreutzwald. St. Petersburg, Buchdruckerei der Kaiserlichen Akademie der Wissenschaften. 1854."

The first is curious, not only as showing the prevalence of Tree Worship in Esthonia at a very recent date, but more so as containing a form of prayer addressed to the Tree God which I have not met with elsewhere.

Dr. Kreutzwald's account of the Serpents, and their annual parliaments, accords with that reported by Castrén as occurring in Sweden (vide supra, p. 26). He does not profess to have seen snakes worshipped himself, but he quotes the late Provost Masing (I. 39.) as having in his boyhood seen tame snakes (unterirdishe Hauswirthe), who were fed and nourished by the peasantry and honoured as household gods:—

"Die *Baumverehrung* der Esten lässt sich aus der jüngsten Vergangenheit nachweisen und wird ohne Zweifel auch heutiges Tages manche Anbeter finden, obzwar—seit die ungläubige Spottsucht unter den Nationalen selbst grösseren Spielraum gewonnen, und durch Aufhebung der Leibeigenschaft manche frühere Verhältnisse verändert worden, die Zahl der baum- und quellgläubigen Seelen jährlich mehr einschmelzen und bei Ausübung ihrer alten Gebräuche noch vorsichtiger werden dürfte, wodurch nach wenigen Jahren vielleicht alle sichtbaren Spuren verschwinden. Indessen möchten wir nicht verbürgen, dass bei dieser spiegelglatten Oberfläche auch der Meeresgrund überall ein ungetrübter sei. In den beiden ersten Decennien des laufenden Jahrhunderts, wo in solchen Dingen weniger Zurückhaltung herrschte, haben wir in Allentacken, Weirland, Jerwen und Harrien heilige Bäume mehrfach gesehen; sie standen unweit des Wohnhauses an einem geschützten Orte, genossen eine sorgfaltige Pflege und wurden gegen Beschädigungen in Acht genommen. Es waren in der Regel alte Linden, Eichen oder Eschen, erstere am häufigsten. Nach der Mittheilung eines glaubwürdigen bejahrten Nationalen wurden solche Bäume wenigstens einmal im Jahre mit frischem Thierblut begossen, desgleichen musste, wenn eines geschlachteten Thieres Herzschlag zur sogenannten "frischen Suppe" *wärske leem*—benutzt worden war, bevor ein Mensch davon gekostet hatte, eine Portion über des heiligen Baumes Wurzeln verschüttet werden, damit der Viehstand besser gedeihe. Am Johannis—Abend hing man in Wierland einen mit "Glücksblumen" *õnne lilled*—durchwundenen Farrenkraut-Kranz in des heil. Baumes Zweige. Am folgenden Morgen wurden die "Glücksblumen" aus dem Kranze genommen und auf jegliches Hausgenossen Glück ein Blümchen zwischen Wandritzen gesteckt, um zu erfahren, wessen Glück in diesem Jahre am schönsten sich entfalten werde.—Der Farrenkraut-Kranz blieb am Baum hängen bis er verwelkte, dann erst ward er abgenommen und bis zur Neujahrsnacht sorgtältig aufgehoben, wo der Abends unter das Kopfkissen gesteckte welke Kranz die Träume dieser Nacht ominös machte. Zu gleichem Zweck streute man in der Johannis-Nacht blühende Blumen unter das ruhende Haupt, die hier, wie der welke Kranz am Sylvester-Abend, für den Schläfer weissagende Vorbedeutung gewinnen sollten. Die Auslegung der Traumorakel besorgten hier—wie's auch anderweitig geschicht—alte Weiber, denen selbst im Volksliede das Prädikat "*targad*" (weise) beigefügt wird, wenn's etwas zu rathen giebt, was über den kleinen hausbackenen Verstand hinausgeht. Es ist uns nicht erinnerlich, Steine unter den heiligen Bäumen bemerkt zu haben, auch wussten wir damals keine besondere Aufmerksamkeit diesem Gegenstande zu widmen, daher, falls wirklich welche vorhanden gewesen, sie leicht unbeachtet können geblieben sein. Nach den Mittheilungen des *Herrn Lagus* aus der Fellinschen Gegend, soll unter dem "Linden-Altar"—*pärna altari al*—immer ein Stein gestanden haben, auf den der Opferbringer seine Gaben hinstellte, nachdem er vorher auf blossen Knien drei Mal von Osten nach Westen, und drei Mal wieder zurück gerutscht war, wobei er sprechen musste: "Empfange die Speise zur Opfergabe." Dann wurden dem Stein zur Besiegelung des Bundes noch drei Küsse gegeben und nun konnte man fortgehen. Auch sollen die Fellinschen Linden—was in Estland nicht der Fall war—auf einem "Hügelchen" gestanden haben. In einem darauf bezüglichen Volksliede hören wir den Opferbringer sprechen:

Saada ônne sarwikuile,	Sende Glück du den Gehörnten,
Kaitse meie kabjajalad,	Wahre unsre Hufenfüssler,
Warja meie warwaskannad,	Schirme unsre Zehenhacken,
Sôrgaliste sigidusta.	Das Gedeihen auch der Klauer.

Wir wollen hier einen Estnischen "Opfergebrauch" ausführlicher beschreiben. Der Opferbringer musste aus seinem Zeigefinger einige Blutstropfen ritzen und dabei sprechen: "Ich nenne Dich " mit meinem Blute und verlobe Dich mit meinem Blute, und bezeichne Dir meine Gebäude zum " Segnen, als Pferdeställe und Viehstadeln und Hühnerstangen; lasse sie gesegnet sein durch mein " Blut und deine Macht."

"Sei mir zur Freude, Du Allermächtigster, meiner Eltern Erhalter, mein Beschützer und " meines Lebens Beschirmer! Ich flehe zu Dir aus Fleisches und Blutes Kraft: Empfange die " Speise, die ich Dir darbringe zu Deinem Unterhalt und zu meines Leibes Freude; bewahre mich " als Dein gutes Kind, und ich werde Dich dankend preisen. Bei des allmächtigsten, meines " eigenen Gottes Hilfe, erhöre mich! Was ich aus Nachlässigkeit etwa Unvollkommenes gegen " Dich gethan habe, das virgiss! Aber bewahre es treu im Gedächtniss, dass ich meine Gaben " auf ehrbare Weise meinen Eltern zu Ehren und zur Freude und zur Vergeltung abgetragen habe. " Ueberdies küsse ich drei Mal niederfallend die Erde. Sei mit mir schnell im Thun und Friede " sei mit Dir bis hierher."

In Wierland wurden die heil. Bäume *Hie-* oder *Pelgepuud*, in Harrien *warjo-puud*—"Schutzbäume" genannt. Das *hie* wird von unsern Sprachkennern gemeiniglich durch *heilig* übersetzt, andere wollen darunter einen Hain verstehen; von unserm Nichtkennerstandpunkte müssen wir bemerken, wie letztere Erklärung bezüglich auf den einzelnen Baum durchaus unstatthaft erscheint.[2] *Pelg*[3] soll nach *Herrn Lagus Taara's* Namen in der Kindersprache bedeuten."

The following two invocations to the Serpent are translations from the Finnish, which are given in the original work in parallel columns.

"O du Schlange, Unterird'sche,
Erdkuchen, Erdbrötchen,
Unter die Erd' hinab neun Klaftern,
In den Fels hinein acht Ellen!
Hülfe, Kehl', Hülfe, Seel',
Hülfe, lieber, Herr Gott!
Hülfe, Hülfe helfe dir,
Den gesund *Taara* geschaffen
Von der Mutter Leib bis sum Lebensend'!
Silber auf des Argen Zipfel,
Weisses Silber sei dem Feinde!

Spruch gegen den Unterirdischen.

Erdväterchen,
Erdmütterchen,
Erdjüngferchen.
Rasengrossmütterchen,
Euch des Silbers Weisses bring' ich:
Gebt mir Helle gegen Schmerzen,
Gebt Gesundheit ihr dem Siechen,
Bringe dann euch meinen Dank dar!

---

[1] Wortgetreu aus dem Estnischen übersetzt, wie Hr. Lagus das Opfergebet aus dem Munde eines Fellinschen Esten niedergeschrieben.

[2] Das Wort *Hie* hängt mit dem Finnischen *Hiisi* zusammen. Vgl. *Neus*, Ehstnische Volkslieder, S. 208. *Sj.*

[3] *Pelg* bedeutet eigentlich "Furcht," im Dorpater Dialekt. *S.*

Streckt sich jemand erhitzt auf den feuchten Erdboden, oder setzt er sich oder ein Glied seines Leibes im heissen Dampfbade dem kalten Luftzuge aus, so entsteht nicht selten ein feiner, brennend juckender Hautausschlag, der ausschwitzt und später eine Kruste bildet. Mit dem Abfallen dieser ist die Krankheit beendet und ohne weiteres Genesung eingetreten (vgl. *Hupel*, nord. Miscel. III. 227). Diese Krankheit schreibt aber der Ehste dem Anhauche der Unterirdischen zu, die er gestört zu haben vermeint, und soll sie nach ihnen *maa alused* oder *maa hingamine* (Erdhauch; das norweg. *alvgust*, Elbhauch, s. *Grimm* a. a. O. S. 430) benennen (s. *Rosenpl.* a. a. O. I. 33 f.). Um den Zorn der Unterirdischen zu besänftigen und von ihnen Heilung zu erlangen, schabt er nun als Opfer auf die Stätte etwas von seinem Silberschmuck oder einer Silbermünze, nachdem er sie dreimal mit der Sonne um den erkrankten Theil bewegt (vgl. unten die Ammerkung zu No. 31, welches letztere jedoch auch scheint unterlassen zu werden (s. *Hupel*, topogr. Nachricht, II. 141). Dazu spricht er dann die Formel. Dieses Opfer geschabten Silbers ist bei ähnlichen Anlässen auch in Schweden üblich; der Opfergebrauch indess umständlicher, s. E. M. *Arndt*, Reise durch Schweden III. 15 f.

Dass aber zu diesem Opfer das edle Silber genommen wird, scheint sich aus der Vorstellung zu erklären, welche Ehsten und Schweden von den Unterirdischen haben. *Lagus* erhielt von den felliner Ehsten folgendes Bruchstück:

Sie, die kleinen Unterird'schen,
Die geheimen Schmid' Allvaters,
Schafften ihr Geschäft in Nächten,
In den Nächten Mühgeschäfte;
Tags, da war der Ruhe Weile.

Nach anderer Angabe hört man in schweigsamer Mitternacht, hält man das Ohr an die Erde, das Schmeiden der Unterirdischen in den sieben Nächten von Weihnachten bis zum Neujhar und kann selbst unterscheiden, ob unter den Hämmern Eisen, Silber oder Gold erklingt. Nach einer dritten Angabe, die auch als Lied vorhanden war, waren es wieder die Unterirdischen, welche dem Schlangenkönige seine Krone geschmiedet hatten. Der blendende Glanz dieser Krone lockte sämmtliche Schlangen heran, dass sie in dem Sirtsosoo westlich vom Peipussee um den Konig einen Haufen von der Höhe eines grossen Heuschobers bildeten, aus welchem das Haupt des Königs gleich der Sonne hervorleuchtete."

APPENDIX B.

Abstract of the Níla-Mata, by Professor E. B. Cowell.

It is mentioned in the Rájatarangiṇí that "the Bauddhas, in their hatred of the Śástras, "abolished the ceremonial laid down by the Níla-puráṇa;" but the work entitled the Níla-Mata can hardly be the puráṇa there alluded to.[1] It is written in a very modern style, but, like other similar recent compilations, it may be founded on old materials. Much of it is occupied with the instructions of the Snake-king Níla to the people of Kashmir; but it is singular that Snake Worship is hardly alluded to in the copious list of offerings there enjoined throughout the Hindu year. The earlier portion of the work wears a partially Vaishṇava character, but some Śaiva legends occur in the latter portion.

---

[1] Similarly the *Nandi-puráṇa* mentioned in the Rájat. I. 123, can hardly be the work described by Professor Aufrecht, in his Catalogue of the Bodleian MSS., p. 81.

The two manuscripts used for the present analysis contain respectively 81 pages and 312 pages; each manuscript has 15 lines in a page, but in the latter manuscript the pages are much smaller and the letters much larger. Both are very inaccurately written, and there are many variations in their respective texts. The poem seems to contain about 1,450 ślokas. It is written in the ordinary Anushṭubh metre, and is supposed to be a continuation of the Mahábhárata, and consequently to be recited by Vaiśampáyana to Janamejaya, the great-grandson of Arjuna.

The poem opens with Janamejaya's asking Vaiśampáyana why the king of Kashmir is not represented as joining in the Mahábhárata war, although the maṇḍala of Kashmir was the principal one in the world. Vaiśampáyana replies by relating that the king of Kashmir, Gonanda, had been slain by Kṛishṇa among the Gándháras on the Indus. Kṛishṇa appoints his rival's widow as regent, and her son (Gonanda according to one manuscript, Govinda according to the other,[1]) did not join either Páṇḍavas or Kauravas on account of his youth. This leads to some questions on the mythological history of Kashmir, and Vaiśampáyana then repeats a dialogue which had taken place between King Gonanda II. and the sage Brihadaśwa. This dialogue is properly the Níla-Mata.

Bṛihadaśwa commences with an account of the destruction of the world by water at the end of the previous Manwantara, the preservation of Manu and his seeds in a ship which is fastened to the mountain now called Nau-bandhana, in the west of Kashmir; and when the world of living creatures is created again, Deví, as Kaśmírá, becomes the land of Kashmir. The snakes, persecuted by Garuḍa, take refuge in the lake Satídeśa, and anoint Níla as their king. Kashmir is subsequently ravaged by a demon named Jalodbhava, who is at length killed by Vishṇu. Kaśyapa then asks Vishṇu that the country may be inhabited by gods and men, but the snake-king demurs. Kaśyapa threatens him with Piśáchas as his neighbours, and tells him that there is an island in "the sea of sand" inhabited by Piśáchas, Daityas, and Yakshas. Their king, Nikumbha, always sets out on the full moon of the month Chaitra, for an annual expedition of six months against his rebellious subjects; he passes the remaining six months in peace on the Himálaya. In future he threatens these six months will be passed with the snakes. Níla is in great distress, until at last Vishṇu, pitying him, promises that the arrangement shall only last one set of four ages, and after that time the snakes shall be allowed to have only men as their neighbours. "In whatever place " belonging to any snake men shall dwell, men shall honour him with flowers, incense, and unguents, " with various offerings of food and dances. And whatever people shall keep the good customs " declared by thee, they shall dwell in this country, blessed with cattle, corn, and wealth." The country is thenceforward inhabited for six months in every year by men who come in on the full moon of Chaitra, and sow and reap their corn, but clear off in Áświayuja, when the country is again given over to the Piśáchas. The various deities become the different rivers; thus Umá becomes the Vitastá, Lakshmí the Viśokí, &c.

This predicted occupation of Kashmir by the Piśáchas continues for four ages. At the end of that time the human inhabitants had, as usual, reaped their grain and cleared off from the country before the full moon of Áśwayuja; but a certain Brahman named Chandradeva remained with the Piśáchas. One day he wanders disconsolate, till he comes to the place in the mountains where Níla holds his court. He propitiates the Snake-king by a hymn of praise, and Níla grants him a boon. He asks that Kashmir may thenceforth be inhabited by men without fear of perpetual emigrations. Níla grants it: "Thus be it, O best of Brahmans; let men always dwell " here, but observing my words revealed to me by Keśava." The Brahman dwells at his court until the month Chaitra comes round, and the human inhabitants flock in from all sides with their king Víryodaya. Chandradeva goes to him and declares what he has seen and heard, and the king and his people agree to observe the words of Níla, and thenceforth they dwell undisturbed in Kashmir (cf. Rájat., I. 182), which gives a somewhat different legend.

[1] This is the Gonarda II. of the Rájat., I. 62–82.

Gonanda then asks Bṛihadaśwa what "the words of Níla" were. The sage then repeats the lesson as it was uttered by Níla himself to the Brahman. Here follows a long list of the principal rites and ceremonies throughout the year, beginning with the full moon of Áśwayuja; it contains some curious matter, but the Nâgas are hardly ever mentioned.

At the close, Vaiśampáyana interrupts the original dialogue by the remark that Gonanda did not obey these laws, and consequently fell at Mathurá, being slain by Balabhadra (cf. Rájat., I. 59–63).

Gonanda then asks for some account of the principal Nâgas who dwell in Kashmir. A long list of names follows, and some legends; and also a list of the principal deities worshipped there, and the benefits derived from visiting their shrines. Bṛihadaśwa then relates some legends connected with several holy places in Kashmir.

The poem winds up with a return to the original interlocutors. Janamejaya asks Vaiśampáyana to eulogize the glory of the river Vitastá, which closes the work.

APPENDIX C.

THE following translations of the rock-cut edicts of Aśoka are reproduced here without note or comment, but literally, as they have already appeared several times in print. None of those yet given to the public can be considered as either perfect or complete, but the sense can in all cases be gathered from them, and they are sufficient for our present purposes. Two other copies of these edicts have been discovered since these translations were made,—one at the foot of the Himalayas, north of Meerut, and another in Cuttack. When these are published a more perfect translation may be possible. Those who desire further information are referred to Prinsep's translation, J. A. S. B., VII. p. 219, et seqq.; to Professor Wilson's, J. R. A. S., XII. 153, et seqq.; to Burnouf, "Lotus de la Bonne Loi," Appendix, p. 659, et seqq.; and to Mrs. Speir's Life in Ancient India, p. 230, et seqq. The object for which they are introduced here is neither to explain their text nor to comment on their doctrines, but to afford the reader of the previous pages a picture of Buddhism as it existed B.C. 250, in the words of its most ardent devotee and its principal promoter. This is done in order that he may compare it with Buddhism as presented 300 years afterwards in the sculptures at Sanchi; or as it appears 300 years after that time, in A.D. 350 at Amravati. This completes the means of comparison in so far as this work is concerned; but, as already mentioned, the frescoes at Ajanta afford a fourth picture 200 years more modern than Amravati; and again, 300 after that we have the Thibetan Lalita-Vistara. Unfortunately we still want, and it is feared are little likely to obtain, any contemporary record at the beginning of our series, 300 years before Aśoka, but it is satisfactory to know that materials now exist for illustrating the other five epochs of Buddhism.

TABLET I.

This is the Edict of the beloved of the Gods, the Raja Piyadasi. The putting to death of animals is to be entirely discontinued, and no convivial meeting is to be held, for the beloved of the Gods, Raja Piyadasi, remarks many faults in such assemblies. There is but one assembly, indeed, which is approved of by the Raja, * * * which is that of the great kitchen of Raja Piyadasi; every day hundreds of thousands of animals have been slaughtered for virtuous purposes, but now, although this pious Edict is proclaimed that animals may be killed for good purposes, and such is the practice, yet as the practice is not determined, these presents are proclaimed, that hereafter they shall not be killed.

TABLET II.

In all the conquered territories of the Raja Piyadasi, even unto the ends of the earth, as in Chola, in Pîda (the kingdom of Satyaputra), in Keralaputra (or Malabar), and in Tambapanni (or Ceylon), and to Antiochus the Yona Raja, and to those princes who are allied with him, it is proclaimed that two designs have been cherished by Piyadasi,—one regarding men, and one relating to animals,—that everywhere wholesome vegetables, roots, and fruit-trees shall be cultivated, and that on the roads wells shall be dug and trees planted, to give enjoyment for both men and animals.

TABLET III.

King Piyadasi says:—This was ordained by me when I had been twelve years inaugurated in the conquered country; that amongst those united in the law, whether strangers or my own subjects, quinquennial expiation shall be held for the enforcement of moral obligations, as—duty to parents, friends, children, relations, Brahmins, and Sramans. Liberality is good, non-injury of living creatures is good, abstinence from prodigality and slander is good. The Assembly itself will instruct the faithful in the virtues here enumerated, both by explanation and by example.

TABLET IV.

In past times, during many hundreds of years, there have prevailed destruction of life and the injury of living beings, want of respect for kindred, Brahmins and Sramans. But now King Piyadasi practises the Law, the drum sounds, and the Law is proclaimed by processions of cars and elephants, and displays of fireworks. That which had not been seen for centuries is now seen * * * in consequence of King Piyadasi's commands that the Law be practised * * * And Piyadasi will cause the observance of the Law to increase; and the sons and grandsons and great-grandsons of Piyadasi will cause its observance to increase until the *Kalpa* of destruction.

TABLET V.

They (the Mahâmâtra) shall also be spread among the warriors, the Brahmins, the mendicants, the destitute, and others, without any obstruction, for the happiness of the well-disposed, in order to loosen the bonds of those who are bound, and liberate those who are confined, through the means of holy wisdom disseminated by pious teachers, and they will proceed to the outer cities and fastnesses of my brother and sister, and wherever are any other of my kindred; and the ministers of morals, those who are appointed as superintendents of morals, shall, wherever the moral law is established, give encouragement to the charitable and those addicted to virtue. With this intent this Edict is written, and let my people obey it.

TABLET VI.

Hitherto attention has not been given to reports and affairs incessantly, or at all times, and on this account I decree that at all times,—even when I take recreation in the apartments of the women and children, or in conversation, or in riding, or in gardens, in all places,—there shall be informers (*Prativedaka*) to make known to me the wishes of the people; and everywhere I will occupy myself with the welfare of the people; and whatever I declare, or whatever the Mahâmâtra shall declare, shall be referred to the Council for decision. Thus shall reports be made to me. This have I everywhere and in every place commanded, for to me there is not satisfaction in the pursuit of worldly affairs; the most worthy pursuit is the prosperity of the whole world. My whole endeavour is to be blameless towards all creatures, to make them happy here below, and enable them hereafter to attain *Swarga*. With this view this moral Edict has been written: may it long endure; and may my sons and great-grandsons after me also labour for the universal good; but this is difficult without extreme exertion.

The small figures in the text mark the beginnings of the lines of the different inscriptions.

I. . . . . gahapatisa Maditisa duhutuya Uvasikâya, Sagha-Rakhitâya, Sabhâsakâya, Sabhagirinaya, tina ka putana cha Dâsa Ajunasa, cha Dâsa Ghasa, bhatiyâna . . .

I. (Gift) of the householder *Maditi's* daughters *Urvâsika*, *Sangha-Rakshitâ*, *Sabhâsakâ*, (and) *Sabhâgirinâ*, together with their sons, and the slave *Arjuna*, and the slave (*San*)*gha*, . . .

II. Bodhiya Nâgamuliya cha Balinada Bodhiya Pusiliyayam deya dhama. Bhagineyânam, Jâmâtukânam, cha natitam natukânam, cha savasa cha hidâswa, ghatha Bhagavata mahâchetiye yaghâ paṭâ sabada kosa dantisa dânam.

II. Pious gift of the Buddhist *Nâgamuli*, and of the Buddhist *Balinanda*, Pusiliyas (? descendants of Pusili).

Gift of their sisters, of their sons-in-law, and of their (—?—), and of all friends, to the great Chaitya of Bhagavata of a slab . . . . enshrined tooth (?) . . . .

III. . . . . tara giha rega . . nadera vathadi parachitikaya (2) ghadhayaya hâlikaya napachitika . . hodiyada . . (3) nâgiyatama dhamateri thapita (6 letters) ta deya (4) dhama d(—?—) thabho.

III. Pious gift of a pillar (the remainder is unintelligible).

IV. Sidham ! Tunulaurakasa Gahapatisa Pusilisa-putasa, Sethivadi-cha Sasivakasa,(2) gharaniya cha Munuriya, Jâmâtukasa-cha Vachitasa, jâmâtukasa-cha Vichitasa, jâmâtuka-(3)sa cha Mahajevasa, Bâlikaya Budhâya, Bâlikaya Chandapusaya, Bâlikaya Chamaya, deya-dhama (4) pataka ba.

IV. Be it auspicious ! Pious gift of two slab-pillars of *Tunulauraka*, the householder, son of *Pusili*, and of *Sasivaka*, the chief Banker, and of his wife *Munuri*, and of his son-in-law *Vachita*, and of his son-in-law *Vichita*, and of his son-in-law *Mahajeva* ; his daughter *Budhâ*, his daughter *Chandrapusa*, (and) his daughter *Charmâ*.

V. Gadhikasa haghasa, (2) saputakasa, saduhu-(3)-tukasa chetiya thabho (4) dânam.

V. Pillar gift to the Chaitya of *Hagha* of Gadhika, together with his son and his daughter.

VI. . . (Nâ) râyana dhama . . . latiputasa . . gahapatisa Dhana Mi(trasa) . . (j)âmâtrika . . . . sa saduhu(trika)sa putana dhisa . . prapuri . . . putra.

VI. Imperfect,—but enough remains to show that the inscription is of the usual form, and records the gift of the householder *Dhana-mitra*, and of his son-in-law, his daughter, &c.

VII. Most illegible.

VII. At the end of the last line but one I read the word *Mahâchetiya*.

VIII. Kabu 5 ravatha vasa Budhi sama . . . ya putasa mulihiri Sagha-Mitrakasa Akhatisa Dhawa Siriya Ba- . . siriya Saghaya Ayabaniga sava.

VIII. This inscription is engraved on five small pillars or stelæ, on one of the sculptured representations of a Stupa. Many of the letters are quite clear and distinct; but no part can be read with certainty.

IX. Munâkala . . kumudaputa rakasa Vâhilasa Kanhiya putasa ta . . ye . . Budhika sa Bhâriya . . . sa . . . Kusuma dhudu Kanayatasa dâsadati mita badavasa deya dhama. Maharaja Yâdnya Siri Sadakani vatha.

IX. This is the most valuable of all the Amravati inscriptions ; but unfortunately the slab has not come to England, and there is only a copy made by a draughtsman to refer to. The title of Maharaja is distinct in the last line but one, and the name following it appears to be *Yâdnya*, who was one of the last of the Andhra kings.

X. radahapachepaya . . kasayanadha . . . kasapanoraya.

X. Not read.

XI. . . patiputasa gahapatino Haghasabhaya cha Savanaya Chetiya vetika cha paṭâ deya dhama.

XI. Pious gift to the Chaitya of a *Vetika* and a slab, of the householder ——*patiputra,* and of *Haghasabhâ,* and of *Savanâ.*

XII. Rakhadiya cha Datiya padaka pata patitatha.

XII. Not read.

XIII. Lonavalavakasa, Saghirakhitasa-cha, Maritisa-cha, Bhâriyayo Saghaya-cha, Sagha-dâsiya-cha, Kamudaya-cha, danam.

XIII. Gift of *Lonavalavaka,* and *Sanghirakshita,* and *Mariti,* and of their wives *Sanghâ,* and *Sanghadâsi,* and *Kumâdri.*

XIV. Akarâ Mâtriya dânam patika.

XIV. Gift of Akarâ's mother of a slab-pillar.

XV. . . daki chasa gahapatisa rana aswas, putasa . . . . na, saBhariyasa, sa-Putakasa sakhatakasa deya dhama.

XV. Pious gift of ——*dakicha,* the householder, son of *Rana-Aswa,* . . . together with his wife, and his son, and his (—?—).

XVI. Akhasavâdi cha Samariti gahapatina tuno Ajunasa deya dhama unisa.

XVI. Nineteen pious gifts of *Akhasavâdi* and *Samariti,* householders.

XVII. Valikachakasa gahapatino Pâpino bhâriya-cha Kanhâya paputikasa dânam.

XVII. Gift of *Pâpi,* householder of *Valikachaka,* and of his wife the grand-daughter of Kanhâ.

XVIII. Therasa Chetiyavadakasa Bhayata Budhino, Bhaginiya Bhikhuniya Budhaya-cha dana deya dhama Siha-thâna.

XVIII. Pious gift of a Lion-pedestal of the *Thera* (*Sthâvira* or Elder) *Bhayata Budhi,* the enlarger of the Chaitya, and of his sister the Nun *Budhâ.*

XIX. . . . virapurakana puma devaputana dulena krita.
Agheya Vachakiṭa Vira Budharakhitasa atevasinaya deya dânam.

XIX. ——(first part not read.)
Pious gift of *Agheya Vachakita Vira,* pupil of Budha Rakshita.

XX. Bâlikâhi sahina tihisa nitya sanigama Khatana gena sahadama deya dhamana Dhankakata mahachetiya chetiya paṭâ be 2, bataka 3, datisa pupha gatiya paṭasa . . cha . . hâ cha nebatasa tha . . ṭḥa Râjagiriyanam nata vadâre paditha pita sanasa dânam chahitasa pathati.

XX. Parts of this inscription are not intelligible; but enough has been made out to show that it records the gift of two slabs and three slab pillars by certain persons of *Râjagiri,* the ancient capital of Bihâr.

A. Cunningham,
Major-General, R.E.

NOTE.

The principal points of interest in these inscriptions, with reference to the preceding text, are the allusions to the Tooth relic in No. II., to Yâdnya Śri in No. IX., and to the Mahâ Chaitya of Dhanakakata in the last. If on further investigation their correctness should be established, the history of the monument can hardly be considered doubtful.—J. F.

TABLET VII.

The beloved of the Gods, the Raja Piyadasi, desires that the ascetics of all the different beliefs (the *Pâshaṇḍa*) may everywhere dwell (unmolested): they all aim at moral restraint and purity of disposition; but men have various opinions and various desires, and the ascetics obtain either all or merely a part (of what they want). However, even for him who does not obtain a large gift or alms, purity of disposition, gratitude, and steady devotion is desirable.

TABLET VIII.

In past times Kings were addicted to travelling about, to companions, to going abroad, to hunting, and similar amusements; but Piyadasi, the beloved of the Gods, having been ten years inaugurated, by him easily awakened, that moral festival is adopted (which consists) in seeing and bestowing gifts on Brahminas and Sramanas, in seeing and giving gold to Elders, and overseeing the country and the people; the institution of moral laws and the investigation of morals. Such are the devices for the removal of apprehension, and such are the different pursuits of the favourite of the Gods, King Piyadasi.

TABLET IX.

The beloved of the Gods, the Raja Piyadasi, thus says:—Every man that is, celebrates various occasions of festivity, as,—on the removal of incumbrances, on invitations, on marriages, on the birth of a son, or on setting forth on a journey,—on these and other occasions a man makes various rejoicings. Such festivals are fruitless—are vain; but the festival that bears great fruit is the festival of duty (the *dharma mangala*), such as the respect of the servant to his master; reverence for holy teachers is good; liberality to Brahmins and Sramanas is good. These and other such acts constitute verily the festival of duty, and this is to be cherished as a father by a son, or a dependant by his master; * * * for the establishment of this object virtuous donations are made, for there is no donation equal to the gift of duty; * * * benevolence contracted between friends * * * is mere chaff; * * * by these means let a man seek *Swarga*.

TABLET X.

The beloved of the Gods, the Prince Piyadasi, does not esteem glory and fame as of great value; and besides, for a long time it has been my fame and that of my people that the observance of moral duty and the service of the virtuous should be practised, for this is to be done. This is the fame that the beloved of the Gods desires; and, inasmuch as the beloved of the Gods excels (he holds) all such reputation as no real reputation, but such as may be that of the unrighteous,—pain and chaff; for it may be acquired by crafty and unworthy persons, and by whatever further effort it is acquired it is worthless and a source of pain.

TABLET XI.

Thus says the beloved of the Gods, King Piyadasi: There is no gift like the gift of virtue, whether it be the praise of virtue, the apportionment of virtue, or relationship of virtue. This (gift) is the cherishing of slaves and dependants, pious devotion to mother and father, generous gifts to friends and kinsmen, Brahminas and Sramanas.

Respect for the life of creatures is good; this is what ought to be said by a father, by a son, by a brother, by a friend, by an acquaintance, by a relation, and even by mere neighbours: this is well; this is to be done. He who acts thus is honoured in this world, and in the other world infinite merit results from this gift of the Law.

TABLET XII.

Piyadasi, the beloved of the Gods, honours all forms of religious belief, whether professed by ascetics or by householders, both by giving alms and by other modes of showing respect. But the beloved of the Gods does not esteem alms and marks of respect so highly as the increase of that which is the essence of renown. Now the increase of that which is essential for all forms of belief is of many kinds, but nevertheless the base of it is, for each of them, praise in words. Further, a man must honour his own faith without blaming that of another, and thus will but little that is wrong occur. There are even circumstances under which the faith of others should be honoured, and in acting thus, according to circumstances, a man increases his own faith and injures that of others. He who acts differently diminishes his own faith and injures that of others; he, whoever he may be, who honours his own faith and blames that of others out of devotion to his own, and says, moreover, Let us make our faith conspicuous; that man, I say, who acts thus merely injures the faith he holds: concord alone therefore is desirable. Further, let men listen to each law and follow it with submission, for such is the desire of the King, beloved of the Gods. Further, may men of all faiths abound in knowledge and prosper in virtue! And those who have faith in this or that religion should repeat this:—The King, beloved of the Gods, does not value alms or marks of respect so much as the increase of that which is the essence of renown and the multiplication of all beliefs. To this end great ministers of law, and superintendents of women * * * and other officers are appointed, and the fruit of this institution will be the speedy increase of all religions, as well as the illumination of the law.

Extract from Tablet XIII., the rest being so injured that it does not admit of continuous translation:—

"There is not in either class of the heretics of men, a procedure marked by such grace * * * nor so glorious, or friendly, nor even so extremely liberal as Devánampiyo's injunction for the non-injury and content of living creatures; * * * and the Greek king besides, by whom the kings of Egypt, Ptolemaios and Antigonos and Magas, * * * both here and in foreign countries, everywhere wherever they go, the religious ordinances of Devánampiyo effect conversion. Conquest is of every description, but the conquest which bringeth joy, springing from pleasant emotions becometh joy itself. The victory of virtue is happiness * * * such victory is desired in things of this world and things of the next world. (J. R. A. S., XII. 233.)

Translation of the Bhabra Inscription, by Professor Wilson.

Piyadasi, the King, to the venerable Assembly of Magadha, commands the infliction of little pain and indulgence to animals.

It is verily known, I proclaim, to what extent my respect and favour (are placed) in Buddha, and in the Law, and in the Assembly.

Whatsoever (words) have been spoken by the divine Buddha, they have all been well said, and in them verily I declare that capability of proof is to be discerned; so that the pure law (which they teach) will be of long duration, as far as I am worthy (of being obeyed).

For these I declare are the precepts of the Law of the principal discipline (Vinaya), having overcome the oppressions of the Aryas and future perils, (and refuted) the songs of the Munis, the Sûtras of the Munis, (the practices) of inferior ascetics, the censure of a light world, and (all) false doctrines.

These things, as declared by the divine Buddha, I proclaim, and I desire them to be regarded as the precepts of the Law.

And that as many as there may be, male and female mendicants, may hear and observe them, as well also as male and female followers (of the laity).

These things I affirm, and have caused this to be written (to make known to you) that such will be my intention.

APPENDIX D.

THE Hindu races worship three classes of deities,—the Grâma devatâ, or village god; the Kula devatâ, or household god; and the Ishṭa devatâ, the personal or patron god.

Snake Worship is general throughout peninsula India, both of the sculptured form and of the living creature. The sculpture is invariably of the form of the Nag or Cobra, and almost every hamlet has its Serpent deity. Sometimes this is a single snake, the hood of the Cobra being spread open. Occasionally the sculptured figures are nine in number, and this form is called the "Nao nag," and is intended to represent a parent snake and eight of its young, but the prevailing form is that of two snakes twining in the manner of the Esculapian rod.

Some Hindus hold that the living snake is not worshipped as a devatâ by any Hindu sect, but is reverenced in commemoration of some ancient event. If this be correct, it has, perhaps, relation to some astronomical occurrence. Others, however, maintain, that it is as a devatâ that it is worshipped; but whatever be the origin of the adoration, the living snake is worshipped everywhere throughout Southern India. On these occasions the worshippers resort to the snake's residence, called in Urdu the سانپ کي هوٹ Sāmp kī hūṭ, which they ornament with streaks of vermilion and daubs of turmeric, and of wheat flour, and they hang garlands of flowers near, strung on white cotton thread, and laid over wooden frames. Also, in the ninth Sravan, which occurs in the rainy season, the "Nâg panchamî" festival occurs, on which Hindus go in search of snakes, or have them brought to their houses by the "Sanpeli," the snake charmers who snare them. The snakes are then worshipped, and offerings are made to them of milk and in nearly every house, figures of snakes, drawn on paper, are fixed on the walls and worshipped. Those who visit the snakes' hūṭs, plant sticks around the hole, and wind white cotton thread around and over the sticks. The Mahratta women go, a number together, to the snakes' hut, and, joining hands, circle five times round and round it, singing songs, and then prostrate themselves. They pour milk into the hole (they ought to give it to the snake). They hang festoons of Chernhela flowers and cucumber fruit, and sprinkle a mixture of sugar and flour (Sakr Suji.)

On the 25th January 1868 I halted in the temple of the Grâma devatâ of Assaye, where Sir A. Wellesley defeated the Bhonslah. I there saw Hanuman with a lingam, and Bassava, the bull, and the tulsi plant, and on the western wall of the temple was a cobra snake. drawn in white, which the worshippers said was travelling to Ceylon or Lankâ. They laughed when I said he would be long on his journey.

In Southern India the deity under whose name the snake is worshipped in Subrāmănī, whose shrine is said to be in the western part of Mysore, and the image there is described as a shapeless lump of earth.

I have only once seen living snakes in the form of the Esculapian rod. It was at Ahmednuggur, in 1841, in a clear moonlight night. They dropped into the garden from over the thatched roof of my house, and stood erect. They were all cobras, and no one could have seen them without at once recognizing that they were in congress. Captain Havelock, to whom I showed these remarks, mentioned in reply that he once, in broad daylight, in the jungles, saw pythons, just as I have sketched them,[1] in the singular form of the Esculapian rod, but many natives mention having seen this sight. Natives of India believe that it is most fortunate to witness snakes so engaged, and they believe that if they can throw a cloth at the pair to touch them with it, the cloth becomes a representative form of Lakshmî of the highest virtue, and is taken home to their houses and preserved as such.

---

[1] A sketch of the serpents in this attitude accompanied the letter, but not sufficiently perfect to enable a woodcut to be made from it.—J. F.

No Hindu, ordinarily, will kill a snake, but turns aside on seeing it. Young men who have been educated at English schools, however, have no such reserve; and a Mahratta Brahmin has informed me that he has killed three of them.

Snakes are kept in houses in Ceylon and Guzerat, partly seemingly as objects of worship, and partly to destroy rats, but no similar practice prevails in the south-eastern parts of peninsula India.

CH. ED. BALFOUR, M.D.

Secunderabad, 23d January 1868.

MEMORANDUM ON SNAKE WORSHIP.

On the Nâg Panchmee festival, which occurs, I think, on the fifth day of the Hindu month Bhadoon, in the rainy season, Nâgs (Cobras) are worshipped by most of the lower classes of the people in the Deccan, and more particularly in the Shorapore country. The principal of those classes in Shorapore are the Beydars, who are decidedly an aboriginal tribe, which is numerous in Mysore and in the southern Mahratta country. The Shorapore class came from Mysore and settled in Shorapore and the Rachore Doab, under chieftains who were originally servants of the Rajas of Beejanugger, but who became subjects of the Kings of Golburgah and Beedar, and of Beejapore after the fall of the Beejanugger state. The Beydars have not mingled with other Hindu castes, and though they profess to be Hindus, they adhere to many of their original superstitions and ceremonies, which have nothing to do with Hinduism; they have little or no reverence for Brahmins, what there is indeed being sparingly afforded, except by the higher classes among them, who have adopted them as priests. The Snake festival, therefore, has very little of the elements of Brahminism in it, if there are any. The ceremonies are very simple: the worshippers bathe, mark their foreheads with red colour, and in small parties, generally families who know each other, go to places where Cobras (Nâgs) are known to live or to frequent. There are generally sacred stones in such places, to which offerings of flowers, ghee, &c., are made, and the stones are anointed with red colour and ground turmeric, prayers and invocations being made to the local spirit of the place and to the Serpents. Small new earthen saucers, filled with milk, are then placed near the stones, or near the Snake's hole, if there be one. Cobras are fond of milk, and are believed to watch the ceremony, coming out of their holes and drinking the milk, even while the worshippers are near, or sitting at a little distance to see if their offering is received. Should the Snake appear and drink, it is esteemed a very fortunate circumstance for the worshippers. Should the Snake not appear, the worshippers after waiting awhile, depart, and visit the place next morning, when the result is anxiously examined; if the milk has disappeared, the rite has been accepted, but not in so marked a degree as if the reptile had come out at once. These ceremonies end with a feast.

Snake Worship is especially resorted to on behalf of children; and the women and children of a family invariably accompany the male head, not only at the annual festival, but whenever a vow has been made to a Serpent Deity. The first hair of a child which is shaved off when it has passed teething, and other infantile ailments, is frequently dedicated to a Serpent. On such occasions the child is taken to the locality of the vow, the usual ceremonies are performed, and with other offerings of flowers, &c., the child's hair is combined. In every case a feast follows, cooked near the spot, and Brahmins who attend receive largess and alms, and relations and friends receive invitations.

In the Shakti ceremonies, Poorna-abhishék, which belong, I think, to aboriginal customs, the worship of the Snake forms a portion, as emblematical of energy and wisdom. Most of these ceremonies are, however, of an inconceivably obscene and licentious character. They are not confined to the lowest classes, though rarely perhaps resorted to by Brahmins; but many of the middle class sects, of obscure origin and denomination, practise them in secret, under a strange delusion that the divine energy of nature is to be obtained thereby, with exemption from earthly troubles.

Although Snake Worship ordinarily belongs professedly to the descendants of aboriginal tribes, yet Brahmans never or rarely pass them over, and the Nâg Panchmee is observed as a festival of kindly greeting and visiting between families and friends—as a day of gifts of new clothes or ornaments to wives or children, &c.

The worship of Grâm Deotas, or village divinities, is universal all over the Deccan, and indeed I believe throughout India. These divinities have no temples nor priests. Sacrifice and oblation is made to them at sowing time and harvest, for rain or fair weather, in time of cholera, malignant fever, or other disease or pestilence. The Nâg is always one of the Grâm Deota, the rest being known by local names. The Grâm Deota are known as heaps of stones, generally in a grove or quiet spot near every village, and are smeared some with black and others with red colour.

Nâg is a common name both for males and females among all classes of Hindus, from Brahmans downwards to the lowest classes of Sudras and Mléchhas. Nâgo Rao, Nâgojee, &c., are common Mahratta names, as Nâgappa, Nâgowa, and the like among the Canarese and Telugoo population.

No Hindu will kill a Nâg or Cobra willingly. Should any one be killed within the precincts of a village, by Mahomedans or others, a piece of copper money is put into its mouth, and the body is burned with offerings to avert the evil.

It is, perhaps, remarkable that the Snake festival is held after the season or at the season of casting the skin, and when the Snake, addressed or worshipped, is supposed to have been purified. Some Brahmans always keep the skin of a Nâg in one of their sacred books.

In reference to the lower castes alluded to, I may mention those who practise Snake Worship with the greatest reverence:—1. Beydars. 2. Dhungars or shepherds, Aheers or milkmen, Waddiwars or stone-masons, Khungins or rope-makers, Brinjaras and other wandering tribes, Mangs, Dhérs, and Chumars, Ramoosees, Bhils, Gonds, and Koles, all which I believe, with many others, to be descendants of aboriginal tribes, partly received within the pale of Hinduism.

Lingayets, who are schismatics from Hinduism, and who deny *in toto* the religious supremacy of the Brahmans, are nevertheless Snake Worshippers, many of them bearing the name Nâg, both male and female.

I cannot speak of the North of India, but in the whole of the South of India, from the Nerbudda to Cape Comorin, Snake Worship is now existent.

MEADOWS TAYLOR, Col. M. N. I.

The festival of the Moonsa Poojah takes place each year about the end of August.

The tribes that I have seen present at it were Bhowries, Dhangas, and Santhals, and the locality was at a large jungle village beside a range of low hills, to the west of the hill Beharînath, and to the south of the hill of Pachete.

The snake catchers and charmers, at this period of the year, assemble and make a tour of the neighbouring villages, carrying snakes twisted around their necks and bodies, the chief of the procession being either carried on men's shoulders, or riding on a buffalo. He generally has a rock boa or python hanging over his shoulders. The usual amount of beating of the Nagara, playing the flute, and singing, attends the procession, and large quantities of the favourite spirit "Mowha" and sweetmeats are consumed.

Presents are also made to the snake bearers, and general dissipation prevails.

A. VANS BEST, M.D.
Bengal Establishment.

NOTE.

In August last, when the first edition of this work was going to press, Professor Goldstücker brought me a note on the Nâga tribes of Cashmere which he had received from H.S.H. Prince Frederick of Schleswig-Holstein, who was then residing in the valley. My intention was to have added this note to this Appendix, but it now turns out most unfortunately that it has been mislaid and cannot be found. This is to be regretted, not only because it was an account of the Nâgas of the present day by a most intelligent and competent observer, but also because the Prince insisted most strongly on the medical qualities of the tribe, and their possession of nostrums which had been handed down from remote antiquity. This retention of the Esculapian character by the Snake Worshippers is one of the most curious points connected with the subject, but it is one that, now that attention is directed to it, will I trust meet with full elucidation from some inhabitant of the valley.

J. F.

APPENDIX E.

By General Cunningham, R.E.

The Amravati inscriptions are similar to those on the Railings and Gateways of the Buddhist Stupas and Monasteries at Bhilsa and other places. They are all written in the Pali language; and, where not injured by weather or breakage, they are generally clear and legible. With two exceptions they have been all copied by myself from the sculptured slabs, and have since been compared with the photographs. The two exceptions are Nos. II. and XI., which have been taken from Colonel Mackenzie's drawings. The former is a good copy, and is mostly legible; but the latter is unfortunately a very corrupt transcript of the most important of all the Amravati records, as it certainly contains the name of a King, which, if it had been faithfully copied, would most probably have enabled us to fix the date of the inscription.

The following translations are not offered as critical renderings of the inscriptions, but simply as free versions conveying their general meaning, which is usually confined to the specification of certain gifts made to the sacred edifice by various individuals, both priests and laymen, in which they were frequently joined by their wives and children. The same practice is still common in Burmah and in other Buddhist countries.

Some of the words which are of unusual occurrence require explanation. In No. IV. I have rendered *gharani*, by "wife," that is, the mistress of the house. The present Hindi form is *gharwâli.* The word *paṭâ* occurs three times in Nos: II., XI., and XX., and the word *pataka* three times in Nos. IV., XIV., and XX. As both words are combined with figures in No. XX., I take them to be the names of the particular gifts thus recorded, and consequently that they refer to the sculptured stones themselves. *Paṭâ* is most probably the same word as the present Hindi *Paṭao,* which means a "broad stone slab," and is specially applicable to the Amravati railing stones, in which the breadth is equal to three times the depth. Both names are derived from the Sanskrit *pâṭa,* breadth, from the root *paṭa,* to spread or extend. The word *pataka,* or in No. XX. *bataka,* is spelt with the dental *t,* and is most probably therefore not connected with *paṭa,* which invariably has the cerebral *ṭ.* I conclude that it must be the name for a railing pillar, because it is found in Nos. IV. and XIV. recorded on the tops of two of them. The name used for a square or octagonal pillar is *thabho* (see No. III.) from the Sanskrit *stambha.* In No. XX. we have a record of two *Paṭas* and three *Patakas,* which I believe to refer to three broad slab pillars of the railing, and the two architrave slabs that covered them. I cannot suggest any explanation of the word *vetika,* which occurs in No. XI., but I conclude that it is the name of some one of the sculptured slabs, as it is coupled with *paṭa.*

APPENDIX F.

WHEN I published, with the first edition of this work, the Chronological Table contained in this Appendix, I stated that it was my intention to publish elsewhere the grounds on which I had arrived at the conclusion therein summarized. That promise I have since redeemed by a paper which appeared in the Journal of the Royal Asiatic Society, (N.S. Vol. IV. pp. 81 to 137). Since then I have had occasion to go over again some of the principal points, but see no reason for deviating from the conclusions then arrived at. Of course corrections in detail here and there may be necessary, but the data on which the reasoning is based appears to me to admit of very little doubt.

The Ceylonese and Burmese date for the death of Buddha (543 B.C.) may possibly be open to correction to the extent of a few years, but there is so much more to be said for it than for any other date that has been proposed, that it must be allowed to stand for the present.

The Mauryan chronology may admit of correction to the extent of ten years, but my belief is that the dates here given for it and the succeeding dynasties down to the Christian era are very nearly certain. Nor do I see any reason for doubting the correctness of the dates of the Andhra or Andhrabitya dynasty, as taken from the Puranas.[1] It seems so consistent with all other historical facts, and all that we gather from architectural progress, or the development of the arts that I place the utmost confidence in it.

The dates of the Sâh kings are taken from Justice Newton's paper in the Journal of the Bombay Asiatic Society (Vol. VIII. p. 1 et seqq.), and agree so well with the Puranic dates of their contemporaries, the Andhras, that I have no doubt of the general correctness, and, lastly, I see nothing whatever to make me doubt that the Guptas dated from their era (318 A.D.) and the Ballabhi kings from the same era, which bore also their name. We are thus enabled to fix with very fairly approximative certainty the dates of all the kings who reigned down to the middle of the eighth century, when a revolution took place which altered the face of India, though, strange to say, we have hardly a hint of its existence in any written authority. The results, however, were that Buddhism ceased to be the religion of the state, and no known Buddhist building was erected after that date, and the religion of Jaina, with the worship of Vishṇu and Śiva, took its place. All the old dynasties came to an end, and the new Rajpoot dynasties took their rise. A new state of things was then inaugurated, which, in so far as the Hindus are concerned, where uninfluenced by the Moslem conquest, continues to the present day.

All the dynasties here quoted will be readily recognised as those published by Prinsep,[2] Wilson,[3] Thomas,[4] and others. No novelty in this respect has been attempted. It is only the arrangement that is, in some instances, somewhat different from that usually accepted. The newest list is that of the Sâh kings, which is copied with its dates from one by Mr. Justice Newton, which appeared in the "Bombay Times of India" in July last.

There are several of the dates in these tables which I would like to adjust arbitrarily to the extent of four or five years, and when I can give my reasons I shall probably do so. For the present I prefer leaving them as I have found them. They are near enough the truth for the purposes of the present work.

---

[1] General Cunningham, in the second edition of his reports just received, demurs to my conclusions regarding Gotamiputra and these Andhras by quoting Pliny against me (Reports, Introduction, p. xxiv). I most distinctly, however, decline to admit Pliny as a competent witness regarding events which, if I am right, took place more than 200 years after his death!

[2] Useful Tables, Calcutta, 1834.

[3] Vishṇu Purâṇa. London, 1840.

[4] Prinsep's Indian Antiquities. London, 1858.

20 Descents from Kaliyuga.	37 Descents in 600? Years from Yudhishṭhira.		
Kritanjaya, 1st emigrant from Kos'ala.	S'ais'unâga Dynasty.		
	S'is'unâga	691	
Raṇanjaya.	Kâkavarṇa.		
Sanjaya.	Kshemadharman.		
S'âkya.	Kshetraujas.		Buddha born, 623.
S'uddhodana.	Bimbisâra	603	„ attained Buddhahood sixteenth year of this king.
Râhula, son of S'âkya Muni.	*Kaṇwâyana, 9.*		
	Bhûmiputra, 14.		
Prasenajit.	Ajâtas'atru	551	„ died eighth year of this reign 543. First Convocation held that year.
Kshudraka.	Udayâs'wa	519	
Kuṇḍaka.	Das'aka	503	
Suratha.	Nâgadâs'oka	495	
Sumitra.	Sis'unâga	471	
	Kâlâs'oka	453	Second Convocation 100 years after Buddha's death.
	Mahâ Nanda	425	
	Sumâlya. } 100 years.		
	7 Nandas.		
	Interregnum, Kautilya.		Alexander in India, 327.
	Maurya Dynasty, 137 *years.*		
	Chandragupta	325	
	Bimbisâra	301	
	As'oka	276	Third Convocation, 255 B.C. in 17th year after his inauguration. Stûpa at Sanchi.
	Suyas'as	240	
	Das'aratha	230?	Caves at Behar.
	Sangata	220?	
	Indrapâlita	212?	
	Somas'arman	210	Hasti Gumpha Cuttack?
	S'as'adharman	203	
	Virhadratha	195	
	S'unga Dynasty, 112 *years.*		
	Pushpamitra	188	Caves at Bâjâ?
	Agnimitra	152	
	Sujyeshṭha	144	
	Vasumitra	137	
	Ârdraka	129	
	Pulindaka	127	No. 2 Tope at Sanchi?
	Ghoshavasu	124	
	Vajramitra	121	Caves at Beḍsa.
	Bhâgavata	112	
	Devabhûti	86	Great Cave at Kârlâ.
	Kâṇwa Dynasty, 45 *years.*		
	Vâsudeva	76	
	Bhûmimitra	67	
	Nârâyaṇa	53	Ganesa Gumpha Cuttack?
	Sus'arman	41	
	„ died	B.C. 31	

ANDHRA DYNASTY.	SÂH KINGS.	KINGS OF MAGADHA.	KINGS OF CASHMERE.	
	Nahapana - - - B.C. 57			
S'ipraka - B.C. 31			Hushka, Jushka, Kanishka } Tartar Princes established Buddhism	Great Caves at Kârlâ. Cave at Nassick.
	Ushavadâta - - - 11			
Krishṇa - A.D. 8	Swâmi Chastana - A.D. 10			
	Jaya Dâmâ.			Nâgârjuna.
S'âtakarṇi I. - 10			Abhimanya, A.D. 21	South Gateway, Sanchi.
Pûrṇotsanga - 28	Jiva Dama - - - 38		GONARDAYA DYNASTY.	
S'rîvaswâmi - 46	Rudra Dâman.		Gonarda. *Nâga worshipped.*	
	Rudra Sinha - - 45–47		Vibhîshana.	
S'âtakarni II. - 64	Rudra Sâh.			
	Srî Sâh.	S'akrâditya.	Indrajita.	S'âlivâhana, A.D. 78.
Lambodara - 120	Sangha Dâman.			West Gateway, Sanchi.
	Dâman Sâh.		Râvaṇa.	Early Caves at Ajanta.
Apítaka - - 138	Yas'a Dâman.		Vibhîshaṇa.	
	Dâmajâta S'rî - - - 97			
Sangha - - 150	Vîra Dâman.	Buddhagupta.	Nara.	
	Îs'vara Datta.			
S'âtakarṇi III. 168	Vijaya Sâh - - - 115		Siddha.	
	Dâmajâta S'rî.			
Skandhaswâti - 186			Utpalâksha.	
	Rudra Sâh - - 131, 141			
Mrigendra - 193	Vis'va Sinha - - - 143	Tathâgatagupta.	Hiraṇyâksha.	
	Atri Dâman - - 153, 157		Hiraṇyâkula.	
Kuntalaswâti - 196	Vis'va Sâh - - 160, 168			
	22. Rudra Sinha 173 or 213		Vásúkulo.	
Swâtikarṇa - 204	Âs'â Dâman.	Balâditya.	Mihirakula, 200?	Central building, Amravati.
	Svâmi Rudra Sâh - 223, 235			
Pulomâvit - 205	Svâmi Rudra Sâh II.			
Gorakshâs'was'rí 241	Svâmi Rudra Sâh - 223, 235		Vaka.	
	Svâmi Rudra Sâh.			
Hâla - - 266			Kshitinanda.	
Mantalaka - 271		Vajra.	Vasunanda.	
Purîndra sena - 276			Nara.	
Sindara - - 281			Aksha.	
Râjâdaswâti - 6 ms.			Gopâditya, 290?	
S'ivaswâti - 284			Gckarṇa.	
Gautamiputra - 312	GUPTA, OR BALABHI Era - 318		Narendrâditya.	Cave at Nassick.
Vásithi putra 333			Yudhishṭhira.	Outer rail, Amravati.
Pulomat - - 335	Gupta.			
		Kings of OUGEIN and CANOUGE.	ÂDITYA DYNASTY.	
S'ivas'rî - - 363	Ghaṭotkacha.			
Skandaswâti - 370			Pratâpâditya, 350?	
Yadnyas'rî - 377	Chandra gupta I. - 400, 411	Vasudeva.	Jalaukas.	
Vijaya - - 406			Tunjîna.	Inner rail, Amravati.
	Samudra gupta - - - 420?	*Bahram-gaur.*	Vijaya.	Buddha ghosha.
Vadas'rî - - 412			Jayendra.	Great Cave at Kanheri.
Pulomat - 422			Ârya Râjâ.	
„ died - 429 or 436	Chandra gupta II. - - 430?	Ramadeva.		
			GONARDAYA LINE *restored.*	
	Kumâra gupta - - - 442	Harsha.		
	Skanda gupta - - 448, 459		Meghavâhana, 434?	
CHÂLUKYA KINGS.	Buddha gupta - - - 463		S'reshṭasena.	
Jaya Sinha Vijayâditya - 430?		Vikramâditya - 490?		
	Toramâṇa - - - - 498		Hiraṇya, Toramâṇa } 498	Buildings at Eran.
Raja Sinha.				
Vijayâditya II.		S'îlâditya - - 530	Mâtrigupta, 525	
Pulakes'î I. - 489?			Pravara sena, 530	Zodiac Cave, Ajanta.
Kîrtti Varman I.	BALABHI KINGS.	Prabhâkara.	Yudhishṭhira II.	
Mangalîs'a.	Nine kings from Bhaṭârka Senâpati - - - - 493?		Nandravat.	
VishṇuVardhana 605 founds Vengi.	S'rîdhara Sena.	Râja varddhana 607?	Raṇâditya.	Temple at Martand.
		S'îlâditya - - 610	Vikramâditya, 30th year, 622	
Pulakes'î II. - 609 founds Kalyân.	Dhruva Sena II. - - 628	„ died - 650	Balâditya, cotem. Yezdigerd and Hiouen Thsang.	Temple at Bhuvanes'war.
	Dhruva Sena III. - - 640			
Vikramâditya - 660?	Sîlâditya II. - - - 656			
	Three names obliterated.			
Vinayâditya - 680	Charagriha II. - - - 700?		Durlabha, 645	Temple at Iwulli.
			Pratâpâditya, 681	
Vijayâditya - 695	Sîlâditya III. - - - 715?		Chandrapira, 731	
			Tarapira, 739	
Vikramâditya - 733	Sîlâditya Musalli IV. - 730?	Yasovigriha - 712	Lalitâditya, 743	Ballabhi destroyed and Anhulwara founded.
„ died 750?	„ died - 745?		„ died 779	

APPENDIX G.

BIRTH OF ŚÂLIVÁHANA.

THE following two extracts from a paper by Colonel Wilford in the ninth volume of the "Asiatic Researches" are of little value from any historical point of view, but being derived from Brahmanical sources, they are curious as an unconscious testimony to the prevalence of Nâga traditions at the time the Sanchi Gateways were being erected.[1]

"Towards the end of his reign, Vicramarca sent secret messengers through all the world to "inquire whether a child were born of a virgin one and half year old. The messengers returned "to Ujjayini with the news that a male child was born of a virgin, the daughter of a potmaker, "begot by the King of Snakes (called Tacshaca or the Carpenter in the original), while she was "in her cradle. They informed him also that the child named Śâliváhana had attained the "age of five years, and that his grandfather had made numberless figures of soldiers to amuse "him.

"Vicramarca marched at the head of an army, but the protecting Snake came to the "assistance of the child, and inspired the figures of clay with life, who started up as able "warriors, attacked Vicramarca and his army, and defeated them" (p. 120).

"There were two Brahmans, who had a sister who lived with them in a state of widow-"hood—her husband having died while she was yet very young. She conceived by a Nâga "Cumâra (or Tacshaca), and the brothers, ashamed of this seemingly disorderly behaviour of "their sister, left the country. The unfortunate young widow thus deserted found an asylum "in the humble cottage of a potmaker, where she was delivered of a male child, whom she "called Śâliváhana."

After some irrelevant matter, the story reaches the battle, and goes on thus:—"They "fought on both sides with courage, but the Nâga Cumâra, or son of the Great Serpent, "stupefied Vicramarca's army, who, finding his soldiers asleep, implored the assistance of the "Serpent Vâśuki, who gave him some Amrit, with which he revived his troops, and Śâliváhana, "hearing of this, sent two of his men for some of it, and Vicramarca complied with his "request, and here ends the legend" (p. 130).

---

1 Śâliváhana died A.D. 78. His capital is said to have been situated 300 miles south-west from Sanchi, but his kingdom extended to the eastward of Nagpore (vide supra, p. 154). If I am not very much mistaken, Nâgârjuna, Kanishka, and Śâliváhana, who were contemporary or nearly so with each other, are the three persons who had the greatest share in engrafting on Buddhism that modern form of Serpent Worship which gave rise to those developments which it has been the object of the preceding pages to investigate.

SCULPTURES IN UDYAGIRI CAVES.

APPENDIX H.

In a little group of sandstone hills, called the Udaya Giri or Khaṇḍagiri Hills, not far from Cuttack in Orissa, there is a series of caves which, though not so extensive as some of those found in other parts of India, are full of interest, and if properly investigated would throw considerable light on many of the questions mooted in the preceding pages.

They were first described by Stirling in his invaluable paper on Orissa in the fifteenth volume of the Asiatic Researches, and were afterwards visited and drawn by the indefatigable Kittoe, and the results of his visit published in the seventh volume of Prinsep's Journal. When I visited them in 1836, the principal cave, the Râj Rânî, was inhabited by Fakirs, who would allow no one to approach them, and I had not then that intimate knowledge of Indian art which would enable me to draw all the requisite conclusions from their examination. In the spring of last year a series of casts were made of all the sculptures by Mr. Locke, the Superintendent of the School of Design at Calcutta, and I have photographs of these casts, and also photographs which he and Capt. Murray made of the exterior of the caves. These are most valuable contributions to our knowledge, but they do not quite supply all that further familiarity with the spot would now afford; but they suffice for such a general notice as is here attempted, and which it is hoped may, at all events, attract attention to their more remarkable features.[1]

The oldest cave in the Udaya Giri hill is known as the Hasti Gumpha or Elephant cave; it is an extensive natural cavern, unimproved by art, but containing the celebrated Aira inscription, which, from the form of its characters and the events it narrates, may be as old as the time of Aśoka,[2] and certainly at all events is earlier than the Christian era. In the rock around it are several small cells, each of which might accommodate a single hermit; and one close alongside has the image of a great three-headed serpent over its entrance.[3] It is so placed that if it is not an object of worship it must at least be considered as the tutelary numen of the place.

Passing from these primitive excavations, we come to one known as the Ganeśa Gumpha, which contains an inscription in the character of the 10th century recording the dedication, of the cave to the service of Jagannâth, evidently, however, the work of a much later age.[4] The bas-relief, Fig. 1, Plate C., is taken from this cave.

The most important excavation of the place is that known as the Râj Rânî, from a tradition that it was last inhabited by the Rânî of Lelat Indra Keśari (A.D. 617). It is two storeys in height, and the façade extends 64 or 65 feet between the wings, which project forward on either side. The sculptures and architectural ornaments on the outside have been dreadfully disfigured and cut away by its modern inhabitants to accommodate their rude additions, but inside the upper verandah, is a bas-relief, extending nearly its whole length, and with returns on either side. Fig. 2, Plate C., is a specimen of this sculpture.

Next in importance to these is the Ananta Cave in the Khaṇḍagiri Hill. Figs. 3 and 4, Plate C. are specimens of its sculptures. The last illustration on Plate C. is from a cave called Jaya Vijaya in the Udaya Giri hill. Besides these there are several other caves in these hills, such as the

---

[1] I do not here allude to Dr. W. W. Hunter's description of these caves and their sculptures, in his "Orissa." It is very eloquent, but has no claim to be considered as anything like scientific archæology.

[2] J. A. S. B., VI. p. 1080, et seqq.

[3] J. A. S. B., VII., Plate XL. I have a photograph from Mr. Locke's cast of this sculpture, but unfortunately it is taken so directly in front, and with the light direct upon it, so as to be unintelligible to those who do not know the image from other sources.

[4] J. A. S. B., VI., p. 1073, Plate LIV., and J. R. A. S., VIII., p. 41, Plate I.

Tiger cave and various nameless ones, which need not be described here, as they have no direct bearing on our subject.

On reviewing these caves and their sculptures the first question that arises is, why are they called Buddhist? The Aira of the great inscription seems to have oscillated between Brahmanism and Buddhism, and the other old inscriptions translated by Prinsep are Buddhist in form, though it can hardly be said they are so in doctrine; and when we turn to the sculptures it is hard to find any trace of Buddhism in them. Buddha himself nowhere appears, either in his conventional form or as an ascetic. That we might expect from our experience at Sanchi. But there are no Dagobas, no Wheels, and only by the most careful inspection can we detect any of those Buddhist symbols we are now familiar with. But on the other hand, if they are not Buddhist, they certainly are not Hindu. No god or goddess of that Pantheon appears anywhere, except Śrî, who appeared so frequently at Sanchi, and she as clearly belongs to both religions as to either, while no four-faced or many-armed personages appear anywhere.

Still these caves must have been excavated for some religious purposes; we can hardly suppose they were the residences of laymen, and the only reasonable conclusion seems to be that they were early Buddhist of a type co-eval, or it may be even anterior to what we find at Sanchi.

Among the sculptures one of the most remarkable is the left-hand one of the two that adorn the Ganeśa Gumpha (Fig. 1, Plate C.). The subject is purely historical, and represents the rape of some Orissan Helen, or rather some Hippolita, who is carried off on the right, in spite of the fighting prowess of her companion in arms, or the tardy succour of the sleeping hero on the left. This evidently is some favourite Orissan legend, for we have the same story repeated in the Râj Rânî cave without any variation, except differences of costume and style. As will be observed (Fig. 2, Plate C.) his wife sits watching by the sleeper on the left, this time, however, in a hut or house instead of under a tree, as in the upper bas-relief. As in Fig. 1, a woman introduces a man, and further on a man and woman are engaged in single combat; while on the extreme right a naked woman is borne off. In the lower bas-relief she retains her shield, which she has dropped in the upper. It is difficult to guess whether we shall ever recover the legend thus portrayed, nor do the other bas-reliefs in these caves give us the smallest hint who the persons are who are here represented. The other bas-relief in the Ganeśa cave seems to represent quite different people, and another story altogether, and though the bas-relief in the Râj Rânî is certainly continuous, it represents scenes of hunting, eating, drinking, dancing, and such other scenes as we are already familiar with at Sanchi, but which hardly aid us in ascertaining who the individual performers are.

The three lower examples in Plate C. are of a more religious character, and of a class we are now tolerably familiar with. The sculpture on the head of the doorway, Fig. 3, is our old friend Śrî,[1] with her elephants and lotuses; and in the next, Fig. 4, is the sacred tree with its enclosure and the usual attributes of worship. Above these two arches are the guardian three-headed Serpents, and over the centre of the one the shield, and over the other the Trisul, which we find in combination on the Gateways at Sanchi. The lowest bas-relief in this Plate (No. 5) is the only one in the cave in which it is found, and is wholly devoted to Tree Worship.

In so far, therefore, as the sculptures of these caves are concerned, the only emblems or indications of worship are the Trees or Serpents, or the Lotus Lady, and the compound Trisul ornament. No Dagobas, and no figures of Buddha, or of any Bodhisatwas appear anywhere, nothing indeed that can be called Buddhism in the ordinary or modern sense of the word.

A much more difficult question to determine than either the historical or religious import of these sculptures is their age. The inscriptions on the Snake and Tiger caves prove them, from the form of their characters, to be not far removed from Aśoka's time;[2] but except the one above alluded

[1] In his translation of the Aira inscription (J. A. S. B., p. 1081) Prinsep suggests that "Śrî Kaḍâra may "denote the servant of Śrî, the goddess of beauty." If this can be sustained, this cave sculpture forms a singularly appropriate illustration of the epithet.

[2] J. A. S. B., VI., Plate LIV.

to in the Ganeśa cave, I am not aware of the existence of any other inscriptions which are of any use in this matter.

All the caves mentioned above must be older than the Great Rail at Amravati, because the simple Buddhist Rail is used as a string course in all, and because the style of the sculpture is so much more nearly allied to that of Sanchi than to that of the more southern Tope.

Here again a curious question arises, which of the two editions of the story of the rape is the older? That in the Ganeśa cave is the purer and the more nearly allied to Greek art. That in the Râj Rânî, though fully as vigorous and full of life, is inferior in style, and much more Indian in detail and costume. Sculpture in itself, however, is much more uncertain in its progress than architecture, and depends so much on local and individual and personal circumstances for its development, that it would be almost impossible to decide this question if it stood alone. But it seems hardly doubtful that the architecture of the Ganeśa is earlier than that of the Râj Rânî cave; while the simplicity of its one-celled plan, as compared with the many-celled two-storeyed magnificence of the other, is so marked that it is impossible to mistake the progress between the two. We thus, it appears to me, arrive at the conclusion that some of the Yavana invaders mentioned above (page 173) introduced Greek art into this remote corner some time, it may be, before or about the Christian era; but that instead of becoming more delicate and refined as it did at Amravati, it became here more vigorous and more local in its manifestations.

This account of these caves is from the circumstances of the case necessarily incomplete and liable to modification on more detailed information being obtained,[1] but it is sufficiently interesting and sufficiently germane to our subject to merit a place here. It is, so far as I know, the only other place in India where that Buddhism without Buddha is found in the same or even greater completeness than at Sanchi.

It presents us with a new form of religion not before recognized in India, which, no doubt, was Buddhism; but in which the Tree, the Serpent, and Srî figure much more prominently than Buddha or even his emblems.

---

[1] Babu Rajendra Lâla accompanied the first expedition to Orissa more than two years ago, and announced his intention of publishing immediately the result of his investigation. Nothing, however, has yet appeared, which is to be regretted as he has, no doubt, collected some inscriptions with which he is perfectly competent to deal, and which may throw light on the subject. I am afraid, however, he is hardly sufficiently grounded, either as an architect or archæologist, to settle many questions we would like to see scientifically discussed, but on which inscriptions shed but the faintest and most uncertain glimmer.

APPENDIX I.

After the text of this work had been completely printed off, and the sheets were in the hands of the binder, it occurred to me that I had once dreamt of something very like the Gateways at Sanchi being connected with the Temple at Jerusalem.[1] I consequently turned back to the passages in Josephus and the Talmud bearing on the subject, read them with more care than I had hitherto done, and having protracted these descriptions on paper, I very soon arrived at the conclusion that I was not mistaken. An erection very similar to the Sanchi Gateways certainly stood in front of the Temple as re-erected by Herod, and was meant to have been a reproduction of the brazen arrangements of Solomon's Porch, as executed by Hiram of Tyre.[2]

The passages in Josephus bearing on the subject are the following :—" The Temple had " doors at the entrance with lintels above, extending to a height equal to that of the Temple. " They were adorned with coloured veils or curtains, on which purple flowers with trellis work " were embroidered. Upon this, but lower than the crowning moulding of the wall, a golden " vine was spread out, with its branches hanging down from a great height, and executed with " such a profusion of material as to strike the spectator with astonishment as well from the art " displayed as from its magnitude."[3]

The corresponding paragraph in the Wars of the Jews is as follows :—" The first Gate of " the Temple was 70 cubits high by 25 broad, but this gate had no doors, for it symbolized the " heavens, every way open and everywhere visible. Its front was covered with gold all over, and " through it the first part of the house itself, which was the largest, was everywhere visible ; as well " as those parts about the inner doors which were also covered with gold . . . . But the Gate " of this Temple, as already mentioned, was all covered with gold as was the whole wall about it. It " also had golden vines upon it, from which clusters of grapes hung down, equal in height to that of " a man."[4]

These passages are too rhetorical for the purposes of a restoration, and the heights, as usual with Josephus, are very much exaggerated. The Talmud is, in this instance at least much more exact and detailed. Its description is as follows :—" The Gates of the propylon were 40 cubits in height and " 20 cubits broad, and above these were five richly carved beams of ash or oak. The lowest of these " extended one cubit either way beyond the pillars of the doorway, while the one next above this was " one cubit longer either way than that below it, so that the upper beam of all extended to 30 cubits. " Between each beam there was a row, or course of stones.

" Transverse beams of cedar (in the Venetian edition of the Talmud it is said " of stone ") were " carried from the wall of the Temple to this portico or propylon to support it "—literally, that it might not start from the perpendicular. " Golden chains were hung to the beams of the portico, " by which the candidates for the priesthood went up to see the crowns, because it is said by " 'Zachariah, vi. 14., And the crowns shall be to Helem, &c. for a memorial in the Temple of the Lord.' "

" A golden vine was spread over this Gateway of the Temple, and was carried upon the supporting " beams. Whoever vowed a leaf or grape, or bunch of grapes brought and suspended it from it (the " vine). Eliezer, the son of Zadok, says, it thus happened the 300 priests were told off as necessary on " occasions when it had to be removed."[5]

---

1 True Principles of Beauty in Art, by the Author, p. 295.

2 The translators of the Vulgate, and of our English version of the Bible, were so entirely ignorant of architecture or of architectural terms that it is impossible to restore Solomon's porch from their translations. Our knowledge of the subject has so immensely increased of late years that, with the assistance of a good Hebrew scholar, I would have no hesitation in undertaking it, with great confidence of success.

3 Antiquities of the Jews, XV. 3.

4 Bell. Jud., V. v. 4.

5 Middoth of the Mishna, III. 7 and 8. Professor Chenery, than whom no one is more competent, has kindly assisted me by revising this translation, and approves of it as it now stands.

From these paragraphs it seems perfectly evident that the object therein described was not a door or gateway in the ordinary sense of the term, but a frontispiece or propylon, partly in wood and partly in stone, standing by itself in front of the main building. When protracted with the dimensions given in the Talmud it does not seem that it could in any essential respect be different from the representation of it in the annexed woodcut. In so far as the restoration is concerned it is not of the least consequence whether the tranverse beams of support were of stone, as the Venetian copy has it, or of wood as they are said to have been in all the more modern editions I have had access to. If of wood, they would have been morticed into the five beams. If of stone, the ends of them are the square blocks over the pillars seen between the beams.

The pillars were certainly in stone, and it is probable that the square block represented as the centre of them was also carried back to the wall. Indeed without these constantly recurring points of support the whole could not only have been, but would have looked frail and unstable to an unpleasing extent. With them there is no difficulty either in the construction, or in artistic effect.

No. 30.

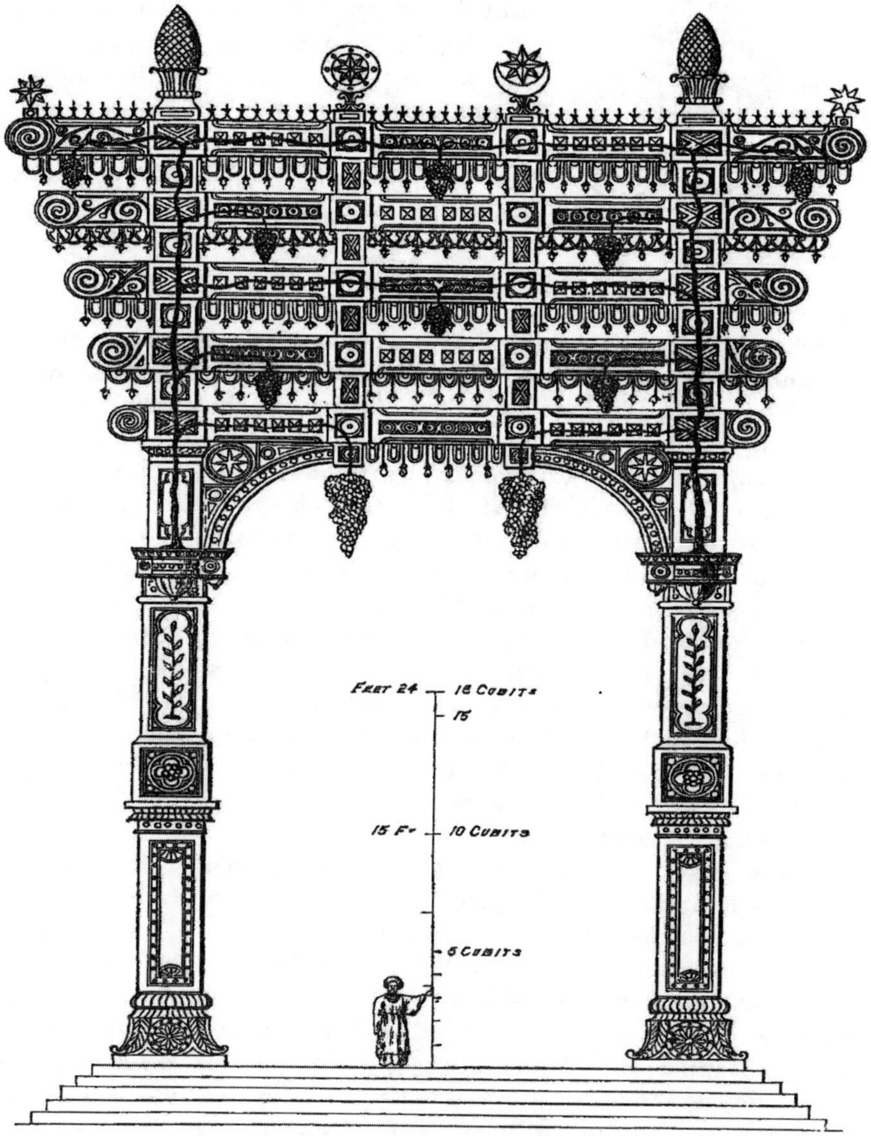

DIAGRAM OF THE GATEWAY OF HEROD'S TEMPLE AT JERUSALEM.

The golden chains that hung from the beams are easily understood. Their forms are repeated so often and in such variety in the stone architecture of the East, that many other varieties might have been chosen besides those represented in the diagram. Nor is the vine a difficulty. As, however, the drawing is meant to explain the construction, not to illustrate the beauty of the object, I have represented the vine realistically and without leaves, though aware that its treatment must have been conventional, and leaves an indispensable accompaniment. It would, however, be easy to add these and to double the number of bunches of grapes if necessary; but, as it stands, the diagram is probably sufficient to explain the form and construction, and to show that it really was only a gigantic and elaborately adorned trellis placed in front of the Temple to support the Sacred Vine.[1]

From various indications it is easy to perceive that such a form of architecture must have been familiar to the Jews at the age of Herod, even supposing that the frontispiece of Solomon's

[1] The Vine is used realistically, as in this diagram, as an architectural ornament to the doorway of the Temple of Baalsamin at Siah, belonging to the time of Herod (De Vogüé, Syrie Centrale, Plates II. and III.), and both realistically and conventionally in the recently discovered palace of Chosroes at Meshita (Land of Moab, by Dr. Tristram, woodcuts 22, 38, and 39). Where are the connecting links between the two ?

Temple was not of a similar construction. There are, for instance, in the British Museum, a series of imperial coins of Cyprus, all of which represent, with more or less distinctness, just such a gateway, as forming the entrance to the Temple of the tutelary goddess of that island. The

No. 31.

COIN OF SEPTIMIUS SEVERUS.

annexed copy of a coin of Septimius Severus is even more like the gateways at Sanchi than that at Jerusalem, inasmuch as it is attached to a circular enclosure, which, making allowances for the defects of coin representations of architecture, may fairly be assumed to be intended for a similar temenos.

In this instance there seems to have been five beams, as at Jerusalem, but the two upper and two lower are joined together without any intermediate blocks, and it is only the centre one which is separated from the others by these characteristic features whether in wood or stone.

The interest of this form of gateway with reference to the present work arises, in the first instance, from finding an almost forgotten form of architecture existing at Jerusalem and in Cyprus, which attained its highest development at Sanchi, but which now prevails in China and Japan and the Indo-Chinese countries to an almost unlimited extent, though long ago forgotten in the West.

The form is alone sufficient to prove that these gateways were originally always executed in wood, but we have also numerous representations of them in the bas-reliefs at Sanchi and Amravati, which are unmistakeably wooden erections, without any admixture of the more permanent material. The example at Jerusalem may thus be regarded as a transitional example, being composed partly of wood and partly of stone, and the Sanchi Gateways still therefore maintain their positions as the first examples known to have been wholly executed in stone.

It is also curious to observe how nearly the Syrian and Indian examples approach each other in date. Herod began to rebuild the Temple in the 11th year of his reign, 19 years before the Christian era, and finished it in eight years. This gateway would certainly have been one of the last adornments added, if indeed it is not wholly subsequent; but at all events we may assume that it belongs to the 10th or 12th year preceding our era. The South Gateway at Sanchi, as explained in the text, was erected during the reign of the first Śâta Karṇi, A.D. 10 to 28. The two examples are consequently certainly within 40 years of one another. They may be even more nearly contemporary.

The great interest, however, of this Gateway, as connected with our present subject, is rather mythological than architectural. At all events, it certainly does not seem to be stretching the argument too far to say, that the Sacred Vine, which was the principal cause of its erection, was a reminiscence of that Tree Worship, which under the name of the Asheerah or Groves, played so important a part in early Jewish history anterior to the time of Hezekiah. Whatever its meaning may have been, this Vine certainly was the principal object that met the eye of the worshipper on approaching the Temple of Jerusalem, and it was for its display that this richly adorned Gateway was erected. Nor can it be said that an image, to which it was considered a meritorious religious act "to vow a leaf, or a grape, or bunch of grapes," and which was entrusted to the charge of 300 priests,[1] was a mere architectural adornment. Whether it symbolized the heavens, as Josephus seems to insinuate,[2] or whether it had any deeper or more recondite meaning may be left for future investigations. In the meanwhile, however, there is certainly more in it than has hitherto "been dreamt of in our philosophy."

[1] The commentators are generally agreed in considering this expression as hyperbolical, and suggest 30 instead of 300. There is, however, no mistake in the words of the text, nor, so far as I can see, any improbability in the number assigned.

[2] The expression in the "Wars of the Jews," V. v. 4, it must be confessed seems to refer rather to the curtain which hung from it, than to the structure itself, but the words quoted above from the "Antiquities," seem to refer to the Gateway.

INDEX.

A.

B.

C.

D.

L.

M.

N.

O.

P.

Q.

R.

S.

T.

U.

V.

W.

X.

Y.

Z.